The Critical Study of Work

Labor, Technology, and Global Production

EDITED BY

Rick Baldoz, Charles Koeber,
and Philip Kraft

TEMPLE UNIVERSITY PRESS

PHILADELPHIA

Temple University Press, Philadelphia 19122
Copyright © 2001 by Temple University
All rights reserved
Published 2001
Printed in the United States of America

Library of Congress Cataloging-in-Publication Data

The critical study of work : labor, technology, and global production / edited by
Rick Baldoz, Charles Koeber, and Philip Kraft.
    p.   cm.
    Includes bibliographical references.
    ISBN 1-56639-797-9 (cloth : alk. paper) — ISBN 1-56639-798-7 (pbk. : alk. paper)
    1. Working class—History—20th century. 2. Work environment—History—
20th century. 3. Technological innovations—History—20th century. I. Baldoz,
Rick, 1969– II. Koeber, Charles, 1967– III. Kraft, Philip, 1944–
    HD4854 .C75   2001
    331—dc21   00-057726

Contents

Part III: Production and Industrial Workers

Part IV: Professional and Technical Workers

Acknowledgments

Every book is a collaboration, none more so than a collection of essays by a dozen or so authors. We are grateful to our collaborators for their patience and their readiness to revise. Thanks go also to Mike Ames and to all the people at Temple University Press who helped produce the book. The essays were inspired by the conference "Work, Difference, and Social Change: Two Decades After Braverman's *Labor and Monopoly Capital*," which was organized by the editors and held at the State University of New York at Binghamton in May 1998. In that effort we were joined by Phoebe Godfrey, Carol Jansen, and Reiko Koide. Neither the conference nor this collection would have been possible without them.

We are happy to acknowledge the crucial early support we received from the Ray Glass Society and the Conversations in the Discipline Program of the State University of New York. We would like to add our individual acknowledgments as well. Rick Baldoz is grateful to his mother, Desne Baldoz, who offered unequivocal support throughout her life. He also thanks Jim Geschwender and Martin Murray for their advice and encouragement. Chuck Koeber thanks his partner, Jerri, and his parents, William and Valerie, for their love and support. He thanks Nicole McFadden and Brenda Henman for their editorial assistance. Nancy Zimmet and Sarah Zimmet have sustained and challenged Phil Kraft through this project and all the others that have mattered.

Introduction

Making Sense of Work in the Twenty-First Century

Rick Baldoz, Charles Koeber, and Philip Kraft

Two broad developments reshaped work at the end of the twentieth century. The first was the implosion of the Soviet Union and the worldwide triumph of market capitalism. The second was the widespread use of computer-based production technologies and management command-and-control systems. The much-anticipated global economy seemed, at long last, to have arrived (Castells 1996). Local and regional economies became parts of international production chains tightly bound by freely moving capital. Computer-based information systems coordinated in unprecedented detail the movement of capital, goods, and people. The effects were visible everywhere. Asian agricultural economies metamorphosed into large and small economic "tigers." Mexico became the industrial partner of its two North American neighbors, and Brazil energetically turned itself into an exporter of computers, cars, and pharmaceuticals. The former Soviet Union embarked on a process of speedy privatization, and once-peripheral European economies such as Ireland and Italy reinvented themselves as niche producers of high-tech goods and services. Only sub-Saharan Africa remained largely untransformed by the revolution in global markets and technologies.

Some of the transformations were indeed dramatic:

- By the end of the 1970s work and production innovations had catapulted Japan into the front rank of economic superpowers, second only to the United States in terms of gross domestic product. Japanese competition forced European and U.S. producers to make radical changes in work relations and production systems. A new and often bizarre polyglot vocabulary entered the discussions of managers and workers worldwide: "lean production," "just-in-time," "*kaizen*," "statistical process control," "Total Quality Management," "*kanban*," "reengineering," "six sigma," "empowerment," "Toyota system," "synchronous production," and "team-based work groups" (Berry 1991; see also Jones 1994; Kraft 1999). In spite of continuous "downsizing," extensive subcontracting, and increasingly global production chains, U.S. and European producers of electronic consumer goods and, most especially, cars were widely written off as the inevitable victims of relentless and superior Japanese manufacturing organization (Womack, Jones, and Roos 1990). Japanese "software factories" threatened even the American redoubt of computer software production (Cusumano 1991).

- Other East Asian nations, notably Singapore, Malaysia, Hong Kong, Taiwan, and Korea, rapidly industrialized. The People's Republic of China managed to talk socialist and act capitalist in ways that won the trust—and investment—of financiers in Tokyo, London, and New York. Labor markets that provided both cheap industrial workers and highly educated technical and scientific specialists gave local and international producers the perfect base from which to enter the global market. Mexico's formal incorporation into a U.S.–dominated trade zone—and the promise to enlarge the North American Free Trade Agreement (NAFTA) to include much of Latin America and the Caribbean—further expanded the arena for U.S. financial and productive investment.

- Former economic or political colonies of rich industrial nations provided special opportunities for investors eager to employ workers who were both cheap and well educated. For example at the end of World War II, Ireland and India were economic backwaters, agricultural economies that imported food and exported people. By the end of the twentieth century, however, these Anglophone nations were important if unlikely producers of computer software for the international market (see Sharpe, Chapter 10; Ó Riain, Chapter 12). Employment also rapidly expanded in the manufacture of computer and telecommunications equipment, and in export-centered service sectors such as insurance claims, data processing and product servicing. Ireland, moreover, had reversed its centuries-old tradition of exporting people and saw more immigrants return than leave. The success of medium- and small-scale manufacturers in Italy's Veneto region had turned northern Italy into an unexpected global power in niche manufacturing and finance. U.S. management theorists such as Piore and Sable (1984) invoked Italian-inspired "flexible specialization" nearly as often as "empowerment" and "process reengineering" as the key to production efficiencies and global competitiveness

- Thus encouraged, European, Japanese, and U.S. manufacturers accelerated the shift of manufacturing out of the metropolitan countries. By century's end General Motors and Daimler-Chrysler, although rapidly shedding workers in the United States and Canada, were both among the largest employers in Mexico. Brazil, once Latin America's largest agricultural economy, transformed itself virtually overnight into its largest industrial economy, and became a major exporter of cars, computers, and aircraft, sometimes with Brazilian names and sometimes with names like Volkswagen, Chrysler, IBM, Bayer, and Goldstar. On the other hand, production workers in the United States and other high-wage countries were advised to stop working with things and learn how to work with ideas or people. A progressive former U.S. secretary of labor regularly celebrated the shift of the U.S. economy away from mass production to "symbolic analysis" (Reich 1991). Everyone in the United States (and by implication, the United Kingdom, Germany, and other high-wage industrial economies) was to become a computer programmer, or perhaps a lawyer.

But tightly coupled economic and production systems also globalized two of the less celebrated outcomes of market economies. First, the benefits have been unevenly distributed. Wealth and income have concentrated among the very rich. Typically the top 5 percent of the population own 60–80% of all assets and receive 30–40% of all income. Even in the richest industrial country—the United States—the majority of the population has been able to maintain consumption levels only by sending more household members, mainly women, into the paid labor force; by taking on more debt; and by making an astounding increase in hours worked (Schor 1991; Mischel, Bernstein, and Schmitt 1999). The world's seven leading industrial (G7) countries in particular have experienced a surge in service sector employment and thus a simultaneous expansion of female employment and downward pressure on the family wage.

Second, the triumph of the global market has meant the globalization of cyclical busts and booms. The euphoria that greeted the collapse of the Soviet Union in 1989–91 led to excited talk among economists of new market paradigms in which the economic laws of gravity were repealed. Production, consumption, and stock prices went only up.

The talk was premature. The triumphal march of Asian capitalism was halted, at least temporarily, in the wake of successive speculative bubbles, currency collapses, and gluts of everything from raw materials to sophisticated consumer and industrial goods. By the end of the 1990s the Asian tigers were experiencing a series of unpleasant "structural readjustments" mandated by nervous central bankers. The "Asian flu" quickly spread to other "emerging markets," meaning the poor countries of the former Soviet Union and Latin America, places where North American, European, and Asian capital had also invested heavily. Russia in particular seemed perpetually on the brink of economic collapse and social chaos. As this is written, some of the Asian economies, notably Korea, Hong Kong, and Taiwan (although not Japan), have recovered some lost ground—but just as the U.S. stock markets are entering a particularly erratic and unstable period and the Chinese "miracle" seems to be coming apart.

In short, the postwar triumph of global market capitalism played out more or less the way both its supporters and critics said it would: bringing prosperity and polarization, more consumption and less leisure, more wealth and more debt, expansion and contraction.

Explanatory Frameworks

The explanations offered for these rapid and often contradictory developments have usually stressed the same large-scale processes: (1) the abolition of barriers to the worldwide movement of capital and commodities, including intellectual property (Porter 1990; Stalk and Hout 1990); (2) the formal or effective integration of nonmarket economies, notably China and the former Soviet Union, into the international production chain (Castells 1996); and (3) large increases in productivity based on varying combinations of technological and workplace innovation, such as information technologies and "business process reengineering." (Hammer 1990; Hammer and Champy 1993; Davenport and Short 1990) Supporters and opponents of NAFTA, of high-tech global production chains, and of unregulated markets disagreed only about the desirability of the outcomes, not the centrality of the processes.

These and other large-scale transformations have influenced but by themselves do not explain the mechanisms that organize and change work and work relations. How could they, when the changes have been so contradictory and defy easy categorization? For example, the global production chain made possible by cheap and reliable computer-based telecommunications technologies has opened employment opportunities to Anglophone Indian and Irish contract software writers, airline reservationists, and data entry and insurance claims clerks. These high-tech and service workers found themselves employed in what amount to "virtual" branch plants of British and U.S. firms. In effect they were and are contract workers, whose earnings are one-quarter to one-tenth of equivalent workers in the United States and the United Kingdom. "Fringe" benefits such as health and unemployment insurance and pensions, where they exist, are underwritten by their governments, not by their U.S. or U.K. employers. Many are disposable "contingent" workers whose organizational role is to relieve the wage pressures on IBM, Hewlett-Packard, Microsoft, British Air, Barclays, and other firms based in advanced industrial countries (see Chun, Chapter 6; Meiksins and Whalley, Chapter 11).

Similarly, the unexpected success of industry in the Italian Veneto is based on something at least as unexpected: the labor of Senegalese and other West African emigrants who work in northern Italian factories, mills, and foundries, even as southern Italy continues to have one of the highest unemployment rates in the European Union. In surprising numbers these Senegalese teachers, civil servants, and small farmers have migrated to Italy as a result of the dismantling of family agriculture and the "structural readjustment" policies of the World Bank and International Monetary Fund (Colatrella 1998). Their willingness to respond to the demands of "flexible specialization" rests in part on their vulnerability as illegal workers with few options in either their old or new countries.

Although it is true that manufacturing has continued its long, post–World War II move out of the rich industrial countries, it is not true that that these countries ceased to make things and devoted themselves instead to symbolic analysis and service work. It is more accurate to say that in these nations the relations between workers, managers, and employers were radically transformed, sometimes in ways that made them hard to recognize. For example, the Japanese manufacturing juggernaut of the 1970s and 1980s did not, in the 1990s, come to dominate the global production of telecommunications equipment, machine tools, semiconductors, or, for that matter, cars. Japan's economic stagnation, brought about in part by speculation and financial sector manipulations, began early in the 1990s and quickly reduced it to a shaky regional hegemony. By 1995 Japan was only one of numerous "core" economies in a global system of many regional economies, challenged by a resurgent American manufacturing sector. From below, other East Asian producers, notably Korea, Taiwan, Singapore, and Malaysia, were steadily chipping away at whatever quality and cost advantages the Japanese still claimed. The short-lived Japanese tradition of lifetime employment for male workers in major enterprises disappeared virtually overnight. Japanese workers are currently being asked by the International Monetary Fund and World Bank to surrender much of what is left of the modest post–World War II social safety net.

We have now arrived at perhaps the most unexpected development of all: the fate of manufacturing in the United States. By the late 1990s U.S. manufacturing as a whole had, quite unexpectedly, reestablished itself as one of the most efficient and responsive in the world. U.S. producers had ruthlessly reorganized production during the early 1990s—the phrase "lean and mean" became popular among U.S. managers about this time—and successfully challenged the Japanese precisely where they were strongest: efficient manufacturing of both mass-production and small-batch high-quality commodities (see Stalk and Hout 1990; Parker and Slaughter 1994; Rinehart, Chapter 8). However, apart from the U.S. business press, few seem to have noticed this phenomenon. Still other factors were also at work. Thanks to aggressive corporate and state policies, American industrial wages and corporate taxes steadily fell to near the bottom of G7 averages, making U.S. manufacturing relatively cheap as well as efficient.

Again defying expectations and common sense, manufacturing employment in the United States remained essentially stable during 1990s. The most spectacular case has been the car industry. Government data for the last forty years show that, in spite of widespread predictions of the collapse of the U.S. auto industry, more Americans are now employed making cars, trucks, buses, and parts than at any time since the end of the Vietnam War (U.S. Department of Commerce, various years; Mischel and Bernstein 1994; Mischel, Bernstein, and Schmitt 1999).

The reasons for this resurgence are not hard to find. The majority of U.S. autoworkers employed in vehicle and parts production no longer work for the "Big Three" U.S. producers (General Motors, Ford, and Daimler-Chrysler), nor, as a consequence, are they likely to be covered by collective bargaining agreements. While the Big Three together shed over half their manufacturing workers in the "downsizings" of the 1980s and early 1990s, even more were hired for lower wages and fewer benefits by "union-free" transplant manufacturers like Toyota, Honda, Nissan, Mitsubishi, and Daimler-Benz. Some unionized Big Three workers also found themselves employed by "new" parts manufacturers, such as American Axle and Delphi, spun off by General Motors in part to weaken the autoworkers union. Ford has similarly recently spun off a large segment of its parts production. U.S. subsidiaries of foreign parts manufacturers (e.g., Germany's Bosch) have also provided employment to nonunion workers.

The autoworkers who still work for the Big Three have felt the effects of the changes. Ford, often cited as the "friendliest" of the Big Three to organized labor, convinced the United Autoworkers Union to accept a precedent-shattering tiered wage system. New hires now get significantly lower wages and fewer benefits than more senior workers. The agreement also increases management discretion in the assignment of job tasks and workloads, bringing Ford workers nearer to the pay levels of workers in the nonunion parts makers and in foreign transplants.

Autoworkers everywhere face a new world of work relations (Rinehart, Chapter 8). In Brazil, for example, Volkswagen operates a truck and bus factory that essentially directly employs no production workers. Production is instead carried out by subcontractors who provide not only vehicle subassemblies, such as dashboards, electrical harnesses, and chassis, but also nonunion assembly workers to install them, and at wages considerably lower than those of Brazilian autoworkers. The Brazilian metalworkers union, which represents auto production workers, opposed the arrangement for obvious reasons, but was unable to stop it. Among VW's subcontractors are several U.S.-based companies. Both Ford and Chrysler are experimenting with similar systems in their Latin American plants. General Motors has announced it intends to build all of its new North American facilities on a variation of Volkswagen's Brazilian model.

In Mexico, the Korean Hyundai company and its local suppliers have relied on direct and indirect government intervention to prevent unionization in plants that make vehicles and parts for sale in the United States. In the United States the United Autoworkers Union, invoking the labor protection provisions of NAFTA, has filed complaints about such Mexican practices, but the U.S. government has yet to take any formal action against either the companies or the Mexican government. Hyundai workers in Korea also went on strike, in part to save production jobs that are being exported to Mexico.

The Politics of Technological Change

The worldwide explosion in productivity is often attributed to recent technological developments, particularly those in computer-based telecommunications and command-and-control systems. The changes we have just described, however, have one thing in common: they are all, in the broadest sense, political or organizational in nature, whether driven by new technology or not. The best-known forms of work reorganization—Total Quality Management, business process reengineering (BPR), team-based high-performance work groups—in fact require little or no technological innovation. Even BPR, which makes the most aggressive use of information technologies, relies at least as much on "flattened hierarchies," compulsory "brainstorming," and production quotas as it does on advanced command-and-control systems to reduce cycle times (Kraft 1999).

Sophisticated information technologies are important, but they are hardly more important than state economic policies that equate corporate profit with general social progress. As socialist states give way to market systems, this transformation simultaneously enlarges markets for goods and the supply of labor, which leads to a downward pressure on wages worldwide along with gluts in raw materials and commodities. Even in the United States average wages continued to sink for a whole generation after the Vietnam War. Increased labor supplies and market competition also provide employers everywhere with both the opportunities and the incentives to reduce wages and experiment with new forms of work organization, with or without advanced production technologies. Managers and engineers learn to achieve higher output through constantly shifting combinations of speedup and ingenious reorganizations of work processes.

Increased productivity, in short, is also the product of old-fashioned work intensification, increasingly systematic appropriation of worker knowledge, and group pressure grounded on threats of unemployment. In contrast to predictions made by academic and business researchers who foresaw the "end of work" and a "jobless future" only a few years ago, the United States now has a larger percentage of the labor force working for wages than at any time since the 1950s—and for astoundingly long hours (Schor 1991; Mischel, Bernstein, and Schmitt 1999). This is in part because the drop in real wages between 1973 and 1996 has made U.S. manufacturing workers extremely attractive to employers in comparison to European, Japanese, and Korean workers.

Clearly, then, a very important "global" change is occurring. But what is it exactly? Without doubt, technological and scientific advances have played a major role. The explosion of technical-scientific knowledge since World War II, particularly in computer-based information technologies, has affected workers and employers around the world in very specific ways. These science-based work innovations require, therefore, very close inspection, which reveals that they are experienced—and confronted—in different ways depending on the time, place, and circumstances.

For example, "virtual" corporations, "virtual" production systems, and even "virtual" education ("distance learning") had emerged as significant components of business enterprises in North America, Europe, and parts of Asia by the mid-1980s. With the help of computer-based telecommunications, firms were able to decouple capitalization, research and design, production, marketing, and customer service from each other and from specific products and enterprises (Stalk and Hout 1990; Castells 1996). The pieces could then be selectively distributed throughout the world, to either branch plants or contractors. In effect, some producers were able to create a high-tech-based system of global sourcing. Enterprise subcontracting, in turn, has its counterpart in the growing numbers of "contingent," that is, temporary, workers called in and dismissed as firms continually shift products and production methods. To complete the loop, integrated "backroom" and "enterprise" software, which controls production scheduling, logistics, process modeling, inventories, quality control, and other end-to-end business activities, now dominates operations and planning departments in postmodern factories, insurance companies, and mass merchandisers, as well as in the transport and telecommunications sectors. The making of backroom and enterprise software by transnational firms like SAP, Oracle, Baan, and IBM has itself become a major commercial product of British, German, and U.S. information technology companies.

Tightly coordinated global production chains, extensive subcontracting, and contingent labor—the linchpins of the international movement of capital and commodities—have meant increased flexibility for multinational enterprises (Porter 1991). Increased flexibility for employers translates into longer work days not just for minimum-wage contingent workers in sweatshops, but also for technical and administrative workers in twenty-four-hour-time-zone production chains (Kraft and Roux 1998). Global production processes enabled by computer technologies also mean profound employment insecurities for all workers, now made vulnerable to global whipsawing. Firms with marketing and sales departments in New York or Frankfurt and research and design facilities in the Silicon Valley or Geneva can continually shop for the cheapest contract manufacturers in Ireland or Brazil or Penang or China. High-fashion clothing designers in New York and Milan hire manufacturing subcontractors in the United States and Italy, who in turn can choose between sweatshops in China—or Chinatown. In the end, the return of sweatshops, as much as the free flow of capital, information technologies, and virtual organizations, may prove to be the defining characteristic of the new global system of production (see Bonacich, Chapter 7).

From Labor Process to the Critical Study of Work

How then are we to make sense of these often contradictory developments? Most of the essays in this volume trace at least some of their roots to the class-based labor process theories of, among others, Michael Burawoy, Richard Edwards, Andrew Friedman, Paul Thompson, and Hugh Wilmott. Labor process analysis is most closely identified, however, with Harry Braverman's *Labor and Monopoly Capital* (1998), which confronted conventional industrial sociology with a powerful if largely unexpected challenge. Braverman's unapologetic gloss on the first volume of Karl Marx's *Capital* reasserted the primacy of some old-fashioned—and for some, even quaint—Marxist propositions. Human labor is purposive and thus a two-edged sword: it makes possible the ability to plan both our own work and the work of others. The uniquely human capacity to separate mental and manual labor thus provides both the means and the opportunity to exploit people as well as nature. Furthermore, the logic of production in capitalist systems is grounded ultimately in neither efficiency nor even productivity, but in the need to protect and extend class relations: the organization of production must guarantee not merely an adequate level of production but also an acceptable form of social reproduction. The relations and tools of capitalist production, therefore, follow no inevitable laws of nature or trajectories of scientific progress. They are bound only by the requirement to continuously replace each generation of workers with another and to expand "productive," that is waged, relations to all spaces, public and private, where they do not yet exist. All efforts by capitalists and their agents—managers, engineers, human relations specialists—to organize and manage production must satisfy these dual requirements of production and social control. The whole capitalist labor process is simultaneously technical, ideological, and political: the production process itself is a form of class struggle (Baldoz et al. 1998).

Braverman's emphasis on "scientific management"—the continuous and systematic decomposition of work carried out by managers—was one of two issues that quickly came to be identified with the entire argument in *Labor and Monopoly Capital* (*LMC*). The other was "deskilling," a term that, as far as we have been able to tell, does not even appear in *LMC*, but which was effectively added to the text by Braverman's readers. It has taken the better part of two decades for Braverman's other insights—the use of production organization and technologies as class weapons, the blurring of the line dividing the personal from the public, the incorporation of more and more activity into productive labor—to find their rightful place in both academic research and practical application (Baldoz et al. 1998).

The essays in this collection demonstrate the ways in which a new and more fully developed critical study of work extends and qualifies traditional labor process analyses. Most were written for the "Work, Difference, and Social Change" conference held at the State University of New York at Binghamton in May 1998. The essays are more likely than earlier discussions of labor process to incorporate race, gender, and other forms of social inequality in their analyses. Several address household and emotional labor as well as the original labor process distinction between mental and manual labor. Most of the essays recognize that production has become more fluid and decentered, venturing out from factory floors and office cubicles to virtual workplaces and computer-era cottage labor. At the same time they pay attention to the intersections of local, regional, and global economies and labor markets. Finally, they acknowledge that the world includes Asia, Africa, and South America as well Europe and North America. In short, while these examples of the critical study of work retain from labor process theory its focus on the unequal social relations of capitalist production, they individually and collectively offer a more flexible approach to the study of workplace relations and the organization of production—and indeed of the notion of work itself.

Part I considers whether labor process analysis can help us make sense of the social relations of work in constantly changing production processes. The essays in this section reflect both the rich legacy of labor process theory and equally provocative approaches in the more recent critical study of work. In so doing, it links the organization of work at the local level of the shop floor and community to larger processes at the wider level of the state and global economy.

Michael Burawoy (Chapter 1) maintains that the labor process research inspired by Braverman's *Labor and Monopoly Capital* played a necessary role in refocusing attention on the specifics of the production process. He reviews the ethnographic research he has completed over the past twenty years as an active participant at various work sites across the globe. He focuses on his comparative studies of different work regimes in both capitalist and socialist countries, seeking to understand the fragility of socialism during the twentieth century. Of particular concern for Burawoy is the "flexibility of capitalism," or its ability to adapt and transform itself in an ever-changing global economy. Finally, his essay provides welcome insights into the nonproductive and subjective aspects of work and work relations, notably workers' consciousness and the role of state policies.

The essay by Jeffrey Haydu (Chapter 2) reminds us that the emergence of a class of modern managers at the end of the nineteenth century required self-conscious class awareness on the part of what he calls the "business community." Managers needed more than to gain the prerogatives over design, pacing, and detail they now take for granted; they also had to learn they needed these things in order to prevail over workers. The details of work organization and work relations, therefore, must be carefully examined and understood in the context of ongoing struggles between workers and employers. Haydu challenges the tendency of labor process theory to treat employers as individual vehicles for larger economic forces. He argues that employers' collective identities are also important ingredients in the development of the labor process. Using a historical case study, Haydu examines how struggles over worker control were influenced by the formation of a business community, an important strategic and ideological weapon used to impose capitalist discipline in the workplace.

The essays in Part II examine work relations in the burgeoning service sector, whose growth has compelled scholars to ask new questions. For example, the interactive nature of service work raises important issues about the standardization and routinization of workers' emotions and attitudes into just another product to be bought and sold on the market. Because so much service work falls to women (and often to immigrants as well), the essays pay particular attention to the intersections of race, gender, and ethnicity. Their topics range from the gendered and racial organization of reproductive labor, to the emotional labor carried out by women working at cosmetics counters in Taiwan, to the subtle forms of resistance practiced by female supermarket cashiers in Brazil and Quebec. The studies address jobs that are high-tech and low-tech, work that requires either relatively little or a great deal of self-conscious activity from workers, and work that is hardly considered work at all.

Evelyn Glenn (Chapter 3) examines how reproductive labor—the array of activities and social relations involved in maintaining people on a daily basis as well as intergenerationally—is both gendered and racialized. In the United States, black, Latina, and Asian women historically have performed reproductive labor not only for their own families but also for white families. The particular forms of race and gender divisions have changed over time as production and reproduction have been continuously reorganized under capitalism. Glenn identifies three major eras of such work: (1) the period before World War II, when reproductive labor was still centered in the household and women of color were concentrated in domestic work; (2) the period after the war, when reproductive labor was increasingly commodified and women of color were shifted into public reproductive work in institutional settings; and (3) the current period, when globalization is creating transnational divisions of labor and women from the "periphery" are migrating into metropolitan centers.

The essay by Pei-Chia Lan (Chapter 4) explores issues of control in the workplace through her ethnographic research of cosmetics counter saleswomen and direct sales vendors of beauty products in Taiwan. Lan combines a structural analysis of the political economy of work with an analysis of the symbolic practices and emotional labor involved in selling beauty products. In order to be successful, cosmetics saleswomen must use their bodies to display themselves in a manner that projects a commodified and idealized image of beauty. Lan argues that control mechanisms are embodied in the discipline and performance of the body that these workers must exhibit.

Angelo Soares (Chapter 5) examines the subtle forms of resistance used against both managers and demanding customers by supermarket cashiers in Quebec and Brazil. Soares found that the interactive nature of the cashiers' jobs makes the organization of worker resistance more complex compared to traditional forms, such as strikes and other collective action. Cashiers are situated at the focal point of supermarket work, simultaneously mediating the demands of store managers and customers. Traditional notions about the passivity of the job, which is generally considered to be "women's work," tend to render invisible the largely individualized forms of resistance. Soares amplifies and clarifies the more subtle forms of resistance in the workplace and enables us to appreciate the complexities of performing interactive service work.

Part III considers the nature and organization of industrial work. Here too there is a welcome emphasis on the interplay of cultural, ethnic, and gender differences. As a group these essays underline the continuing relevance of production and industrial workers in the global economy. Although essays by Jennifer JiHye Chun, Edna Bonacich, James Rinehart, and Edward Webster examine very different kinds of industrial employment, from the manufacturing of computer parts to the production of automobiles and garments, they share a concern with how flexible production affects workers. Academics, policy makers, and media commentators often celebrate the advantages of flexible production for employees, employers, and the "new" economy. The authors, however, find that the "new" workplace bears a strong resemblance to the old: in spite of changes in names and labels and the introduction of "quality circles" and "empowered" workers, managerial control is still ultimately grounded in some combination of Taylorism and fear. Flexible production often intensifies employment instability and insecurity while diminishing the wages and organizational power of workers.

Chun (Chapter 6) reports on her ethnographic fieldwork of computer component assembly in the Silicon Valley. What she calls "despotic" management often characterizes work relations in this field as firms strive to be "flexible." She examines two different types of "flexible despotism" that correspond to subcontracting regimes and contract manufacturing regimes. Subcontractors use numerical flexibility to quickly expand and contract their workforce, exploiting ethnic and community ties both to recruit and to elicit the workers' consent. In the more technologically advanced and automated assembly lines that dominate the Silicon Valley, contract manufacturers deemphasize informal ties and discipline workers using a well-rehearsed rhetoric of "global competition" to threaten workers with job loss. Chun does more than debunk the mythology associated with the Silicon Valley and flexible specialization, however, for she also highlights the complex social dynamics of work relations under coercive "flexible" production.

Bonacich (Chapter 7) focuses on sweatshop workers in the Los Angeles–area apparel industry. Although the conditions of sweatshop work are relatively well documented, she examines problems and prospects associated with organizing workers in this growing yet largely invisible sector of the American economy—indeed, one that is not supposed to exist in a high-tech economy. According to Bonacich, the mobility and flexibility of production systems in the apparel industry hinder trade union organizing. Through subcontracting, firms become decentralized to the extent that workers often do not know the identity of their employers. The apparel industry also disproportionately employs an immigrant workforce made up predominately of women who are economically and politically marginalized. In spite of these and other barriers, organizers have achieved success by linking the interests of apparel workers with those of consumers concerned with the conditions under which clothing is manufactured. The results have been a series of successful campaigns organized by Union of Needle Trades, Industrial, and Textile Employees (UNITE) to reform and challenge apparel industry employers.

Rinehart (Chapter 8) examines the gap between descriptions and realities of "post-Fordism" in the Canadian and U.S. auto industry. The automobile industry represents an ideal case study, because it, more than any other, has embraced and developed the principles and practices of post-Fordism, such as worker participation programs, reengineering, benchmarking, and lean production programs. Rinehart concludes that the combination of post-Fordist restructuring and the introduction of advanced technologies does not improve the quality of work life. Neither does it create a worker-friendly environment or provide the framework for harmonious labor-management relations. In the North American auto industry, in spite of—or because of—new production technologies and management programs to help workers "work smart," the new system of control looks remarkably like the old one.

Edward Webster (Chapter 9) adds a cross-cultural perspective to the essays in this section by studying the effects of one of the most significant global historical events of the decade: the end of official apartheid in South Africa. According to Webster, black shop stewards were among the most politically active South Africans, both within the workplace, in their opposition to (white) management, and beyond the workplace, in their resistance to apartheid. Yet following the end of official apartheid, many of them became highly cooperative with management. Relying on a nationwide survey of shop stewards, Webster concludes that their willingness to cooperate with management was a result not merely of their "contradictory class locations" but also of the often contradictory intersections of race, class, and resistance in the workplace. The militancy of the shop stewards was in large part fueled by the structure of segregated workplaces. The end of apartheid, however, removed an important element of solidarity between workers and their shop stewards. As overt racial conflict decreased, management became more equipped to elicit cooperation and compromise of shop stewards. Consequently much of the informal workplace structure of apartheid remains in place.

The essays in Part IV examine global and local implications of the proliferation of advanced technology and high-tech work. In doing so they appropriately bring together many of the recurring themes of the book. The worldwide spread of new technology, flexibility in production and organization, and the rapid growth of service and information work require an appreciation of the complexity of the social nature and organization of work. Richard Sharpe analyzes changes in structural employment of the worldwide computer software industry. Peter Meiksins and Peter Whalley and Seán Ó Riain examine microlevel work relations within high-tech, contingent employment and in "virtual" high-tech organizations. This final group of essays also reminds us that many of the most optimistic accounts of the new world of work are premature. If new technology in old workplaces has not eliminated old problems, workplaces boasting new products and new production regimes don't seem to have fared much better.

Sharpe (Chapter 10) discusses the growth of the worldwide software and computer industries. According to him, the content of work and the organization of production are contingent upon a constantly shifting balance of investment capital and the availability of an "appropriate" workforce. "Primary" software production creates software development tools, the intellectual equivalent of capital goods that are sold chiefly to other software companies. These tools in turn enable "secondary" production, in which firms design and develop software applications for corporate or individual consumers. A workforce of elite technical workers in core countries produces the design and short-run prototypes. In the early stages of this process management cedes control over production, motivating professionals with "inspiration," largely because they have no choice. Following the initial period of development, management attempts to regain control of the production process by adopting selective measures that weaken the organizational power of workers. Secondary production—using the products of primary production to make shrink-wrapped "applications"—opens new possibilities for taking back control. Chief among these are contingent employment and the use of routine intellectual labor, which offer a perfect opportunity to move production offshore and to manage using more traditional forms of control. Former economic or political colonies with English-speaking elites are the preferred destination for such secondary production, a situation that literally shapes the industrial geography of software production. By its very nature, the value chain of this most symbolic of high-tech work thus cannot be global at all, but selective.

Meiksins and Whalley (Chapter 11) report on interviews with a subset of U.S. technical professionals employed in contingent work arrangements. They, like Sharpe, find that the high-tech industry has shifted the composition of its workforce, employing fewer traditional full-time and salaried technical workers and more part-time, temporary, or contract employees. Meiksins and Whalley examine specific methods U.S. employers use to control this growing segment of the high-tech workforce. Because traditional techniques, such as career ladders and loyalty measures, seem inappropriate for workers employed in alternative arrangements, managers use a variety of other control methods. For example, employer networks are often used to locate and evaluate prospective workers. Hence a temporary or contracted worker is compelled to meet or exceed work requirements to solicit a favorable recommendation from her or his employer. Management may place contingent workers in project teams, subjecting them to performance pressures placed upon them by their peers. Management also uses sophisticated communications technologies to monitor the work of contingents. Employers may increase market pressures to perform by strategically limiting opportunities for alternative work, thereby increasing competition for jobs. These and other measures enable more effective managerial control of employees who, because of their alternative employment arrangements, may have no direct stake in the future of the organization in which they are employed.

Ó Riain (Chapter 12) turns to another form of high-tech employment: a transnational and "virtual" software firm. A participant-observer, he worked as a technical writer on a team of software developers in an Irish branch plant of a Silicon Valley company. Discussing the dynamics of globalization, he challenges the argument that transnational firms and new technologies diminish the significance of place and break down traditional organizational hierarchies. Ó Riain found that one of the main structural characteristics of production relations was the project deadline. In spite of the physical absence of a manager, the deadline effectively compelled team members to work long hours to complete a project on time. Place became more salient as team members worked closely and developed complex interdependencies. Although solidarity and work intensification characterized the predeadline phase of the project, team members, some of whom were contract workers, became fragmented during the postdeadline period as they jockeyed for position on forthcoming assignments. The frantic pace of work also burned some workers out. Thus, fragmentation, instability, and reorganization of the team in the postdeadline phase allowed the firm to reassert its hierarchical control, even in the absence of direct supervision.

This collection of essays brings together a set of richly nuanced accounts of the changing nature of work in an increasingly integrated international economy. Although wide-ranging in geography and workplace, they are unified in their concern for the predicament of workers in the global workplace. Much of the current discussion of the benefits of globalization, technological innovations, and the opportunities for the unfettered movement of capital ignores the injuries visited by the global "boom" on the majority of the world's population who work longer hours for declining wages. The essays in this volume give voice to the growing ranks of those whose daily experiences with globalization require a more balanced and critical assessment.

Whether in a circuit board factory in San Jose, a supermarket checkout in São Paulo, or a cosmetics counter in Taipei, the nature and organization of work will continue to shape and be shaped by evolving technologies, new forms of work intensification, and ever more tightly managed commodity chains. The complexity of these issues is reflected in the variety of approaches taken by the essays in this volume. Together, they demonstrate that a revitalized critical study of work can help us make sense of both the complexity of global production and the details of workplace relations.

References

Baldoz, Rick, et al. 1998. "Introduction." Pp. 1–3 in *Proceedings of the Conference on "Work, Difference, and Social Change: Two Decades After Braverman's 'Labor and Monopoly Capital,'"* edited by Rick Baldoz, Phoebe Godfrey, Carol Jansen, Charles Koeber, and Philip Kraft. Binghamton: Department of Sociology, State University of New York.

Baskerville, Richard, et al., eds. 1994. *Transforming Organizations with Information Technology.* Amsterdam: North Holland.

Berry, Thomas H. 1991. *Managing the Total Quality Transformation.* New York: McGraw-Hill.

Braverman, Harry. 1998. *Labor and Monopoly Capital: The Degradation of Work in the Twentieth Century*. 25th anniversary ed. New York: Monthly Review Press.

Castells, Manuel. 1996. *The Rise of the Network Society*. Malden, MA: Blackwell.

Colatrella, Steven. 1998. *The Working Class "Web": Immigrants in Italy and the Making of the Worldwide Labor Market*. Ph.D. dissertation, Department of Sociology, State University of New York, Binghamton.

Cusumano, Michael A. 1991. *Japan's Software Factories: A Challenge to U.S. Management*. New York: Oxford University Press.

Davenport, Thomas H., and James E. Short. 1990. "The New Industrial Engineering: Information Technology and Business Process Redesign." *Sloan Management Review*, 31(4): 11–27.

Economic Report of the President. Various years. Washington, DC: U.S. Government Printing Office.

Hammer, Michael. 1990. "Reengineering Work: Don't Automate, Obliterate." *Harvard Business Review*, July–August: 104–112.

Hammer, Michael, and James Champy. 1993. *Reengineering the Corporation: A Manifesto for Business Revolution*. New York: HarperBusiness.

Jones, Matthew. 1994. "Don't Emancipate, Exaggerate: Rhetoric, Reality, and Reengineering." Pp. 357–378 in *Transforming Organizations with Information Technology*, edited by Richard Baskerville, Steve Smithson, Ojelanki Ngwenyama, and Janice I. DeGross. Amsterdam: North-Holland.

Kraft, Philip. 1999. "To Control and Inspire: U.S. Management in the Age of Computer Information Systems and Global Production." Pp. 17–36 in *Rethinking the Labor Process*, edited by Mark Wardell, Thomas L Steiger, and Peter Meiksins. Albany: SUNY Press.

Kraft, Philip, and Angela Roux. 1998. "Globalization, Flexibility, and Work and Family Time." Paper presented at the annual meeting of the Association for Social Economics, Chicago.

Mischel, Lawrence R., and Jared Bernstein. 1994. *The State of Working America, 1994–1995*. Armonk, NY: M. E. Sharpe.

Mischel, Lawrence R., Jared Bernstein, and John Schmitt. 1999. *The State of Working America, 1998–99*. Ithaca: Cornell University Press/ILR Press.

Parker, Mike, and Jane Slaughter. 1994. *Working Smart: A Union Guide to Participation Programs and Reengineering*. Detroit: Labor Notes.

Piore, Michael J., and Charles F. Sable. 1984. *The Second Industrial Divide: Possibilities for Prosperity*. New York: Basic Books.

Porter, Michael. 1991. *The Competitive Advantage of Nations*. New York: Basic Books.

Reich, Robert B. 1991. *The Work of Nations: Preparing Ourselves for 21st-Century Capitalism*. New York: Knopf.

Schor, Juliet. 1991 *The Overworked American*. New York: Basic Books.

Stalk, George, and Thomas M. Hout. 1990. *Competing Against Time: How Time-Based Competition Is Reshaping Global Markets*. New York: Free Press.

U.S. Department of Commerce, Various years. *Statistical Abstract of the United States*. Washington, D.C.: Economics and Statistics Administration, Bureau of the Census.

Womack, James P., Daniel T. Jones, and Daniel Roos. 1990. *The Machine That Changed the World*. New York: Rawson and Associates.

Part I

Continuity and Change

CHAPTER 1

Dwelling in Capitalism, Traveling Through Socialism

Michael Burawoy

Until the appearance of Harry Braverman's *Labor and Monopoly Capital* in 1974, the renaissance of Marxism in the 1960s and 1970s had confined itself either to theories of the state, ideology, or education or of capitalism as an economic system, leaving Marx's analysis of production largely untouched. It was the unproblematic prop for the Marxian edifice. It was Braverman who took up the challenge of rewriting volume one of Marx's *Capital,* producing a history of capitalism's expropriation of control from direct producers. First proletarianized, then deskilled, the working class—Braverman among them—was subject to the inexorable logic of capital.

Where industrial sociology and industrial psychology aimed to attune workers to work, Braverman focused on the transformation of work itself. For the empirical exploration of the subjective side of work—attitudes, perceptions, consciousness, and even conflict—he substituted a critique of capitalism from the standpoint of its artisans. In expelling the craftworker, the capitalist labor process divided mental from manual labor so that workers could no longer imaginatively fabricate the products of their labor. In his historical analysis of the degradation of work, Braverman was simultaneously recounting the objective experience of the worker and the recomposition of class structure.

My own work took up the challenge of studying both these tracks—the experience of the worker and its relation to class formation—but from the subjective side. *First, how do managers elicit the cooperation of workers in the production of surplus value?* Why should workers offer capitalists more than was required for their own reproduction? With nineteenth-century England as his laboratory, Marx explained the extraction of surplus value in terms of coercion, the need to survive, and thus the fear of job loss. With the organized sector of postwar America in mind, I argued that management could rarely fire their workers at will and, even where they could, unemployment compensation and alternative work cushioned the impact. More subtle means of extracting surplus were required. Therefore, where Braverman regarded monopoly capitalism as the consolidation of work degradation, I saw it as new techniques for regulating work, techniques in which consent prevailed over coercion.

This analysis fed directly into the second question: *what is the role of production in working-class formation?* I found it puzzling that in studying class for itself, class as an actor, so much attention was devoted to the realm of superstructures—education, political parties, ideology, and above all the state. This was putting the cart before the horse. If production was not the crucible of class formation, then the significance of superstructures must be seen in a very different light. They no longer exist to counteract political challenges rising from the bowels of the economy. My research pointed to the realm of production as having its own superstructures, what I first called the *internal state* and later the *political and ideological apparatuses of production* or, more broadly, the *regime of production. There were ideological effects of the labor process, but there were also distinct apparatuses that regulated the labor process and shaped a politics of production.*

The concept of production regime offers a conceptual framework for studying divergent struggles and identities emerging around work. I used this framework, for example, to reinterpret my ethnographies of the racial division of labor in Zambia and South Africa as an expression of a production regime I called *colonial despotism.* Others have used the same framework to explore gender regimes in different periods of history and in different parts of the world (see, for example, Milkman 1987; Thomas 1985; Lee 1997; and Salzinger 1997). The idea of production regime allows us to comprehend the political and ideological effects of work in a richer and more variegated way than Braverman's unidimensional notion of control based on deskilling.

My own interest, however, lay in the specificity of capitalist production regimes and the meaning of socialism. Braverman never stated his own vision of socialism, but, from his critique of capitalism, I inferred that it entailed the reunification of mental and manual labor at the collective level in the realm of necessity and at the individual level in the realm of freedom. The production of material necessities would be organized through factory councils themselves and coordinated through a democratic planning mechanism, thereby creating the foundation for craftlike self-realization beyond the realm of necessity. Along these lines I speculated about a socialist production politics as a council communism, hints of which emerged embryonically in the Soviets of the Russian Revolution of 1917, in the Turin factory occupations of 1919, and in the Hungarian workers' committees of 1956.

Important though such speculation might be, the projection of a utopian vision of socialism based on the inversion of capitalism was unsatisfactory. It entailed the false comparison of the reality of one regime with an idealization of another. It was false in two senses. First, in confining oneself to capitalism, one could not appreciate what was specific to capitalism and what might be the ineluctable imperatives of industrialism. Second, it was dangerous to dismiss capitalism in the name of an unspecified, unelaborated utopia without examining whether the latter was either viable (i.e., self-sustaining) or feasible (i.e., reachable). I instead decided, therefore, to study actually existing socialism, or what I called *state socialism.* How might such research help us comprehend what was intrinsically capitalist about work and its regulation, and what, in turn, might this tell us about the possibilities of a democratic socialism, a socialism in which producers governed their own lives?

I searched for the different production regimes of state socialism. What do they share that distinguishes them from capitalist production regimes? How might we think of production regimes in a workers' socialism? To investigate such regimes required access to the everyday world of production, the experiential moment of work and its regulation. Beginning with my research in Africa, my preferred technique had always been participant observation. I had then found a job in a South Chicago plant, where I worked for a year (1974–75) as a machine operator. From this experience emerged the concept of *hegemonic production regime*, which I contrasted with a *despotic regime*, a notion I derived from my reinterpretation of Donald Roy's (1952) earlier ethnography of the same plant. Like so much of the Marxism of the 1970s, my focus was on the durability of capitalism—how it withstands threats to its own demise, how it overcomes its own internal contradictions. I speculated that regimes under state socialism might produce a more volatile working class. Since we knew so little about production regimes in Eastern Europe and the Soviet Union, and what we did know was so heavily refracted through ideology and counterideology, it was even more imperative that I pursue my ethnographic propensities there. Thus between 1983 and 1985 I found jobs in a Hungarian champagne factory, spinning factory, and autoplant. During the next three years I worked intermittently for about a year *in toto* as a furnaceman in Hungary's largest steel plant. I was so focused on the distinguishing traits of socialist production that I didn't pay much attention to the disintegration of the wider political regime. When that time arrived, I didn't hang around to watch socialism's denouement but jumped ship for the Soviet Union, which was then opening up to foreign researchers. In 1991 Kathryn Hendley and I studied a rubber plant in Moscow, and later that year I found a job in a furniture factory in the northern Republic of Komi. The storm from the paradise that we call capitalism seemed to follow me everywhere. Therefore, I decided to stay put, abandoning the holy grail of a democratic socialism to study the tyranny of an unfettered market. Since 1991 I have been following the destruction—what I call the *involution*—of Komi's timber, coal, and construction industries.

In the essay that follows I recapitulate how my trajectory over the last twenty years was driven by abiding Marxist concerns, and how migration from country to country, from workplace to workplace, reshaped the theory I carried with me and thus also my comprehension of the trail I left behind. I investigate the durability of advanced capitalism, the fragility of state socialism, and the peculiarities of emergent postsocialism—all through the eye of an itinerant worker-academic. Finally, I shall show how this dialectic of experience and interpretation, of practice and theory, was itself reconfigured by profound changes in national and global political economies, crystallized in the Polish Solidarity movement (1980–81), the collapse of communism first in Eastern Europe (1989) and then in the Soviet Union (1991), and the concomitant worldwide ascendancy of neoliberal policies and ideologies.

Hegemony Is Born in the Factory

My journey begins with a theoretical puzzle to be found in the writings of Marx. To make the analysis of capitalism plausible, Marx has recourse to a model of feudalism in which surplus labor takes the form of labor rent, separated in space and time from necessary (subsistence) production. The lord always knows, because he sees, what he is getting from his serfs. Under capitalism, by contrast, there is no separation of necessary and surplus labor. Workers appear to be paid for their entire labor time and not only that proportion corresponding to the wage. If surplus value is invisible, capitalists never know whether they have realized a profit until after the fact. But if surplus labor is obscured, how is it secured? If industrial sociology sought to ask why workers don't work harder and why they "restrict output," I asked the opposite question: why do they work as hard as they do?

The theoretical puzzle was born not just out of theory but also out of practice. From July 12, 1974, the day I began work in Allied's South Chicago machine shop, I was struck by how hard my fellow machine operators worked. Advisedly I say "they" since it took me quite a few months before I could even begin to keep up with them. There seemed no good reason for all this effort. Certainly, as my day man would say, "No one pushes you around here. You are on your own." The piece rate system, moreover, guaranteed everyone a minimum wage. Promotion and transfers were decided by a bidding system that favored experience and seniority rather than diligence. So why did everyone stretch and strain to produce those extra pieces that only marginally increased income?

When I asked my fellow workers why they worked so hard, they either looked at me in blank incomprehension or responded indignantly that they were not working hard at all and demonstrated the point by goofing off. They would admit to no such sin. They seemed happier to endorse the managerial view that workers would try to get away with anything than to believe that they were hard workers. I wondered how it was that workers so freely concurred with management's image of them. How was it that management not only exercised domination over workers but won their active consent? My answer borrowed from contemporary analyses of the state, and I showed how similar mechanisms were at work in production (Burawoy 1979).[1]

Management elicited consent to its own domination by allowing work to be organized as a game. To survive in the factory eight hours a day, five days a week, doing monotonous, exhausting, and often dangerous work, laborers turn their work into a game of making out with carefully elaborated rules, sanctioned by shop floor management. Sometimes you made the rate from the job, sometimes you didn't, but always your reputation and self-esteem were on the line. As long as there was work to do, the day sped by. Work as game was framed by two other institutions. One, the *internal labor market*, constituted workers as individuals with rights to job mobility within plant, based on seniority and experience. The longer employees remained at Allied, therefore, the greater their interest in staying with the firm, and the greater their interest in its profitability. The second, the *internal state*, regulated relations between workers and managers. On the one hand collective bargaining forged a common interest between management and union, embodied in the collective contract. On the other hand grievance machinery allowed workers to defend their rights against violations of the emergent legal order of the workplace polity.

Here in the factory opposed class interests were being coordinated as, at the same, time workers were being constituted as industrial citizens. I found myself in the midst of what I called a hegemonic production regime. How typical was it? From all I had learned about postwar U.S. industrial relations, the three features I described above were quite general in the monopoly sector of industry. In locating the regime historically, I was aided by a remarkable coincidence: I had landed in the same factory studied thirty years earlier by Roy (1952), Chicago's great ethnographer of the workplace. Because the labor process was still quite similar, I could concentrate on explaining changes in the regime of production. Examining the rise of hegemony on the shop floor forced me to consider factors beyond the factory: the absorption of Roy's old Geer Company into the multinational corporation I called Allied as well as postwar changes in the broader system of industrial relations. In this way I was able to contextualize the hegemonic regime, recognizing both its *sectoral* and *historical* specificity.

Further, from Roy's study I was able to extrapolate the archetypal *despotic regime of production*, where managers deploy force arbitrarily, and where workers are subject to ad hoc and oppressive penalties, dished out by the capricious overseer. Managers hire and fire at will under market compulsion. Workers have no rights except those they win on the basis of raw power exercised through the monopoly of skill or knowledge. Under the despotic regime political and ideological apparatuses of production have a purely negative function, coercing effort and repressing dissent.

The comparison allowed me to elaborate the ideal type of hegemonic regime in which the application of coercion, whether in the form of fines or firing, is bound by rules that constrain managers as well as workers, rules that are themselves the object of consent. With force limited to infractions of a negotiated order, workers can carve out an arena of self-organization—the first condition of spontaneous consent to managerial domination. The second condition for consent lies in the concrete coordination of interests of managers and workers, based on their interdependence, organized through such institutions as the internal labor market and the internal state. The impetus to consent, however, lies not only in the possibility of future material gain but also in the immediate alleviation of boredom and drudgery at work.

In *Manufacturing Consent* (Burawoy 1979) I sought to turn industrial sociology upside down by inverting its motivating question and Marxism outside in by installing a superstructure within its base. The original inspiration came from Antonio Gramsci (1971, 277–318). Writing of Western Europe, he argued that the distinctive feature of advanced capitalism lay not in its economy but in the rise of civil society and the expansion of the state. Through these superstructures the capitalist class not only justifies and maintains its domination but also wins the active consent of workers. However, Gramsci claimed that the situation was different in the United States, where, without the burden of feudal legacies, the superstructures are "simplified and reduced in number," and hegemony is born in the factory.

This became the leitmotif of my own work, but it begged the question of American exceptionalism. Was there such a thing as an American "Fordist" production regime? If so, how did it differ from other production regimes? What were the conditions of existence of different regimes, both hegemonic and despotic? Above all, did they have different consequences for class struggle?

A Comparative History of Despotism

If it was a fluke that I had stumbled into the same South Chicago factory that Donald Roy had studied, it was no less fateful to discover Miklos Haraszti's (1977) depiction of his trials and tribulations in Hungary's Red Star Tractor Factory. While I was marveling at the effort of my fellow machine operators in South Chicago, Haraszti—an intellectual who had been banished to the factory—had scaled unimaginable heights of work intensity in Budapest. His piece rates were based on running two machines at once. His descriptions violated all the stereotypes of socialist production—socialist workers as slackers, noted only for their indolence, who had retained only one right, the right not to work hard. If Roy's work had forced me to theorize the despotic regime under capitalism, Haraszti's *A Worker in a Worker's State* called for theorization of the despotic regime under state socialism.

The secret of all factory despotism lies in the dependence of workers' material survival outside work on their performance at work. It is this dependence that gives managers their coercive whip. But it can assume different forms. Under early capitalism workers were subject to the whim of their overseer or managers who could hire and fire at will. They had no welfare system to fall back on in the case of unemployment. Under state socialism job guarantees came with wage uncertainty. Where at Allied I was guaranteed a minimum wage regardless of what I produced, at Red Star Haraszti had to work for every forint. To earn a living he had to run his two machines, butter up his supervisor to get a continuous flow of work, and grapple with piece rates that he could not make. His supervisor became his tormenter and the almighty norm his dictator. Far from restraining managerial despotism, the state was always on his back, surveilling, calculating, punishing. The party controlled promotions and transfers, the trade union denied workers their rights, and managers bullied workers into submission with their discretion over every petty reward and penalty. Party, trade union, and management conspired to extract the maximum effort from workers. Instead of market despotism, he was held prisoner to *bureaucratic despotism* (Burawoy 1985, 156–208).

Haraszti's account forced me to think more seriously about early capitalism and its despotic regimes. I had been working with the lurid images of this period that are found in *Capital*. Returning to Marx's original descriptions of the satanic mills of the English textile industry, I unearthed a plurality of production regimes—patriarchal and paternalistic—as well as the original market despotism.[2] Comparing these with the early textile industries in the United States and Russia, I tied regime type to class

struggle in the second half of the nineteenth century in all three countries—the spo-
radic struggles in the United States, the reformist struggles in England, and the revo-
lutionary struggles in Russia (Burawoy 1985, 85–121).[3]

Paying greater attention to early capitalism inevitably led to a deeper understanding of the hegemonic regime of advanced capitalism. Two factors distinguished hegemonic from despotic regimes, both related to the expansion of the state. First, under
advanced capitalism workers had alternative sources of livelihood, in particular minimal social security provided by the welfare state. This meant that since workers were
less vulnerable to despotism, managers had to adopt hegemonic strategies to elicit
cooperation. Second, managers were now restrained from exercising despotic rule by
legally enforceable provisions for trade union recognition, compulsory collective bargaining, regulation of the length of the working day, health and safety guarantees,
and so on. The extension of the state in these two directions—regulation of industrial
relations and the provision of welfare—took on different configurations in different
advanced capitalist countries, giving rise to different hegemonic regimes, again with
different implications for class struggle (Burawoy 1985, 122–155).

At least in the United States, the Reagan years brought a new regime of production,
hegemonic despotism, that restored the coercive mode of early periods but, paradoxically enough, in a hegemonic form. Under this regime, global competition gives the
impetus to intensify control over labor on pain of capital flight. The transition to the
new regime is engineered through a double retreat of the state—on the one side cutting back welfare and the guarantees of livelihood outside production, and on the
other side weakening restraints on the managerial temptation to despotism. Workers
may still be protected from arbitrary firing, but they lose their jobs through regularized layoffs. They can strike, but they are subject to permanent replacement. They can
organize, but their unions are subject to decertification. Hegemony now operates in
reverse: instead of capital making concessions to labor, labor makes concessions to
capital in order to hold on to their jobs. Hegemonic despotism is the unchallenged
rule of capital, measured by declining strikes and union membership.[4]

One arena in particular still seemed to have escaped the strictures of hegemonic
despotism: public employment, where unions continued to expand, and strikes
joined workers and consumers against the state. Here, in a sector that is exempt from
direct effects of global competition and relatively immobile, budget constraints were
softer and subject to political negotiation. State employment was inherently political,
offering a clear target, as well as opportunities and resources for class struggle (see
Johnston 1994).

This brought my comparisons back to state socialism. Were the struggles that
erupted periodically in Eastern Europe similar to the social movement unionism of
state workers of advanced capitalism? Certainly there was a convergence in the
noneconomic goals pursued by both sets of workers; certainly in both cases those
goals might be traced to the direct presence of the state at the point of production. On
the other hand, it was equally plausible that the struggles within state socialism
stemmed not from its *bureaucratic* character but from its *despotic* character, and so the

parallels are better made with working-class movements of the nineteenth and early twentieth centuries.

This was certainly the conclusion that Haraszti wanted to convey in his fascinating observations about the utopian yearnings of his fellow workers. Whereas Allied workers could enact a game within the framework of capitalist domination, Red Star workers could give free reign to their creativity only outside and in opposition to bureaucratic domination. They would carve time out of the working day to produce anticommodities, imaginative and useless objects called "homers." By extension the Polish Solidarity movement was the Great Homer—a national, collective effervescence forced by despotism into "untamed exteriority."

However, whether it was the bureaucratic or the despotic aspect of the production regime that invited class mobilization could not be determined on the basis of one manicured ethnography of the socialist shop floor! Although Haraszti presented Red Star as the universal socialist factory, this claim was only accomplished by artificially severing the factory from its very specific historical, political, and economic context. As I shall show below, Red Star was a quite unusual enterprise, calling into question the generality of bureaucratic despotism as the archetypal regime of state socialism. In any case, if I wanted to determine the nature of production politics and its link to class struggle, I seemed to have no alternative—I had to end my sojourn into comparative history and return to ethnography.

Socialism Too Can Be Efficient

Solidarity erupted in Gdansk, Poland, in August 1980. Not even my wildest theorizing of bureaucratic despotism had prepared me for such an epochal event—the first sustained, nationwide revolt of a working class. But before I could pack my bags and search for work in Poland, General Wajciech Jaruzelski had declared martial law on December 13, 1981. Instead I eventually wormed my way into Hungarian factories in the fall of 1983. I began where it looked most feasible, that is in the rural areas, working first in the champagne factory of a state farm and then in various auxiliary workshops on a cooperative farm.

Wherever I went the gender division of labor was startling—women were driven by the relentless pace of a bottling line or enslaved by piece rates to spinning bobbins while the men loafed around as inspectors, mechanics, supervisors, and the like. For the men, as I soon discovered, work was often a place to rest while their true labors took place in the more entrepreneurial second economy, rearing pigs and poultry, growing vegetables, building new houses. It seemed to be bureaucratic despotism for women and self-organization for men.

This was the case in the rural areas, but what about the industrial plants of the towns? It seemed that working-class life was one of socialism's best-kept secrets. It was difficult enough to set foot inside a real socialist factory, let alone work in one. Only the organizational genius of my friend János Lukács made it possible. We first visited the factory of Bánki in November 1983, at the end of my first extended field trip to Hungary. I returned in the summer of 1984 to work there for two months as a radial drill operator. I couldn't believe my luck until I found myself holding down steel flanges with one bare hand, while trying to control an immense, shaking drill with the other. They had been waiting for a sucker like me (see Burawoy and Lukács 1992, 35–58).

Still this was not Haraszti working on two parallel mills. I was in a machine shop like his, but my experience was very different. Comparing our situations, I began to understand the peculiar context that created his isolation, alienation, and intense work under bureaucratic despotism. First, I quickly found myself at the center of attention. Who, after all, had worked with an American professor, even if he was incompetent? On the shop floor I was protected by Anna, Klára, and Ági of the Dobó Katica Brigade, and outside I occasionally joined my workmates in their wine cellars. Haraszti, by contrast, as a Budapest intellectual and dissident, was shunned and cut off from the social life of the factory. *A Worker in a Worker's State* is indeed about only one worker, and a peculiar one at that.

Second, just as I was delivered to the worst job in the shop, with the most difficult piece rates and conditions, so the same would be true of any newcomer, Haraszti included. More generally, it is often the case that socialist production divides into a core of key workers, usually male, skilled, and experienced, who bargain their way to comfort but at the expense of peripheral workers, unskilled, inexperienced, often women, shackled by impossible piece rates and subject to despotic rule. *Thus, regimes of bureaucratic despotism and what I call "bureaucratic corporatism" reproduce each other within the same workplace.*

Third, there is an historical component to the difference between Red Star and Bánki that accounts for the overall diminution of the despotism and its continuation in particular for women. With the economic reforms of the late sixties came the opening of a second economy, which gave many workers, particularly skilled workers, access to alternative sources of livelihood and therefore greater bargaining strength on the shop floor. Self-organized cooperatives were introduced within the factory in an attempt to halt the drain of key workers into the cooperative sector. This further complicated and diminished despotism. Women, however, were usually excluded from both external and internal second economies, and so they remained as vulnerable as ever.

Fourth, and finally, Bánki was part of a relatively successful concern that produced buses and other heavy vehicles that were often exported. By contrast, Red Star Tractor Factory had been one of the first large enterprises to be subject to the economic reforms in the late 1960s, and when Haraszti arrived it was in deep trouble, soon to be liquidated. He thus experienced the pressure of working in a factory that had lost favor with the state.

Does deconstructing Haraszti's study lead to the conclusion that there is nothing unique and distinctive to socialist production? Obviously not. Despite much internal heterogeneity within both state socialism and advanced capitalist, the former production regimes are *bureaucratic* with variation governed primarily by relation to the state, whereas the latter are *hegemonic* with variation governed primarily by relation to the market. The great Hungarian economist János Kornai (1980; 1992) concluded that the soft budget constraints occasioned by bureaucratic bargaining with the state lead to shortages and supply-side constraints, while market forces and the pursuit of profit tend to stimulate surplus production and demand-side constraints. Extending Kornai led me to the conclusion that Braverman's theory of managerial expropriation of control was indeed specific to capitalism. The widely touted "flexibility" of contemporary capitalism, which Michael Piore and Charles Sabel (1984) link to changes in demand, is more likely to create a despotic workplace than their "yeoman democracy." Under state socialism, on the other hand, uncertainties in supply side, that is, in materials, machinery and labor, call for flexible autonomy on the shop floor. There the exercise of managerial control through the expropriation of skill is counterproductive.

Certainly, I was impressed how well self-organization on the shop floor could work. There was always work for me, even at my wobbly radial drill. There was none of the chaos that plagued life on the shop floor at Allied—the hot jobs that had to be done yesterday, the queues outside the inspector's office and the crib, the eternal waiting for the truck driver to deliver some needed parts, the disappearing set-up man, the half-completed engines lining the aisles. Bánki, it turned out, was a capitalist paradise next to Allied, which was more the socialist nightmare. Why?

Once more my experiences in Hungary forced me to rethink my conception of production in the United States. (Burawoy and Lukács 1992, 59–80). Allied was a division in a larger corporation and had a relationship to the center based on bureaucratic bargaining and soft budget constraints, and, as in socialism, the result was shortages on the shop floor, shock work, wastage, and inefficiency. Allied's management was always seeking to control the shop floor and always with devastating consequences for production. If Allied was like a socialist factory in a capitalist economy, Bánki was the capitalist factory in the socialist economy. It benefited from competitive pressures for export and exploited the autonomy the state had granted it.

The theoretical lesson is as follows. It's a bad idea to compare an idealization of one system with the reality of another. That is to say, it is no less misguided to critique actual socialism for failing to live up to an idealization of capitalism than to attack actual capitalism for falling short of a socialist utopia. Better discern the rationality or logic of each system and use it to evaluate the corresponding reality. Better still, recognize that actual capitalism and actual socialism contain elements of both types. Both orders contain markets *and* hierarchies but in an inverse relation. Just as the dominant principle in capitalism is the market whose malfunctioning requires compensation by corporations and states, so in socialism hierarchies prevail whose dysfunctions require the complementarities of inside contracting systems, external cooperatives, and private production.[5] Each pure system contains too many internal contradictions to exist without restitution from the other.

So much for the distinctive features of socialist work organization and its regulation, but how did this shape the formation of a working class and its propensity to class action? Why did Solidarity erupt in Poland and not in Hungary? To discern the multiple layers of class consciousness required a deeper immersion in working-class life.

Painting Socialism: The Ritual Enactment of Class

As I made my way from Budapest to the medieval town of Egér, where Bánki was located, I had to pass through Hungary's second biggest city, Miskolc, the capital of its eastern industrial heartland. There, sprawling along the valley, lay the giant Lenin Steelworks, employing fifteen thousand workers and marking the pulse of the city. The soul of the socialist proletariat lay here—capable of heroic feats of endurance, celebrated in posters of the Stalinist past, carriers of that radiant future that was to be communism. To join the army of workers that swarmed through the gates three times a day was my secret dream. Miraculously, János Lukács arranged it, and I won a place at the heart of the steelworks as a furnaceman, tending the state-of-the-art German basic oxygen furnace. I'd finally graduated from an individualistic machine operator to a team worker. I joined the October Revolution Socialist Brigade for about the year over the period 1985–88.

The Lenin Steel Works was a nightmare of coordination. From Japan there were a continuous caster and an electric arc furnace, from Germany a basic oxygen furnace, from Sweden a vacuum degasser, and from Austria technicians to help maintain this newfangled goulash technology. The combination was not only difficult to negotiate in itself but underlined the incongruence of capitalist technology in a socialist order. The technology all presumed that material inputs could be accurately calibrated and punctually delivered. In a shortage economy that was simply impossible. You took what you got and when it arrived. There was no way of sending back the iron or the scrap if it was the wrong quality or contained unwanted impurities. You were lucky to have the materials at all. When the Japanese came to repair the continuous caster and correct the computerized system, they could only scratch their heads, bemused by the anarchy of production. They couldn't cope with this socialist variant of "just in time" (Burawoy and Lukács 1992, 87–110).

Ideally, the steelworks was supposed to be controlled from above through computerized systems. In reality this system was effective only when skilled supervisors and workers on the shop floor ignored the computer and improvised to ward off continual crises. Middle managers were superfluous at best and meddling at worst. They compensated for their ineffectiveness with despotic rule that continually broke down as they relied so heavily on spontaneous cooperation on the shop floor. When Lukács and I reported on this state of affairs, middle managers had a tantrum, called a public meeting to condemn our study, and told us to do the study again. Managers could never be blamed for inefficiency; any problems were outside their control, and we simply didn't understand what was going on. My fellow October Revolutionaries chuckled in amusement.

Slowly I began to assimilate the steelworkers' socialist "culture of critical discourse," to play back their cynicism to them. They were steeped in socialist imagery expressed in endless jokes about socialist irrationality, relentlessly drawing attention to the gap between ideology and reality. For them reality appeared to be more the inversion of ideology than its realization. I made much, perhaps too much, of the rituals that workers had to perform in celebration of the wonders of socialism, which included political and production meetings; the circus organized for visiting dignitaries; the badges, flags, and medals that we'd win for outstanding performance. In their joking their cynicism was much in evidence, but in their outbursts of anger I detected a continuing commitment to socialist ideals.

Still vividly etched in my memory was the visit of the prime minister. We had to volunteer a "communist" shift to paint the slag drawer a bright yellow. My fellow October Revolutionaries got out their paintbrushes, but I could only find one with black paint and so I proceeded to paint our shovels black. Along came the superintendent, wanting to know what the hell I was doing. I told him, as innocently as I could, that I was helping to build socialism. ET, the brigade's wit, turned to me and said, "Misi, Misi, you are not building socialism, you are painting socialism, and black at that." All of us roared with laughter, except the superintendent, who stalked off.

It was true: workers had to paint socialism as efficient, egalitarian, and just, while all around them was waste, class privilege, and favoritism. They criticized the socialist regime, the party, the system for failing to realize its promises. They turned the ideology against the regime it was supposed to legitimate. Workers developed a strong sense of class hostility to the red directors and their managerial lackeys, exuding a socialist consciousness at the very same time that they rejected actually existing socialism (Burawoy and Lukács 1992, 111–114).

Behind their cynicism lurked the shadows of a working-class movement, or so I thought. At least Hungarian workers talked the language of socialism. The missing ingredient, I thought, was an effective working-class solidarity. Here in Hungary, there were so many avenues for workers to realize their material interests through the second economy, whether at work in the VGMKs or outside in cooperatives or odd jobs.[6] Working-class consciousness was layered with strong petty bourgeois inclinations that subverted class unity. Class solidarity was more likely in Poland, where workers still spent time standing in queues rather than working on their dachas, where second-economy activities were less well organized, and where the church acted as a solidifying umbrella, a symbol of an oppressed nation. As individual outlets were less available, so class interests were realized in collective organization against the Polish regime.

While I was busy working out why Solidarity occurred in the east and not the west, in Poland and not Hungary, the regime was crumbling from above. I was riveted to my search for socialist symbols and rituals. With my limited historical perspective, I did not recognize—or did not want to recognize—just how attenuated they had become. As I scraped away the dust from the slogans of yesteryear, I didn't appreciate that workers were holding a ruling elite accountable to an ideology in which it no longer believed. The *nomenclatura* was getting ready to cast off the trappings of socialism. When the appropriate moment arrived in 1989, there was surprisingly little resistance to emancipating the economy, at least from the atrophying socialist *ideology*.

There were those like Jancsi, our devoted shop steward, who now saw the chance to create a real trade union. For three years I had chided him for selling his soul to a bankrupt company union. When communism disintegrated, he was one of the first to become active in the burgeoning factory council movement—a throwback to 1956. He promised to build a real union. But in the end these were lone voices. Socialist ideology had been so pummeled, distorted, and deployed against the working class that it could awaken few people's imagination.

If ideology could evaporate, institutions were more obdurate. As I was to discover in Russia, reality lagged behind the new market religion, sometimes even following in reverse. It has been difficult to liberate the Hungarian economy from the industrial dinosaurs that dogged its past. Lenin Steelworks, albeit with a different name, lived on, receiving subsidies from the state until it was finally sold to a Slovakian company in 1997, but not before its labor force was decimated. Of the original fifteen thousand employees, only a couple of thousand remain, including my comrades from the October Revolution Brigade who are still stoking the furnace. Unemployment is up to 25 percent in Hungary's industrial wastelands. For many in Miskolc, the past does indeed look more radiant every day.

The theoretical lesson is that state socialism rests on the central appropriation and redistribution of surplus. Domination and exploitation are transparent and therefore require *legitimation*. Transparency calls for an ideology that presents the party state as all-knowing and embracing the universal interest embodied in the plan.[7] Legitimation based on a radiant future, rather than immemorial tradition, however, invites criticism on its own terms—a criticism that demands that the party state live up to its promises. State socialism cannot live without legitimacy, but in the end it could not live with legitimacy. As pressure mounted, so the ruling class abandoned its socialist project and parachuted into a market economy.

Capitalism, by contrast, is blessed with flexible patterns of accumulation and the invisibility of exploitation so that legitimation plays second fiddle to *hegemony*—the coordination of material interests of all classes with the general interest of the dominant class. The power of hegemony is to channel dissent into struggles at the margins rather than the center, over compromises rather than principles. Hegemony may be strengthened by but does not rely on the capricious belief in legitimacy. It depends on practices that organize consent in production, in school, in family, and so on. Hungary tried to bolster the fragility of its socialist legitimacy with the robustness of hegemony organized in civil society. But even this substructure could not prevent the outer shell from cracking.

On the Cusp Between Perestroika and Privatization

I migrated to Hungary to experience socialism and its work regime firsthand. I had wanted to know why the first societywide workers' revolution took place in a socialist rather than a capitalist society. I was curious about the prospects for the democratization of state socialism, the possibilities of workers' socialism.[8] I had not come to study the transition to capitalism, so I packed my bags and made my way to the bastion of communism. It was not only a matter of escaping Hungary, for just as important was

the appeal of the Soviet Union, which, in the period of late perestroika, was undergoing momentous political change. For the first time foreigners could travel and talk freely
in the country.

I began the exploration of Soviet enterprises with Kathryn Hendley at the beginning
of 1991. For two months we spent every day at Rezina, a famous rubber plant in the
center of Moscow. Through the enterprise trade union she had managed to gain unlimited access in exchange for a couple of computers for their kindergartens. We were
promised that Rezina was a "drop of water" through which we could study the turbulent seas of perestroika. We were not disappointed (Burawoy and Hendley 1992).

Rezina was a dreadful place, an apparition arisen from the last century. It was just
as I imagined those Victorian satanic mills to be, with workers, mainly women, toiling in dark, dank dungeons without ventilation or light, suffering respiratory dis-
eases from the fumes of resin and paid a pittance for the privilege. Whenever we
wanted to talk to workers, we were accompanied by managers, and the conversation
quickly fell into a sullen silence. Even if they could speak freely, what was there to
say to a couple of foreigners? Their humiliation and degradation were palpable.

We managed to inveigle ourselves into the morning planning meetings attended
by all the managers and shop chiefs. It was quite a scene to behold, with insults and
innuendo thrown from one end of the table to the other, managers fulminating at each
other for this failure or that. Usually the manager for supplies bore the brunt of verbal abuse. He had the unenviable task of begging, cajoling, bribing, coercing suppliers from all over the Soviet Union. But that was only half the job. He then had to wave
his magic wand over truck drivers and railroad officials to transport the materials. He
would never reveal to us the secret of his trade.

With the entire planning system in disarray, winter 1991 was a particularly bad time
to coordinate production. It was further complicated by the burgeoning second economy within the enterprise. The director was funneling funds from the state into the
pockets of supervisors, managers, and suave, young entrepreneurs who ran the so-
called cooperatives and small enterprises within the plant. These semi-autonomous
units used the materials, machinery, and labor of the official enterprise at discounted
rates, set by the director, and could sell or barter the products very profitably at so-
called contractual prices, boosted by the pressures of a shortage economy. Workers
never saw these profits—they were expected to consider themselves lucky for the
opportunity to work over time.

I'd seen it all before in Hungary in 1988 and 1989, when managers at the Lenin Steelworks had made themselves (in cooperation with foreigners) share owners of limited
companies that they had created from the potentially profitable parts of the enterprise. The state continued to own the company shell and was billed for overheads and
the escalating losses, while the limited companies and their shareholders pocketed
handsome profits. No wonder workers were cynical about so-called privatization, or
what was euphemistically called "spontaneous privatization."

Over their heads but in the name of the labor collective, struggles were tearing apart
Rezina's management—a microcosm of the wider Soviet polity. On the one side there

were the defenders of the integrity of the Soviet Union, which included the director of the enterprise, his chief engineer, and much of the old guard. They argued that Rezina's dependence on supplies from all over the Union meant that fragmentation would be suicide. They urged continued allegiance to the Soviet ministries who guaranteed their livelihood. The young Turks, headed by the leader of the factory council (STK), argued for changing the enterprise's affiliation to Russia and Yeltsin's government. They attacked the Soviet ministries as the source of Rezina's economic crisis. A market economy and privatization, as proposed for Russia, could not be worse than the existing planning system. While we were there, factory civil wars broke out in public meetings, with each side pressing its interest in the name of the labor collective while accusing the opposition of particularism and corruption.

So much for the legendary unity of the labor collective, so beloved by Western treatises on the planned economy that had regarded the enterprise as an integral entity bargaining with the state over success indices and plan targets. In the classic pictures of David Granick (1967), Alec Nove (1965), and Joseph Berliner (1957), the enterprise was like a machine operator—restricting output below 100 percent (goldbricking) to signal a plan that was too tight and keeping output to only a little above 100 percent (quota restriction) to hide a plan that was too loose. Enterprises would try to restructure themselves to enhance their power vis-à-vis the center, integrating backward into supplies to overcome shortages or expanding into key products that would enhance their leverage with the center. In every analysis the enterprise acted as a unit, and the interests of all lay in minimizing what they had to give up to the state and maximizing what they took from the state. Apart from literary accounts, we never heard of struggles within the factory over divergent interests and strategies, like those that overwhelmed Rezina. As the coherence of the state broke down and dual power emerged on the national scene, so the enterprise itself split into two, an organic crisis in which the old is not yet dead and the new is struggling to be born.

The symbol and guarantor of enterprise unity had been the party organization. Under the Soviet order it sought to build internal unity and align the interests of enterprise with the state. By January 1991 the party had already disintegrated at Rezina. We were perhaps the first and the last to visit Rezina's new party secretary in his spacious office, now stripped of all furniture. A lonely old man sat all by himself behind a desk, with an enormous telephone switchboard—symbol of bygone power—at arm's length. Its connections, however, had all been ripped out of the wall. He reminisced about the past and his long-standing ambition to become a party secretary. He had realized his dream now, when the party, except for a handful of obdurate old-timers, was already defunct. The power struggle was raging all around, but it never blew through his hollow chambers. Long before August 1991 he had been consigned to the museum of communist history.

Rezina lay on the fault line of a low-intensity earthquake that was rumbling through the Soviet economy. Dependent on supplies from all over the Union, the factory was itself a major supplier of rubber products to the all-important auto industry. When the economy shook, Rezina threatened to fall apart at its seams. The collapse of the Soviet Union was catastrophic, so different from the molecular transformation of Hungary. Even though I was at the center of Hungary's largest steel plant, the politics of disintegration seemed remote from the workplace. For twenty years Hungary had been grooming an alternative political economy, a rudimentary hegemony that coordinated disparate interests and that lay in waiting when the party state crumbled. In Russia, however, there was no legitimate alternative ready to take over, and so the forces of the past would quickly regroup to exploit the new opportunities of disintegration. But that is getting ahead of myself. For now I fled the scene of the Rezina disaster for the north, where things were still tranquil and from where I could get a better glimpse of the past and future.

Industrial Involution: Russia's Descent into Capitalism

Syktyvkar, with a population of 250,000, is the capital of the Komi Republic, lying to the west of the Urals in the far north of European Russia. Sparsely populated, it is rich in natural resources—coal, bauxite, oil, and gas—and covered in a rich forest, much of it still inaccessible. Komi has always been a land of exiles from the period of Catherine the Great. Under communism it was an integral part of the gulag, with labor camps feeding the timber and coal industries. The area had long been essentially closed to foreigners, but in the spring of 1991 it was already possible to migrate there to continue my peripatetic vocation as an incompetent factory worker. With the help of a local sociologist, Pavel Krotov, I obtained a job drilling holes at Polar Furniture, the city's model furniture factory (Burawoy and Krotov 1992).

Whereas Rezina's management was divided into warring factions, Polar Furniture had a tightly knit managerial team that capitalized on its favorable economic position. It had a regional monopoly of the production of poor quality wall units, an item of furniture found in every Soviet apartment. Because they were in such demand, wall units were easily bartered for other goods in short supply—places in holiday camps in the Crimea, housing, sugar, and tinned meat. The chief barterer was the trade union boss, who acted like a feudal baron, dispensing his loot to keep peace among his minions.

Wall units are simple to manufacture, providing one can guarantee the supply of materials. At Polar Furniture this presented few problems for two reasons. First, the supplies were simple and for the most part locally accessible, namely pressed wood that was produced nearby from the Komi forests. Second, Polar had a privileged relation to the Komi Timber Conglomerate that distributed resources throughout the industry.

Polar's charmed existence gave its general director the self-assurance to hire me, when every other place had closed their doors. On the shop floor, however, it was a different matter. There the lack of enthusiasm toward me was palpable, and I was shunned from most collective activities. I speculated at the time that I was too much of an oddity for people to accept—an American professor who wanted to work on the shop floor. My work mates had never met an American, let alone one as strange as I. My Russian was still embryonic, and my mechanical ineptitude put me at the very bottom of the status hierarchy. To add insult to injury I was paid more or less the same as everyone else in the brigade. Still, under not too different conditions, Hungarian workers had embraced me. At the time, I speculated that cultural factors must be at work—the legacy of Stalinist suspicion as well as the solidarity of the labor collective. Later I learned the reason was simpler: management, in particular my shop floor supervisors, were using me to discipline the workforce. Sveta, my "master," would say, "Hey, lads, get to work. There's an American watching us!"

But even this warning didn't seem to have much effect. To the contrary, workers would straggle in late and leave early. There were all sorts of stoppages in work. At the end of the month there would be a desperate surge of production to fulfill the plan, the legendary shock work lived on. At last I'd arrived in a "real" socialist factory! The tempo of production was too unstable for the work games I had known at Allied. Instead we played cards and dominoes to while away the time. We were not constituted as individuals with rights and obligations but as a labor collective. The trade union did not patrol a grievance machinery nor even bargain with management, but instead was unambiguously part of management. If there was a production game, it was between the brigades on the shop floor and the enterprise managers over plan fulfillment. It was not an individual game as at Allied or Bánki, but part of a bargain in which management ceded control of production yet provided conditions of work in return for workers' best effort to meet plan targets. From here bargaining spiraled up the hierarchy to successive levels.

As controls from the republic's planning centers relaxed in the spring of 1991, I could already discern capitalism incubating within socialism. As the party lost its grip on powerful monopolies such as Polar, they became more autonomous and better able to exploit their market position, dictating terms of exchange. Barter relations that had always existed but under the auspices of party supervision spread like weeds through the economy. Management, which before had devoted its attention to garnering supplies, now strategized to maximize the returns on trade. At the same time autonomy of the shop floor increased. Always great because flexible specialization was needed to adapt to supply uncertainty and because workers could not be fired, autonomy now increased even more because the party as the one organ of control had all but vanished. It was as if managers had become merchants subcontracting work to the labor collective. This *merchant capitalism* was a far cry from modern bourgeois capitalism with its focus on accumulation and investment, on process and product innovation. Still it was capitalism—profit had come to rule the day—even if it was not Max Weber's sober, Western bourgeois version.

Incipient merchant capitalism set the parameters for enterprise response to economic reforms promulgated from Moscow. I stopped work two months before the failed coup of August 1991 that signaled the disintegration of the Soviet Union, and the ascendancy of Boris Yeltsin and his economic reformers. I returned to Polar in the following summer of 1992, six months after price liberalization and the dismantling of planning organs. Polar was still doing very well, exploiting its newly won freedom by raising prices to capture the unfulfilled demand for wall systems. But by the fall of

1992 the reforms were taking their toll. Wage increases were falling behind those in neighboring enterprises, Polar was losing money on its export contract with IKEA, and privatization was looming ahead. A revolt from the shop floor threw out the wily old director for dictatorial and corrupt practices. Most of the old managerial team left with him. They could see the writing on the wall.

In 1993 Polar's fortunes took a nose dive. Furniture from different parts of the ex–Soviet Union and even elsewhere in Europe was appearing in the shops, often cheaper and of vastly better quality than Polar's. Then came the disintegration of the Komi Timber Conglomerate and Polar's privileged access to credit and material resources. The effects came slowly through 1993 and then escalated in 1994, first in the form of falling real wages, and then through furloughs and nonpayment of wages. Once more, in the spring of 1994, the labor collective, now owners of the enterprise, installed a new director. But there was not much he could do. The enterprise had accumulated such enormous debts that credit was unobtainable. It tried to sell its reserve shares, but no one would buy them. The enterprise was bankrupt but maintained limited operations through bartering its products for raw materials. Decline was now irreversible. When I returned in the summer of 1995 I found most of the factory in darkness.

The experience of Polar was quite typical of companies all over Russia. The decline of the Russian economy has been unprecedented; since 1989 every year has seen a decline in gross domestic product, sometimes by as much as 20 percent. Far from promoting accumulation, liberalization, privatization, monetization, and stabilization have come at the cost of production. A process of involution governs the decline of an economy that eats itself up. Dynamism in the sphere of exchange—shopkeepers, merchants, financiers, mafia—funnels resources from production, forcing workers to retreat into subsistence and petty commodity production. In a reversal of Soviet industrialization that had been purchased at such great human cost, Russia today is marked by primitive disaccumulation. Involution is not so much an enduring legacy of the past as the outcome of neoliberal policies applied to an administered economy. In the first phase of transition—disintegration—monopolies were strengthened. Freed of party control, they could now exploit their market position. The second phase—liberalization—continued to feed enterprise coffers through inflation. With privatization, managers appropriated the benefits, whether through asset stripping or price gouging, while workers turned to stealing. Under pressure from monopolistic industry, the state expanded enterprise credits, channeling them through newly independent banks that raked in their share of the profit. These newly constituted banks were, after all, owned by the same enterprises that received the credit. Budget constraints were not hardened but monetized. The third phase—stabilization—saw the credit supply dwindle, interest rates turn positive, and inflation rates fell. Rather than disappear into bankruptcy, enterprises exited the financial sphere and returned to barter relations. Banks collapsed or were absorbed by the mafia, which came into its own as a shadow state to guarantee transactions. The fourth phase—consolidation—saw the concentration of wealth in financial industrial groups, closely tied to government and organized around the export of raw materials, energy, and the media. In return for supporting local and national cliques descended from the communist nomenclature, the new Russian managers were rewarded with ownership of the most lucrative public enterprises. Untold wealth accumulated at one pole and poverty at the other.

Now workers retreat rather than resist. Wages are not paid, but workers still turn up for work in the vain hope that something will trickle their way. Socialism has been so effectively discredited that it provides no more than nostalgia for the past. There is no ideology to cement opposition or to imagine alternatives. Production politics have been eviscerated, and commodity fetishism has won undisputed allegiance.

The Grave Diggers of Communism

One thousand kilometers north of Syktyvkar lies Vorkuta, a city of some two hundred thousand inhabitants on the Arctic Circle that has had one and only one reason for existing—its rich supply of coal. It is a living artifact of the gulag, an internal colony cut out of the frozen tundra by prison labor in the 1930s. No one could escape from this valley of death—as one of its communities is called—because there was simply nowhere to go. Vorkuta also became a critical supply of metallurgical coal during World War II, when the Ukraine was occupied by the Germans. Because prisoners from all over Russia were dispatched to Vorkuta, it became a veritable international community. Many were political prisoners—writers, painters, scientists, and musicians—and the city became famous for its artistic talent and its theater. Aspiring apparatchiki would do their sacrificial stint in the inhospitable Vorkuta before being promoted into the higher circles of Moscow or Leningrad. After the camps were closed in the 1950s, workers migrated to Vorkuta from all over the Soviet Union, and especially from the mining towns of the Ukraine, in search of higher wages. Accustomed to horrific working conditions underground and storms, blizzards, and arctic temperatures on surface, the people of Vorkuta developed their own rugged culture, a sense that they could confront any adversity, even communism.

In 1989, together with the miners from Kuzbass in Siberia and Donbass in the Ukraine, Vorkuta miners stunned the world with their sustained and militant strikes. In their first set of demands, they called for improved wages, pensions, longer vacations, Sunday as a holiday for all, better housing, guaranteed supplies of basic food, and the termination of the feudal code that held workers in bondage to a single mine. The second set of demands attacked the economic order, calling for enterprise autonomy, the right to dispose of 25 percent of foreign earnings, and most broadly the introduction of a market economy. The third set of demands were political: dismantling the command economy, and revoking Article 6 of the Constitution, which gave the party its monopoly of power. They also called for free elections to all official positions, the right to form independent trade unions and parties, a free press, and recognition of their own strike committee. In short, this was an all-embracing radical program for a new society.

The protests lasted through the summer of 1989 and were renewed in 1991 when Yeltsin, already leader of the Russian Federation, used them in his battle against Mikhail Gorbachev and the Soviet regime. The miners were the dynamite that brought down the Soviet system, but they were also among the first victims of the new order. Their anarcho-syndicalist platform was appropriated as a program for a capitalist economy and liberal democracy. In 1992 the economic reforms brought inflation rates of 30 percent per month, wiping out the miners' life savings. Allowed to sell 17 percent of their coal at any price, mine management and the new independent trade unions competed for access to the world market. Vorkuta was flooded with Western consumer goods—televisions, videos, refrigerators, and clothes—a sop to the miners who had fought for much more. The strike committee abandoned its followers for sinecures in local and federal government or found their way into lucrative "commercial structures."

In Vorkuta, at least, socialism had created its own grave diggers, the very proletariat the regime had celebrated. No sooner had they put down their spades than their captains grabbed the inheritance, abandoning their followers to their fight for daily bread. Vorkuta spawned its own mafia—the merchants of coal—who spread their nodes across the former Soviet Union and from there across Europe, arranging chains of barter, exploiting the as-yet low production costs based on handsome subsidies and low wages. As with timber, however, coal prices very quickly caught up with the merchants, and the inrushing capitalism brought world prices to the Russian hinterland.

But in the coal industry, involution never caused the destructiveness it did in timber. The timber industry was a vertically integrated commodity chain, with the lumber villages and timber centers exploited at the bottom of the hierarchy. When the reforms came, those at the bottom exited the chain in the expectation that they could only do better in the open market. Their departure brought about the collapse of the industry, leaving them destitute without buyers for their raw timber. The coal industry, by contrast, controled a scarce resource that it could parlay into political muscle. Once the initial flurry into the world market was over, the mines and the trade unions regrouped around the conglomerate to demand increased subsidies and wage payments from the federal government. Strikes were orchestrated to draw attention to the miners' plight. Theirs was a strategy of voice rather than exit, and for the time being it has contained the rate of involution.

Under the supervision of the World Bank, the Russian coal industry is downsizing. Vorkuta Ugol´, the local coal conglomerate, has already closed five of the thirteen mines. The World Bank proceeds as rationally as possible, determining how best to implement a safety net and how best to allow the community to participate in its own demise, trying to ensure that the government does not create false expectations. The World Bank's strategy of environmentally sustainable development seeks to implant a hegemonic production politics wherever protest threatens the global expansion of capitalism (see Cernea and Kudat 1997; Goldman 1997; Ferguson 1994). To promote the mobility of capital, the enlightened are now trying to transport Western apparatuses of production, organizing consent on inhospitable soils. But so far there is no sign that hegemonic regimes are so portable!

Flexible Capitalism, Fragile Socialism, and the Aftermath

Braverman captured the rhythm of capitalist expansion, its capacity to reconstitute itself through the recomposition of work in a dialectic of deskilling, reskilling, and further deskilling. But he didn't capture the source of capitalism's political and ideological sustainability, which, I argue, lay first in its despotic and then in its hegemonic apparatuses of production. Capitalism has proved to be as durable as socialism has been fragile. As I scampered away from under Gulliver's feet, migrating from Hungary to Russia, from Moscow to Syktyvkar to Vorkuta, everywhere capitalism caught up with me. Why did socialism keel over, for the most part without even a murmur or a gasp? Too much has been said about the flexibility of capitalism and not enough of the fragility of socialism.

There are, of course, many theories. Some relate the internal economic contradictions of socialism that had begun to make themselves felt in the 1970s, but all economic orders face contradictions. Others argue that socialism was too rigid to adapt to the information order. But this does not explain the absence of resistance to the collapse of the social order. Then there are globalism arguments, but they too stress the strength of an irrepressible international capitalism rather than the feebleness of socialism. In addition to such economic arguments, there are the political theories that portray socialism as a pack of cards waiting to collapse. No order can live for ever by repression alone. But it did live for seventy years, and it crumbled when repression was at its weakest. Ken Jowitt (1992) offers a more prescient analysis of a regime that had lost its sense of purpose with the routinization of its charismatic powers.

From the standpoint of my own odyssey from capitalism to socialism, I see the political and the economic as inextricable. The hegemonic regimes of advanced capitalism work through the coordination of interests, operating at all levels of society, and not least in production. The bureaucratic regimes of socialism work through the legitimation of a transparent exploitation and domination. Hegemony organizes and isolates struggles on its own terms, while legitimacy invites critique that challenges its own order. To speak of a legitimation crisis in advanced capitalism or a hegemonic crisis of state socialism is to confound their distinctiveness.

But understanding the economic foundations of political crisis and continuity is more complicated than simply pinning hegemony to one regime and legitimacy to the other. Each system can only exist when complemented by the other. Capitalism calls on states to compensate for the irrationality of its economy. The fragility of capitalism, therefore, lies with its weakest link, the state, which politicizes its own regulation. Equally, socialism requires an elaborate private sphere, coordinated by market-type relations, to compensate for the malfunctioning of the administered economy. In this complementary world of real socialism, interests can be organized and coordinated, and hegemony can be constituted to bolster legitimacy. This was developed furthest in Hungary and is the mainstay of the Chinese order. Private, market-like coordination may be necessary to sustain socialism, but it may be labeled antithetical to socialism, so deepening the crisis of legitimacy. This was the case in Russia. In short, each system incubates its opposite, which can in turn either reinforce or undermine the dominant order.

How do these comparisons help us comprehend the postsocialist order? Does the specific combination of administered and market coordination prefigure the emergent political economies? No such determining-path dependency can be established. To try to do so would be to confuse the dynamics and collapse of the old order with the very different process of the genesis of the new. It is much better to focus on the transition as a *sui generis* process with its own combined and uneven logic in which government interventions are as important as their unintended and unexpected consequences. Still this process does not take place in a vacuum—its origins lie in the breakdown of the socialist order, just as its direction is influenced by global capitalism. Where the breakup of the socialist order does not reveal a sturdy structure of civil society and hegemony, as it did not in Russia, so an alternative legitimacy has to be fabricated out of a new ideology, in this case neoliberalism, which carries its own unanticipated consequences and immanent critiques.

Notes

1. This book was heavily influenced by Antonio Gramsci and by the French structuralist Marxism of Louis Althusser and Nicos Poulantzas.

2. I had also studied a different type of despotism—colonial despotism—in the Zambian copper mines. Based on four years of fieldwork, from 1968 to 1972, I analyzed the uneven persistence of colonial despotism even after political independence. See Burawoy, 1985, 209–252.

3. For elaborations of this comparative approach showing the links between factory politics and wider struggles, see Richard Biernacki's (1995) comparison of the nineteenth-century textile industry in England and Germany, and Jeffrey Haydu's (1998) comparisons of metalworkers in England and the United States at the turn of the twentieth century.

4. For more recent analyses of this phenomenon see Gordon 1996; Blum 2000; and Chun, Chapter 6.

5. This idea of mirrored comparisons derives from Iván Szelényi 1981.

6. VGMKs were work collectives based on a form of inside contracting. See Stark 1986.

7. Here I am indebted to George Konrád and Iván Szelényi's classic *The Intellectuals on the Road to Class Power* (1979).

8. Linda Fuller (1992), for example, shows how Cuba's economic decentralization in the late 1960s led to a democratization of production politics and how this in turn fed back into national politics.

References

Berliner, Joseph. 1957. *Factory and Manager in the USSR*. Cambridge: Harvard University Press.

Biernacki, Richard. 1995. *The Fabrication of Labor: Germany and Britain, 1640–1914*. Berkeley: University of California Press.

Blum, Joseph. 2000. "Degradation Without Deskilling: Twenty-Five Years in the San Francisco Shipyards." Pp. 106–136 in *Global Ethnography*, edited by Michael Burawoy et al. Berkeley: University of California Press.

Burawoy, Michael. 1979. *Manufacturing Consent: Changes in the Labor Process Under Monopoly Capitalism*. Chicago: University of Chicago Press.

———. 1985. *The Politics of Production: Factory Regimes Under Capitalism and Socialism*. London: Verso.

Burawoy, Michael, and Kathryn Hendley. 1992. "Between Perestroika and Privatization: Divided Strategies and Political Crisis in a Soviet Enterprise." *Soviet Studies*, 44: 371–402.

Burawoy, Michael, and Pavel Krotov. 1992. "The Soviet Transition from Socialism to Capitalism: Worker Control and Economic Bargaining in the Wood Industry." *American Sociological Review*, 57(2): 16–38.

Burawoy, Michael, and János Lukács. 1992. *The Radiant Past: Ideology and Reality in Hungary's Road to Capitalism*. Chicago: University of Chicago Press.

Cernea, Michael, and Ayse Kudat. 1997. *Social Assesments for Better Development: Case Studies in Russia and Central Asia*. Washington, DC: World Bank.

Ferguson, James. 1994. *The Anti-Politics Machine: "Development," Depoliticization, and Bureaucratic Power in Lesotho*. Minneapolis: University of Minnesota Press.

Fuller, Linda. 1992. *Work and Democracy in Socialist Cuba*. Philadelphia: Temple University Press.

Goldman, Michael. 1997. "Green Hegemony." Unpublished manuscript, Department of Sociology University of Illinois Urbana-Champaign.

Gordon, David. 1996. *Fat and Mean: The Corporate Squeeze of Working Americans and the Myth of Managerial "Downsizing."* New York: Free Press.

Gramsci, Antonio. 1971. *Selections from the Prison Notebooks*. New York: International Publishers.

Granick, David. 1967. *Soviet Metal-Fabricating and Economic Development*. Madison: University of Wisconsin Press.

Harastzi, Miklos. 1977. *A Worker in a Worker's State*. New York: Penguin Books.

Haydu, Jeffrey. 1988. *Between Craft and Class: Skilled Workers and Factory Politics in Great Britain and the United States*. Berkeley: University of California Press.

Johnston, Paul. 1994. *Success While Others Fail: Social Movement Unionism and the Public Workplace*. Ithaca: ILR Press.

Jowitt, Kenneth. 1992. *New World Disorder: The Leninist Extinction*. Berkeley: University of California Press.

Konrád, George, and Iván Szélenyi. 1979. *The Intellectuals on the Road to Class Power*. New York: Harcourt Brace Jovanovich.

Kornai, János. 1980. *The Economics of Shortage*. 2 vols. Amsterdam: North Holland Publishing.

———. 1992. *The Socialist System*. Princeton: Princeton University Press.

Lee, Ching Kwan. 1997. *Gender and the South China Miracle*. Berkeley: University of California Press.

Milkman, Ruth. 1987. *Gender at Work: The Dynamics of Job Segregation by Sex During World War II*. Urbana: University of Illinois Press.

Nove, Alec. 1965. *The Soviet Economy*. New York: Praeger.

Piore, Michael, and Charles Sabel. 1984. *The Second Industrial Divide*. New York: Basic Books.

Roy, Donald. 1952. "Restriction of Output in a Piecework Machine Shop." Ph.D. dissertation, University of Chicago.

Salzinger, Leslie. 1997. "From High Heels to Swathed Bodies: Gendered Meanings Under Production in Mexico's Export Processing Industry." *Feminist Studies*, 23(3): 549–574.

Stark, David. 1986. "Rethinking Internal Labor Markets: New Insights from a Comparative Perspective." *American Sociological Review*, 51(4): 492–504.

Szelenyi, Ivan. 1981. "The Relative Autonomy of the State or the State Mode of Production?" Pp. 565–591 in *Urbanization and Urban Planning in Capitalist Society*, edited by M. J. Dear and Alan Scott. London: Methuen.

Thomas, Robert. 1985. *Citizenship, Gender, and Work*. Berkeley: University of California Press.

CHAPTER 2

Do Capitalists Matter in the Capitalist Labor Process? Collective Capacities, Group Interests, and Management Prerogatives, c. 1886–1904

Jeffrey Haydu

A common and early criticism of Harry Braverman's *Labor and Monopoly Capital* (1974) was its neglect of workers. Labor appeared in his story, of course, but largely as a generic victim of capital's relentless quest for control. What critics found missing in Braverman's account was a dialectic between the labor process and its victim. They called for more attention to the impact of production relations on workers' ideology and action, and they insisted that workers' resistance to capital also shaped the development of the labor process (Thompson [1989] reviews the debates). Sympathetic scholars soon filled the gap. Ethnographic and historical research has given us a richer sense of how the labor process influences labor consciousness and politics (Burawoy 1979; Vallas 1993; Hanagan 1980; Haydu 1988a). That research also restored workers' agency, celebrating the ways in which working-class action altered the technologies and control strategies deployed by management (Edwards 1979; Hyman 1980; Noble 1986).

As the 1998 conference on Braverman's legacy has demonstrated (see Baldoz et al. 1998) this scholarly tradition is alive and well. Contemporary research investigates the subtleties of management control in new arenas of labor, from software designers to part-timers and workfare recipients (Ó Riain 1998; Whalley and Meiksins 1998; Krinsky 1998). And in exploring the interaction of the labor process with worker identities and resistance, scholars have broadened the scope of the field to include race, ethnicity, and gender along with class (Webster 1998; Baldoz 1998; Heide 1998).

In this chapter I argue that students of the labor process owe employers the same kind of attention they have lavished on workers. Much as workers' solidarities and identities mediate their impact on the labor process, so do employers' ties with their peers. The character of those ties, I argue, shapes their policies vis-à-vis employees and modifies their ability to implement those policies. For both reasons, our understanding of the labor process requires that we treat employers as we treat workers: as agents and as members of larger communities.

This recommendation clearly applies to turn-of-the-century struggles over craft control, the same struggles that provided the basic story line for Braverman's theory of the labor process. Drawing on recent research in business history and on various local histories of business elites, I argue that employer class formation mattered in these workplace transformations. It mattered for both collective capacities and for common definitions of employer goals. At a time when many employers were by no means settled on how they should deal with craft regulations, a realignment in their solidarities and identities favored a belligerent assertion of "management rights." And at a time when "capitalists" were mostly proprietary employers with limited individual resources, local class formation gave business interests the ability to defeat craft control. After developing these arguments about employer class formation and the labor process in the late nineteenth century, I will briefly illustrate their relevance to capitalists and models of management in the late twentieth century.

Capitalists and the Labor Process

The strengths and weaknesses of labor process theory can be illustrated by two brief anecdotes. When machinists struck the Coe and Stanley Company in 1913, the Manufacturers' Association of Bridgeport, Connecticut, rallied behind one of its own. Secretary F.A. Bennett arranged to import and house scabs; the Executive Board agreed to cover Coe and Stanley's strikebreaking expenses; and board members, recognizing the special difficulty of replacing highly skilled workers, increased their subsidy to the firm by $1.50 a day as a bonus for each toolmaker employed. By early 1914, Secretary Bennett was pleased to report Coe and Stanley "progressing with its work with practically no outside interference" (Manufacturers' Association, June 5, July 2, November 6, December 4, 1913; January 8, 1914 [quote] *Machinists' Monthly Journal* 1913, 680). Another dispute that year did not go as well for the association. Members of the International Association of Machinists at American Graphophone in Bridgeport raised the same demands as machinists at Coe and Stanley: a fifty-hour week with no reduction in pay. In this case, however, management capitulated. Officials of the Manufacturers' Association protested that this concession "would have a very injurious effect on the interests of the other members," and they organized a special meeting with American Graphophone's manager to discourage this breach of open-shop principles. But not even the added moral weight of guests from the New Jersey and New York branches of the National Metal Trades Association and from the American Anti-Boycott Association was enough to reverse the company's decision. (Manufacturers' Association, April 25, 28, 29, 1913; April 2, 1914).

The literature on the labor process illuminates some aspects of these two disputes. That literature has long been concerned with management control and occupational deskilling. These theoretical interests converge in historical studies of craft control in the late nineteenth and early twentieth centuries. Employers' offensives at this time targeted both workers' skills and customary mechanisms of workplace control. Their victories paved the way for the dilution of labor and the elaboration of open-shop management techniques (Montgomery 1979; Nelson 1975; Haydu 1988a). Coe and Stanley's troubles with toolmakers and employers' alarm over American Graphophone yielding to a union clearly fit this model. Graphophone's heresy can also be accommodated by more recent contributions to the labor process literature. Management strategies now tend to be thought of as more varied and less sure to succeed than Braverman imagined (Littler 1990; Friedman 1990; Guillén 1994).

Where the literature on the labor process is less helpful for understanding these two disputes is in its tendency to treat employers in the singular rather than the plural. Management strategies are many (Friedman 1977; Burawoy 1985), of course, as are managerial factions. These differences may, in turn, be linked to diverse external influences, such as professional ideologies (Burawoy 1979, 183) or "elite mentalities" (Guillén 1994, 22–27). The unit of analysis, however, typically remains the single firm. Contributors to the 1998 conference often refer to "employers," as in "employers perpetuate workers' conditions of dependence" (Chun, Chapter 6), but the plural form does not signify employers as a group so much as employers in the aggregate. Neither in case studies nor in surveys of capitalist labor policy does this aggregate shape employers' capacities or dispositions. Instead, it reflects the assumption that individual employers respond to external market forces or internal labor relations needs in similar ways. Indeed, nothing is lost by substituting for "employers" the abstract "capitalist," whose behavior can be explained in terms of systemic pressures and imputed interests. One conference paper reminds us that "what is of interest to the capitalist . . . is the amount of labour time taken to produce each unit of value." The necessity of reducing labor time is what "drive[s] and structure[s] the character of the capitalist labour process at *all* stages of its development" (Cohen 1998, 93, 94 [emphasis in original]).

This asymmetry in studies of the labor process—agency and group dynamics for workers, stick figures and atomization for employers—has many sources. The field attracted scholars seeking to understand divisions and quiescence among workers, not employers. Lembcke's (1995) recent and welcome proposal to reintegrate labor history with studies of the labor process, for example, presents joint organization and collective capacity as problems for workers. For employers, by contrast, neither power nor goals have seemed problematic. American intellectuals in particular, surveying postwar industrial relations, find little reason to doubt capital's ability to organize the labor process and exclude unions from workplace control. And while different management strategies for controlling the labor process did become a major focus of the literature, employers' underlying interests are still either taken for granted or deemed irrelevant, given the constraints of the market. What varies are the problems facing employers and thus the strategies they adopt to exert control and extract surplus—not employers' own understandings of their priorities. Two more examples from the 1998 Braverman conference illustrate this logic. James Rinehart (1998, 337) invokes the external forces of "heightened international competition, declining profits, and fiscal crises" to explain management's shift from Quality of Work Life reforms in the 1970s to an emphasis on teamwork and participation in the 1980s. And Peter Whalley and Peter Meiksins (1998) analyze the dilemmas created by different types of employees (technical professionals working either as independent contractors or as on-site part-timers) to explain differences in employer control strategies. In both cases, the explanation can move directly from problems to employer policies because each employer's underlying interests and goals are known and constant, accepted as givens within the capitalist system.[1]

Whatever the reasons for this skewed analysis, however, labor process theory obscures the formidable influence of the business *community* on individual employers. Coe and Stanley could count on the support of competitors as well as managers in other industries. An even broader coalition of local, regional, and national employers sought to steer American Graphophone toward particular industrial relations objectives. If these employers were wage earners, their encompassing solidarities, joint organization, and shared understanding of industrial conflict would surely be labeled "class consciousness."[2] It is the role of employer class formation in battles over craft skills and craft unions that is largely missing from debates on the labor process.

In the remainder of this chapter, I offer a preliminary exploration of two links between employer class formation and the labor process. In the first section, I examine collective capacities. My focus will be not on large corporations and their managers but on the smaller firms and proprietors that were most strident in their attacks on craft control and union interference around the turn of the century. These employers did not necessarily have the clout to triumph over craft customs and unions.[3] The obvious alternative of cooperation with other employers to control work practices, labor markets, and employee representation was easily undermined by competition or mutual indifference. The cultural practices and collective organization associated with employer class formation helped overcome these obstacles. In the second section, I turn to the ideological side of employers' offensive against craft regulation. Class formation for employers, as for workers, involved the construction of both differences (from other classes) and similarities (among members of a putatively common community). The ideological lines along which employers drew distinctions and extended solidarities, I argue, were also peculiarly favorable to belligerent assertions of management prerogatives. In turn, this common rallying cry reinforced employers' collective capacities. Contemporary class alliances and ideologies of work, I will suggest, may be analyzed in similar terms.

Employer Class Formation and Collective Capacity

Craft Control and the Problem of Collective Action Among Employers

One of the most common criticisms of Braverman is that he overestimated management's ability to have its way with wage labor. Through formal organization and informal work group practices, employees often thwart capital's drive to separate conception from execution. With or without the boss's knowledge, workers also may exert control over the methods, pace, and remuneration of production tasks, even when those issues have been declared management prerogatives or officially settled off the shop floor by corporate executives and union bureaucrats (Burawoy 1979; Zetka 1992; Zuboff 1984). The political effects of this stubborn attachment to customary job controls vary and may (as Burawoy argues) even benefit employers. It remains the case, however, that these controls are not easily or inevitably overcome by management.

This general criticism of Braverman applies to turn-of-the-century as well as more recent conflicts over craft control. Much like Braverman's work, early surveys in the new labor history highlighted pivotal battles in which large firms like Carnegie or Ford vanquished craft unions and revolutionized the labor process (Brody 1960; Nelson 1975; Meyer 1981). More recent historiography, however, has found these epics doubly misleading. First, they obscure the persistence of craft practices in hatmaking shops, stove foundries, pottery plants, construction sites, and textile factories, among others (Bensman 1980; Cebula 1976; Stern 1994; Christie 1956; Scranton 1983). Even in the heart of the second industrial revolution and the open shop—early twentieth-century Detroit—craft practices persisted in smaller metalworking shops, and many employers quietly accommodated union representation for their skilled employees (Klug 1993, 762, 767–768). Ford and Carnegie are misleading examples for another reason. Most employers lacked the financial resources and strength in product and labor markets to single-handedly abolish craft work practices and purge unions. The typical firm in the late nineteenth century was still a small one, owned and managed by a single proprietor or a few partners (Bruchey 1980; Roy 1997). More than 80 percent of all manufacturing firms in 1880 had fewer than fifty employees, and in most cities these modest establishments accounted for a clear majority of the workforce (Griffen and Griffen 1980, 124). Such firms got the better of craftsmen if and when employers acted together—honoring the same blacklists, establishing vocational training programs to replace union apprenticeships, fusing political resources to limit union influence in municipal government, and maintaining a united front against strikes (Ramirez 1978; Harris 1991; Cohen 1990; Klug 1993).[4]

Neither employers nor business historians needed game theory to recognize the obstacles to such cooperative action (Akard 1992; Bowman 1989). Common organization and collective action among firms could be every bit as problematic as solidarity among workers, but for rather different reasons. In contrast to wage earners, employers were not usually divided by ethnicity or religion in late-nineteenth-century America:

most were native born and high Protestant (Zunz 1982, 204–206; Folsom 1981, 77; Ing-ham 1978). Nor did personal hardship drive them to put immediate needs ahead of col-lective interests. Still, cooperative action often proved difficult. In any given industry, employers might profit by *not* coming to the rescue of competitors under siege from union demands or strikes. If one firm made concessions to unions, others gained a com-petitive advantage in production costs; when one company suffered a strike, rivals could poach market share. At various times, employers did make agreements to curb "ruinous competition" by standardizing labor costs and conditions, but these pacts were vulnerable to free riders and defection (Bowman 1989; Haydu 1988c). Managers of rail-roads in the Chicago area, for example, organized in 1886 to combat railway union demands. Rival lines, however, spurned the General Managers' Association's efforts to cooperate on a wider scale (Stromquist 1987, 251–252; McMurry 1953).

Cooperation among employers in different economic sectors was not sabotaged by direct competition. Employer unity across trades, however, was no more "natural" than solidarity among workers. The uneven development of markets and the labor process put employers in very different strategic positions. Shop owners who still worked at the trade might have little in common with full-time managers; custom and large-batch producers did not have the same labor needs; and firms manufacturing for local markets experienced different opportunities and constraints than did those that sold their wares nationally. Even among employers in closely related indus-tries—stove and general foundries, for example, or general and "sanitary" pottery—differences in product markets and ownership patterns could rule out common action (Barnett 1912, 441–442; Stern 1994).

Whether their relations were competitive or merely distant, two additional consid-erations made employers wary of collective organization. One concerned proprietary rights. Employers who inveighed against union attempts to "run their businesses" were also reluctant to to cede authority to employer associations. Detroit managers, for example, often declined to share personnel information with the Employers' Asso-ciation's Labor Bureau or even to establish administrative mechanisms for gathering this information (Klug 1993, 792–793, 802–806). Walter Drew of the National Erectors' Association added that collective action against labor was bad politics. Arguing against proposals to establish a national federation of open-shop employers after World War I, Drew warned that such "class organization" might stimulate workers to follow suit (Fine 1995, 202).

Solidarity and Organization Among Employers

Despite these obstacles, formal organization among employees to deal with labor spread rapidly from the mid-1880s (Bonnett 1922, 1956). It was often a common threat from the labor movement that first drove employers to organize or to adapt existing trade associations to industrial relations tasks. Reflecting both the speed of mobiliza-tion and its roots in confrontation with the Knights of Labor, employer associations accounted for 75 percent of lockouts in 1884–86, compared to 30 percent in 1881–83

(Bonnett 1922, 22). Many of these early combinations faltered once labor insurgency ebbed. By the turn of the century, however, employer organizations assumed a more permanent footing and more regularized functions, including local employment services, data gathering, and industrial boosterism, as well as ad hoc strike-fighting assistance.[5] These organizations also commonly exacted substantial dues and even the posting of bonds to guarantee compliance with association policies.

The fact that employer associations spread, institutionalized, and acquired significant authority over member firms even in the absence of immediate labor challenges suggests that employer solidarity had deeper roots than the contingencies of class struggle. When labor historians seek to explain worker solidarities and divisions, the usual suspects are social networks and cultural practices rooted in residence, leisure, and politics (Faler 1981; Rosenzweig 1983; Wilentz 1984). Students of the middle classes (Blumin 1989; Gilkeson 1986) and upper classes (Baltzell 1964; Jaher 1982; Domhoff 1974; Roy 1991) have followed their lead, substituting for pubs, mechanics institutes, and ward politics the elevated realms of social clubs, prep schools, and civic reform associations. Through such institutions, local upper classes developed common codes of behavior, regulated entry into both business and social circles, and stigmatized the rabble. And most studies highlight the 1880s and 1890s as the key decades in which local employers, bankers, and professionals actively differentiated themselves as a distinct class, withdrawing into separate neighborhoods, cultivating the fine arts, organizing country clubs, and steering their children into the right schools and colleges (Gilkeson 1986, 136–174; Couvares 1984; Ingham 1978; Eggert 1993). Naturally, the character and timing of class formation varied. The three major metropolises (Boston, New York, and Philadelphia), for example, displayed more social differentiation between older elites and an emergent middle class than was common in newer, middle-sized manufacturing cities such as Pittsburgh, Detroit, or Cleveland (Jaher 1982).

Personal ties and status conventions developed in elite schools, private clubs, and local charities may have smoothed the way for joint organization among men otherwise divided by business competition or by the industry-specific concerns of their workaday lives (Rosenzweig 1983, 14–15; Roy 1991).[6] Case studies of urban elites during this period point to an overlap in the membership of cultural institutions and business associations. Members of San Francisco's Industrial Association, for example, came from varied business backgrounds but shared service with the local art association and Boys' Club; most activists in Detroit's Employers' Association, similarly, belonged to the same high Protestant churches and Republican party organization (Issel and Cherny 1986, 96; Klug 1993, 745–752). And the development of common cultural institutions and social identities among businessmen, professionals, and the upper crust of the white-collar workforce, in turn, had clear implications for employers' collective capacities. As Herbert Gutman (1997) emphasized, it became more likely that employers could count on "community" support and municipal government backing in their battles with labor.

Under these conditions, the trend was toward more inclusive organization for dealing with labor. Often, early employer associations were local branches of industry-specific bodies like the National Founders' Association, National Metal Trades Association, United Typothetae, and National Erectors' Association. By the early 1900s, however, a growing number of citywide employers associations combined representatives from different trades (Jackson 1984; Cohen 1990; Harris 1991; Klug 1993). Even without formal peak organizations, sectional bodies were increasingly linked by a dense network of interlocking memberships, mutual endorsements, circulating newsletters, and rotating guest speakers (Bonnett 1922, 362–377, 551–552; Cohen 1990, 170).

Employer Class Formation and Collective Interests

Employer class formation was important not only for the balance of power in labor relations, but also for employers' understandings of their interests and rights at work. A variety of competitive pressures and technological opportunities led employers to attack craft practices and unions in the late nineteenth and early twentieth centuries. The ideological terrain of class formation, however, may have helped turn practical considerations into uncompromising moral principles.

In their dealings with craft control and unions, late-nineteenth-century employers pursued different policies and justified them in different ways. Alongside the familiar pattern of deskilling, textile proprietors in Philadelphia and specialty steel manufacturers in Pittsburgh treated handicraft skills as a resource for innovation and "flexibility" rather than as obstacles to management control (Ingham 1991). And amid movements for the open shop, stove founders, coal mine owners, and pottery manufacturers relied on unions to help stabilize their industries rather than driving them from the workplace (Klug 1993; Bowman 1989; Stern 1994; Haydu 1988b).

The range of strategies for organizing work and labor relations can be explained at least in part by the constraints that technology, markets, and ownership patterns imposed on employers. But this diversity also suggests that individual capitalists had more discretion in their approach to unions and workplace control than labor process theory would allow.[7] The *convergence* of employer policies vis-à-vis craft regulation toward the turn of the century also suggests that there were forces at work *other* than competitive pressures and capital's unvarying quest for control. Businessmen who had seemingly taken a more pragmatic stance with regard to craft unions now insisted that they would in no way compromise their management prerogatives. And at least in their public statements, this antiunion consensus brought together employers in very different economic circumstances. To explain this shift, we should take our cue not from studies of the labor process but from reinterpretations of labor politics. Those accounts have emphasized the links between social networks, collective identities, and the framing of group interests (Melucci 1989; Berlanstein 1993; Hall 1997). We might thus ask if employers' definitions of proper labor policies (as well as their capacity to implement them) also reflect the "imagined communities" to which they belong.

Community Standards Versus Managerial Prerogatives

Proprietary capitalists in much of the nineteenth century were constrained by two sorts of communities, those of the town and those of the trade. Status honor in their local communities might reinforce rational economic strategy in encouraging employers to meet union representatives. For example, the president of New York City's Typothetae justified his decision to confer with International Typographical Union officials on the grounds that "the simplest rules of good breeding . . . would compel us to give a respectful hearing and answer" (Tichenor 1980, 182). Late-nineteenth-century Pittsburgh iron masters took a similar tact for more complex reasons. As part of a long-standing urban elite, they regarded honorable dealing with local unionists as both a social obligation to their men and as a reprimand to low-born outsiders like Carnegie (Ingham 1991).

Within the trade, a variety of vertical ties continued to link "master and men," ties that persisted longer in medium-size and diversified manufacturing cities than in one-industry factory towns or the largest metropolitan centers. Case studies emphasize different factors bringing owner and employee together despite their presumed economic antagonisms. These include "Christian capitalism" in the 1840s–50s (Wallace 1972); the crusade for free labor before the Civil War (Steinfeld 1991); a persistent nineteenth-century republicanism (Faler 1981; Ross 1985; Licht 1995); and post–Civil War ethnicity (Zunz 1982), fraternalism (Clawson 1989), and machismo (Bensman 1980). Such interpretations are generally designed to explain the limits of working-class solidarity and militancy. But the same ties constrained employers, too. Owners often fought with their men over wages and working conditions. Even the strikes and lockouts that sometimes ensued, however, were recognized and ritualized parts of an ongoing work relationship (Ingham 1991). Employers were reluctant to sever relations with men who were not only familiar and skilled employees but also fellow Masons, Swedes, and citizens of the republic. More important, the producer ideology associated with these class alignments endowed mechanics with some acknowledged (if not welcomed) rights both to control their work and to participate in workplace governance (Bensman 1980; Hoffecker 1974; Eggert 1993). When machinists petitioned a Connecticut manufacturer of cutting tools for higher wages in 1833, he declined to pay them more but commended their collective action. The machinists' "candid manly course" is "worthy of yourselves and the high character you have always sustained as a community," and it confirms both "the prospects of our Republic" and the wisdom of hiring "none but Americans" (Larson 1944, 135). The language of republicanism was much fainter by the 1880s, but in many workplaces some sense of shared membership in a common community of producers persisted (Trachtenberg 1982, 73–76, 97; Salvatore 1982; Licht 1995, 108).

Late-nineteenth-century class formation shaped the construction of employer interests by realigning community solidarities, thus both altering employers' reference groups and redefining membership and rights in the workplace community. The grounds on which employers distanced themselves from employees and constructed a broader business community of proprietors, professionals, and executives, I would argue, favored a more belligerent assertion of management prerogatives as against craft rules and union interference. And developments at both the community level and within the labor process fueled this realignment.

Class Distinctions, Business Communities, and Workplace Governance

By the early 1920s, the Employers' Association of Detroit was broadcasting its views on industrial relations to a mailing list of six thousand businessmen, schoolteachers, bankers, and professionals. Few manual workers, however, received the Association's *Industrial Barometer* (Klug 1993, 832–833). The demographics of its mailing list suggest that the organization had ties to a broad coalition of middle- and upper-class groups and made little effort to cultivate even the skilled employees of its own member firms. These priorities typify a more general class realignment—underway in many manufacturing centers in the late nineteenth century—that frayed lingering vertical ties and broadened horizontal ones. Both dimensions of this process were important for reorienting employers' thinking about workplace control and unionism.

The severing of ties involved what Pierre Bourdieu (1984) might describe as the cultivation of distinctions. Owners and craftsmen had often seen themselves as sharing membership in a community of producers, with craftsmen's skills and voice entitled to some measure of respect. Class reformation emphasized instead the differences in character and value between management and labor and between brain and hand. The change is mirrored in the post–Civil War decline of mechanics institutes, associations that combined proprietors and craftsmen in a common commitment to "progressive" industry (Gilkeson 1986, 95; Kornblith 1983). It appears as well, John F. Kasson (1976, 223) suggests, in the nostalgia of late-nineteenth-century utopian novels for lost republican bonds between employer and workman. This social realignment seems to have diminished employers' scruples and provided a rationale for more uncompromising claims to unilateral management rights as against craft control and union representation.

A wider fellow feeling among employers of different trades, extending to professional and managerial elites, complemented vertical differentiation. Here too the ideological side of class formation had direct implications for industrial management. First, highlighting attributes that united employers across trades simultaneously underscored what set them apart from wage earners. This included, of course, the ownership and rights of private property, an increasingly strident theme of late-nineteenth-century employer discourse (Thimm 1976). It also included the division between brain and hand. This vertical division was reinforced from within the new business community by professionals' glorification of mental labor (Gilkeson 1986, 100–101). These ideological lubricants for broadened employer solidarity thus provided a favorable setting for more generalized assertions of a "right to manage" shared by proprietors and managers throughout industry.

Second, a particularly important arena for the cultivation of local solidarities and organization among employers at the turn of the century was civic reform (Sturges

1915, 354; Schiesl 1977). The pursuit of more "efficient," nonpartisan government had obvious practical benefits for employers. But it also helped bring employers, professionals, and white-collar workers into a common civic community, one with a very different center of gravity than the old producer community. The respectable citizenry defined by civic reform, Rotaries, philanthropy, and local boosterism was nearly indistinguishable from the "business community." It conferred neither membership nor rights on craftsmen, at least not in their roles as practitioners of a trade. It is this reorientation that helps explain the close links drawn by Law and Order Leagues in the 1880s and 1890s between anti-unionism, the promotion of local industry, and the public good (Bonnett 1956, 248–259; Ross 1985, 272). "Give to the world the assurance that here labor and capital, which are mutually dependent upon each other and essentially the same, are fully protected," announced St. Louis's League, and "that enterprises of all kinds can be safely entered on, because every opportunity for success will be offered, and immediately the stream of immigration that is spreading over the great West will flow to St. Louis as surely as the magnet turns to its pole" (Bonnett 1956, 249–251; see also Jaher 1982, 505–507). In this framework, unions did more than violate the ideal of nonpartisanship. They also appeared as outsiders subverting the community interest. Extirpating them thus became a civic responsibility. According to International Harvester managers in 1903, it was "a duty for this company, as a large employer of labor, to take some action [against unions] which may be . . . an example for the community" (Ozanne 1967, 57). Freedom from union interference, a 1907 National Association of Manufacturers' report emphasized, is not a matter of "capital against labor, nor employers against employees, but . . . of good citizenship against bad citizenship" (Brady 1972, 278).

All of these ideological supports for class formation *among* local elites, then, (1) provided a cultural setting favorable to more strident assertions of generalized employer rights; and (2) excluded skilled workers from the communities—of civic reformers, brain workers, or property owners—entitled to control or voice.[8] Redrawing the lines of collective solidarity was crucial for the redefinition of employers' interests at work in the late nineteenth century. Labor process theories that treat employers as individual cogs in a particular mode of production miss this source of capital's offensive against craft control.

The Contributions of the Labor Process

Thus far I have emphasized the links between the labor process and employer class formation in only one direction: from realignments in employers' social networks and collective identities to individual employers' industrial relations policies. Might these links also be traced in the other direction? At first glance, it appears reasonable for labor process theory to make this connection only for workers, not employers. A single firm, after all, includes few "employers" but many employees, so we can easily follow the effects of production methods, supervision, or employment systems on worker solidarities and ideology. The influence of these variables on employers as a group is not so clear.[9] It is possible, of course, that similarities in the roles played and challenges faced by late-nineteenth-century capitalists engendered common "feelings, purposes, traditions, and hopes" (Livingston 1986, 246). There is another way that workplace arrangements shaped employer ideology, however. Changes in the labor process complemented community realignments in constructing new boundaries between labor and capital. And these social distinctions, in turn, helped redefine employers' collective interests. Understanding the turn-of-the-century offensive against craft control thus requires that we consider the impact of the labor process on employer class formation.

Historians such as Daniel Nelson (1975; see also Jacoby 1985) have documented common changes in relations between management and workers in the four decades straddling 1900. These shifts included a much lamented loss of the "personal touch" and the accretion of intermediate layers of management separating (and increasing the social distance between) owner and employees. Although changes like these developed furthest in large corporations, they also affected the proprietary firms that dominated midsize manufacturing centers and that spearheaded the open-shop movement. The experience of other countries and of New Deal industrial relations reminds us that more bureaucratized workplace management is not incompatible with craft production or union recognition. But changing workplace administration may have complemented class formation outside the factory gates in realigning employer identities.

Two sorts of workplace-based realignment deserve a closer look. First, the decline of direct participation in industrial management by proprietors, together with new career paths insulating managers from the shop floor (Noble 1977), helped replace the rhetoric of "our trade" with the language of "our business." The former, like republicanism, included craft employees in a common community of "ironmakers," "potters," and the like. Thinking of production activities as "my business" surely favors, instead, a preoccupation with unilateral control and an opposition to outside interference. Certainly by 1900, when W. J. Chalmers testified before the U.S. Industrial Commission (1901–2, 7), employers were harping on the theme that they would never "allow any walking delegate . . . to come into our shop and . . . tell a person how wide or how deep his cut shall be . . . or what wage we shall pay him for doing a specified amount of work." Second, there was a redefinition of just who qualified as an "outsider." Case studies of Philadelphia, Pittsburgh, and Wilmington, among others, find late-nineteenth-century proprietors defining outsiders as those foreign to the *local community* (Scranton 1989, 23, 207; Ingham 1991, 130–137; Mapes 1973, 157–158, 163–165). During an 1886 dispute at a Wilmington railroad car works, the owner denounced not unions in general but the fact that "the local Knights had invited a committee of Knights from Philadelphia to meet with him. [The owner] Jackson regarded this step as unfair and objected to outside interference" (Hoffecker 1974, 129). The aversion to outsiders might even include outside *capital*, which proprietors sometimes blamed for upsetting harmonious labor relations (Mapes 1973, 77; Hoffecker 1974, 134–135). By the end of the century, the circle of insiders had narrowed: nonemployees or external organizations speaking through employees had no legitimate standing in workplace governance. In the characteristic rhetoric of early twentieth-century open-shop employers, the director of North Grinding Company insisted that he would not permit "any outside person or interest to interfere with its business, tell us how to run it, or interfere with our honest endeavor to have a happy working family of all of us employed by the company" (Crawford 1995, 102). Here again, the redrawn boundaries of the workplace community justified a vigorous repudiation of "externally" imposed craft standards and representatives.

Contemporary Parallels

In the late twentieth century, too, the political ideologies around which earlier business leaders rallied are clearly echoed within the workplace, but there are striking differences in political rhetoric and in the calls for change in the labor process. What has sometimes been called "populist conservatism" (Phillips 1983; Rieder 1989; Kazin 1995) now repudiates both the bureaucratic model and the activist role for government championed by late-nineteenth-century reform movements. The immediate targets are New Deal and Great Society programs. One charge is that the government has undertaken regulatory tasks (e.g., preserving endangered species) or social programs (e.g., providing housing for the poor) that are none of its business. Even if the goal is worthy, conservatives reject the state as an appropriate means to achieve it. Government bureaucracies, by their very nature, can do little good. Federal agencies are too big, too distant, and above all too encumbered by red tape to respond quickly and effectively. The national government should instead leave many of its customary tasks to state or local governments or, better still, to the private sector's "thousands points of light." This redefinition of "efficiency" in the public sector thus involves not only a critique of bureaucracy but also a celebration of market alternatives. The prospects of market rewards for innovation, together with the harsh discipline of market competition, would yield more effective solutions than government could provide, whether in running prisons, teaching children, or employing welfare recipients.

All of these themes, of course, stretch far back in American political history. Indeed, antistatism and a preference for market solutions are sometimes considered the defining elements of American exceptionalism (Shafer 1991). Two additional features of populist conservatism are more novel and especially important for capitalist class alliances. First, the themes of antistatism and individual freedom based on the rights of property were, for most of the twentieth century, championed by small business, often in opposition to (among others) "corporate liberals." During the 1980s, corporate capital, represented by such formidable organizations as the Business Roundtable, rejoined smaller businesses on a laissez-faire platform (Akard 1992; Edsall 1989). Indeed, along with the political preference for market solutions went a new celebration of entrepreneurship. Small firms, we were often reminded, contribute most of our economy's job growth and innovation. And in an echo of Gilded Age Horatio Algerism, scrappy entrepreneurs and start-up companies (along with the occasional maverick CEO) once again became the idols of economic progress. In George Gilder's (1981, 52) paean to unfettered capitalism, the heroes were even reassuringly multicultural: "immigrants in every American city—Cubans in Miami, Portuguese in Providence and Newark, Filipinos in Seattle, Koreans in Washington, D.C., Vietnamese in Los Angeles, to mention the more recent crop—have performed . . . feats of commerce, with little help from banks or government or the profession of economics."

Second, the movement combines conservative goals with populist politics, and this too helped rally together capital of different types and scale. Prior to the 1970s, America's populist impulse tended to use democratic government as a popular weapon against economic elites. The Republican Party in the 1970s succeeded in making business values the core of an electoral realignment that encompassed a substantial majority of the white middle class. Building on the economic frustrations and racial resentments of a declining middle class, the GOP redrew political dividing lines. On one side stood business and hard-working white Protestants, mad as hell. On the other stood big government, liberal elites, and racial minorities. The demographics were not this neat, but the political rhetoric did help bring together a remarkable coalition of middling-income whites and capital, large and small. With Reagan's 1980 victory, downsizing government and liberating the private sector seemed to have become popular crusades (Phillips 1983; Rieder 1989; Kazin 1995; Edsall and Edsall 1991).

The political strategy and the rhetoric of reformers thus gave different factions of capital common ideological ground. They also highlighted a common enemy in organized labor, albeit in different ways than in the late nineteenth century. The GOP's political strategy was to put together an electoral majority based on southern and western states, where Democrats were least able to rely on support from organized labor (Phillips 1970). And in appealing to the "Reagan Democrats"—white, male, often ethnic, working-class voters who had been a bastion of both unions and the New Deal Democrats—the GOP's campaign rhetoric further marginalized union labor. Organized labor became a "special interest," a resonant populist term for groups with power and access but with neither regard for the public interest nor a wide base of support among the "American people." During the 1984 presidential campaign, for example, Walter Mondale was repeatedly attacked for being a "captive" of the AFL-CIO (Edsall and Edsall 1991, 202–204). GOP political rhetoric also sought to discredit organized labor by associating unions, with some historical accuracy, with the "big government" programs, bloated public sector employment, and extortionate tax policies of the New Deal Democrats. These electoral appeals reinforced the more general message that downsizing government not only improved efficiency but also returned power to ordinary Americans.

Management rhetoric in the realm of work echoes this populist conservatism.[10] The flexible workplace, like the revamped welfare system, is said to be more efficient by virtue of its decentralization. A global marketplace requires firms nimble enough to adapt quickly to shifting demands and opportunities; this, in turn, requires less specialized job categories and less fat in middle management. Enlarging lower-level workers' authority to monitor quality or streamline production methods makes fuller use of employee skills and, like block grants, allows them to adopt general policies and techniques to local conditions. "'Customization' is a watchword here: economic changes . . . allow business to personalize their products and services to the identities of specific groups of people" (Gee, Hull, and Lankshear 1996, 28). In order to customize a firm's products, skills and authority also have to be placed on the front line. "You just can't manage a fast-growing, fast-moving organization in detail from the top," a Digital Equipment vice president told Gideon Kunda (1992, 62), "so we've continually tried to push decision making functions down inside the organization."

Advocates of flatter management hierarchies and more flexible deployment of workers, like champions of lean government, also invoke the wisdom of the market to legitimate changes. Much as welfare reformers recommend the lash of the market to encourage independence and hard work among welfare recipients, so it is for the benefit of the company as a whole to expose employees or corporate units to the competitive struggle. "One hundred percent of employees turned into 'business people' is . . . no mere pipe dream," exults management guru Tom Peters. "Every job can become an entrepreneurial challenge. Letting go [i.e., decentralizing responsibility] means letting the person alone to experience those Maalox moments—that is, true, genuine, no-baloney ownership in the gut" (quoted in Gee, Hull, and Lankshear 1996, 30). Loyalty to the firm and security of employment, we are told, are virtues for a (diminishing) core of valued employees. And even for these employees, an increasing proportion of pay is based on performance-based bonuses, which sometimes add up to zero. ("You can't count on it," one employee notes, "but that's business. Stockholders don't always get dividends, either" [Bucholz 1996, 10]). Beyond this charmed circle of valued employees, work must incur the lowest cost and the least encumbrance. Those requirements are usually taken to mean some combination of temporary employees, subcontractors, and foreign operations, all of which can be reassigned or discontinued on short notice (Shostak 1996).

In celebrating decentralization and market principles as the keys to flexibility, contemporary management publicists find no greater role for unions than did late-nineteenth-century advocates of bureaucratic governance. And today, as then, indictments of unions echo prevailing political rhetoric. At work, as in public governance, unions appear as an egregious special interest using their entrenched power at the expense of the common good. Flexible firms are said to rely on teamwork and a willingness to put in extra effort or make occasional sacrifices to give the company a competitive edge. Most employees, in this view, are willing to make concessions on wages or work rules; they understand, after all, that their own fortunes rise or fall with the firm's. Unions are demonized for blocking these concessions. Their "philosophy of ever-shorter hours, narrow job classifications and artificial workload limits is at odds with the work ethic and drags down the nation in its fight to stay competitive" (Peterson 1987, 2). More generally, unions are seen as sabotaging direct cooperation between employees and management for fear of being cut out of industrial relations altogether. The ideal of flexibility is turned against unions in another way. Much as the Democratic Party is seen as the party of big government, bureaucratic regulation, and red tape, so unions are viewed as the source of rigidity in workplace governance. In a remarkable fit of historical amnesia, managers attribute narrowly defined job categories, due process employment protections, and formalized grievance procedures to union demands. Contractual regulation of labor relations is incompatible with flexibility; the flexible workplace, accordingly, must be union free (Amberg 1991; Kaus 1983). "A web of rules," Kaus (1983, 30) argues, "is often the enemy of economic progress. . . . It was only by defeating the skilled workers at Homestead, alas, that Andrew Carnegie was able to introduce the technology that . . . made American steel manufacturers the most efficient in the world."

These comparisons between the late nineteenth and twentieth centuries are merely suggestive. A self-standing study of capitalist class formation and the labor process today would require a closer look at the social networks and collective identities through which political movements and the workplace interact. It seems clear, however, that changes in capitalist class solidarities and political alignments remain relevant to employer ideology and practice within the factory gates.

Conclusion

Students of the capitalist labor process need to pay more attention to capitalists to understand the labor process better. We have long since abandoned the theoretical fiction that a worker's consciousness can be inferred from his or her place in relations of production. Employers deserve the same courtesy. Their policies at work are not structurally determined in detail, either by competitive pressures or by some essentialized capital-labor conflict. Employer policies also reflect their definitions of "the labor problem" and their understanding of what options are available to deal with it. Those definitions and perceptions, in turn, are mediated by employers' social ties and collective identities. Although these ties and identities are forged largely outside the workplace, they have direct implications for the inner sanctum of the labor process.

The parallels in identities and discourse between polity and workplace that I have illustrated here are not what either Marxist or liberal sociologists would lead us to expect. Both have long argued that a separation of political and economic authority helped sustain capitalist democracy. The legal and ideological walls between polity and economy kept democratic states from attacking the power of capital and kept citizens—in their 9-to-5 roles as wage labor—from invoking democratic rights on the job. Historians have traced the construction of these walls in labor laws (such as legal doctrines of conspiracy and liability [Tomlins 1993]) and in statutes of incorporation (whereby socialized capital freed itself from public control [Roy 1997]). A closer look at the late nineteenth and twentieth centuries, however, suggests that in other respects the boundary between authority at work and in politics is quite porous. In both periods, ideals of efficiency held up as goals for managers or justifications for management practices drew on ideals of government reform. And in both cases, those ideals may be traced to broader political and class realignments. If movements for municipal reform or deregulation did not *cause* employers to advance new agendas for workplace governance, they at least created opportunities for employers to publicly legitimate their authority in new ways.

Whether in the late twentieth or the late nineteenth century, those tools for legitimation have also served as weapons against labor. Looking back to the period examined most closely here, the grounds on which employers forged more encompassing identities and the lines along which they distinguished themselves from employees put craft control at odds with the rights of individual employers and the interests of the business community. I have stressed how class realignments in industrial cities generally fostered a redefinition of interests and solidarities. That influence also ran in the opposite direction: a new rhetoric of management prerogatives and freedom from outside interference provided a common rallying cry for employers otherwise divided by competition and industrial setting. In this way, redefined interests also enhanced collective capacities. The collective lives of capitalists thus matter a great deal more than the literature on the labor process would suggest.

I should emphasize again that proprietors and managers had many and varied incentives for repudiating craft regulation and union representation. The relative weight of employer class formation and of economic constraints impinging on individual employers is neither fixed nor quantifiable. At the very least, however, the ways in which class formation reconstructed interests and identities account for most of the language and much of the vehemence with which employers mounted their offensive. The importance of anti-unionism to American employers' identities and collective organization, in turn, may help explain why alternative approaches to regulating production and representing workers were adopted, if at all, only grudgingly and as a last resort. In this respect, at least, the differences in political and managerial rhetoric between the 1890s and 1990s are less striking than the continuities.

Notes

Acknowledgments: Kathy Mooney, Phil Kraft, Rick Baldoz, and Tom Klug contributed in various ways to this chapter. I'm grateful for their help.

1. Claus Offe and Helmut Wiesenthal (1980) offered theoretical support for these assumptions, arguing that employers, unlike workers, had no need of collective action either to construct or to implement their interests.

2. For a comparison of working-class and capitalist class formation, see Roy and Parker-Gwin (1999) and Haydu (1999b).

3. Bruno Ramirez (1978), in particular, emphasizes that smaller firms dealt with their labor problems collectively, while large corporations could afford to be the rugged individualists in their labor policies.

4. Larry Griffin et al. (1986) also emphasize the importance of collective action in fighting unions and abolishing craft restrictions. But they do not see common action and organizations as especially important, or particularly difficult to achieve, for small firms in competitive industries.

5. I have not found figures for the total numbers of employer associations, but their spread probably matched the growth of less specialized Chambers of Commerce, which numbered 30

in 1850, 2,944 in 1898, and 3,356 in 1913 (Sturges 1915, 44–45). By 1920, about two-thirds of all industrial cities had active employer associations (Derber 1984, 89).

6. Roger Gould (1995) reviews the theoretical rationale for attributing changing identities to new social networks.

7. The history of production techniques has been reinterpreted as a story of multiple paths pursued by employers as they creatively adapted to their environment. Leading proponents of this approach include Michael J. Piore and Charles F. Sabel (1984), Philip Scranton (1997), and Sabel and Jonathan Zeitlin (1997). In explaining why particular industries followed specific paths, these scholars sometimes emphasize networks of trust and reciprocity among economic actors. They do not investigate class formation and collective identities among industrialists, however.

8. For a more extended discussion of correspondence between the rhetorics of political reform and anti-unionism, see Haydu (1999a).

9. For *both* workers and employers, however, relations among individuals across workplaces are at least as important for class formation as relations among individuals at a single site.

10. Celebrations of flexibility and surveys of contemporary "best practices" include Piore and Sabel (1984), Appelbaum and Batt (1994), Bernstein (1997), Gee, Hull, and Lankshear (1996), and Hirschhorn (1997).

References

Akard, Patrick J. 1992. "Corporate Mobilization and Political Power: The Transformation of U.S. Economic Policy in the 1970s." *American Sociological Review,* 57(5): 597–615.

Amberg, Stephen. 1991. "Democratic Producerism: Enlisting American Politics for Workplace Flexibility." *Economy and Society,* 20(1): 57–78.

Appelbaum, Eileen, and Rosemary Batt. 1994. *The New American Workplace: Transforming Work Systems in the United States.* Ithaca: ILR Press.

Baldoz, Rick. 1998. "Filipino Migrant Workers in the United States: Incorporation, Class Formation, and the State, c. 1908–1970." Pp. 4–17 in *Proceedings of the Conference on "Work, Difference and Social Change: Two Decades After Braverman's 'Labor and Monopoly Capital,'"* edited by Rick Baldoz, Phoebe Godfrey, Carol Jansen, Charles Koeber, and Philip Kraft. Binghamton: Department of Sociology, State University of New York.

Baldoz, Rick, Phoebe Godrey, Carol Jansen, Charles Koeber, and Philip Kraft, eds. 1998. *Proceedings of the Conference on "Work Difference and Social Change: Two Decades After Braverman's 'Labor and Monopoly Capital.'"* Binghamton: Department of Sociology, State University of New York.

Baltzell, E. Digby. 1964. *The Protestant Establishment: Aristocracy and Caste in America.* New York: Vintage Books.

Barnett, George. 1912. "National and District Systems of Collective Bargaining in the United States." *Quarterly Journal of Economics,* 26 (May): 425–43.

Bensman, David. 1980. "Economics and Culture in the Gilded Age Hatting Industry." Pp. 352–365 in *Small Business in American Life,* edited by Stuart W. Bruchey. New York: Columbia University Press.

Berlanstein, Lenard R., ed. 1993. *Rethinking Labor History.* Urbana: University of Illinois Press.

Bernstein, Paul. 1997. *American Work Values: Their Origin and Development.* Albany: State University of New York Press.

Blumin, Stuart M. 1989. *The Emergence of the Middle Class: Social Experience in the American City, 1760–1900*. Cambridge: Cambridge University Press.

Bonnett, Clarence E. 1922. *Employers' Associations in the United States: A Study of Typical Associations*. New York: Macmillan Company.

———. 1956. *History of Employers' Associations in the United States*. New York: Vantage Press.

Bourdieu, Pierre. 1984. *Distinction: A Social Critique of the Judgement of Taste*. Cambridge: Harvard University Press.

Bowman, John R. 1989. *Capitalist Collective Action: Competition, Cooperation, and Conflict in the Coal Industry*. Cambridge: Cambridge University Press.

Brady, Robert A. 1972. *Business as a System of Power*. Freeport, NY: Books for Libraries Press.

Braverman, Harry. 1974. *Labor and Monopoly Capital: The Degradation of Work in the Twentieth Century*. New York: Monthly Review Press.

Brody, David. 1960. *Steelworkers in America: The Nonunion Era*. New York: Harper and Row.

Bruchey, S.W., ed. 1980. *Small Business in American Life*. New York: Columbia University Press.

Buchholz, Barbara B. 1996. "The Bonus Isn't Reserved for Big Shots Anymore." *New York Times*, 27 October, section 3, p. 10.

Burawoy, Michael. 1979. *Manufacturing Consent: Changes in the Labor Process Under Monopoly Capitalism*. Chicago: University of Chicago Press.

———. 1985. *The Politics of Production: Factory Regimes Under Capitalism and Socialism*. London: Verso.

Cebula, James E. 1976. *The Glory and Despair of Challenge and Change: A History of the Molders Union*. Cincinnati: International Molders and Allied Workers Union.

Christie, Robert. 1956. *Empire in Wood: A History of the Carpenters*. Ithaca: Cornell University Press.

Clawson, Mary Ann. 1989. *Constructing Brotherhood: Class, Gender, and Fraternalism*. Princeton: Princeton University Press.

Cohen, Bruce. 1990. "Worcester, Open Shop City: The National Metal Trades Association and the Molders' Strike of 1918–1920." Pp 168–198 in *Labor in Massachusetts: Selected Essays*, edited by Kenneth Fones Wolf and Martin Kaufman. Westfield: Institute for Massachusetts Studies, Westfield State College.

Cohen, Sheila. 1998. "Ramparts of Resistance: Rank-and-File Unionism and the Labour Process." Pp. 93–105 in *Proceedings of the Conference on "Work, Difference, and Social Change: Two Decades After Braverman's 'Labor and Monopoly Capital,'"* edited by Rick Baldoz, Phoebe Godfrey, Carol Jansen, Charles Koeber, and Philip Kraft. Binghamton: Department of Sociology, State University of New York.

Couvares, Francis G. 1984. *The Remaking of Pittsburgh: Class and Culture in an Industrializing City, 1877–1919*. Albany: SUNY Press.

Crawford, Margaret. 1995. *Building the Workingman's Paradise: The Design of American Company Towns*. London: Verso.

Derber, Milton. 1984. "Employers Associations in the United States." Pp. 79–114 in *Employers Associations and Industrial Relations: A Comparative Study*, edited by John P. Windmuller and Alan Gladstone. Oxford: Clarendon Press.

Domhoff, William. 1974. *The Bohemian Grove and Other Retreats: A Study in Ruling-Class Cohesiveness*. New York: Harper Torchbooks.

Edsall, Thomas Byrne. 1989. "The Changing Shape of Power: A Realignment in Public Policy." Pp. 269–293 in *The Rise and Fall of the New Deal Order, 1930–1980*, edited by Steve Fraser and Gary Gerstle. Princeton: Princeton University Press.

Edsall, Thomas Byrne, and Mary D. Edsall. 1991. *Chain Reaction: The Impact of Race, Rights, and Taxes on American Politics*. New York: W.W. Norton.

Edwards, Richard. 1979. *Contested Terrain: The Transformation of the Workplace in the Twentieth Century*. New York: Basic Books.

Eggert, Gerald G. 1993. *Harrisburg Industrializes: The Coming of Factories to an American Community*. University Park: Pennsylvania University Press.

Faler, Paul G. 1981. *Mechanics and Manufacturers in the Early Industrial Revolution: Lynn, Massachusetts, 1780–1860*. Albany: SUNY Press.

Fine, Sidney. 1995. *"Without Blare of Trumpets": Walter Drew, the National Erectors' Association, and the Open Shop Movement, 1903–1957*. Ann Arbor: University of Michigan Press.

Folsom, Burton W., Jr. 1981. *Urban Capitalists: Enterpreneurs and City Growth in Pennsylvania's Lackawanna and Lehigh Regions, 1800–1920*. Baltimore: Johns Hopkins University Press.

Friedman, Andrew. 1977. *Industry and Labour: Class Struggle at Work and Monopoly Capitalism*. London: Macmillan.

———. 1990. "Managerial Strategies, Activities, Techniques, and Technology: Towards a Complex Theory of the Labour Process." Pp. 177–208 in *Labour Process Theory*, edited by David Knights and Hugh Willmott. London: Macmillan.

Gee, James Paul, Glynda Hull, and Colin Lankshear. 1996. *The New Work Order: Behind the Language of the New Capitalism*. Boulder, CO: Westview Press.

Gilder, George. 1981. *Wealth and Poverty*. New York: Basic Books.

Gilkeson, John S., Jr. 1986. *Middle-Class Providence, 1820–1940*. Princeton: Princeton University Press.

Gould, Roger V. 1995. *Insurgent Identities: Class, Community, and Protest in Paris from 1848 to the Commune*. Chicago: University of Chicago Press.

Griffen, Clyde, and Sally Griffen. 1980. "Small Business and Occupational Mobility in Mid-Nineteenth-Century Poughkeepsie." Pp. 122–141 in *Small Business in American Life*, edited by Stuart W. Bruchey. New York: Columbia University Press.

Griffin, Larry J., Michael E. Wallace, and Beth A. Rubin. 1986. "Capitalist Resistance to the Organization of Labor before the New Deal: Why? How? Success?" *American Sociological Review*, 51(2): 146–167.

Guillén, Mauro F. 1994. *Models of Management: Work, Authority, and Organization in a Comparative Perspective*. Chicago: University of Chicago Press.

Gutman, Herbert. 1977. *Work, Culture, and Society in Industrializing America*. New York: Vintage Books.

Hall, John R., ed. 1997. *Reworking Class*. Ithaca: Cornell University Press.

Hanagan, Michael P. 1980. *The Logic of Solidarity: Artisans and Industrial Workers in Three French Towns, 1871–1914*. Urbana: University of Illinois Press.

Harris, Howell John. 1991. "Getting It Together: The Metal Manufacturers Association of Philadelphia, c. 1900–1930." Pp. 111–131 in *Masters to Managers: Historical and Comparative Perspectives on American Employers*, edited by Sanford M. Jacoby. New York: Columbia University Press.

Haydu, Jeffrey. 1988a. *Between Craft and Class: Skilled Workers and Factory Politics in Great Britain and the United States, 1890–1922*. Berkeley: University of California Press.

———. 1988b. "Employers, Unions, and American Exceptionalism: A Comparative View." *International Review of Social History*, 33(1): 25–41.

———. 1988c. "Trade Agreement vs. Open Shop: Employers' Choices Before WWI." *Industrial Relations*, 28(2): 159–173.

———. 1999a. "Counter Action Frames: Employer Repertoires and the Union Menace in the Late Nineteenth Century." *Social Problems*, 46(3): 313–331.

———. 1999b. "Two Logics of Class Formation? Collective Identities Among Proprietary Employers, 1880–1900." *Politics & Society*, 27(4): 505–525.

Heide, Margaret. 1998. "The Impact of Corporate Restructuring on Women in Customer Service Jobs: A Case Study of Female Customer Service Representatives." Pp. 170–184 in *Proceedings of the Conference on "Work, Difference, and Social Change: Two Decades After Braverman's 'Labor and Monopoly Capital,'"* edited by Rick Baldoz, Phoebe Godfrey, Carol Jansen, Charles Koeber, and Philip Kraft. Binghamton: Department of Sociology, State University of New York.

Hirschhorn, Larry. 1997. *Reworking Authority: Leading and Following in the Post-Modern Organization.* Cambridge: MIT Press.

Hoffecker, Carol E. 1974. *Wilmington, Delaware: Portrait of an Industrial City, 1830–1910.* Charlottesville: University Press of Virginia.

Hyman, Richard. 1980. "Trade Unions, Control, and Resistance." Pp. 303–334 in *The Politics of Work and Occupations*, edited by Geoff Esland and Graeme Salaman. Toronto: University of Toronto Press.

Ingham, John N. 1978. *The Iron Barons: A Social Analysis of an American Urban Elite, 1874–1965.* Westport, CT: Greenwood Press.

———. 1991. *Making Iron and Steel: Independent Mills in Pittsburgh, 1820–1920.* Columbus: Ohio State University Press.

Issel, William, and Robert Cherny. 1986. *San Francisco, 1865–1932: Politics, Power, and Urban Development.* Berkeley: University of California Press.

Jackson, Robert Max. 1984. *The Formation of Craft Labor Markets.* Orlando, FL: Academic Press.

Jacoby, Sanford M. 1985. *Employing Bureaucracy: Managers, Unions, and the Transformation of Work in American Industry, 1900–1945.* New York: Columbia University Press.

Jaher, Frederic Cople. 1982. *The Urban Establishment: Upper Strata in Boston, New York, Charleston, Chicago, and Los Angeles.* Urbana: University of Illinois.

Kasson, John F. 1976. *Civilizing the Machine: Technology and Republican Values in America, 1776–1900.* New York: Grossman Publishers.

Kaus, Robert. 1983. "The Trouble with Unions." *Harper's*, June, 23–35.

Kazin, Michael. 1995. *The Populist Persuasion: An American History.* New York: Basic Books.

Klug, Thomas A. 1993. *The Roots of the Open Shop: Employers, Trade Unions, and Craft Labor Markets in Detroit, 1859–1907.* Ph.D. dissertation, Wayne State University.

Kornblith, Gary John. 1983. *From Artisans to Businessmen: Master Mechanics in New England, 1789–1850.* Ph.D. dissertation, Princeton University.

Krinsky, John. 1998. "Work, Workfare, and Contention in New York City: Recombinant Repertoires and Multiple Accounts of Worker Identity and the Opposition to Workfare." Pp. 214–228 in *Proceedings of the Conference on "Work, Difference, and Social Change: Two Decades After Braverman's 'Labor and Monopoly Capital,'"* edited by Rick Baldoz, Phoebe Godfrey, Carol Jansen, Charles Koeber, and Philip Kraft. Binghamton: Department of Sociology, State University of New York.

Kunda, Gideon. 1992. *Engineering Culture: Control and Commitment in a High-Tech Corporation.* Philadelphia: Temple University Press.

Larson, Henrietta M. 1944. "An Early Industrial Capitalist's Labor Policy and Management." *Bulletin of the Business Historical Society*, 8 (5): 132–141.

Lembcke, Jerry Lee. 1995. "Labor History's 'Synthesis Debate'." *Science and Society*, 59(2): 137–73.

Licht, Walter. 1995. *Industrializing America: The Nineteenth Century.* Baltimore: John Hopkins Press.

Littler, Craig R. 1990. "The Labour Process Debate: A Theoretical Review." Pp. 46–94 in *Labour Process Theory,* edited by David Knights and Hugh Willmott. London: Macmillan.

Livingston, James. 1986. *Origins of the Federal Reserve System: Money, Class, and Corporate Capitalism, 1890–1913.* Ithaca: Cornell University Press.

Machinists' Monthly Journal. 1913. Reports from Business Agents. Published by the International Association of Machinists.

Manufacturers' Association of the City of Bridgeport. Various dates. *Minutes of Executive Board and Committee Meetings.* Bridgeport Public Library, Accession 1981.06, Box 1.

Mapes, Lynn Gordon. 1973. *Iron Age: An Iron Manufacturers' Journal and the "Labor Problem" in the Age of Enterprise.* Ph.D. dissertation, University of Rochester.

McMurry, Donald. 1953. "Labor Policies of the General Managers' Association of Chicago, 1886–1894." *Journal of Economic History,* 13(2): 160–178.

Melucci, Alberto. 1989. *Nomads of the Present: Social Movements and Individual Needs in Contemporary Society.* Philadelphia: Temple University Press.

Meyer, Stephen. 1981. *The Five Dollar Day: Labor Management and Social Control in the Ford Motor Company, 1908–1921.* Albany: State University of New York Press.

Montgomery, David. 1979. *Workers' Control in America: Studies in the History of Work, Technology, and Labor Struggles.* Cambridge: Cambridge University Press.

Nelson, Daniel. 1975. *Managers and Workers: Origins of the New Factory System in the United States, 1880–1920.* Madison: University of Wisconsin Press.

Noble, David F. 1977. *America by Design: Science, Technology, and the Rise of Corporate Capitalism.* New York: Alfred A. Knopf.

———. 1986. *Forces of Production: A Social History of Industrial Automation.* New York: Oxford University Press.

Offe, Claus, and Helmut Wiesenthal. 1980. "Two Logics of Collective Action: Theoretical Notes on Social Class and Organizational Form." *Political Power and Social Theory: A Research Annual,* 1: 67–115.

Ó Riain, Seán. 1998. "Networking for a Living: Irish Software Developers in the Global Workplace." Pp. 278–291 in *Proceedings of the Conference on "Work, Difference, and Social Change: Two Decades After Braverman's 'Labor and Monopoly Capital,'"* edited by Rick Baldoz, Phoebe Godfrey, Carol Jansen, Charles Koeber, and Philip Kraft. Binghamton: Department of Sociology, State University of New York.

Ozanne, Robert. 1967. *A Century of Labor-Management Relations at McCormick and International Harvester.* Madison: University of Wisconsin Press.

Peterson, William H. 1987. "Putting An End to Adversarial Unionism." *New York Times,* 26 July, section 3, p. 2.

Phillips, Kevin. 1970. *The Emerging Republican Majority.* Garden City, NY: Anchor Books.

———. 1983. *Post-Conservative America: People, Politics, and Ideology in a Time of Crisis.* New York: Vintage Books.

———. 1990. *The Politics of Rich and Poor: Wealth and the American Electorate in the Reagan Aftermath.* New York: Random House.

Piore, Michael J., and Charles F. Sabel. 1984. *The Second Industrial Divide: Possibilities for Prosperity.* New York: Basic Books.

Ramirez, Bruno. 1978. *When Workers Fight: The Politics of Industrial Relations in the Progressive Era, 1898–1916.* Westport, CT: Greenwood Press.

Rieder, Jonathan. 1989. "The Rise of the 'Silent Majority.'" Pp. 243–268 in *The Rise and Fall of the New Deal Order, 1930–1980*, edited by Steve Fraser and Gary Gerstle. Princeton: Princeton University Press.

Rinehart, James. 1998. "Transcending Taylorism and Fordism? Two Decades of Work Restructuring." Pp. 336–349 in *Proceedings of the Conference on "Work, Difference, and Social Change: Two Decades After Braverman's 'Labor and Monopoly Capital,'"* edited by Rick Baldoz, Phoebe Godfrey, Carol Jansen, Charles Koeber, and Philip Kraft. Binghamton: Department of Sociology, State University of New York.

Rosenzweig, Roy. 1983. *Eight Hours for What We Will: Workers and Leisure in an Industrial City, 1870–1920*. Cambridge: Cambridge University Press.

Ross, Steven J. 1985. *Workers on the Edge: Work, Leisure, and Politics in Industrializing Cincinnati, 1788–1890*. New York: Columbia University Press.

Roy, William G. 1991. "The Organization of the Corporate Class Segment of the U.S. Capitalist Class at the Turn of This Century." Pp. 139–63 in *Bringing Class Back in: Contemporary and Historical Perspectives*, edited by Scott G. McNall, Rhonda F. Levine, and Rick Fantasia. Boulder, CO: Westview Press.

———. 1997. *Socializing Capital: The Rise of the Large Industrial Corporation in America*. Princeton: Princeton University Press.

Roy, William G., and Rachel R. Parker-Gwin. 1999. "How Many Logics of Collective Action?" *Theory and Society*, 28(2): 203–237.

Sabel, Charles F., and Jonathan Zeitlin, eds. 1997. *World of Possibilities: Flexibility and Mass Production in Western Industrialization*. New York: Cambridge University Press.

Salvatore, Nick. 1982. *Eugene V. Debs: Citizen and Socialist*. Urbana: University of Illinois.

Schiesl, Martin J. 1977. *The Politics of Efficiency: Municipal Administration and Reform in America, 1800–1920*. Berkeley: University of California Press.

Scranton, Philip. 1983. *Proprietary Capitalism: The Textile Manufacture at Philadelphia, 1885–1900*. Cambridge: Cambridge University Press.

———. 1989. *Figured Tapestry: Production, Markets, and Power in Philadelphia Textiles, 1885–1941*. Cambridge: Cambridge University Press.

———. 1997. *Endless Novelty: Specialty Production and American Industrialization, 1865–1925*. Princeton: Princeton University Press.

Shafer, Byron E., ed. 1991. *Is America Different? A New Look at American Exceptionalism*. Oxford: Clarendon Press.

Shostak, Art, ed. 1996. "The Impact of Changing Employment: If the Good Jobs Go Away." *The Annals of the American Academy of Political and Social Science*, 544.

Steinfeld, Robert. 1991. *The Invention of Free Labor: The Employment Relation in English and American Law and Culture, 1350–1870*. Chapel Hill: University of North Carolina Press.

Stern, Marc Jeffrey. 1994. *The Pottery Industry of Trenton: A Skilled Trade in Transition, 1850–1929*. New Brunswick, NJ: Rutgers University Press.

Stromquist, Shelton. 1987. *A Generation of Boomers: The Pattern of Railroad Labor Conflict in Nineteenth-Century America*. Urbana: University of Illinois Press.

Sturges, Kenneth. 1915. *American Chambers of Commerce*. New York: Moffat, Bard, and Company.

Thimm, Alfred L. 1976. *Business Ideologies in the Reform-Progressive Era, 1880–1914*. N.P.: University of Alabama Press.

Thompson, Paul. 1989. *The Nature of Work: An Introduction to Debates on the Labour Process*. Basingstoke, England: Macmillan.

Tichenor, Irene. 1980. "Master Printers Organize: The Typothetae of the City of New York, 1865–1906." Pp. 169–191 in *Small Business in American Life*, edited by Stuart W. Bruchey. New York: Columbia University Press.

Tomlins, Christopher L. 1993. *Law, Labor, and Ideology in the Early American Republic.* Cambridge: Cambridge University Press.

Trachtenberg, Alan. 1982. *The Incorporation of America: Culture and Society in the Gilded Age.* New York: Hill and Wang.

U.S. Industrial Commission. 1901–2. *Reports.* Vol. 8. Washington, DC: U.S. Government Printing Office.

Vallas, Steven Peter. 1993. *Power in the Workplace: The Politics of Production at AT&T.* Albany: SUNY Press.

Wallace, Anthony F. C. 1972. *Rockdale: The Growth of an American Village in the Early Industrial Revolution.* New York: W. W. Norton.

Webster, Edward. 1998. "The Dynamics of Race and Class Among South African Shop Stewards in the Nineties." Pp. 462–474 in *Proceedings of the Conference on "Work, Difference, and Social Change: Two Decades After Braverman's 'Labor and Monopoly Capital,'"* edited by Rick Baldoz, Phoebe Godfrey, Carol Jansen, Charles Koeber, and Philip Kraft. Binghamton: Department of Sociology, State University of New York.

Whalley, Peter, and Peter Meiksins. 1998. "Controlling Technical Workers in Alternative Work Arrangements: Rethinking the Work Contract." Pp. 475–488 in *Proceedings of the Conference on "Work, Difference, and Social Change: Two Decades After Braverman's 'Labor and Monopoly Capital.'"* edited by Rick Baldoz, Phoebe Godfrey, Carol Jansen, Charles Koeber, and Philip Kraft. Binghamton: Department of Sociology, State University of New York.

Wilentz, Sean. 1984. *Chants Democratic: New York City and the Rise of the American Working Class, 1788–1850.* New York: Oxford University Press.

Zetka, James R., Jr. 1992. "Mass-Production Automation and Work-Group Solidarity in the Post–World War II Automobile Industry." *Work and Occupations*, 19(3): 255–271.

Zuboff, Shoshana. 1984. *In the Age of the Smart Machine: The Future of Work and Power.* New York: Basic Books.

Zunz, Olivier. 1982. *The Changing Face of Inequality: Urbanization, Industrial Development, and Immigrants in Detroit, 1880–1920.* Chicago: University of Chicago Press.

Part II

Service and Service Sector Workers

CHAPTER 3

Gender, Race, and the Organization of Reproductive Labor

Evelyn Nakano Glenn

Feminist sociologists and historians have revolutionized labor studies by making gender a central concept in the analysis of work. One of their most significant contributions has been to expand the concept of labor to include activities that were not previously recognized as forms of work, especially unpaid work in the household. In this chapter, I present a race-gender analysis of one form of nonmarket work—the labor of social reproduction—which has been extensively explored as a form of gendered labor, but not as labor that is simultaneously racialized.

Gender and Reproductive Labor

The term "social reproduction" was coined by feminist scholars to refer to the array of activities and relationships involved in maintaining people on both a daily basis and intergenerationally (Laslett and Brenner 1989). Reproductive labor includes such activities as purchasing household goods, preparing meals, washing and repairing clothing, maintaining furnishings and appliances, socializing children, providing emotional support for adults, and maintaining kin and community ties. Marxist feminists in the 1970s and 1980s (e.g., Bose et al. 1987) placed the gendered construction of reproductive labor at the center of women's oppression. They pointed out that this labor is performed disproportionately by women and is essential to the industrial economy. Yet because it takes place mostly outside the market, it is invisible, not recognized as "real work." Men benefit both directly and indirectly from this arrangement—directly in that they contribute less labor in the home while enjoying the services women provide as wives and mothers, and indirectly, in that, freed of domestic labor, they can concentrate their efforts in paid employment and attain primacy in that area. Thus the gender division of reproductive labor in the home interacts with and reinforces the gender division in the market.

These analyses drew attention to the way the gender construction of reproductive labor helped to create and maintain inequality between men and women, and conversely how their unequal power has enabled men to avoid doing reproductive labor and hampered women's ability to shift the burden. When feminist scholars represent gender as the sole basis for assigning reproductive labor, they imply that all women have the same relationship to it and that it is therefore a universal female experience. And while feminists increasingly are aware of the interaction of race and gender in stratifying the labor market, they have rarely considered whether race might interact with gender in shaping reproductive labor; thus they have failed to examine differences across race, ethnic, and class groups in women's relationship to that labor.

The Racial Division of Labor

Because scholarship on race and labor has been, consciously or unconsciously, male centered, it has focused exclusively on the paid labor market and especially on male-dominated areas of production. U.S. historians have documented the way in which race has been integral to the structure of labor markets since the beginnings of the nation. In the 1970s, several writers (e.g., Blauner 1972; Barrera 1979), seeking to explain the historic subordination of peoples of color, pointed to dualism in the labor market—its division into distinct markets for white workers and for racial-ethnic workers—as a major vehicle for maintaining white domination. According to these formulations, labor systems have been organized to ensure that racial-ethnic workers are relegated to a lower tier of low-wage, dead-end, marginal jobs; institutional barriers, including restrictions on legal and political rights, prevent workers from moving out of that tier.

Writers have differed in their views about the relative agency of capitalists and white workers in the creation and maintenance of color lines. Some have interpreted the color line as a divide-and-conquer strategy of capital to prevent workers from organizing (e.g., M. Reich 1981); others have depicted white workers as active agents in drawing color lines in order to secure a privileged position in the market (e.g., Bonacich 1972; 1976). Both camps see class conflict as generating race conflict. Whatever the ultimate cause of the conflict, labor struggles in the United States have often taken the form of racial exclusion movements. William Forbath (1999) describes how European American male workers in the nineteenth century constructed their identities as whites and claimed their rights in contrast to blacks around racialized notions of work: skilled versus unskilled, free versus unfree, and dirty versus clean. These studies draw attention to the material and ideological advantages whites gain from the racial division of labor. However, the studies either take for granted or ignore women's paid and unpaid household labor and fail to consider whether this work might also be racially divided.

Reproductive Labor as Raced and Gendered

In short, the analysis of the racial construction of reproductive labor has been miss-ing from the literatures of both race and gender, because of their focus on either race or gender alone. Only by viewing reproductive labor as simultaneously raced and gendered can we grasp the distinct exploitation of women of color. Using a race-gender lens reveals that reproductive labor has divided along racial as well as gender lines, with white and racial-ethnic women having distinctly different responsibilities for social reproduction, not just in their own households but in other work settings. The specific characteristics of the division have varied regionally and over time with changes in the organization of production and reproduction.

I examine three major periods. In the first, from the mid-nineteenth century until World War II, reproductive labor remained organized at the household level. Racial-ethnic women were employed as servants to perform reproductive labor in white households, thus relieving white middle-class women of more onerous aspects of that work. After World War II parts of reproductive labor were increasingly transformed into commodified forms; reproductive labor was turned into commercial products or activities to produce profit for capital. As this occurred, racial-ethnic women were brought into this reorganized form of labor as well. Black and Latina women were disproportionately employed as service workers in institutional settings to carry out lower-level "public" reproductive labor, while cleaner white-collar supervisory, as well as lower professional positions, were filled by white women. In the most recent period, with economic globalization there has been a growing demand for reproduc-tive services among the expanding professional, technical, and managerial sector concentrated in metropolitan centers. Concomitant with globalization has been the economic impetus for women from the periphery to migrate to metropolitan centers to fill demands for both private and public reproductive services. The race-gender division of reproductive labor has thus become a transnational race-gender division of labor. In all three periods less desirable or more onerous aspects of reproductive labor have devolved on disadvantaged women of color, "freeing" more privileged women for higher-level pursuits. Thus the organization of reproductive labor has been as much a source of division and hierarchy as it is of unity and commonality among women both nationally and internationally.

The Race and Gender Division of Private Reproductive Labor

From the late nineteenth century to the mid-twentieth century, poor and working-class women did reproductive labor not only in their own homes, but also for middle-class families. The division between white women and women of color grew in the latter half of the nineteenth century, when the demand for household help and the number of women employed as servants expanded rapidly (Chaplin 1978). Rising standards of cleanliness, larger and more ornately furnished homes, the sentimentalization of the home as a "haven in a heartless world," and the new emphasis on childhood and mother's role in nurturing children all served to enlarge middle-class women's responsibilities for reproduction at a time when technology had done little to reduce the sheer physical drudgery of housework (Cowan 1983).

By all accounts, middle-class women did not challenge the gender-based division of labor or the enlargement of their reproductive responsibilities. To the contrary, as readers and writers of literature, and as members and leaders of clubs, charitable organizations, associations, reform movements, religious revivals, and the cause of abolition, they helped to elaborate and refine the domestic code (Epstein 1981). Instead of questioning the inequitable gender division of labor, they sought to slough off the more onerous tasks onto more oppressed groups of women.

In the United States, the particular groups hired for private reproductive work varied by region. In the Northeast, European immigrant women, especially Irish, were the primary servant class. In areas with a substantial racial minority population, the servant caste consisted almost exclusively of women of color. In the early years of the twentieth century, 90 percent of non-agriculturally employed black women in the South were servants or laundresses, constituting over 80 percent of female servants (Katzman 1978). In Southwestern and Western cities, such as El Paso and Denver, where the main division was between Anglos and Mexicans, approximately half of all employed Mexican women were domestic or laundry workers (Deutsch 1987; Garcia 1981). In the San Francisco Bay area and in Honolulu, where there were substantial numbers of Asian immigrants, a quarter to half of all employed Japanese women were private household workers (Glenn 1986; Lind 1951).

Women of color shouldered the burdens not only of household maintenance, but also of family nurturing for white middle-class women. They did both the dirty, heavy manual labor of cleaning and laundering and the emotional work of caring for children. By performing the most onerous or time-consuming tasks, they freed their mistresses for supervisory tasks, leisure, and cultural activities, or, more rarely during this period, a career. Ironically, then, many white women were able to fulfill white society's expectation of feminine domesticity only through the domestic labor of women of color.

For the domestic worker, the other side of doing reproductive labor for white families was not being able to perform reproductive labor for their own families. Unlike European immigrant domestics, who were mainly single young women, racial-ethnic servants were usually wives and mothers (Stigler 1946). Yet, the code that sanctified white women's domesticity did not extend to them. In many cases, servants had to leave their own children in the care of relatives in order to "mother" their employers' children. A six-and-a-half-day work week was typical. A black children's nurse reported in 1912 that she worked fourteen to sixteen hours a day caring for her mistress' four children. Describing her existence as a "treadmill life," she said she was allowed to go home

> only once in every two weeks, every other Sunday afternoon—even then I'm not permitted to stay all night. I see my own children only when they happen to see me on the streets when I am out with the children [of my mistress], or when my children come to the "yard"

to see me, which isn't often, because my white folks don't like to see their servants' children hanging around their premises. (Katzman 1982, 179)

The dominant group ideology naturalized the mistress-servant relationship by portraying women of color as particularly suited for service. These racialized gender constructions ranged from the view of African American and Mexican American women as incapable of governing their own lives and requiring white supervision to the image of Asian women as naturally subservient and accustomed to a low standard of living. Although racial stereotypes undoubtedly preceded their entry into domestic work, household workers were also induced to enact the role of race-gender inferiors in daily interactions with employers. Domestic workers interviewed by Judith Rollins (1985) and Mary Romero (1992) described a variety of rituals that affirmed their subordination and dependence; for example, employers addressed the household workers by their first names, and required them to enter by the back door, eat in the kitchen, wear uniforms, and accept with gratitude "gifts" of discarded clothing and leftover food.

The lack of respect for racial-ethnic women's family roles stood in marked contrast to the situation of white middle-class women in the late nineteenth and early twentieth centuries, when the cult of domesticity defined white womanhood primarily in terms of wifehood and motherhood. While the domestic code constrained white women, it placed racial-ethnic women in an untenable position. Forced to work outside the home, they were considered deviant according to the dominant gender ideology. On the one hand, they were denied the buffer of a protected private sphere; on the other, they were judged deficient as wives and mothers compared to white middle-class women who could devote themselves full-time to domesticity (Pascoe 1990). Women of color had to construct their own definitions of self-worth and womanhood outside the standards of the dominant culture. Their efforts to maintain kin ties, organize family celebrations, cook traditional foods, and keep households together were crucial to the survival of ethnic communities.

The Race and Gender Division of Public Reproductive Labor

Due to the expansion of capital into new areas for profit-making, the fragmentation of families and the breakdown of extended kin and community ties, and the squeeze on women's time as they moved into the labor market, the post–World War II era saw the expansion of commodified services to replace the reproductive labor formerly performed in the home (see, e.g., Braverman 1974). Among the fastest-growing occupations in the economy from the 1970s to the 1990s were lower-level service jobs in health care, food service, and personal services (U.S. Bureau of Labor Statistics 1993). Women are the main labor force in these occupations. Within this new realm of "public reproductive labor," we find a clear race-gender division of labor. Women of color are disproportionately assigned to do the dirty work, as nurses' aides in hospitals, kitchen workers in restaurants and cafeterias, maids in hotels, and cleaners in office buildings. In these same institutional settings white women are disproportionately employed as supervisors, professionals, and administrative support staff. This division parallels the earlier division between the domestic servant and the housewife.

As in the case of domestic service, allocation to lower-level service occupations has followed racial-ethnic caste lines in regional economies.[1] Census data for 1990 show that black and Latina women were overrepresented among service workers in every city where they were a significant part of the population. African American women were more than twice as likely to be employed in service occupations in Northern and Southern cities than white women. For example, the relevant percentages of black versus non-Latina white women employed in service occupations were: Atlanta, 27.4 percent versus 10.2 percent; Memphis, 27.7 percent versus 10.5 percent; Chicago, 17.4 percent versus 12.5 percent; New York, 25.4 percent versus 8.5 percent. In Western and Southwestern cities where Mexican Americans are concentrated, Spanish-origin women were much more likely to be service workers than Anglo women. In San Antonio 24.1 percent of Spanish-origin women were so employed, compared to 11.3 percent of non-Spanish-origin white women; in El Paso the percentages were 21.0 percent versus 10.1 percent; and in Los Angeles, 29.1 percent versus 8.8 percent. In Hawaii, Asian and Pacific Islanders are disproportionately found in these occupations: 18.9 percent of Asian and Pacific Islander women in Honolulu were employed as lower-level service workers, compared to 13.1 percent of non-Latina white women.[2]

Particularly instructive is the race and gender division of labor in the health care system. In an effort to "contain costs," more and more care was shifted out of hospitals and into nursing and convalescent centers and private homes. In these settings health care aides, including nursing aides and home health workers, were the primary caregivers for those with severe disabilities and the feeble elderly. These aide positions were overwhelming a specialty of women of color. The jobs were defined as unskilled and menial; hence the women who do it were too. This point was brought home to Timothy Diamond (1988, 41) during the training course he attended as the sole white male in a mostly black female group:

> We learned elementary biology and how we were never to do health care without first consulting someone in authority; and we learn not to ask questions but to do as we were told. As one of the students, a black woman from Jamaica, used to joke, "I can't figure out whether they're trying to teach us to be nurses' aides or black women."

Yet, these jobs were physically and emotionally demanding and tiring: aides helped patients dress, took vital signs, bathed and fed them, moved them to prevent bed sores, emptied bedpans, changed diapers and bedsheets, and kept the area tidy. There was much dirty work, but there was also unacknowledged mental and emotional labor: listening to the reminiscences of elderly patients to help them hold onto their memories, comforting frightened patients about to undergo medical procedures, providing the only human contact some patients get (Diamond 1992). The women were assuming work that would otherwise devolve on female relatives or on "real" nurses.

Whether the shift from domestic service to service work represented an improvement for these women is debatable. In many ways minority women were performing the same kinds of dirty work they did before in a new setting. Service work occupied a similarly low position in the occupational hierarchy and was, aside from private household work, the lowest-paid category of work. Service workers made up nearly two-thirds of all workers earning minimum wage or less (Mellor 1987). Because of low pay, many service workers moonlighted. This sector has had low rates of unionization, and in many cases employers were subcontractors who did not provide any benefits.

With the shift of reproductive labor from the household to market, face-to-face race and gender hierarchies were replaced by structural hierarchies. In institutional settings, race and gender stratification was now built into organizational structures, including lines of authority, job descriptions, rules, and spatial and temporal segregation. Distance between higher and lower orders was ensured by structural segregation. Much routine service work was organized to be out of sight. It took place behind institutional walls, where outsiders rarely penetrated (nursing homes, chronic care facilities), in back rooms (restaurant kitchens), or at night or other times when occupants were gone (office buildings and hotels). Although workers may have appreciated this time and space segregation, which allowed them some autonomy and freedom from demeaning interactions, it also made them and their work invisible. In this situation, more privileged women did not have to acknowledge the workers or their own privilege at the expense of other women.

Globalization and the Transnational Race-Gender Division of Reproductive Labor

The speedup of economic globalization in the 1990s has meant a partial breaking down of barriers to the movement of capital, people, goods, and labor processes. With globalization the race-gender division of labor has become more transnational as corporate capitalism has moved labor-intensive manufacturing processes to the periphery while keeping financial, design, and distributional control in the core countries. One dimension of this division is the familiar one between core and periphery. Specialized professional services that employ managerial, financial, technical, engineering, legal, accounting, and other high-level service personnel are increasing in industrialized countries, where they are concentrated in large global cities of the first world, such as Los Angeles, Tokyo, London, and New York. By contrast, low-wage unskilled labor for labor-intensive manufacturing processes has been moved to peripheral countries, where the work is often concentrated in export processing zones (EPZs) set up to corporate specifications to bypass environmental and labor regulations.

A second dimension of this division is manifested in the core itself, where skilled and semiskilled manufacturing jobs are being lost at the same time that semiskilled and unskilled service jobs are expanding. The latter expansion is associated with the above-mentioned growth of specialized professional services in metropolitan centers "both directly, through the structure of the work process, and indirectly, through the structure of the high income lifestyles of those therein employed" (Sassen 1988, 158).

Among the occupations meeting the lifestyle demands of the professional managerial class are both private reproductive workers—such as housekeepers, nannies,
maids, and general domestic workers—and public reproduction workers—such as
cleaners, porters, waiters, and chambermaids (Cohen 1992). Former U.S. Secretary of
Labor Robert Reich (1991) notes that 30 percent of all workers in the new U.S. economy provide "routine personal services"—for example, restaurant and hotel workers, taxi drivers, nurses, and sales clerks. This work, unlike manufacturing, cannot be
exported. It has to be done on site.

As the drive for profits heats up with a capitalism ever more unfettered by globalization, the industries that arose and expanded to provide commodified services,
such as health care and elderly care, are undergoing pressures to increase profitability. They have done so by a two-fold strategy of reorganizing the labor process
so as to transfer more of the work onto lower-paid workers while sloughing off
parts of the labor altogether by shifting it back to the consumer (Glazer 1989). The
health industry in particular has been undergoing a continuing round of cost-cutting in response to pressures from other sectors of capital to reduce both insurance
and government payments for medical care. As this happens, hospital and nursing
home stays are being shortened, and patients are being released before they can
take care of themselves. Although much of the care is being taken up by relatives,
particularly wives and daughters as unpaid work, some of the gap is being filled
by home health aides, who work for minimum wage and without benefits. Many
are employed by state-funded programs under the rubric of "in-house support services"; although funded by the state, these programs nonetheless save enormous
amounts over the cost of nursing home care. The home health care aide provides
both housekeeping services, including cleaning, laundry, shopping, and cooking,
as well as hands-on personal care by helping with bathing, dressing, grooming,
medication, and exercise. The U.S. Bureau of Labor Statistics (1998) projects this
field to be among the fastest-growing occupations through the year 2006, although
it admits that it is highly demanding, poorly paid, and offers little opportunity for
advancement.

Although historically, as mentioned in the previous section, the ranks of these jobs
have been drawn mainly from native minorities, the turnover is high and demand
outstrips the supply of workers who are skilled, reliable, and desperate enough to
stick with the work. As a result, the demand for such services is spurring transnational migration from the periphery to the metropolitan center. Many of these workers are drawn from the same countries where transnational corporations have
located production facilities. Thus the transnational division of labor includes several sets of low-wage workers: those employed in transnational corporate manufacturing processes located in third countries, those who migrate to the cities where
transnational corporate headquarters are located to provide services for the profes-
sional-managerial elite involved in the control of the corporations, and, increasingly,
immigrant workers who are brought into core countries to do low-wage work in
manufacturing sweatshops. Indeed, these phenomena are all concomitant conse-

quences of unequal relations among nations. While some low-wage jobs that inject money into the economy are created, the huge profits extracted from the labor of workers in manufacturing processing zones go back to the core, further enriching it in relation to the periphery.

With the exception of a few newly "modernized" countries, which have managed to develop some export-led industrialization of their own, peripheral countries involved in export-led manufacturing remain stuck as the bottom link in the commodity chain of global production (Ong, Bonacich, and Cheng 1994). Furthermore, the effort to obtain Western goods and military armaments has enmeshed the economies and governments of both newly industrialized and peripheral countries in enormous debt. One result is that the International Monetary Fund, the World Bank, and other First World institutions can impose structural adjustment policies that involve cuts in even the scantiest of social welfare provisions as a condition for refinancing debt. As welfare is cut, the economic circumstances of poor families in the Third World becomes ever more dire. Sending one family member abroad to work and send remittances back home becomes one way to deal with the plight. In turn, governments in the Third World encourage migration abroad, since remittances infuse foreign currency into their debt-ridden economies (Chang 1997).

The Philippines is one of the largest exporters of migrant labor, having adopted "manpower export" as a strategy of economic growth, first under the Marcos government in the 1970s and then under its successors (Basch, Schiller, and Blanc 1994). Although the actual figures involved are in dispute because of the large number of migrants who evade official channels, estimates range up to 4.5 million Filipino workers in 120 countries. Taking only the official numbers of those workers deployed through the Philippine Overseas Employment Administration, 700,000 contract migrants were going abroad each year in the late 1990s. Some 55 percent of them were women, of whom over two-thirds were employed as nannies, housekeepers, or maids in middle- or upper-middle-class homes in the United States, Europe, the Middle East, Japan, Hong Kong, and other parts of Asia (Karp 1995). In many countries they are "guest" workers, which means they are allowed to remain only as long as they stay in their jobs and cannot move into other jobs.

In the United States, Filipinas are more often concentrated in nursing, nursing aide, and home health aide work than in private household work, because of both greater opportunities for mobility in the health care field and the availability of Latina women for domestic work. As Rhacel Parrenas (2000) has discovered from interviewing Filipina immigrants in Rome and Los Angeles, Filipina workers tend to be relatively well educated; indeed, they are often overqualified for their jobs. Typically, Filipina workers have left their own children behind; because of the lower standard of living in the Philippines, a Filipina maid in Rome or a home health aide in Los Angeles can afford to pay an even poorer Filipina to care for her family back home. According to Parrenas, the racial division of female reproductive labor has been transformed by economic globalization into what amounts to an "international transference of mothering."

Implications

Both historically and contemporaneously, the racial division of reproductive labor has created fundamental differences in women's relationship to job segregation, wage inequality, and the double day. Further, it has meant an interdependence between the subordination of some women and the higher standard of living of other women. This analysis suggests that if these special forms of exploitation were to cease, more favorably positioned women as well as men would have to give up certain privileges and benefits that rest on the reproductive labor of other women. We may have to accept the idea that improving the lot of racial-ethnic and Third World women necessarily involves a loss of privilege or status for white women.

Moreover, as we enter the twenty first century the demographic trends quite dramatically point toward more unequal distribution of economic resources, both within the United States and in the global economy. Accordingly, the potential supply of Third World women to perform public or private reproductive work for mostly white First World women is projected to greatly increase, while the financial resources available to white women for buying reproductive labor will also expand. If present efforts to breakdown borders for the benefit of "free markets" continues, we may expect ever larger numbers of Third World women working in the United States and other developed countries.

The interdependence between richer and poorer women calls into question the feasibility of formulating national or global policies for "working women." Given historic and continuing divisions, identifying universal solutions to problems of "working women" may be fruitless. Instead, we need to acknowledge the divergent and often contradictory interests of different groups of women and confront potential sources of resistance to change from women as well as men.

Notes

1. The U.S. Labor Department and the U.S. Bureau of the Census designate as service occupations three major subgroupings of jobs: private household, protective services, and service occupations except private household and protective services. I want to set aside private household workers, who have been covered above, and protective service workers, who include firemen and police. These jobs, in addition to being male dominated and relatively well paid, carry some degree of authority, including the right to use force. Thus, in the discussion that follows the term "service occupations" refers to the remaining subgroup, "service occupations except private household and protective services". This classification includes the following subcategories: food preparation and service, health care service, cleaning and building service, and personal service.

2. Figures computed from Tables 174 and 185 in each of the state volumes of U.S. Bureau of the Census (1993). Vol. 12, Georgia; Vol. 44, Tennessee; Vol. 15, Illinois; Vol. 33, New York; Vol. 45, Texas; Vol. 6, California; Vol. 13, Hawaii. The figures for Latina and Anglos in the Southwest are estimates, based on the assumption that most "Spanish-origin" women are Mexicans

and that Mexicans are counted as whites (they are supposed to be); therefore the "Spanish-origin" totals are subtracted from the white total to leave the remainder as "Anglo."

References

Barrera, Mario. 1979. *Race and Class in the Southwest.* Notre Dame, IN: University of Notre Dame Press.

Basch, Linda, Nina Glick Schiller, and Christina Szanton Blanc. 1994. "Different Settings, Same Outcome: Transnationalism as a Global Process." Pp. 225–265 in *Nations Unbound: Transnational Projects, Postcolonial Predicaments, and Deterritorialized Nation-States.* Langhorne, PA: Gordon and Breach Publishers.

Blauner, Robert. 1972. *Racial Oppression in America.* New York: Harper and Row.

Bonacich, Edna 1972. "A Theory of Ethnic Antagonism: The Split Labor Market." *American Sociological Review,* 37(5): 547–559.

———. 1976. "Advanced Capitalism and Black/White Relations in the United States: A Split Labor Market Interpretation.' *American Sociological Review,* 41: 34–51.

Bose, Chris, Roslyn Feldberg, and Natalie Sokoloff, with the Women and Work Research Group (eds.). 1987. *Hidden Aspects of Women's Work.* New York: Praeger.

Braverman, Harry. 1974. *Labor and Monopoly Capital: The Degradation of Work in the Twentieth Century.* New York: Monthly Review Press.

Chang, Grace. 1997. "The Global Trade in Filipina Workers." Pp. 132–152 in *Dragon Ladies: Asian American Feminists Breathe Fire,* edited by Sonia Shah. Boston: South End Press.

Chaplin, David. 1978. "Domestic Service and Industrialization." *Comparative Studies in Sociology,* 1: 97–127.

Cohen, Robin. 1992. "Migration and the New International Division of Labor." In *Ethnic Minorities and Industrial Change in Europe and North America,* edited by Malcolm Cross. Cambridge: Cambridge University Press.

Cowan, Ruth Schwartz. 1983. *More Work for Mother.* New York: Basic Books.

Deutsch, Sarah. 1987. *No Separate Refuge: Culture, Class, and Gender on an Anglo-Hispanic Frontier in the American Southwest, 1880–1920.* New York: Oxford University Press.

Diamond, Timothy. 1988. "Social Policy and Everyday Life in Nursing Homes." Pp. 39–55 in *The Worth of Women's Work,* edited by Anne Statham, Eleanor M. Miller, and Hans O. Mauksch. Albany: SUNY Press.

———. 1992. *Making Gray Gold: Narratives of Nursing Home Care.* Chicago: University of Chicago Press.

Epstein, Barbara. 1981. *The Politics of Domesticity: Women, Evangelism, and Temperance in Nineteenth-Century America.* Middletown, CT: Wesleyan University Press.

Forbath, William. 1999. "Caste, Class and Equal Citizenship." *Michigan Law Review,* 98 (2).

Garcia, Mario. 1981. *Desert Immigrants: The Mexicans of El Paso, 1880–1920.* New Haven: Yale University Press.

Glazer, Nona Y. 1989. *Women's Paid and Unpaid Labor: The Work Transfer in Health Care and Retailing.* Philadelphia: Temple University Press.

Glenn, Evelyn Nakano. 1986. *Issei, Nisei, War Bride: Three Generations of Japanese American Women in Domestic Service.* Philadelphia: Temple University Press.

Karp, Jonathan. 1995. "A New Kind of Hero." *Far Eastern Economic Review,* 158: 42–45.

Katzman, David. 1978. *Seven Days a Week: Women and Domestic Service in Industrializing America.* New York: Oxford University Press.

———. 1982. *Plain Folk: The Life Stories of Undistinguished Americans.* Urbana and Chicago: University of Illinois Press.

Laslett, Barbara, and Johanna Brenner. 1989. "Gender and Social Reproduction: Historical Perspectives." *Annual Review of Sociology,* 15: 381–404.

Lind, Andrew W. 1951. "The Changing Position of Domestic Service in Hawaii." *Social Process in Hawaii,* 15: 71–87.

Mellor, Earl F. 1987. "Workers at the Minimum Wage or Less: Who They Are and the Jobs They Hold." *Monthly Labor Review,* 110 (July): 34–38.

Ong, Paul, Edna Bonacich, and Lucie Cheng. 1994. "The Political Economy of Capitalist Restructuring and the New Asian Immigration." Pp. 3–35 in *The New Asian Immigration in Los Angeles and Global Restructuring.* Philadelphia: Temple University Press.

Parrenas, Rhacel. 2000. *The Global Servants: Filipina Servants in Rome and Los Angeles.* Ph.D. dissertation, University of California, Berkeley.

Pascoe, Peggy. 1990. *Relations of Rescue.* New York: Oxford University Press.

Reich, Michael. 1981. *Racial Inequality.* Princeton: Princeton University Press.

Reich, Robert. 1991. *The Work of Nations.* New York: Vintage Press.

Rollins, Judith. 1985. *Between Women: Domestics and Their Employers.* Philadelphia: Temple University Press.

Romero, Mary. 1992. *Maid in the U.S.A.* New York: Routledge.

Sassen, Saskia. 1988. *The Mobility of Labor and Capital: A Study in International Investment and Labor Flow.* Cambridge: Cambridge University Press.

Stigler, George J. 1946. *Domestic Servants in the United States, 1900–1940.* Occasional Paper 24. New York: National Bureau of Economic Research.

U.S. Bureau of the Census. 1993. *1990 Census of the Population: Social and Economic Characteristics.* Washington D.C.: US Government Printing Office.

U.S. Bureau of Labor Statistics. 1993. *Occupational Outlook Quarterly,* Fall.

———. 1998. "Homemaker-Home Health Aides." In *Occupational Outlook Handbook.* Washington, DC: Government Printing Office.

CHAPTER 4

The Body as a Contested Terrain for Labor Control: Cosmetics Retailers in Department Stores and Direct Selling

Pei-Chia Lan

Contemporary sociologists, unfettered by the Cartesian mind/body dualism, finally turn to a topic that has been ignored for centuries: the body (Turner 1984; Frank 1991). As many theorists have argued from different perspectives, the body is not only a biological existence, but also a historical and social construct. It is inscribed by the articulation of knowledge and power (Foucault 1977, 1980), it embodies social distinctions and class taste (Bourdieu 1984), and it reproduces social construction of gender differences (Cornell 1987; Bordo 1993). However, the body is still an overlooked dimension in labor process theory. The blindness to the body is an even more serious flaw in analyzing service workers who interact with customers via their bodily performances. This chapter therefore aims to investigate contested practice of labor control exerted on the bodies of service workers employed in contemporary consumer societies.

This essay is composed of two parts: a theoretical discussion and an empirical comparative study. In the first half, I argue that orthodox labor process theory has not yet adequately analyzed the microphysics of labor control in regard to constructing workers' bodies. Its lopsided emphasis on manufacturing workplaces has obstructed the theoretical investigation of the special features of service labor process. I then propose a typology to analyze multiple dimensions of body control involving different management strategies. In the second half of the essay, I apply this theoretical typology to examine two work settings of cosmetics retailers: department stores and direct selling. Due to their divergent accesses to customers, these two groups of service workers encounter different forms of control practices along the four dimensions of body control. I also argue that the practices of body control intersect with the reproduction of gender difference and inequalities. Although these two work settings hold distinctive employment relations, they share a similar gendered pattern of body control. Male and female cosmetics retailers are assigned to different components of bodily labor parallel to hierarchical gender relations in the workplace. The implications for further research are addressed in the conclusion.

Toward a Corporeal Labor Process Theory

The central concern of labor process theory is about what types of management strategies are developed to overcome the "central indeterminacy of labor potential" (Littler 1982, 31). Karl Polanyi (1957, 72) identifies the indeterminacy emerging from the rise of market society as a "great transformation." Human labor now becomes a thing that can be sold and bought in the market, despite its characteristics that contradict the nature of commodity exchange: labor power cannot "be detached from the rest of life, be stored or mobilized." Karl Marx (1976) further argues that the essential contradiction of capitalism lies in the distinction between "labor power" and "labor": the commodity sold by the worker is not a fixed amount of labor but rather labor power, that is, a capacity to conduct labor activities. As labor power is not the same entity that enters into the production process (labor), the central concern of employers/managers is thus to minimize the uncertainties existing in the transformation from abstract labor power to labor embodied in a completed product (Littler 1982).

On the shoulders of Marx, Harry Braverman (1974) develops his famous deskilling thesis, and Richard Edwards (1979) distinguishes three "systems of control" in a chronological historical development: simple, technical, and bureaucratic control. These two scholars share a similar focus on how the development of scientific management decreases the uncertainties in the labor process and brings about the subordination of workers. Nevertheless, both theories are harmed by their reliance on a linear model of labor control driven by technological transformation. They thus fail to represent a dynamic contestation of social forces (Thompson 1983) or to explore the constitution of workers' agency and subjectivity in their daily work (Knights 1990).

Michael Burawoy (1979; 1985) has made a theoretical breakthrough beyond Braverman's focus on the *objective* moments of labor process. Burawoy points out that labor control, even under the most coercive technology, rests on ideological structures that frame and organize workers' *subjective* consciousness. Manufacturing workers' consent further becomes a primary component of labor control in response to the recent transformation of workplaces. As Fordist and Taylorized mass production no longer brings in significant competitive advantages, the locus of authority in a decentralized workplace is transferred from rational rules and bureaucratic hierarchy to the coordinated participation of worker. For example, James Barker (1993) raises the concept of "concertive control" in his study of self-managed teams to describe how team workers developed a system of normative rules out of their value consensus.

Nevertheless, the image of workers in the above literature remains a being of mind and consciousness that has no sexuality, no emotions, and no body (Acker 1990). How workers, as embodied subjects, experience body control and corporeal resistance has not yet been under the scrutiny of labor process theory. I find Michel Foucault's (1977, 25) theory useful in this aspect, especially his theoretical agenda of the "political economy of the body." The introduction of Foucault into labor process theory has generated controversy. Some praise him for providing a theoretical approach to exploring workers' subjectivity and resistance (Knights 1990; Willmott 1990; Knights and Vurdubakis 1994); however, for others, postmodernists like Foucault who reject the Marxist framework and challenge the theoretical primacy of labor and production represent nothing but a distraction for labor process theory (Thompson 1993). In my view, Foucault's work provides valuable insights that we may use to reconstruct the concept of labor control. He leads us beyond a *repressive* notion of economic power and reveals the *productive* exercise of "disciplinary power" in the workplace, which is "not a control functionally oriented to capitalist exploitation but to the creation of obedient bodies" (Clegg 1994, 279).[1]

To further theorize the corporeal nature of labor control, I argue that workers' bodies constitute a crucial source for the indeterminacy of labor potential in the labor process. Drawing on Foucault, I look at labor control not merely as *repressive* violence that is related to capitalists' economic power, but as a *productive* and *discursive* exercise to produce workers as appropriated subjects. Workers' bodies become a crucial target of labor control, since "the body becomes a useful force only if it is both a productive body and a subjected body" (Foucault 1977, 26). The core issue of labor process theory can be translated as follows: the uncertainties in transforming labor power into labor lie in the reproduction of worker's *productive* bodies (being healthy and strong) and *docile* bodies (conforming to management rules and disciplines). The *productivity* and *tractability* of workers' bodies are the necessary preconditions for appropriating the value of their labor activities.[2]

Such a theoretical approach allows us to investigate heterogeneous practices of labor control that cannot be subsumed under the economic logic of efficiency and capital accumulation. For example, workers' dress codes (the "decoration" of worker's bodies,) are often part of management rules in both manufacturing and service workplaces. These rules, however, do not directly serve the goal of productive efficiency, but aim to preserve symbolic domination by reproducing differences and hierarchies among workers, or between workers and employers. In Karen Hossfeld's (1990) study of the Silicon Valley microelectronics industry, she found that male workers' smocks are color-coded according to their occupations, while female workers' smocks are color-coded by sex regardless of occupation. In other cases, androgynous uniforms are used to unmark and suppress (especially female) workers' sexual identities in the workplace (Wendt 1995; Salzinger 1998). Another example is that domestic workers are often prohibited from wearing makeup and are required to wear uniforms, especially in the presence of guests. This control practice aims to underscore a class and racial hierarchy between employers and domestic workers, and to "desexualize" workers' bodies that may otherwise threaten a female employer's roles as wife and sexual partner (Glenn 1986; Romero 1992; Constable 1998).

The above examples also reveal that workers' bodies are inscribed by their social differences in gender, race/ethnicity, and culture. Arguing against a universalistic nature of traditional labor process theory, recent scholars point out that "workers' subjectivities cannot be predetermined as rooted solely and always in class terms" (Lee 1998, 19). Employers or managers often establish a hierarchical division of labor based on workers' social differences, which facilitates economic exploitation, or racist/sexist domination, or both (see Ong 1987; Hossfeld 1990; Salzinger 1997; and Lee 1998). Workers' differences, especially gender differences, constitute an integral part of body control that simultaneously reproduces gender differences and inequalities on a daily basis. This point is particularly crucial in analyzing service work that is predominantly performed by women. The next section briefly reviews relevant literature on service work and illustrates why service work settings involve more comprehensive and complex body control than manufacturing workplaces.

Service Labor in Contemporary Society

The volume of service labor has overtaken its manufacturing counterpart in most industrialized societies nowadays. However, the topic of service work remains an Achilles' heel for labor process theory as this field is grounded on the experience of (generally male) manufacturing workers. Service labor is difficult to systematically theorize for many reasons. First, it covers such a broad range of diversified occupations that no universal theoretical model is possible. Second, its "labor product"— providing services or making deals—is difficult to assess and measure, and third, its performance—interacting with customers or clients—is difficult to subdivide or standardize (Benson 1986). Finally, the presence of customers or clients adds a new source of uncertainty to the routinization of the service labor process (Leidner 1993). To pursue theorization in this aspect, I once again recall the core questions raised by Polanyi and Marx: what is the "central indeterminacy of labor potential" in the service labor process? What kinds of control strategies are utilized to overcome these uncertainties? What kinds of power dynamics, other than capital-labor contradictions, are involved in this process?

In late capitalism, the value of a commodity is not determined solely by its utility in the circuit of production, but also by its semiotic meanings in the circuit of exchange. Many contemporary theorists try to reconstruct Marx's value theory to fit with today's more complicated picture of commodity exchange. For example, in his early work Jean Baudrillard (1988) expands Marx's concept of value (use value and exchange value) by adding two other logics of value: "sign value," based on the principle of difference, and "symbolic value," based on the principle of ambivalence. The production of sign values is best exemplified by the proliferating varieties of commodities and services around body maintenance. Contemporary consumer culture constructs the body as an object for display and a vehicle of pleasure, rather than a vessel of sin to be covered (Featherstone 1991). The growing body industries not only attract and discipline consumers' bodies, but also employ the bodies of service workers in the gym, hair salon, diet center, and at the cosmetics counter. A cosmetics manager vividly described the logic of value production in this industry: "In factories we produce lipsticks, in stores we sell hope!"[3] While manufacturing workers create use value while producing a commodity in the factory, the sign value of a commodity is "produced" by advertisements, carried by service workers, and then delivered to customers.

As manipulating and delivering symbols become a vital component of service work, and as personal interaction becomes the raw material for service workers, more dimensions of workers' bodies are incorporated and disciplined in the service labor process. Some studies have insightfully described the specialties of the service labor process and the unique ways of controlling service workers. Arlie Hochschild (1983) proposes the concept of "emotional labor" to describe how service workers are required to produce a particular emotional state in another person, and how their emotions and feelings become the objects of control by employers through training and supervision. Robin Leidner (1993) defines "interactive service work" as the service jobs that require workers to directly interact with customers or clients. Managers use a variety of means to channel and transform the behaviors of these service workers, including the recruitment of service recipients as informal supervisors.

Although these studies have revealed that emotions and interaction are embodied through facial expressions and bodily gestures, the crucial role of the body in the service labor process is not yet sufficiently theorized. To make a further theoretical move, I raise the concept of "body control" to discuss control practices in the service labor process.[4] Body control involves not only the exterior body of service workers (appearance, figure, posture, movement, etc.), but also as the interior bodies (feelings, emotions, etc.), both inseparable and mutually constituted in their labor activities. The different components of body control are explicated in the next section.

Theorizing Body Control

Before getting into the details of a typology of body control, it is necessary to briefly explain my theoretical take on the conception of the body. Chris Shilling 1993 identifies two major approaches to theorizing the body: naturalist and constructionist. The body has often been treated as natural and generic, especially in the field of sociobiology. This naturalistic approach toward the body tends to explain individuals' actions and potentials as an unavoidable result of their physical and genetic characteristics, thereby legitimizing social inequalities of gender and race. Another contrasting approach is a constructionist view of body. Under the influence of Foucault, scholars in this approach view the body as a social construct and an object of knowledge. They are nevertheless criticized for reducing the body to a textual play designating semiotic differences and failing to investigate the materiality of the body.

Shilling (1993, 12) suggests a compromise between these two perspectives by conceptualizing the body as "an unfinished biological and social phenomenon which is transformed, within certain limits, as a result of its entry into, and participation in, society." He agrees that the body consists of biological features and genetic characteristics and forms a basis for shaping social relations, but he also emphasizes that these "natural" features will change over the life time of an individual, and could be transformed by variable social positions and social contexts. In short, the body is the medium of human agency as well as the outcome of social construction.

Shilling's approach enables us to analyze how workers' bodies are constrained by, but also constrain, the practices of labor control. As argued earlier, workers' bodies constitute the "central indeterminacy of labor potential." When employers buy labor power, they buy not only workers' potentiality of conducting *physical* labor activities, but also their capability to embody certain *symbolic* images or messages. The uncertainties mediated by workers' bodies are twofold: First, managers are concerned that the body be both productive (capable of offering sufficient energy and strength to conduct labor activities) and tractable (able to be transformed and disciplined to accommodate job requirements). Second, the body is neither a machine that needs little rest, nor a clay doll that can be shaped in any way. A human body needs to eat, drink, and sleep. It can get old, sick, or pregnant. These corporeal phenomena require maintenance to ensure the reproduction of a healthy and capable body, and to constrain the extent of exploitation and transformation of workers' bodies. In the following, I use some research examples to further explain how different means of labor control are involved to overcoming these corporeal uncertainties.

First, the primary goal of labor control is to assure the appropriation of surplus value produced by workers, that is, *exploitation*. Marx (1976) vividly described how capitalists in the early stages of industrialization nakedly appropriated the value of workers' labor and brutally exploited their bodies by increasing work intensity and expanding work hours. Burawoy (1985) further argues that the appropriation of labor value in monopoly capitalism is usually through the production of *consent* rather than *coercion*. He found that the piece-rate wage system in the factory generated a political effect of "making out," which made work similar to "playing games" and brought about psychological compensation apart from monetary reward (Burawoy 1979). The stock-sharing program adopted in many high-tech firms is another means to bring about workers' consent and self-exploitation. Through this tactic the antagonism between capital and labor is reconciled and molded into a common interest that is in fact unequally distributed between the two parties. All these strategies represent a more complex and ambivalent way of labor control, in which the worker's body is seduced and self-exploited, rather than directly coerced and oppressed.

The second classic strategy of controlling workers' bodies is standardization or routinization, which emerged from the development of scientific management in the early twentieth century. This strategy is best exemplified by Taylorism, which treats workers' bodies as objects under the scrutiny of scientific work-study and disciplines workers to perform standardized bodily actions in a deskilled and fragmented labor process. The strategy of routinization is still applied to many service jobs, even though the standardizing of personal interactions between service workers and their clients is difficult to achieve. Leidner (1993) identifies three methods used to over-come the obstacles of routinization in interactive service jobs. First, employers may try to standardize the behaviors, in other words, the bodies, of customers or clients, this making their interactions with service workers more practicable. Second, they may adopt personalized work routines to disguise the routinization. Third, they may try to transform workers' characteristics, personalities, and thought processes, thereby reducing uncertainties in worker behavior. I shall further discuss these approaches in my empirical research with a focus on body discipline.

The third way for employers to pursue labor control is by maintaining workers' bodies. This strategy is especially prominent in service jobs that involve direct interactions with customers and clients. Although employers aim to maximize exploitation as well as profits, they also need to maintain workers' physical health and emotional well-being. For example, flight attendants may fail to perform emotional labor due to the stress caused by the company's adoption of a speed-up policy (Hochschild 1983). Main-taining workers' bodies becomes a more vital concern for managers in a workplace where symbolic values and body images are emphasized. Workers such as body-build-ing trainers and beauticians are required by their employers to take good care of their bodies, since their bodies serve as living proof of their expertise and services.

Finally, although standardization and routinization have become crucial strategies of labor control, they are not applicable to all workplaces and are not as effective as Taylorists claim.[5] In most cases, employers need to allow a certain degree of *flexibil-ity* and *autonomy* for workers to deal with uncertainties in their daily labor activities. Especially for service workers who encounter unpredictable interactions with indi-vidually diverse customers or clients, an overstandardized work script may become a barrier rather a facilitator. A flight attendant who carries a "standardized" smile may be criticized by passengers as being "phony" or "like a robot" (Hochschild 1983, 135). An insurance agent who only follows a rigid work script will have difficulties in accommodating the needs of various clients and fail to build the personal attachment that is necessary in maintaining a long-term insurance contract (Leidner 1993). In some service settings, employers even authorize workers' autonomy and flexibility to pursue symbolic domination over customers. For example, Debra Gimlin (1996) observes that hair stylists in a Long Island beauty salon use their privileged knowl-edge of fashion and styling methods to position themselves as experts, thereby reduc-ing the status differences between these service workers and their clientele.

To sum up, complex practices of labor control are exerted on four dimensions of service workers' bodily performances: (1) *the exploited body* (offering physical strength for labor activities); (2) *the disciplined body* (serving customers through bod-ily gestures); (3) *the mirroring body* (embodying images to display products); and (4) *the communicating body* (interacting with customers with emotions and feelings).[5] These different strategies of body control contain two sets of potential dilemmas: *exploitation versus maintenance*, and *standardization versus individualization*. The dimen-sions of workers' bodies and the involved labor control strategies are summarized in Figure 4–1 (arrows indicate a contradictory relationship within each pair).

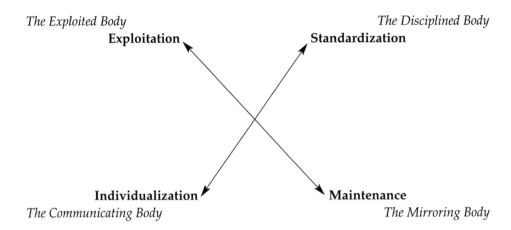

The Exploited Body   *The Disciplined Body*
  Exploitation   **Standardization**

  Individualization   **Maintenance**
The Communicating Body   *The Mirroring Body*

FIGURE 4–1. Typology of body control of service workers

A Comparative Study of Cosmetics Retailers

In the remainder of this discussion, I apply the above theoretical typology to examine two work settings of cosmetics retailers: department stores and direct-selling organizations (DSOs).[7] "Direct selling" or "DSO" in this article refers to "network direct selling" or "multi-level marketing" industry, such as Amway and Mary Kay. The two research projects were conducted in Taipei, the capital city of Taiwan, during the spring of 1995 and the summer of 1997. My research methods included in-depth interviews and participant observation (side observation of department store counters, attendance at DSO training classes and group meetings, etc.). I interviewed twelve saleswomen and two salesmen working in department stores, and twenty units of DSO distributors (ten females, six couples, and four males).[8] I used the methods of snowballing and theoretical sampling to cover sufficient variation in education, ages, and marital status among interviewees.[9]

While selling similar commodities (cosmetics), these two groups of salespeople have different accesses and relationships with their customers. Department stores usually attract anonymous customers with brand prestige and commercial advertisements. In contrast, DSO distributors persuade customers, who are mostly their acquaintances, with personal experiences and mutual trust. As a result, these two groups of salespeople encounter different job scripts and different modes of labor control along the four dimensions of body. The comparative results are summarized in Table 4–1 and discussed in detail in the later sections.

The Exploited Body

Unlike manufacturing workers whose labor value is measured by the products they make, salespeople produce no material output. Their labor performance involves their interaction with customers and the deals they make. The measurement of labor

TABLE 4–1.   Four Dimensions of Body Control over Cosmetics Retailers in
Department Stores and Direct Selling

Dimension	Department Stores	Direct Selling
The Exploited Body	Commission-based wage system; self-exploitation and mutual competition among workers	Retail and organization bonuses; reducing management costs and capital-labor opposition
The Disciplined Body	Body engineering under the supervision of managers and customers	Transforming workers' bodies through self-discipline and network surveillance
The Mirroring Body	Body display; a standard mirror of beauty	Bodily testimony; differentiated mirrors of beauty
The Communicating Body	Surface acting; the carrier of "professional" authority in the workplace	Deep acting; the missionary of everyday lifestyle

output becomes even more difficult when their work settings are scattered and decentralized. For example, saleswomen hired by the same cosmetics company work at different counters located in various department stores; DSO distributors make door-to-door visits with customers as their regular work practice. These features of the sales labor process call for some unique strategies to appropriate the value of salespeople's labor.

In department stores, a commission-based wage system constitutes the most effective political apparatus of labor control. It shifts part of the risk in the consumer market from employers to workers, and pushes the latter to voluntarily work longer and harder on sales. Most saleswomen in this study perceived this wage system as a positive condition that allows them to increase their incomes by maximizing sales. Some identified themselves as "self-employed" or even "petit boss." As more than one informant told me, "We are our own boss, because the more you sell, the more you earn." This explains why few saleswomen complain about the lack of overtime pay when they are required to work extra hours during peak seasons. They see this instead as a good opportunity to earn more commissions, and so agree to *voluntarily exploit their own bodies*—to work harder, stand longer, and greet customers with bigger smiles.

The political effect of self-exploitation is further consolidated by competition among and within counters that is institutionally encouraged by some cosmetics companies. These competitions bring about psychological or symbolic, rather than material, compensation for workers, an effect similar to "making out" (Burawoy 1979). Every morning before business starts, saleswomen are required by their cosmetics company to record the previous day's sales records from counters belonging to other cosmetics companies. While showing me her sales records, a saleswoman told me, "I showed this off to saleswomen at other counters, saying 'Hey, we sold more than you folks yesterday!' When I asked her why she did this, she replied, "Oh, just for fun. Work is boring." The effect of "making out" is more obvious at counters that calculate commission based on the sales records of individual saleswomen.[10] Sometimes saleswomen even compete in soliciting the same customers when there is only a limited number of customers at their counter. "Super-saleswomen" with marvelous sales become the object of envy for other saleswomen, and are often subsequently recruited at a higher wage by other companies. The social relations among saleswomen are characterized by competition, rather than a group identity.[11]

Direct selling exemplifies another way of organizing workers' identities and the capital-labor relationship. Salespeople, categorized as the "independent distributors" of direct-selling companies, actually play three different roles at work: consumer, retailer, and recruiter. The first step for a person getting involved in direct selling is to become a consumer. He or she has to be "recommended" by a salesperson or consume a certain quantity of commodities, and then become a "member," who can purchase commodities at wholesale prices. The person who recruits is called "upline," and the recruited person is called "downline." Every DSO distributor is a previous and current consumer, and every customer to whom he or she sells products is a potential downline whom he or she tries to recruit. In response to the duality of their work content (retailing and recruiting), the DSO payment system is composed of two parts: a retail bonus and an organization bonus (commission). A distributor can gain a retail bonus whenever he or she sells a retail product. After recruiting a certain number of downlines and getting promoted to a higher position, or the distributor starts receiving commission extracted from the retail bonus of his or her downlines. The more downlines an upline recruits, the higher position and commission the upline can receive.

Such an organizational design has many advantages for DSOs. First, it achieves an organizational flexibility by creating a self-expanding labor force recruited from the pool of consumers. A commission system constitutes an auto-regulating mechanism for *screening appropriate workers*. The distributors with good sales and recruitment records are promoted to a higher position with a larger commission proportion, while those who slide down the ladder lose the share of organization bonuses but retain the identity of consumer. Second, such a flexible staffing practice allows DSOs to lower costs for *reproducing workers' bodies,* such as sick leaves, pensions, and other benefits. DSOs also reduce the expenses in *managing workers' bodies,* since workers are responsible for recruiting and training new workers (their downlines). These spared expenses are transformed into a generous commission system that offers the most important incentive for DSO distributors to work hard.

In contrast to the opposing relationship between department store saleswomen and cosmetics companies, a relationship of quasipartnership exists between DSOs and their distributors. Competition among saleswomen in department stores is replaced by cooperation among DSO distributors who share joint interests under the governance of the payment system. Uplines voluntarily play active and multiple roles in training and assisting their downlines, based on the principle that "the more people you help to reach success, the more successful you become."

The political effect of self-exploitation is more obvious among DSO distributors than among their counterparts in department stores. When I asked a full-time distributor how much time he spent working per week, he replied: "What should I say? Almost 100 percent of the time, since this is your own business. Not like before, work was work, and after work, it was your own time." In the absence of a fixed timetable mandated by company management, distributors set up their own schedules. Setting goals and time management are two major topics in direct-selling magazines and training courses. Some distributors even obtain home mortgages or car loans or purchase inventory as a way of increasing their financial pressures and hence their work incentive. As a distributor, recently recruited to the position of manager, proudly told me, "Those who fail in direct selling are expelled by no one but themselves, because they lack sufficient self-discipline!"

The Disciplined Body

What is bought and sold at department stores is not only commodities, but also services and values attached to the behavior of shopping. Saleswomen embody the message that "we provide the best service" in their bodily performance toward customers. Employers attempt to increase control over the interaction process by standardizing saleswomen's gestures and speech. In the work scripts for cosmetics saleswomen, I found many measures of body engineering that subject saleswomen to infinitesimal power over details of their bodily activities (Foucault 1977). Most department stores require saleswomen to stand all day, even when no customers are present. Attitudes toward customers are standardized and instrumentally coded in work scripts. For example, saleswomen have to repeat standardized statements whenever they greet a customer, such as, "How are you doing today?," "Thanks for coming," and so on. Some department stores ask saleswomen to practice these statements in a loud voice before the store opens every morning. A management handbook printed by the department store trade council even specifies the angles of bowing to customers (15 degrees for "please wait a moment," 30 degrees for "welcome," and 45 degrees for "thanks for coming"). The extreme example of body engineering is the elevator lady in Japanese-style department stores. Her only job is smiling, greeting, and bowing to every customer who enters the elevator, just like a beautiful robot.

Body discipline is conducted by company supervisors as well as by customers. Customers' complaint letters and service evaluation forms are often used by department stores as evidence to evaluate or punish saleswomen. An invisible but effective mechanism for overseeing saleswomen comes from customers passing by the counters in department stores. The gazes from male customers are evaluating saleswomen's bodies, and the gazes from female customers represent imitation or envy for their beauty. Some male customers come to the counter to strike up a conversation. There is even the story of Cinderella circulating among saleswomen—how some saleswomen married handsome rich men whom they met at the counter. The disciplinary mechanism over saleswomen's bodies is not centralized or oppressive, but rather dispersed, anonymous, and seductive.[12]

DSO distributors access their customers in a way different from saleswomen in department stores. A distributor analogized the difference as the distinction between spiders and bees. Department stores attract anonymous customers with their spider webs of brand names and fancy counters, while DSO distributors, like bees, approach customers through personal affiliations and social networks. Network-based marketing allows DSOs to decrease uncertainties in the consumer market. Based on the extensive networks of distributors, DSOs are able to approach a great variety of customers with minimal marketing costs. DSOs can also perpetuate a stable pool of consumers, as distributors maintain long-term relationships with their customers through personal referral and frequent contacts.

However, this arrangement increases difficulty for DSOs in controlling distributors who are free of direct supervision in an unbound workplace. Similar to what Leidner (1993, 37) observed in the case of insurance agents, DSOs overcome this difficulty by adopting the strategy of "transforming workers' characters, personalities, and thought process so that their reactions to variable work situations will be predictable." Two DSO slogans succinctly explain this strategy: "The first thing to recommend in direct selling is yourself," and "Let yourself become the *product* of product." DSOs transform distributors' bodies in two aspects. First, they transform distributors' physical bodies by integrating personal consumption and bodily testimony into part of their work. Second, they standardize distributors' feelings, thoughts, and lifestyles by indoctrinating them with a belief in the moral values of direct selling. The next two sections will further discuss the details of these two strategies.

Despite the absence of the direct superintendence of managers, DSOs incorporate peer distributors and customers as agents of supervision. The relationship between uplines and downlines is not only that of a collective corporation but also of mutual surveillance. Motivated by the organization bonus, uplines usually vigorously watch over their downlines' job performance, and keep in frequent contact with them through daily phone calls and weekly meetings. Whenever a downline becomes idle, the upline is the first one pushing him or her to work hard. In addition, since there is no longer a boundary between work and private space, distributors are under the surveillance of potential customers everywhere. In a group meeting, an upline kept reminding her downlines, "Don't forget to wear makeup and the badge of our company, even though you only go to the grocery store at the corner." The purpose of carrying bags or wearing badges with the DSO logo is to attract the curiosity of passersby and to strike up conversations with them. In short, even without the direct supervision of management, DSO distributors are subjugated to body discipline carried out by omnipresent gazes in their everyday lives.

The Mirroring Body

Cosmetic products appeal to consumers with the promises of attaining beauty and maintaining youth; those promises are incarnated by the virtual bodies of advertisement models as well as the corporeal bodies of saleswomen. A central work component of department store saleswomen is displaying commodities and mirroring the beauty image by using their bodies as living mannequins. When hiring, cosmetics companies require certain demands on their youth, weight, and height. Afterward, managers continue monitoring and elaborating saleswomen's bodies inside and outside the workplace. During the working day, saleswomen have to wear stockings, black high heels, and fitted uniforms. Their makeup and nail polish have to comply with the fashionable color that is being promoted that season. Attentive supervisors periodically show up without prior notice to make sure that these regulations are obeyed. Ubiquitous mirrors around the counters also remind saleswomen to check on their makeup and hairdo a dozen times a day. In addition, the company provides them with free makeup and skincare products, to be used both during working hours and after work. They represent not only an employee benefit and a sign of companies' generosity, but also a measure for maintaining their bodies. Like using ammonia to maintain the shine of shop windows, cosmetics companies need to maintain saleswomen's bodies so they can effectively perform the role of the mirroring body.

Nevertheless, human bodies are not mirrors. Human bodies will get old, sick, or pregnant, and thus will no longer be able to perform their functions as mirrors of the beautiful body. In many cases, management intervenes to suspend the work rights of the "disabled" bodies. For example, most cosmetics companies in Taiwan forced pregnant saleswomen to quit their jobs during the 1960s and 1970s. Even now, at least one company continues to require pregnant saleswomen to stay at home for the last six months, with a reduced salary, such as half the basic pay. The natural cycles and reproductive functions of human bodies often contradict the role of the mirroring body, which needs to be pretty and young forever. This contradiction is resolved in direct selling, however. In contrast to department store saleswomen, whose bodies mirror the *standard* body image, DSO distributors, with various ages, genders, and skin types, use their bodies to mirror *differentiated* body images. The role of the mirroring body for the first group of saleswomen is *displaying* fashion products and beauty ideals, while for DSO distributors the role of the mirroring body is bearing the *testimony* of using products to transform their own bodies.

Since most customers in direct selling are acquaintances, the best way for distributors to promote commodities is to use DSO products themselves and then convince customers with their bodily improvement as living proof. A female cosmetic distributor told me: "I have used all the products in this display set. They are designed for four different skin types. I have to experiment with them on myself first." Many male distributors started using skin care products after they got involved in cosmetics direct selling: "Of course I never used skin care products before . . . But I have to use them so I can be confident enough to sell them to others."

A hard-working distributor is not only an industrious worker but also a devoted consumer. Uplines emphasize the importance of personal testimony to encourage the consumption of their downlines. A currently inactive distributor recalled the time when she first joined direct selling: "My skin is not good, so my upline told me to eat pollen, ten grains a day, and to drink aloe juice, two bottles a day. But you know what?

One bottle costs 900 [New Taiwanese] dollars (US$35)!" The DSO payment system further incorporates consumption as a necessary component of labor for distributors. Distributors are required to meet a monthly minimum sales target, or they will lose their position as well as organization bonuses extracted from their downlines. Many distributors thus strategically purchase products to meet the target. They explained to me that, compared to the bonuses they would receive, the cost of buying inventory was not significant. Overstocked products may be used for personal consumption or as free samples given to customers or downlines.

In contrast to the strict regulations of cosmetics companies, DSOs place no demands or restrictions on their distributors in terms of their gender, age, skin condition, physical appearance, or pregnancy. In fact, older or less pretty women may become more successful distributors. More than one distributor told me scenarios similar to this one:

> I know a blue-diamond distributor who's fifty-something. She has really terrible skin! But it was even worse before. At the beginning, when her upline was trying to convince her to get involved, she said, "I can sell anything. It's just this [cosmetics] I cannot sell." But her upline told her, "If you use it and your skin improves, then all the people you know will buy it." So she gave it a try and it worked! Really, all her neighbors and mahjong partners became her downlines.

The emphasis on individual bodily differences helps relieve the anxieties of many women who cannot attain the perfect body image. Many female distributors shared with me their negative experiences when shopping in department stores, such as the following: "I am always intimidated by what those saleswomen tell me about how terrible my skin is. I always end up buying a lot of products I hardly use, because I feel so bad that I could not be as beautiful as [the saleswomen] are." Some middle-aged women feel embarrassed facing young saleswomen at department store counters, as an informant said: "I am worried people will laugh behind my back and wonder why this old woman needs makeup anyway." In contrast, direct selling offers a more private and personalized setting, in which distributors draw in a variety of customers with their bodily testimony, and mitigate customers' anxiety with a display of differentiated body images.

The Communicating Body

Interaction and communication with customers occupy the core of salespeople's work, and also constitute the most uncertain part of the labor process. Body control in this dimension covers not only the physical body but also the interior body, like emotions, feelings, and even values and beliefs. Hochschild (1983) describes the dilemma of service workers in their performance of emotional labor: on the one hand, salespeople try to protect their private feelings from management and manipulation, but on the other hand they also want to avoid being criticized by customers for being "phony" or insincere. Hochschild (1983, 33) also indicates two ways to accomplish emotional labor: "surface acting"— disguising what you feel and pretending to feel what you do not—or "deep acting"—taking over "the levers of feeling production" and actually altering what you feel. These two methods of performing emotional labor are represented in the contrast between department stores saleswomen and DSO distributors.

The emotional labor performed by department store saleswomen includes two contradictory components. Saleswomen are supposed to create a pleasant emotional state for customers, however rude or obnoxious they may be. "Customers first" and "Customers are always right" are the guiding principles of the training program. I also observed that many saleswomen wrote down some slogans and posted them under the counter or on their accounting book, such as, "More patient, more happy," and "Those who get angry are real losers," to remind themselves to suppress their anger and manage their emotions.

In addition to emotional management, the recent trend of "professionalizing" cosmetic sales has further complicated the messages that saleswomen are required to deliver to customers. In contrast to the trend of deskilling in most manufacturing industries, management of cosmetics companies now aim to produce more "skilled" and "professional" saleswomen, who embody the companies' "professional" authority over customers. Cosmetic companies improve upon many aspects of saleswomen's work script to attain professionalization of the selling floor. Saleswomen's titles are euphemized as "beauty counselor" or "beauty director." Some companies' uniforms even imitate the pharmacist's white suit. Their work content expands to include explaining the chemical components of products, providing personal skin care direction, and using skin test technology or even cybernetics (computer skin tests and video makeup simulation). All of these measures help saleswomen pursue emotional manipulation and symbolic domination over customers. However, since saleswomen's "professional" status is bestowed by cosmetics companies, the status power can also be easily stripped by the companies. When a customer treats a saleswoman in a rude manner or challenges her "professional" identity, the managers usually take the side of the customer.

Emotional labor performed by department store saleswomen is generally limited to surface acting, since their interactions with anonymous customers usually involve only brief encounters in the workplace. However, for DSO distributors who approach personally affiliated customers, they have to perform emotional labor in the way of deep acting. As Nicole Biggart (1989) has pointed out, economic transactions in direct selling are transformed into moralized actions such as "teaching," "caring," and "sharing." However, I disagree with her quasi-functionalist argument that explains these moral ideologies merely as a tactic of maximizing profits by "obscuring the economic in the social" (Biggart 1989, 33). Highlighting the agency of DSO distributors, I argue that the performance of "moralized" emotional labor is an outcome of how distributors negotiate their identities when interacting with customers who are at the same time their friends.

The difficulties for DSO distributors in performing emotional labor are bipartite. First, when Hochschild (1983) raises the concept of emotional labor to describe how private feelings or emotions are appropriated to commercial use, she implicitly assumes a dichotomy between the private and public spheres or selves (Wouters 1989). But for DSO distributors, whose personal lives overlap with their work, the boundary between the public and private spheres has become blurred and mutually penetrated. Second, since distributors' interactions with customers parallel business transactions, it is difficult for them to avoid being criticized as "purposive" or "insincere." A substantial proportion of distributors quit due to the personality crisis they go through in doubting the authenticity of their emotions and interactions with customers. Two former-distributors explained to me the reasons they quit: "I often doubted people's motives in making friends in direct selling, even my own." "It seemed that every conversation with others has some other purpose. I don't want to live a life like that."

The best way for distributors to overcome this personality crisis and emotional anxiety is to develop deep commitment to and true belief in the morality of direct selling. An informant told me: "Many people cannot bear the frustration of being rejected. I think you have to believe in yourself first. You shouldn't feel guilty about it. You should believe that this is really something good that you want to share with others, rather than ripping them off." Many DSO distributors analogized themselves as "missionaries" of ideal lifestyles: "We are not only selling products, we are disseminating ideal lifestyles, not only about health, but about the ideal to make your life better and to realize your dreams." "I don't think I am selling cosmetics. I think I am saving a woman's future."

In short, since their networks with customers are simultaneously networks with friends, DSO distributors cannot maintain a clear distinction between front and backstage in their everyday-life performances (Goffman 1959). Department store saleswomen are able to perform emotional labor at the level of surface acting within their fixed working time and space. In contrast, DSO distributors have to perform a deep acting of emotional labor by persuading not only their customers but also themselves. Through developing a belief in the moral values of direct selling, they try to resolve a conflict between their identities at work (as a salesperson) and in the private life (as a friend). As body control over DSO distributors becomes more comprehensive and internalized, distributors lose more and more privacy and safe zones backstage.

Gender Politics in Body Control

Although the job of cosmetics sales is usually defined as a "feminized," my studies, however, found men selling cosmetics in both department stores and direct selling. These men provide us with an experimental group to explore how the practices of body control intersect with the reproduction of gender differences and hierarchies.[3] My findings demonstrate that these two work settings, department store sales and direct selling, have distinct employment patterns but share a similar gendered pattern of body control.

For a young woman who just graduated from high school with little work experience or skills, cosmetics sales is probably one of the best-paid jobs she can get. These women's bodies and beauty constitute a kind of social capital deriving its value in the labor market. However, unlike economic or cultural capital, their body capital cannot be accumulated over time, but will decline with age. Women's bodies are treated as being highly exploitable and disposable in this labor market—a saleswoman becomes unqualified for the job after reaching a certain age, when her body is no longer young and pretty. The disposability of women's bodies is further institutionalized in the organization of cosmetics companies that offer little recruitment and promotion for saleswomen.

Gender differences are reproduced in many dimensions of bodily labor performed by cosmetics saleswomen in both department stores and direct selling. The disciplined body (providing humble service), and part of the communicative body (offering emotional consolation) are the extensions of women's domestic roles. The mirroring body reproduces the status of the female body as an observed object under the male gaze. Body control in the workplace is similar to the discipline that produces a "feminine" body in women's daily lives. Saleswomen are required to maintain their bodies in a certain size and configuration; they are directed toward a specific repertoire of confined body gestures, posture, and movements; they have to attend to skin care habits in their everyday lives to preserve their bodies as ornamented surfaces (Barkty 1988).

In 1991, a cosmetics company in Taiwan decided to recruit eleven men as a strategy to boost its declining sales. Although these men were selling cosmetics as saleswomen were, much differential treatment existed in their qualifications, training programs, and assignments. When hired, men were expected to have a college degree (women needed only a high school diploma), and there were no demands on men's age and marital status (women had to be young and preferably single). These men were called "male make-up artists" (MMAs), whereas the saleswomen were known as "beauty advisors." The company created a vertical segregation within the job along gender lines and assigned different kinds of bodily performance to male and female workers. Men were assigned more "professional" duties, like providing skin care advice or demonstrating makeup techniques, and were not responsible for low-status tasks, like cleaning or emptying the trash. The recruitment of men brought about the revaluation of the originally feminized and degraded job. The upgrading was obviously indicated by the wage differential—the basic salary of a MMA was almost twice that of a saleswoman's.

In fact, the job content of MMAs was very similar to the work of an instructor, a position usually taken by experienced saleswomen after getting married or reaching a certain age. Why did the cosmetics company choose to create a new position of male "professionals" with higher training costs, rather than promoting female instructors who already had adequate experiences and skills? Instead of attributing discrimination only to employers' bias or prejudice, Cass Sustein (1991) argues that discrimination sometimes persists because it is economically rational for employers to rely on a sex-based generalization in order to save "information cost." The cosmetic companies, drawing on gender stereotypes shared by customers, assumed that it was easier to construct men as "professionals." As succinctly represented by the company's slogan for the recruitment plan—"to see women's beauty from men's eyes"—the masculine bodies of MMAs were constructed as the figures of professional and scientific authority. Their bodies are seldom used as the mirroring body (displaying commodities), but rather as the communicative body (pursuing professional domination).

Compared to bureaucratic organizations like cosmetics companies, DSOs provide a better opportunity for women, since they place no restrictions on distributors' education, experience, gender, or full-time/part-time status. It is also commonly perceived that women can integrate work and family better in direct selling than in other work settings, since most DSOs encourage families to form business units, a strategy to incorporate family values and intimate ties for an economic end (Biggart 1989). In 1996, almost 70 percent of DSO distributors in the United States were females, 19 percent were males, and 10 percent were couples.[14] DSOs in Taiwan have attracted a more significant number of men with the masculine promise of "being your own boss." The number of male distributors in Taiwan is only slightly lower than the number of female distributors (Fair Trading Committee 1997). Many male distributors had not joined DSOs or objected to their wives' involvement until their wives had made impressive sales records and the men perceived direct selling as a promising career.

Even though the labor process of DSO distributors is significantly different from the labor process in department store sales, I observed a very similar gender division of bodily labor in both cases. Most male distributors tend to convince their customers with their "scientific" knowledge about the products (chemical components, lab examinations, etc.) and an "objective" analysis of the potential of attaining success direct selling (the communicating body). In contrast, women tend to talk more about their personal experience with the products, and use their own bodies as the medium of bodily testimony (the mirroring body). Within a family unit, the wife is usually responsible for holding home parties to demonstrate commodities as well as retailing commodities on the front line. After she exhausts most of her personal connections, her husband will take over, organizing networks and leading training programs. The wife is then assigned the "clerical," "soft," or "feminine" aspects of work, such as bookkeeping, providing emotional support, or holding social activities for group solidarity.

In short, these two cases present a similar division of bodily labor along gender lines, whether body control is enforced by managers of cosmetics companies or voluntarily conducted among DSO distributors themselves. The male body is usually constructed as a seeing and talking body, playing the role of professional authority, while the female body is mostly constructed as an object to be judged and evaluated, or an embodiment of submissive service and emotional responsiveness. This finding illustrates that body control not only serves the purpose of class domination, but also intersects with other power dynamics, especially inequalities based on gender and sexuality. Labor control cannot be reduced to a one-dimensional, coherent management strategy in reflection of the intention of capitalists. Its practices consist of multiple components conducted by multiple actors, including employers, different levels of managers, customers, clients, and even workers themselves.

Conclusion

This essay examines the body as a contested terrain for labor control, a topic that has not yet been adequately theorized and studied in labor process theory. I propose a typology to analyze multiple-dimensional practices of body control over service workers. It includes four different, and sometimes contradictory, strategies (exploitation versus maintenance, standardization versus individualization) carried out on four major aspects of workers' bodies: the exploited body, the disciplined body, the mirroring body, and the communicating body.

I further apply this typology to compare cosmetics retailers employed in department stores and direct selling. Despite selling similar commodities, these two retail settings appeal to different kinds of customers and organize their labor forces in different ways. Without a fixed retail location or mass-scale advertising, DSOs rely on distributors' personal networks to approach known customers. They avoid uncertainties in the anonymous consumer market by personalizing the interaction process between distributors and customers. Unlike department store saleswomen who follow more standardized job scripts, DSO distributors carry out more flexible and personalized routines; the perfect beauty image maintained at cosmetics counters is replaced with the more differentiated body images conveyed by DSO distributors.

Such an arrangement also increases uncertainties as DSOs attempt to control their agents, who are independent distributors working in an unbound workplace. Unlike cosmetics companies, DSOs do not enforce direct supervision and body engineering: they depend solely on the self-discipline of and mutual supervision among distributors driven by the incentive of generous commissions. Through the transformation of distributors' bodies, behaviors, and values, body control in DSOs is more internalized, invisible, and yet effective than its counterpart in department stores. Labor control practices have moved from coercion to consent, from bureaucratic control to self-discipline, and from surface acting to deep acting.

This study has crucial implications that can be applied to other work settings in a contemporary economic paradigm that is characterized by scholars as "flexible accumulation" (Harvey 1990) or "disorganized capitalism" (Lash and Urry 1987). Non-bureaucratic organizational practices, such as subcontracting, homeworking, and part-time and temporary employment, have not declined but rather have become an integral sector in a flexible mode of capitalist production. These organizational reforms have brought about innovations of labor control techniques, such as teamwork, self-management, quality circles, and group bonuses (Smith 1997). The focus of these labor control practices has shifted from direct supervision and bureaucratic rules to the microdiscipline of workers' bodies and subjectivities. Exploitation and labor control in these decentralized workplaces may become even more effective, despite the absence of managers or centralized supervision.

My study also indicate that workers' bodies are situated in a complex field of power that involves multiple labor control strategies in articulation with other power dynamics like gender and racial inequalities. The theoretical framework of body control allows us to jettison a narrowly defined notion of economic power that reduces contested labor control practices in the logic of capital accumulation. Further research is necessary to explore how workers' bodies constitutes a battleground for female and male workers to resist labor control and negotiate their identities and subjectivities that are locally and constantly constituted in the daily labor process.

Notes

Acknowledgments: I am grateful for the comments of Michael Burawoy, D.S. Chen, Gary Fine, Carol Heimer, Orville Lee, and G.S. Shieh. I also thank Chuck Koeber for his assistance in editing. This paper won an Honorable Mention for the 1998 Braverman Award given by the Labor Studies Division of the Society for the Study of Social Problems.

1. The first standpoint can been seen in Knights (1990), Willmott (1990), and Knights and Vurdubakis (1994). The example of the second standpoint is Thompson (1993).

2. Louis Althusser(1971, 132) makes a similar point by asserting that "the reproduction of labor power requires not only a reproduction of its skills, but also, at the same time, a reproduction of its submission to the rules of the established order." However, he fails to examine the reproduction of labor power within the labor process, since he believes that "the reproduction of labor power takes place essentially outside the firm"(p.130), in, for example, the family, church, and education.

3. A famous comment from a Revlon cosmetics manager, quoted by a Taiwanese cosmetics manager I interviewed.

4. I develop another concept "bodily labor" elsewhere (Lan in press) to describe labor activities of a particular group of service workers employed in body industries. Their major work content is using their bodily postures, expression, display, and movements to provide services or sell products regarding consumption related to the cultural ideals of body. Here I use the concept of body control in a more general sense to discuss labor control adopted by employers to discipline, maintain, and transform service workers' bodies.

5. As Edwards (1979, 101) points out, "the extent and incidence of scientific management has always been something of a mystery, but the available evidence suggests that Taylorism was largely confined to smaller, usually nonunionized enterprises."

6. My naming of these four dimensions is inspired by Arthur Frank (1991). He proposes four types of body use with different mediums of body action: the disciplined body (regimentation), the mirroring body (consumption), the dominating body (force), and the communicating body (recognition). The difference between us is that Frank seeks to create a general theoretical scheme applied to all bodily actions, while my theoretical typology covers a more specific social field and power nexus (labor process and labor control).

7. "Direct selling" or "DSO" here refers to network direct selling or the multilevel marketing industry, such as Amway and Mary Kay.

8. "Distributor" is commonly used to refer to people in direct selling. In some parts of this essay, I use the word "salespeople" to designate both groups of retailers for the purpose of comparison.

9. Here I only present a limited amount of empirical data relevant to the argument of body control. For more details of these two case studies, see my other articles (Lan 1999, in press).

10. The calculation may be based on the sales of each individual salesperson (individual sales) or all the salespeople at the same counter (group sales). Many companies adopt the calculation of individual sales in order to avoid "free riding" by "lazy" workers and to encour-

age mutual competition. However, others adopt the calculation of group sales based on the concern that competition among saleswomen at the same counter may create a bad impression for customers.

11. Fluctuating sales goals are assigned by managers in the beginning of each month, and are sometimes unreasonably high. I also observed how some saleswomen develop invisible strategies to manipulate the goals (Lan in press).

12. Sandra Barkty (1985, 75) argues that Foucault is blind to the different bodily experiences of men and women, especially when the "disciplinary practices of femininity usually lack a formal institutional structure, and create the impression that the production of femininity is voluntary or natural."

13. As Joan Scott (1988, 42) asserts, gender is "a constitutive element of social relationship based on perceived differences between the sexes" and "a primary way of signifying relationships of power."

14. According to the survey of the World Federation of Direct Selling Associations, available at: http://www.wfdsa.org.

References

Acker, Joan. 1990. "Hierarchies, Jobs, Bodies: A Theory of Gendered Organizations." *Gender and Society*, 4: 139-158.

Althusser, Louis. 1971. "Ideology and Ideological Apparatuses." Pp. 127–186 in *Lenin and Philosophy and Other Essays*. New York: Monthly Review Press.

Barker, James. 1993. "Tightening the Iron Cage: Concertive Control in Self-managing Teams." *Administrative Science Quarterly* 38: 408-37.

Bartky, Sandra. 1988. "Foucault, Femininity, and the Modernization of Patriarchal Power." Pp. 61–86 in *Feminism and Foucault: Reflection and Resistance*, edited by I. Diamond and L. Quinby. Boston: Northeastern University Press.

Baudrillard, Jean. 1988. "Consumer Society." Pp. 29–56 in *Selected Writing*, edited by M. Poster. Cambridge: Polity Press.

Benson, Susan. 1986. *Counter Culture: Saleswomen, Managers, and Customers in American Department Stores 1890–1940*. Urbana and Chicago: University of Illinois Press.

Biggart, Nicole. 1989. *Charismatic Capitalism: Direct Selling Organizations in America*. Chicago: University of Chicago Press.

Bordo, Susan. 1993. *Unbearable Weight: Feminism, Western Culture, and the Body*. Berkeley: University of California Press.

Bourdieu, Pierre. 1984. *Distinction: A Social Critique of the Judgment of Taste*. Cambridge: Harvard University Press.

Braverman, Harry. 1974. *Labor and Monopoly Capital: The Degradation of Work in the Twentieth Century*. New York: Monthly Review Press.

Burawoy, Michael. 1979. *Manufacturing Consent: Changes in the Labor Process Under Monopoly Capitalism*. Chicago: University of Chicago Press.

———. 1985. *The Politics of Production: Factory Regimes Under Capitalism and Socialism*. London: Verso.

Clegg, Steward. 1994. "Power Relations and the Constitution of the Resistance Subject." Pp. 274–325 in *Resistance and Power in Organizations*, edited by J. Jermier, D. Knights, and W. Nord. London and New York: Routledge.

Constable, Nicole. 1998. "Sexuality and Discipline among Filipina Domestic Workers in Hong Kong." *American Ethnologist*, 24: 539–558.

Cornell, Robert. 1987. *Gender and Power*. Cambridge: Polity Press.

Covaleski, Mark, Mark W. Dirsmith, James B. Heian, and Sajay Samuel. 1998. "The Calculated and the Avowed: Techniques of Discipline and Struggles over Identity in Big Six Public Accounting Firms." *Administrative Science Quarterly*, 43: 293–327.

Edwards, Richard. 1979. *Contested Terrain: The Transformation of the Workplace in the Twentieth Century*. New York: Basic Books.

Ezzamel, Mahmoud, and Hugh Willmott. 1998. "Accounting for Teamwork: A Critical Study of Group-Based Systems of Organizational Control." *Administrative Science Quarterly*, 43: 358–396.

Fair Trading Committee Administration. 1997. *Annual Survey of Multi-Level Marketing Business*. Taipai: Administrative Yuan, Republic of China.

Faurschou, Gail. 1990. "Obsolescence and Desire: Fashion and the Commodity Form." Pp. 234–259 in *Postmodernism: Philosophy and the Arts*, edited by H. J. Silverman. London and New York: Routledge.

Featherstone, Mike. 1991. "The Body in Consumer Culture." Pp. 170–196 in *The Body: Social Process and Cultural Theory*, edited by M. Featherstone, M. Hepworth, and B. Turner. London: Sage.

Foucault, Michael. 1977. *Discipline and Punish: The Birth of the Prison*. New York: Vintage.

———. 1980. "Two Lectures." Pp. 78–108 in *Power/Knowledge: Selected Interviews and Other Writings, 1972–77*, edited by C. Gordon. Brighton: Harvest Press.

Frank, Arthur. 1991. "For a Sociology of Body: An Analytic Review." Pp. 36-102 in *The Body: Social Process and Cultural Theory*, edited by M. Featherstone, M. Hepworth, and B. Turner. London: Sage.

Gimlin, Debra. 1996. "Pamela's Place: Power and Negotiation in the Hair Salon." *Gender and Society*, 10: 505–526.

Glenn, Evelyn Nakano. 1986. *Issei, Nisei, War Bride: Three Generations of Japanese American Women in Domestic Service*. Philadelphia: Temple University Press.

Goffman, Erving. 1959. *The Presentation of Everyday Life*. New York: Doubeday Anchor.

Harvey, David. 1990. *The Condition of Postmodernity*. Cambridge and Oxford: Blackwell.

Hochschild, Arlie. 1983. *The Managed Heart: Commercialization of Human Feeling*. Berkeley: University of California Press.

Hossfeld, Karen. 1990. " 'Their Logic Against Them': Contradictions in Sex, Race, and Class in Silicon Valley." Pp. 149–178 in *Women Workers and Global Restructuring*, edited by K. Ward. Itacha: Cornell University Press.

Knights, David. 1990. "Subjectivity, Power, and the Labor Process." Pp. 197–335 in *Labour Process Theory*, edited by D. Knights and H. Willmott. New York: Macmillan.

Knights, David, and Theo Vurdubakis. 1994. "Foucault, Resistance, and All That." Pp. 167–198 in *Resistance and Power in Organizations*, edited by J. Jermier, D. Knights, and W. Nord. London and New York: Routledge.

Lan, Pei-Chia. 1999. "Network Control and Emotional Labor in Direct Selling." Paper presented at the annual meeting of American Sociological Association, Chicago.

———. In press. "Working in a Neon Cage: 'Bodily Labor' of Cosmetics Saleswomen in Taiwan." *Feminist Studies*.

Lash, Scott, and John Urry. 1987. *The End of Organized Capitalism*. Cambridge: Polity Press.

Lee, Ching-Kwan. 1998. *Gender and the South China Miracle: Two Worlds of Factory Women*. Berkeley: University of California Press.

Leidner, Robin. 1993. *Fast Food, Fast Talk: Service Work and the Routinization of Everyday Life.* Berkeley: University of California Press.

Littler, Craig. 1982. *The Development of the Labour Process in Capitalist Societies.* London: Heinemann.

Marx, Karl. 1976. *Capital: A Critique of Political Economy.* Vol. 1. Penguin Books.

————. 1978. "Economic and Philosophical Manuscripts of 1844." Pp. 66–125 in *The Marx-Engels Reader,* edited by D. McLellan. 2nd ed. Oxford: Oxford University Press.

Nicholson, Linda. 1995. "Interpreting Gender." Pp. 39–67 in *Social Postmodernism: Beyond Identity Politics,* edited by L. Nicholson and S. Seidman. Cambridge: Cambridge University Press.

Ong, Aihwa. 1987. *Spirits of Resistance and Capitalist Discipline: Factory Women in Malaysia.* Albany: SUNY Press.

————. 1991. "The Gender and Labor Politics of Postmodernity." *Annual Review of Anthropology,* 20: 279–309.

Polanyi, Karl. 1957. *The Great Transformation: The Political and Economic Origins of Our Time.* Boston: Beacon Press. Original edition, New York: Ferrar & Rinehart, 1944.

Romero, Mary. 1992. *Maid in the USA.* London and New York: Routledge.

Salzinger, Leslie. 1997. "From High Heels to Swathed Bodies: Gendered Meanings Under Production in Mexico's Export Processing Industry." *Feminist Studies,* 23: (3) 549–574.

Scott, Joan. 1988. *Gender and the Politics of History.* New York: Columbia University Press.

Sewell, Graham. 1998. "The Discipline of Teams: The Control of Team-Based Industrial Work Through Electronic and Peer Surveillance." *Administrative Science Quarterly,* 43: 397–428.

Shilling, Chris. 1993. *The Body and Social Theory.* London: Sage.

Smith, Vicki. 1997. "New Forms of Work Organization." *Annual Review of Sociology,* 23: 315–339.

Sustein, Cass. 1991. "Why Markets Don't Stop Discrimination." *Social Philosophy and Policy,* 8: 22–37.

Thompson, Paul. 1983. *The Nature of Work: An Introduction to Debates on the Labour Process.* London: Macmillan.

————. 1993. "Postmodernism: Fatal Attraction." Pp. 183–203 in *Postmodernism and Organizations,* edited by J. Hassard and M. Parker. London: Sage.

Wendt, Ronald. 1995. "Women in Positions of Service: The Politicized Body." *Communication Studies,* 46: 176–196.

Willmott, Hugh. 1990. "Subjectivity and the Dialectics of Praxis: Opening up the Core of Labor Process Analysis." Pp. 336–378 in *Labour Process Theory,* edited by D. Knight and H. Willmott. London: Macmillan.

Wouters, Cas. 1989. "The Sociology of Emotions and Flight Attendants: Hochschild's Managed Heart." *Theory, Culture, and Society,* 6: 95–123.

CHAPTER 5

Silent Rebellions in the Capitalist Paradise: A Brazil-Quebec Comparison

Angelo Soares

Where there is power, there is a resistance,

MICHEL FOUCAULT, *L'histoire de la Sexualité*

Introduction

Supermarkets may be considered major exponents of consumer society, a capitalist version of the Garden of Eden, where everything exists for the happiness of men and women. Indeed,

> when a purchase is made in the supermarket, the displays hide all the work involved there: the work of production, distribution, the placement of displays, price labelling, etc. Goods are there like fruits in an orchard, vegetables in a garden, fish in the seas and rivers, ... until one arrives at the checkout to pay; the cash-register is the end of the Garden of Eden and the return to the brutality of the marketplace. (Chauí 1989, 70)

Considered "light and simple," the work of supermarket cashiers is the object of little attention in Brazilian and Québecois supermarkets, and one often hears discrediting and scornful remarks about it. In Quebec, employment as a cashier is often considered a "small summer job." Workers are hired part-time, and their training is often done on the job. However, a closer analysis of this type of work reveals its strategic importance, for besides being responsible for the entry of money into the organization, the cashier is the access point between the customer and the supermarket. Moreover, cashiers' work is situated precisely at the difficult transition between the Garden of Eden and the "brutality of the marketplace." These factors give this kind of work a particular complexity.

My main objective will be to highlight how supermarket cashiers face this complexity, with a particular focus on their encounters with customers in Brazil (São Paulo) and Canada (Montreal and Quebec). The strategies they use in their daily struggles serve as a starting point, a "chemical catalyst," in Foucaultian language, that permits us to put into evidence the power relations present in work, and to highlight the laborious character of a traditional female job and all the (in)visible skills necessary to accomplish it, skills that often remain hidden under the discourse of "light" work and of women's "passivity."

In the first part of this chapter, certain aspects of work organization at the supermarket checkout in Brazil and Quebec will be presented. Then, the role of cashiers will be analyzed, for they are not passive victims of such a reality—they resist! Sometimes their resistance is collective and organized (i.e., strikes), but most of the time resistance is individual and silent. In the second part of this chapter, these silent rebellions will be analyzed to make evident the active role of supermarket cashiers in the production of this service.

Strategies of Resistance

Strategies of resistance are presented by Nino Shapiro-Perl (1984, 194) as "creative acts made with purpose by workers who aim to limit, more than change, what management can do to them, while keeping their job." An important dimension of this definition is that the strategies of resistance aim, at one and the same time, to contest power relations while enabling the worker to keep his or her job. However, one must widen this conception of work, since these creative acts can be used by working women to limit the oppression not only of management, but also that of customers (i.e., in the service sector) and of the work organization. Moreover, these creative strategies enable cashiers to mediate between the demands of the job and the home.

Transposing J. C. Scott's (1985) ideas to the worlds of work, one may say that these daily strategies of resistance form a constant struggle that uses such simple and ordinary weapons as dissimulation, false compliance, pilfering, feigned ignorance, slander, foot dragging, sabotage, work-to-rule, solidarity, absenteeism, and, more radically, quitting. Thus, "just as millions of anthozoan polyps create, willy-nilly, a coral reef, so do the multiple acts of [worker][1] insubordination and evasion create political and economic barrier reefs of their own" (Scott 1985, xvii) and these "barrier reefs," in a certain way, have a shielding effect against oppression, violence, and exploitation at work.

On the other hand, strategies of resistance must not be seen as the panacea against all constraints present in the organization and conditions of work. They are used by workers to help them cope with workplace reality and minimize their perverse effects. This does not mean that these strategies prevent workers from suffering the physical and mental consequences of oppressive work organization or bad working conditions.

Strategies of resistance signal precisely the existence of oppressive working conditions and the active role of workers in their daily struggles to work with dignity and in a healthy environment. However, despite the fact that these resistance strategies radically contest the worlds of work, they have been studied very little. Part of the literature on this topic appeared as a critique of Harry Braverman (1974), who was criticized for not having considered the role of workers' resistance in the deskilling process (Friedman 1977; Elger 1979; Edwards 1979; and Burawoy 1985). Other literature is dedicated to sabotage practices at work, a more visible strategy of resistance (Sprouse 1992; Taylor and Walton 1971). The small number of studies devoted to workers' resistance are even more limited when one takes gender into consideration (Milkman 1987; Paules 1991; Shapiro-Perl 1984; Rosa 1991; Kergoat 1982; Gottfried 1994; Jermier, Knights, and Nord 1994; Souza-Lobo 1995; Soares 1997). One possible reason for the lack of research on women's strategies of resistance at the workplace may be the fact that these strategies do not necessarily conform to those used by white male workers nor to the ideas that the researchers have about what constitutes resistance (Paules 1991; Kergoat 1982).

Recently, Randy Hodson (1995) proposed a model to conceptualize workers' resistance using four categories: (1) the diversion of mistreatment; (2) the regulation of the quantity and intensity of work; (3) the defense of autonomy; and (4) the expansion of the workers' control in participation programs. The author highlighted the interrelationships between forms of resistance and systems of control used by management (direct and personal control, control techniques, bureaucratic control, and diagrams of working involvement, respectively).

Certainly, this model is an important theoretical advancement, as it is a first attempt to categorize workers' resistance, but it must be improved, as it does not consider the influence of different payment systems and forms of control in the shaping of specific forms of resistance. For example, if salary is paid on a piece-rate basis, workers will not use the strategy of slowing down the pace of work (Scott 1985).

Another drawback is that this model does not incorporate the specific strategies of resistance of working women, such as those used in juggling paid and unpaid work (De Koninck 1995; Corbeil and Descarriers 1997; Séguin 1997, Prévost and Messing 1997) and in facing sexual and racial harassment (Yount 1991; Snow, Robinson, and McCall 1991). One must incorporate in the same model not only the convergent forms of strategies of resistance used by men and women at work but also the divergent ones. Thus, the analysis of these strategies permits us to understand, in broader scope, relations not only of social class, but also of sex, race, and ethnicity.

In the next sections I will discuss the work organization of supermarket cashiers in Brazilian and Québecois supermarkets as well as the means with which the cashiers face this soulless work organization — their solidarity, their strategies for coping with violent customers and sexual harassment, and their struggle to keep the limited control that they possess within their work. But first we must discuss some points on the methodology used.[2]

Methodology

To explore these aspects of cashiers' working lives in São Paulo (Brazil) and Montreal and Quebec (Canada), a qualitative approach was used. One of the reasons for choosing a qualitative perspective was that "qualitative methodologies bring into central focus the points of view of those studied and their active participation in constructing worlds that are sometimes quite different from the worlds they are thought to live in by those in power" (Statham, Miller, and Mauksch 1988, 311). In fact, to understand what happens in the worlds of workers, "it is necessary that one knows that the essential knowledge is not in his/her mind but in the workers' mind and that there is a rationality within their behavior" (Foucault 1994b, 422). Therefore, in both societies, 106 cashiers and 32 managers were interviewed in 20 supermarkets. Table 5–1 presents the number of interviews according to geographical location, job, and number of stores.

The choice of these two settings centered on several aspects. First, work at the cash register is considered a pink-collar job in both countries. Furthermore, the historical evolution of supermarkets in Brazil and Quebec followed a similar path of small shops evolving into self-service stores. This resemblance is even more remarkable when one considers that in both societies there is a predominance of independent supermarkets rather than supermarket chains. Moreover, the state of technological development at the time of the present research was similar in each country and included both automated and nonautomated stores. Finally, because I am familiar with both societies, I was able to form a qualitative judgment on the equivalence between them (Niessen 1982; Sears 1961).

The supermarkets were chosen to make sure a variety of chains and store sizes were represented, since the size of the operation may influence work organization and its effects on workers' health (Billette and Bouchard 1986). In addition, the stores were in geographical locations that were socially and economically diversified.

In both societies, the interest shown in this research by the owners enabled me to study their methods of operation. Personal interviews were conducted and recorded in a private room at the workplace during working hours. Each person was informed of the nature of the project, and was assured that the interview would remain anonymous and confidential.

TABLE 5–1.   Interviews per City, Job, and Number of Stores

	Cities			
	São Paulo (Brazil)	Quebec (Canada)	Montreal (Canada)	Total
Cashiers	56	45	5	106
Managers	13	17	2	32
Number of stores	8	11	1	20

Each person solicited was free to accept or refuse the interview and its recording. It was only after receiving the interviewee's consent that the interview was recorded. During the interviews, subjects were never pressured to answer questions, because "the task is never neutral to the workers' emotional life, s/he can talk about her/his job or s/he must be silent about it. Sometimes it is necessary to hide the content of the job from others" (Dejours 1993, 63).

Finally, I interviewed at least one manager (store owners, head cashiers, store managers, or human resource managers) in each supermarket to capture certain dimensions that are not always apparent to or known by cashiers, such as recruitment and selection policies, control over personnel, and other aspects of human resources management. These interviews were conducted in the same manner as the interviews with the cashiers.

One must be conscious of the difficulties that a qualitative approach might engender. For instance, one problematic aspect is the relationship between interviewer and interviewee, which is never neutral and may influence the results of the research. Another potential problem is the number of interviews, since the samples in qualitative studies are typically small. Nevertheless, I was also aware that "the kind of phenomenon we chose to investigate should be achieved through the possible techniques and not through the ones considered as ideal because we risked gaining in formality and losing our object, if we were attached to the most usual proceedings in social research" (Rodrigues 1978, 38).

Cashiers' Work in the Capitalist Paradise

In supermarket cashiers' work one can find the main characteristics of service sector work: relating to the public and performing simultaneous tasks (i.e., providing the customer with information while performing other manual tasks). The encounter between cashiers and customers adds a high level of complexity to this work, which includes emotional, sexual, and class dimensions that do not exist in industrial work.

Work organization at the supermarket checkout is characterized by rigid discipline and control that can be observed in the spatial distribution of cashiers, the control of their bodies, and the control of their emotions (Soares 1995). Most of the time, supervision is placed behind the checkout line or a mirror-window, producing panoptic effect designed to induce in the individual "a state of conscious and permanent visibility that assures the automatic functioning of power, to arrange things so that the surveillance is permanent in its effects, even if it is discontinuous in its action" (Foucault 1975, 234).

The cashier remains stationary at her post and the pace of her work is determined, most of the time, by the number of customers in the supermarket and by the number of checkouts kept open by management. Thus, the cashier has very limited control over the pace of her work. She is pressured by both customers and administrators to work more quickly. A cashier can pass, on average, between twenty-four and twenty-eight items per minute through her checkout. However at times she can manage to pass forty-nine items per minute. Productivity increases as the worker constantly repeats the same movements during the length of the workday:

> It's always the same routine. It's always, "Hello," we pass the order, we take the money, it's always the same thing, it's almost like assembly-line work there, but it is still pretty interesting work. (Québecois cashier 12)

> The customer arrives at the checkout, we automatically say, "Hello," we wrap up the merchandise . . . , did he pay? "Ciao, good-bye, see you later," that's a routine, isn't it? (Brazilian cashier 3)

The "idle times"of production, like the time cashiers wait for customers, are not considered as stressful components of this work by supermarket managers. During slow periods, a whole set of additional tasks are imposed on the cashier: cleaning, filling (especially in Quebec), helping in certain departments (e.g., the bakery). Work is continuous except for breaks, which are taken according to how busy the supermarket is.

In Brazil, a cashier works forty-four hours per week, spread over six days, that is, seven hours per day from Monday to Thursday and eight hours per day on Fridays and Saturdays. The cashiers work full-time, and there is neither part-time work nor work on Sundays.[3] In Quebec, most cashiers work part-time from Monday to Sunday, often accumulating eight to twelve hours of work a day. A cashier can work 25 hours a week or more, depending on how many hours the employer assigns.

In the two societies, one finds strategies adopted by employers that intensify the work of cashiers. This intensification of work must be understood in an economic context in which the rate of unemployment is high, which leaves less maneuvering space for workers. One of the strategies adopted by management consists of opening stores with the least possible number of cashiers, causing a surplus of work for those who are working. A spokesperson from a Québecois supermarket chain articulates the logic of this approach: "Our strategy was to make more with less. Increasing our productivity and producing with the same fixed operating costs, we got closer to our different customers" (Barbès 1995, 30).

In both countries, there are similar management practices, such as the lengthening of cashiers' schedules, especially as related to the time of departures and meals.[5]

> One doesn't have regular hours. . . . It's not a regular schedule like in the offices, when at midday everyone goes to lunch. Here it works depending on the customers; if there's a lot of people, you stay there, even though you've finished your shift, if there's no girl to replace you, you stay there. They won't close a checkout during a big rush, because customers are going to shout. (Québecois cashier 12)

> Finishing is hard, because it feels like a compromise. I am here from 9:00 A.M. and I leave at 5:00 P.M.. We can't do anything else, have another responsibility, . . . I wanted to return to my studies, but the conditions don't permit it, because I don't leave the checkout at 5 P.M. . . . it's 5:30 . . . 6:00 . . . 7:00 . . . it's at the time that they think they should let you go, you understand? (Brazilian cashier 49)

Work at the checkout has become more and more automated with the introduction of the optic reader, direct payment, machines that fill in checks, and the like. The use of all this machinery has the effect of increasing the pace of cashiers' work in addition to deskilling their work (Soares 1996). These new technologies introduce another dimension of time control to cashiers' work through electronic surveillance, for the machines record the activities and time of every task. In this manner, management can control the net sales of a cashier; they know how many and what types of corrections have been made, the number of times that the till was opened, the number of articles and of customers passed during the workday, the amount of time taken to service the customer, customers' waiting time, the average sales per hour and per client, the length of breaks, and so on.

This rigid control of time is associated with other management practices, such as the lengthening of the workday, the intensification of work through underestimated scheduling, and on-call work. These strategies form a discipline that seeks to guarantee that working time is "totally useful," that is, that the "time measured and paid must also be a time without impurities or defects; a time of good quality, throughout which the body is constantly applied to its exercise" (Foucault 1975, 177).

One notes, therefore, that cashiers are submitted to a rigid discipline that seeks to achieve total control over their work. However, one must not believe that the cashier has no control over her work or that administrators are capable of controlling all aspects of work. When one speaks of the cashier's control of work, it is necessary to make the distinction between the horizontal and vertical control of work,[6] because a simplified, one-dimensional concept of control does not consider that relations may be unequal (Aronsson 1989). Thus, cashiers certainly have very little vertical control of work, but they can exercise a certain horizontal control and they fight to keep this control, especially that which exists in their relations with customers.

Finally, one must emphasize that cashiers' work includes a lot of challenging responsibilities, with the relationship to the customer being a clear example. However, very often supermarket cashiers consider and perceive their work as monotonous:

> When the store is empty, no one comes to your checkout, that's terrible. There are times when you feel tired. I don't like staying there doing nothing. (Brazilian cashier 3)

The monotony in cashiers' work includes the two dimensions underlined by Gunn Johansson (1989), that is, repetitive monotony, whose best measure is the length of task cycles, and uneventful monotony. While in industrial work these two types of monotony represent completely different work conditions and do not coexist, in supermarkets one finds an alternation between them, because there can be uneventful monotony when the supermarket is empty and followed by repetitive monotony when the store is full. The latter must be nuanced, for the presence of customers introduces a factor of variability and unexpectedness that minimizes the repetitive monotony of the work.

When the Cashier Meets the Customers

Work organization at the checkout includes the encounter between cashiers and customers, a "relationship adds a new dimension to the pattern of human relations in industry. When the customer takes an active part in business activity, the whole organization must be adjusted to his behavior" (Whyte 1946, 123). In fact, the encounter[7] between cashiers and customers represents the intersection of many social relations, such as sex/gender, race/ethnicity, and class. All of these add complex dimensions to cashiers' work.

Of all employees in a supermarket, the cashier is the one who has the most contact with the public, and it is she who most directly "sells" the company. When customer think of the service in a supermarket, they are unlikely to remember a clerk or a butcher; they will most likely think of the cashier, for it is she with whom they will have had their longest contact. However, despite their importance, encounters between customers and cashiers have not been adequately considered in the analysis of cashiers' work.[8]

Customers occupy a central role in the daily work of cashiers; they are a source of communication and social interaction, of variety that breaks up the monotony, of funny or amusing situations, and of challenges, especially with regard to keeping the customers not only satisfied but happy. To accomplish this, the cashier engages in emotional labor (Hochschild 1983), or the work produced to change her own emotions or those of the customer. Like domestic work, emotional labor is an "invisible" effort that is neither valorized nor recognized unless it is not accomplished. One must be conscious that the emotional labor of cashiers is crucial to the quality of the service rendered.

Customers are also a potential source of violence that can be expressed in several ways, from verbal abuse to physical action. The violence can also take the form of racism or sexual harassment. In fact, the majority of cashiers reported cases of sexual harassment from customers.

Thus, cashier's work includes a paradoxical reality: it is, at the same time, the strategic work of interfacing between the organization and its customers that ensures the entrance of money into the organization, and little-valorized work that includes physical, organizational, and technological constraints. It is work that demands a lot of skills that nonetheless remain invisible under the discourses of "feminine nature" and "unskilled" work." Thus, the main question is how cashiers cope with this paradoxical reality. Are they passive victims of the oppression imposed by the organization of work? By administrators? By customers?

One must emphasize that oppression does not exist as an absolute, outside and independent of the social interactions and their material effects (Martin 1988). Cashiers are not detached from the heterogeneous web of micropowers that form the social relations of our daily lives. However, they also exercise their own powers by using the skills acquired in the accomplishment of their work and the maintenance of control over their relations with customers and administrators. Cashiers are not objects, but real subjects who struggle daily to accomplish their work. Cashiers resist.

Resisting the Capitalist Paradise

Because of the emotional labor performed by cashiers, they are often seen as a very passive and docile population. However, when their daily strategies are analyzed, one can identify several strategies of resistance.[9] Strategies of resistance insert themselves at the heart of relations of power at work and, as Shapiro-Perl (1984, 104) expressed so well, "ironically, these individual acts of economic self-interest are reproduced by worker after worker, side by side, and though performed individually, they nonetheless grow out of a shared class position." Moreover, these strategies share not only class position, but also positions of gender, race, and ethnicity.

Before presenting the strategies of resistance identified in Brazilian and Québecois supermarkets, two points must be highlighted. First, when one speaks of strategies of resistance, one must bear in mind that workers need their jobs and that in both countries, proportionally speaking, there is economic crisis and an elevated level of unemployment. This means that in most cases being a cashier is not a professional choice, but a job that the workers succeeded in acquiring (Soares 1996a). Besides, a "winning strategy" is one that, in the end, enables the worker to maintain her job. In a context of economic recession, management has more room to maneuver because the workforce is abundant. In other words, the pressure of the industrial reserve army is strong, which can render the expression of resistance strategies difficult.

> As one knows, it's difficult to find a job and that was what was available, it was that or nothing, so I took that by default (Québecois cashier 40).

> Because in my domain, I didn't find anything, it was really difficult. So my situation became tighter, and I was obliged to decide to be a cashier in a supermarket. (Brazilian cashier 44)

Second, strategies of resistance must not be seen as the solution to all problems in the organization and conditions of work. Workers undergo consequences of this reality at work, especially with regard to their health. A Québecois cashier confessed that "with the years, we get sick of being a cashier."

Solidarity as a Resistance Strategy

The organization of work at the checkout is characterized, as discussed above, by the existence of a rigid disciplinary system that is reinforced by new technologies and electronic surveillance. Foucault (1994b) suggests that when everyone works under these same conditions of discipline, a collective solidarity against this discipline emerges. Indeed, as workers must collectively solve the problems bound to the organization of work, they form not only production groups but also struggle groups: "It is because their situation in production creates among them a community of interests, attitudes and objectives irremediably opposed to those of management that at the most elementary level workers spontaneously associate together to resist, to defend themselves, to struggle" (Foucault 1994b, 44).

Solidarity among cashiers can appear under several guises. First, it can be bound to the achievement of tasks—cashiers often help each other by packing merchandise, telling each other the prices or codes of products, or borrowing money from one another, a practice forbidden by management.

I ask one colleague, or I ask another, [for price]. Most people that have worked at the checkout for a long time know the prices. (Brazilian cashier 24)

We are very united. Always, when someone needs money, a colleague lends us some. (Brazilian cashier 55)

When we are in a big rush around 5:00, 5:30, the big rush makes it so that as soon as there is one who doesn't have anything to do, she comes and she helps us. (Québecois cashier 9)

Another form of solidarity functions as a type of compensation or support for difficult situations related to emotional labor. Most of the time this solidarity is bound to relations with customers:

The spirit of cashiers is strong. If there is a customer that hurts a cashier, the other cashiers are all there, and cashiers are going to be polite to the end with her, polite to the point of annoying someone. [One difficult customer] never came back. That was just great by me. (Québecois cashier 8)

When we are at the checkout, we hear what happens at the checkout nearby. Sometimes, if there's a problem with money, we say: "How much do you need? Wait. I am going to lend it to you." If it's an unpleasant customer, my colleague will wink and say, "Sorry, I don't have any." One day a customer quibbled over a penny. The girl [colleague] looked for it from everyone, but no one had it. Then she asked me, "Do you have a penny?" I was going to say yes, but she winked at me and I answered, "No, I don't have any," only because she [the customer] was unpleasant. (Brazilian cashier 11)

Resisting in Silence

The maintenance of discipline by administrators in Brazilian and Québecois supermarkets is not free of resistance by workers. According to Andrew Friedman (1977, 51), "the maintenance of discipline has always been a problem for top managers. Resistance is expressed in terms of time by workers arriving after or leaving before the times specified in their employment contracts. . . . More important for top managers are absenteeism and voluntary quits." In fact, strategies that aim at getting a little free time enable workers to recover their strength. Thus, cashiers will arrive late or ask to leave a little earlier. They will also be absent from work. The amplitude of these strategies can be discerned from the discourse of supermarket managers:

The biggest problem is absenteeism . . . It is enough to trouble us . . . Presently, I changed the timetable, I hired some new workers and I believe that I am putting a final end to this problem. (Brazilian manager 1)

Especially Saturdays, when one needs them most, then there were six, seven absences. (Brazilian manager 6)

That happens regularly enough [absences], not every day, but I would say two times per week, either lateness or an absence, but it happens quite often. (Québecois manager 19)

There are always last-minute replacements, it's things we always have to take care of. Today I had three people to replace. It is not always very easy to do. (Québecois administrator 15)

These strategies must not be seen as arising from cashiers' lack of incentive or bad faith but rather from the organization of the work, with its rigid discipline, its poor work conditions, and all its constraints.

There are also strategies that challenge the disciplinary system. The most obvious example of this was chewing of gum or eating candy, which was forbidden to cashiers:

To chew gum? No! No, but we hide it, since we cannot chew gum. (Québecois cashier 4)

To eat candies [is forbidden]—but I eat them all the time, if I take one, it doesn't show. They don't need to know. (Québecois cashier 8)

Not chewing gum or eating candy in front of customers can be understood simply as a question of manners. However, beyond this initial interpretation, it also involves the issue of focusing the cashier's attention on the "main involvement,"[10] that is, serving the customer. Administrators try to make sure that no "subordinate involvements," such as humming, chewing gum, or eating, exist. These activities constitute a deviation from the main activity of waiting for the customer and signal a contestation of discipline, especially since it is the cashier who keeps control over the situation and over her emotions. For the cashier, chewing gum means that the customer is not the master of the situation. She concedes the customer her attention, but she nevertheless keeps a part of it on herself.

Another strategy of resistance that passes through the system of controls imposed by administrators concerns annulments. For example, when the cashier makes a mistake, she can negotiate with the customer and avoid the annulment without being obliged to call the supervisor:

If you know how to dialogue with the customer . . . if I record two products of small value, I tell him, "Can you take another product at the same price or a similar product?" The customer ends up taking it. (Brazilian cashier 3)

Finally, there is an interdiction against conversation between cashiers:

We chat a lot . . . about the customers, about something funny that happened, or when there's an argument at the checkout. (Brazilian cashier 17)

We are not supposed to speak to other cashiers while we have a customer, but we do it anyway, same thing with the packer. (Québecois cashier 10)

These strategies help cashiers not only bypass a rigid work organization, but also keep at least minimal control over their work.

Gender Strategies

Strategies of resistance are employed to face power relations with customers as well as with management. Obvious examples are those strategies used to counter sexual harassment. Such strategies are not a struggle for power, but a refusal to be treated as an object.

It is necessary to remember that sexual harassment, as demonstrated by Cynthia Cockburn (1991, 142), is "a male intervention for the assertion of power. But this time it is a warning to a woman stepping out of her proper place. It is a controlling gesture to diminish any sense of power she may be acquiring and to remind her 'you're only a woman, that's the way I see you, and that you're vulnerable to me and any man.'"

In both countries, cashiers in most cases use two individual strategies, to counter sexual harassment. Humor is one of the most common:

I take that as a joke. I am going to act as if he made a joke, so it goes unobserved. (Brazilian cashier 36)

I prefer to take that as a joke. (Brazilian cashier 41)

That happens regularly, but we must take it as a joke. We often turn it into a joke to show him that I am not interested. . . . Often, men who come to buy the lottery, they will say in any case, "If I win I'll take you away and give the money to your boyfriend so that he lets us leave together." I tell him then, "Well, I hope that you won't win just for having said that." (Québecois cashier 13)

This type of strategy is very complex, for it includes several important measurements. Perceiving the context of inequality inherent in the policy that "the customer is always right," the cashier manages her emotions, and, with diplomacy, succeeds in transforming the situation with humor. It does not mean that she finds the situation funny, but only that with humor she is capable of keeping control and of coping with the dual power of her interlocutor: his power as a customer and his power as a man.

Another strategy of resistance to sexual harassment is silence. Cashiers play the deaf ear. One imagines silence as a mark of passivity; however, as Richard Sennett and Jonathan Cobb (1972, 197) make clear, "silence is not a passive disconnection," and the cashier does not want the respect of a harassing customer. She instead feels that she is exerting her power as a worker when she keeps silent in the face of this taunting; she is protecting her relationship with her work and her own ego. By treating the customer as if he didn't exist, she refuses his power while making her "person foreign to her performance; it is approval from authority rather than the task that is at issue" (Sennett and 1972, 198).

> If they begin to make jokes, I make the deaf ear. (Brazilian cashier 24)

> I pretend that it doesn't concern me. I ignore it. (Brazilian cashier 44)

> I am not a very shy girl, but there are some things that shocked me. I didn't answer. . . . I only said hello. (Québecois cashier 7)

> The thing that aggravates me the most is men with sly comments. . . . I just ignore them, I try to ignore it, because I know they won't like that. (Québecois cashier 44)

Other cashiers preferred direct confrontation as a strategy of resistance against a harassing customer:

> The customer arrived and with his hand, he touched my buttocks, but spontaneous as I am, my hand flew up, and he got it full in the face. The customer looked at me and he told me, "You are mean." Well, I told him never do that to me again. He stopped. . . . You must defend yourself in those situations, the more you let things go, the worse it will be. (Québecois cashier 21)

In the case of sexual harassment, store size and administrative support can influence the type of resistance strategy adopted. In the smaller supermarkets, where there is support from management, some collective resistance against sexual harassment is possible:

> We were talking about it among ourselves, that [the] guy is annoying. He would get us in a corner, take our hands, bump against our buttocks, it was annoying. So we said that some time we will get together and we will tell him: "Are you going to stop taking our hands? Are you finished cornering me?" We did that, we got the manager to come down, we weren't shy. We were about five or six, we told him, and the client felt the harassment in another way. He stopped coming. Then at one point he started coming back and no one said hello to him. We were very cold toward him. We served him—that's all. Hello, goodbye, no help, without being impolite. Today, he doesn't do that any more. (Québecois cashier 21)

In the strategies of humor and silence, cashiers use the principle of "emotive dissonance" (Hochschild 1983) as they make a separation between what they feel and what they display. These two strategies are not only used in cases of sexual harassment but also in interactions with unpleasant customers:

> The best way to remove his bad humor is to speak to him, to joke, to smile. I believe that it is the best way, because if you are going to answer in the same way, it's worse. (Brazilian cashier 56)

> Things always go easier with a little humor. (Québecois cashier 21)

If he wants to argue, we don't speak. We must not try and argue. In the beginning, I tried to argue with them to explain other points of view, except that now it's better to just smile, to shrug your shoulders and just say, "Well, it's like that." (Québecois cashier 13)

Sometimes, it's difficult, but I don't unclench my teeth. (Brazilian cashier 4)

The encounter between cashiers and customers includes two parts: the public transcript and the hidden transcript (Scott 1990). The public transcript is the open interaction between the customer and the cashier, and includes all (non)verbal communication. However, the "public transcript, where it is not positively misleading, is unlikely to tell the whole story about power relations" (Scott 1990, 2). The hidden transcript "consists of those offstage speeches, gestures, and practices that confirm, contradict, or inflect what appears in the public transcript" (Scott 1990, 4–5).

Silence and jokes as forms of resistance constitute part of the public transcript, and thus "an assessment of power relations read directly off the public transcript between the powerful and the weak may portray a deference and consent that are possibly only a tactic" (Scott 1990, 3). For this reason, one cannot agree with Rafaeli's (1989) classification of the strategy of ignoring the customer as a passive one. When one considers the hidden transcript of the encounters between supermarket cashiers and their customers, one realizes that these silent rebellions are not passive but rather a "key survival skill of subordinate groups" (Scott 1990, 3).

In this sense, the offstage speech of cashiers is revealing. Cashiers will speak among themselves of all the situations they have experienced with work and with their customers. In fact, customers occupy an important role in these conversations.

For sure sometimes, when the cashiers meet, we say everything that happened to us. It is incredible all the things we say, you know? That frees us. (Québecois cashier 11)

Still, they do not speak of only the negative dimensions but also of the positive aspects, such as the handsome customer, the kind customer, and so on.

Struggling for Control

Another strategy of resistance employed by cashiers is controlling the speed of their work. For example, cashiers pass an order faster when the customer is unpleasant in order to get rid of the person:

I usually try to get them out as fast as possible. (Québecois cashier 44)

I try to pass their order as fast as possible, to receive payment so that they leave quickly. (Brazilian cashier 30)

The introduction of new technology at the checkout has helped cashiers employ this strategy, since it has appreciably reduced the time needed to pass a client. That is one of the reasons cashiers say they prefer the new technologies despite the deskilling process they cause (see Soares 1996b).

Finally, one can identify another strategy of resistance: politeness:

> I just smile. Before I used to be very defensive, I used to take it like, "Why are you being like this to me?" and I've gotten a lot of headaches from it, so now I just smile. . . . Because it is hard to be mean to someone who is not being mean back to you. That's what I've seen, so I sort of kill. . . . I stop the anger with a smile. (Québecois cashier 44)

> We give a slap, without hitting the customer's face. . . . He arrives in a bad mood, we treat him the same way, but with a lot of knowledge, we ignore his impoliteness. (Brazilian cashier 40)

In effect, this strategy is especially centered on the diplomacy that cashiers employ to change customers' moods and to protect themselves from possible aggression. Although cashiers must perform emotional work to implement this strategy, while using it they cannot be reprimanded if the customer makes a complaint or has a crisis of frustration. This strategy thus allows cashiers to remain within the norms prescribed by management and gives them a feeling of having done what was necessary and what was within their power to do.

Conclusion

The experiences of supermarket cashiers in Brazil and Quebec, demonstrate that women are far from being passive, submissive, or docile at work. The cashiers show us that oppression does not exist as an absolute power, outside and independent of social relations. The strategies of resistance that they use may seem passive or conformist, if analyzed within the domain of the public transcript.

Obviously, there is not just resistance among cashiers; many have internalized the policy that the "customer comes first." In effect, they exhibit a combination of both resistive and consensual practices that are ambiguous and simultaneous. Moreover, one cannot find a dichotomous division between strategies of resistance and consent, for these strategies are constituted by the social practices of cashiers.

However, behind the image of passivity are many silent rebellions aimed at maintaining control over and within work, so that the cashiers may keep their skills and dignity in the performance of their tasks. These workers' struggles carry "a radical contention of the organization of work and the system of values that can be certainly a source of submissiveness but that can also, in another context, be a source of radical contention of this system to the degree that they attack the base of that system" (Kergoat 1982, 133). In this context, cashiers are not passive victims, for they resist each day in order to keep the expertise and skills they have acquired.

One may explain the similarities in the strategies of resistance used by cashiers in Brazil and Quebec in part by the fact that in both societies their work is considered typically feminine work. Moreover, this type of work presents an opposition to the power of men over women. This opposition constitutes, as Foucault (1994d, 226) points out, both a struggle against the authority present in this type of relation, and a "transversal" struggle that "doesn't limit itself to a particular country. Of course, some countries encourage their development, facilitate their extension, but they are not restricted to a particular type of political or economic government."

Finally, despite all the economic, social, and cultural differences between these societies, the similarities in cashiers work in both of them are evidence that these are normalized jobs that use the same technologies, management techniques, and low levels of organized labor. In an increasingly globalized world, where work is becoming more and more casualized and similar, it is good to know that silent rebellions are taking place in the supermarket paradise of capitalist production, a resistance that provides some hope for the future.

Notes

1. In the original text, Scott (1985) uses "peasant insubordination" in this remarkable book on everyday forms of peasant resistance in Malaysia.

2. For a complete description of the methodology, see Soares (1995).

3. As Heidi Hirata (1997) explained, part-time jobs are nonexistent in Brazil because the full-time jobs are sufficiently flexible, not because work conditions are better.

4. In 1994, this supermarket chain had an increase of 41 percent in its net profit.

5. Sometimes cashiers in both societies have only half an hour for lunch.

6. Gunmar Aronsson (1989) makes the distinction between having control *over* work (vertical control) and control *within* work (horizontal control).

7. The encounter is understood here as "all those instances of two or more participants in a situation joining each other openly in maintaining a single focus of cognitive and visual attention—what is sensed as a single mutual activity, entailing preferential communication rights" (Goffman 1963, 89). One must point out that the encounter presupposes the immediate physical presence of the individuals (Goffman 1961), whose actions have a reciprocal influence on one another (Goffman 1983).

8. The exception is Anat Rafaeli and Robert Sutton, who have treated the topic in several articles: Rafaeli (1989, and 1990), Rafaeli and Sutton (1987, 1989), Sutton (1991), and Sutton and Rafaeli (1988).

9. I use the concept of strategy as the choice of winning solutions (Foucault, 1994d, 241).

10. Goffman (1963, 43–44) defined the involvement as the "capacity of an individual to give, or withhold from giving, his concerted attention to some activity at hand. . . . A main involvement is one that absorbs the major part of an individual's attention and interest, visibly forming the principal current determinant of his actions. . . . A subordinate involvement is one he is allowed to sustain only to the degree, and during the time, that his attention is patently not required by the involvement."

References

Aronsson, Gunmar. 1989. "Changed Qualifications Demands in Computer-mediated Work." *Applied Psychology: An International Review* 38(1): 57–71.

Barbès, François. 1995. "Metro: Richlieu Hausse Son Profit Net de 41%." *Les Affaires: Les Plus Importantes Enterprises au Quebec*, 17 June, p. 30.

Billette, André, and Renaud Bouchard. 1986. "Taille des Pools de Travail et Problèmes de Santé: Enquête Après des Opératrices en Saisie de Données." *Sociologie et Sociétés*, 28: 37–46.

Braverman, Harry. 1974. *Labor and Monopoly Capital: The Degradation of Work in the Twentieth Century*. New York: Monthly Review Press.

Burawoy, Michael. 1985. *The Politics of Production: Factory Regimes Under Capitalism and Socialism*. London: Verso.

Castoriadis, Cornelius. 1974. *L'Expérience du Mouvement Ouvrier*. Vol. 2. Paris: Union Générale d'Éditions.

Chauí, Marilena. 1986. *Conformismo e Resistência: Aspectos da Cultura Popular do Brasil*. Sao Paulo: Editora Brasiliense.

———. 1989. "Produtividade e Humanidades." *Tempo Social*, 1(2): 45–71.

Cockburn, Cynthia. 1991. *In the Way of Women: Men's Resistance to Sex Equality in Organizations*. London: Macmillan.

Corbeil, Christine, and Francine Descarries. 1997. "D'Espoirs et de Réalités: Les Stratégies de Conciliation des Mères en Emploi." Pp. 123–149 in *Stratégies de Résistance et Travail des Femmes*, edited by A. Soares. Montréal and Paris: Harmattan.

Dejours, Christophe. 1993. *Travail: Usure Mentale—Essai de Psychopathologie du Travail*. Paris: Bayard Éditions.

De Koninck, Maria. 1995. "Double Travail: Changement Social et Résistance des Femmes Cahiers." *Réseau de Recherches Féministes* 3: 17–25.

Edwards, Richard. 1979. *Contested Terrain: The Transformation of the Workplace in the Twentieth Century*. New York: Basic Books.

Elger, Tony. 1979. "Valorization and 'Deskilling': A Critique of Braverman." *Capital & Class*, 7: 58–99.

Foucault, Michel. 1975. *Surveiller et Punir*. Paris: Gallimard.

Foucault, Michel. 1976. *Histoire de la Sexualité*. Vol. 1, *La Volonté de Savoir*. Paris: Gallimard.

———. 1994a. *Dits et Écrits*. Vol. 1. Paris: Gallimard.

———. 1994b. *Dits et Écrits*. Vol. 2. Paris: Gallimard.

———. 1994c. *Dits et Écrits*. Vol. 3. Paris: Gallimard.

———. 1994d. *Dits et Écrits*. Vol. 4. Paris: Gallimard.

Freidman, Andrew L. 1977. *Industry and Labour: Class Struggle at Work and Monopoly Capitalism*. London: Macmillan.

Giddens, Anthony. 1994. *Les Conséquences de la Modernité*. Paris: Harmattan.

Goffman, Erving. 1961. *Encounters: Two Studies in the Sociology of Interaction*. Indianapolis: Bobbs-Merrill Educational Publishing.

———. 1963. *Behaviour in Public Places*. New York: Free Press.

———. 1983. *A Representaçao do Eu na Vida Cotidiana*. Petrópolis: Vozes.

Gottfried, Heidi 1994. "Learning the Score: The Duality of Control and Everyday Resistance in the Temporary-Help Service Industry." Pp. 102–127 in *Resistance and Power in Organizations*, edited by J.M. Jermier, D. Knights, and W.R. Nord. London: Routledge.

Hirata, Helena. 1997. *Travail et Division Sexuelle du Travailet—Comparaisons Internationales du Travail Industriel*. Saint-Quentin-en-Yvelines: Université de Versailles.

Hochschild, Arlie. R. 1983. *The Managed Heart: Commercialization of Human Feeling*. Berkeley: University of California Press.

Hodson, Randy. 1995. "Worker Resistance: An Underdeveloped Concept in the Sociology of Work." *Economic and Industrial Democracy*, 16: 79–109.

Hughes, Everett. C. 1958. *Men and Their Work*. Glencoe, IL: The Free Press.

Jermier, J. M., D. Knights, and W. R. Nord, eds. 1994. *Resistance and Power in Organizations*. London: Routledge.

Johansson, Gunn. 1989. "Job Demands and Stress Reactions in Repetitive and Uneventful Monotony at Work." *International Journal of Health Services*, 19(2): 365–377.

Kergoat, Danièle. 1982. *Les Ouvrières*. Paris: Le Sycomore.

Martin, Biddy. 1988. "Feminism, Criticism and Foucault." Pp. 3–19 in *Feminism and Foucault: Reflections on Resistance*, edited by I. Diamon and L. Quinby. Boston: Northeastern University Press.

Milkman, Ruth. 1987. *Gender at Work: The Dynamics of Job Segregation by Sex During World War II*. Chicago: University of Illinois Press.

Niessen, Manfred. 1982. "Qualitative Aspects in Cross-National Comparative Research and the Problem of Functional Equivalence." Pp. 83–104 in *International Comparative Research—Problems of Theory, Methodology, and Organisation in Eastern and Western Europe*, edited by M. Niessen and J. Peschar. Oxford: Pergamon Press.

Paules, Greta F. 1991. *Dishing It Out: Power and Resistance Among Waitresses in a New Jersey Restaurant*. Philadelphia: Temple University Press.

Prévost, Johane, and Karen Messing. 1997. "Quel Horaire, What Schedule? La Conciliation Travail-Famille et L'Horaire de Travail Irrégulier des Téléphonistes." Pp. 251–270 in *Stratégies de Résistance et Travail des Femmes*, edited by A. Soares. Montréal and Paris: Harmattan.

Rafaeli, Anat. 1989. "When Cashiers Meet Customers: An Analysis of the Role of Supermarket Cashiers." *Academy of Management Journal*, 32(2): 245–273.

———. 1990. "Busy Stories and Demanding Customers: How Do They Effect the Display of Positive Emotion?" *Academy of Management Journal*, 33 (3): 623–637.

Rafaeli, Anat, and Robert I. Sutton. 1987. "Expression of Emotion as Part of the Work Role." *Academy of Management Review*, 12(1): 23–37.

———. 1989. "The Expression of Emotion in Organizational Life." *Research in Organizational Behaviour*, 11: 1–42.

Rodrigues, Arrakey M. 1978. *Operário, Operária*. Sao Paulo: Simbolo.

Rosa, Kumudhini. 1991. "Strategies of Organisation and Resistance: Women Workers in Sri Lankan Free Trade Zones." *Capital and Class*, 45: 27–34.

Scott, James C. 1985. *Weapons of the Weak: Everyday Forms of Peasant Resistance*. New Haven: Yale University Press.

———. 1990. *Domination and the Arts of Resistance*. New Haven: Yale University Press.

Sears, Robert E. 1961. "Transcultural Variables and Conceptual Equivalence." Pp. 445–455 in *Studying Personality Cross-Culturally*, edited by B. Kaplan. Evanston, IL: Row Peterson.

Séguin, Céline. 1997. "Conjuguer Emploi et Famille en Situation de Monoparentalité: Les Stratégies Déployées par les Mères Seules." Pp. 151–183 in *Stratégies de Résistance et Travail des Femmes*, edited by A. Soares. Montréal and Paris: Harmattan.

Sennett, Richard, and Jonathon Cobb. 1972. *The Hidden Injuries of Class*. New York: W. W. Norton and Co.

Shapiro-Perl, Nina. 1984. "Resistance Strategies: The Routine Struggle for Bread and Roses." Pp. 193–208 in *My Troubles Are Going to Have Troubles with Me: Everyday Trials and Triumphs of Women Workers*, edited by K. B. Sacks and D. Remy. New Brunswick, NJ: Rutgers University Press.

Snow, David A., Cherylon Robinson, and Patricia L. McCall. 1991. "'Cooling Out' Men in Singles Bars and Nightclubs—Observations on the Interpersonal Survival Strategies of Women in Public Places." *Journal of Contemporary Ethnography*, 19(4): 423–449.

Soares, Angelo. 1995. "Les (Més)aventures des Caissières dans Le Paradis de La Consommation: Une Comparaison Brésil." Ph.D. dissertation, Université Laval.

———. 1996a. "Le (Non) Choix d'Etre Caissière." Pp. 125–146 in *Le Travail et l'Emploi en Mutation*, edited by L. Mercier and R. Bourbonnais. Montréal: ACFAS.

———. 1996b. "Nouvelles Technologies = Nouvelles Qualifications? Le Cas des Caissières de Supermarché." *Recherches Féministes*, 9(1): 37–56.

———. 1997 *Stratégies de Résistance et Travail des Femmes*. Montréal and Paris: Harmattan.

Souza-Lobo, Elisabeth. 1995. *Domination et Résistance: Travail et Quotidienneté*. Paris: Cahiers du Gedisst.

Sprouse, Martin. 1992. *Sabotage in the American Workplace: Anecdotes of Dissatisfaction, Mischief, and Revenge*. San Francisco: Pressure Drop Press.

Statham, Anne, Eleanor Miller, and Hans O. Mauksch. 1988. *The Worth of Women's Work—A Qualitative Synthesis*. Albany: SUNY Press.

Sugiman, Pamela. 1992. "'That Wall's Comin' Down': Gendered Strategies of Worker Resistance in the UAW Canadian Region 1963–1970." *Canadian Journal of Sociology*, 17(1): 1–27.

Sutton, Robert I. 1991. "Maintaining Norms About Expressed Emotions: The Case of Bill Collectors." *Administrative Science Quarterly*, 11: 322–336.

Sutton, Robert I. and Anat Rafaeli. 1988. "Untangling the Relationship Between Displayed Emotions and Organizational Sales: The Case of Convenience Stores." *Academy of Management Journal* 31(3): 461–487.

Taylor, Laurie, and Paul Walton. 1971. "Industrial Sabotage: Motives and Meanings." Pp. 219–245 in *Images of Deviance*, edited by Stanley Cohen. New York: Penguin Books.

Whyte, William F. 1946. "When Workers and Customers Meet." Pp. 123–147 in *Industry and Society*, W. F. Whyte. New York: McGraw Hill.

Yount, Kristen R. 1991. "Ladies, Flirts, and Tomboys: Strategies for Managing Sexual Harassment in an Underground Coal Mine." *Journal of Contemporary Ethnography*, 19, (4): 396–422.

Part III

Production and
Industrial Workers

CHAPTER 6

Flexible Despotism:
The Intensification of Insecurity
and Uncertainty in the Lives
of Silicon Valley's High-Tech
Assembly Workers

Jennifer JiHye Chun

In the special fifth-anniversary issue of *WIRED* magazine Po Bronson (1998, 1) issues a simple message: "Be warned: if your imprint of the Silicon Valley was soldered together in the 80s, it's time to upgrade." Competition, innovation, and adrenaline are perpetually transforming this high-tech culture of dynamism. According to Bronson, the Silicon Valley is like a "stew that never comes off the gas heat," and the "*real* work" is "done in silence, sitting in cubicles, staring at screens." Part of the recipe for success certainly entails the creative inspiration needed to design a new software program or a faster microchip. However, Bronson's recipe also needs to be upgraded to include the manufacturing workers who help transform each new innovation into a profitable finished product. Every time a new idea passes from the computer screen to the consumer's hands, it must be routed through mass production lines before the next technological breakthrough renders it obsolete. Silicon Valley's place as the cyberheart of the Digital Revolution depends on the ability of its workforce to produce its high-tech novelties quickly, cheaply, and efficiently.

To successfully turn out a more customized and innovative array of high-tech products, firms have upgraded to more flexible, high-volume production. Proponents of this shift argue that the drive for greater flexibility in the organization of production (Piore and Sabel 1984), the industrial structure (Saxenian 1994), and employment relations (Carnoy, Castells, and Benner 1997) is creating a "win-win" situation for workers as well as employers (Olmsted and Smith 1996). Not only does flexibility give employers a strategic advantage in a highly competitive global market,[1] but it also generates more humanistic and egalitarian opportunities for workers (Womack, Jones, and Roos 1991). Teamwork, job rotation, and quick thinking on the line are replacing the monotony and routinization associated with mass production. Today's flexible firms depend on multiskilled workers who can shift quickly from one product to another on the same line, operate more technologically advanced machinery, and work in cooperative settings (Castells 1996). Nowhere, it is argued, is this new flexible model of labor-management relations more apparent than in the Silicon Valley.

The Changing Conditions of Flexible Work

Despite the reigning popularity of flexibility in today's discourse on global competitiveness, the conceptual versus concrete benefits of flexibility are hotly contested, particularly when debating its effects on workers.[2] Critics of flexibility are highly skeptical of the "newness" of today's workplaces and their ability to generate a "better world" for everyone.[3] They claim that instead of offering training programs and expanding workers' roles in production, flexible firms are reducing the number of stable, permanent jobs and replacing them with more insecure forms of contingent employment, thus simply reproducing existing patterns of social and economic inequality (Gordon 1996; Harrison 1994). In the state of California—a leader in the national growth of key sectors in the information economy—the largest single category of new jobs over the past four years has been temporary jobs. In 1998, 45 percent of temporary workers had held their jobs for two years or less, yet the overwhelming majority expressed a desire for stable, full-time employment (Brenner, Borwnstein, and Dean, 1999). Shop floor accounts of changes in the auto industry reveal that the added stress and insecurity of the production system itself (Parker and Slaughter 1993), or managerial strategies that threaten plant relocation[4] or disguise teamwork principles, simply add to the insecurity of flexible manufacturing work.[5]

By studying the consequences of flexibility through the lens of workers' experiences, these critics expose the despotic character of flexibility. They argue that little has changed in workers' lives for "many of the trendiest workplaces are the same old fashioned factories in disguise" ("New Work Order" 1994, 76). However, they see its underside as the result of either a capitalist system that exacerbates socioeconomic inequality or a production system that generates high stress levels for workers. They do not interrogate how despotism actually operates in the drive for flexibility. Since they assume that flexible production relies on a single, generic production regime and a single, generic pattern of capitalist exploitation, they also fail to acknowledge that flexible production regimes can and do rely on multiple forms of despotism. How do flexible production regimes actually create, maintain, and reproduce worker consent to the stress and insecurity associated with the drive for flexibility, particularly in a global economy in which constant adaptation to change is directly associated with survival?

In this essay, I demonstrate that flexibility for management translates into extreme uncertainty, unpredictability, and insecurity in the lives of high-tech manufacturing workers. Workers intimately experience the tremendous twists and turns of flexible production as an "objective" condition of a fiercely competitive, highly volatile, and constantly changing global market.[6] When workers are dependent on employers for wages, they possess limited ability to contest the erosion of autonomy in their everyday work lives as a result of the drive for flexibility. According to Michael Burawoy's (1985) study of production regimes, in this climate of market despotism employers who are able to connect workers' conditions of economic dependence to their performance on the job can exercise a strong form of labor control. This is clearly evident on the shop floors of the Silicon Valley's high-tech manufacturing plants, where workers—predominantly immigrants with few choices in the regional labor market—labor with few institutional protection against layoffs, occupational health and safety hazards, and wage reductions. However, the character of labor regimes under *flexible despotism* reveals marked differences with Burawoy's account of market despotic regimes. Under market despotism, when anarchy in the market intersects with despotism in production, supervisors simply revert to direct repression and coercion (Burawoy 1985, 88–89). The rigorous, volatile, and unpredictable demands of flexible production, however, require more complex and rationalized coordination of worker consent.[7] Employers in flexible despotic regimes attempt to mask the coercive character of their labor control strategies through two types of labor regimes: subcontracting and contract manufacturing. In both regimes, they tie workers' need for work to their performance on the job by stressing the "voluntary" nature of worker consent to the chaotic and unpredictable demands of flexible production. Yet, their tactics of labor control vary along three key dimensions: (1) the labor process, (2) the internal labor market, and (3) the organizational culture (see Table 6-1).

Employers combine three forms of flexibility in the labor process to streamline operating costs and respond more efficiently to market fluctuations: (1) numerical flexibility—expanding and contracting workforces according to changing production needs; (2) structural flexibility—contracting out or outsourcing operating costs and direct responsibility to other suppliers, producers, and service providers; and (3) functional flexibility—enhancing worker mobility and cooperation across tasks in the work organization. The implementation of each type of flexibility in the labor process enables management to intensify their control over the conditions of production at the expense, not the provision, of worker autonomy. The organization of a firm's internal labor market depends on the types of flexible workers it employs. An informal labor markets relies more heavily on *recruiting* specific kinds of workers, whereas a more formalized internal labor market expends more energy *cultivating* certain types of workers. Internal labor markets vary from firm to firm; however, employers attempt to disarticulate workers' individual interests from their class-based collective interests and realign them with their own interests through practices such as offering bonuses and job promotions. Cultivating organizational cultures that are compatible with a firm's internal labor market provides

TABLE 6-1.   Two Regimes under Flexible Production

Dimension	Subcontracting Regimes	Contract Manufacturing Regimes
Labor process	• Labor-intensive unit assembly • Low capital costs, low barriers to entry • Numerical flexibility • Structural flexibility: squeeze labor through traditional subcontracting methods	• Capital-intensive, highly automated assembly lines • High capital costs, high barriers to entry • Numerical flexibility • Structural flexibility: provide customized, speedy electronic manufacturing services from multinational contract manufacturers who offer a commitment to quality assurance and total customer satisfaction • Functional flexibility: flexible work organization
	Informal	Formal
Internal labor market	• Emphasis on recruiting workers, through ethnic and community networks, who are marginalized in the larger labor market (such as limited-English-speaking immigrant women of color) rather than on cultivating certain kinds of workers through internal labor market practices • Little to no possibility for job mobility within the firm; job mobility externalized across firms in larger segmented labor market • Promote individual competition	• Emphasis on cultivating certain types of workers rather than on recruiting specific kinds of workers; recruitment needs are outsourced to temporary agencies and energies are focused on creating a company team • Possibilities for job mobility within the firm (from temporary to permanent worker and from line assembler to line lead to supervisor) and distribution of quarterly bonuses based on group rather than individual performance • Promote intrafirm competition between customer lines, buildings, and hubs
Organizational culture	• Appeal to ethnic and community ties to create worker-management solidarity along subcontracting community lines • Link wages and job security to job performance by emphasizing workers' and employers' common membership and interests along ethnic and community lines • Emphasize workers' subjectivities as members of ethnic communities	• Appeal to team concept to create company-based solidarity between workers and management • Link wages and job security to job performance by emphasizing a culture of collective survival in which everyone is subject to the volatility of the global market • Emphasize workers' subjectivities as consumers

ideological underpinnings that concretely link the interests of labor and capital. Tying workers' dependence on wages to their performance in the workplace establishes the parameters of the organizational culture; however, management must engage in additional tactics of persuasion to ensure worker consent to the volatility of flexible production. Firms, thereby, create discourses that forge commonalities between workers' experiences and the firm's needs.

Printed Circuit Board Assembly Workers

The printed circuit board (PCB) industry in the Silicon Valley represents the ideal site to examine these three dimensions in different production regimes under flexible despotism. The Silicon Valley is regarded as the prototype of flexible production and the trendsetter of global industrial change (Carnoy, Castells, and Benner 1997). Until the mid-1980s, flexibility simply meant sweating labor, a practice common to the history of labor-intensive work. The majority of PCB assembly work took place in "high-tech sweatshops." Because they are a highly dependent workforce, immigrant women of color were recruited as the primary flexible labor of choice for these anti-union, high-tech companies. Their responsibilities as mothers, wives, and economic contributors to other family members make their wages a vital part of their households. However, workers' struggles in arenas such as the family only multiply their struggles in the workplace (Bookman and Morgan 1988).

A highly dependent workforce continued to be recruited after the regional industry experienced major restructuring in the mid-1980s. A widespread economic depression forced regional firms to dramatically transform production by implementing greater flexibility in the labor process and the organizational structure (Saxenian 1994). Contract manufacturers emerged as a leading force in global PCB production. Today, many high-tech sweatshops have been and are continuing to be replaced by new contract manufacturing plants that combine capital-intensive machinery with PCB assembly. Sleek, technologically advanced, and hyperclean, these contract manufacturers often are touted as model "high-performance workplaces." Yet despite the PCB industry's flexible makeover, the workforce recruited for high-tech assembly still is composed predominantly of immigrants of color and other racial-ethnic minorities, although it is now more diverse in terms of gender and age (Luethje 1997). In addition, the rise of institutionalized temporary employment (Benner 1996b) and the continued absence of organized trade unions in high-tech manufacturing give workers few sources of protection from the volatility of the industry. How do these dramatic changes in regional PCB production, in light of the continued recruitment of a highly marginalized workforce, affect the organization of work? How do workers experience these flexible changes in their everyday work lives? What might these changes reveal about the character of production regimes under diversifying forms of flexible production?

To address these questions, I will conduct a comparative ethnographic case study of flexible production regimes. An existing ethnographic study of PCB subcontractors carried out by Soon-Kyoung Cho (1987) in the mid-1980s creates an ideal comparison between subcontracting and contract manufacturing production regimes in Silicon Valley PCB assembly. Between 1984 and 1986, Cho worked as an electronics assembler at two ethnic-owned PCB subcontracting firms: (1) Chinotech Co., a Chinese-owned PCB assembly shop that employed mainly recently arrived Chinese immigrant women; and (2) Hantronics, a Korean-owned PCB assembly house that employed primarily Korean immigrant women.[8] An interview-based study of Asian entrepreneurs and workers in the same industrial category with roughly the same types of workforces, conducted by Edward Park (1992) and Karen Hossfeld (1988, 1990, 1991, 1994), added valuable empirical evidence about the perceptions and attitudes of employers.[9] To examine the new generation of contract manufacturers, I conducted participant observation at a major contract manufacturer in the Silicon Valley—which I will refer to as FlexTech—during the summer of 1997. A leading regional and global contract manufacturer, FlexTech has received of many awards for being an exemplary "high-performance workplace." I was hired as a temporary worker and received weekly paychecks from a temporary agency. I worked as an entry-level assembler on the graveyard shift, 10:30 P.M. to 7:00 A.M., for six weeks. My hourly wage was $6.00 plus 15 percent for the graveyard, for a total of $7.18 per hour. My coworkers came from diverse racial and ethnic backgrounds, including but not limited to Vietnamese, Chinese, Filipino, Mexican, Hawaiian, Ethiopian, South Asian, African American, white American, and Chicano.

By examining the relationship between specific production regimes and the everyday lives of PCB workers on the shop floor, we can better understand how changes in flexible production are affecting both the organization of work and the workers' experience of the drive for flexibility. In the next section, I will compare and contrast the specific characteristics of each regime under flexible production along three dimensions—the labor process, the internal labor market, and the organizational culture—to highlight the emergence of two distinct types of flexible production regimes: *subcontracting* and *contract manufacturing regimes*.

Subcontracting Regimes

In this section, I will focus on the character of the subcontracting regime and the experiences of workers in this particular kind of flexible production. An in-depth description of the labor-intensive character of assembly, the internal labor market, and the organizational culture for PCB production in the 1980s will show how workers' dependence on employers for their livelihoods provides the material links through which firms are able to elicit workers' compliance to the vagaries and specific needs of subcontracting manufacturing—the first type of despotic production regime.

The Labor Process

PCB assembly factories in the Silicon Valley primarily consisted of small to medium subcontractors until the mid- to late 1980s. During this period large computer manufacturers, or OEMs (original equipment manufacturers), attempted to maximize flex-

ibility and reduce costs by outsourcing their PCB assembly needs to smaller production houses. OEMs employed a smaller core workforce and relied on outside subcontractors during periods of intense demand. This allowed OEMs to cut costs while
passing on the legal responsibility for just wages, safe working conditions, and fair
employment contracts to subcontractors. Since many subcontracting firms had to
compete for the same contracts, they squeezed labor costs to outbid other firms. They
expanded and contracted their labor force, paid substandard wages, frequently violated health and safety regulations, and often demanded that employees work overtime but refused to compensate them accordingly. Subcontractors whose survival
was dependent on obtaining customer contracts combined sweatshop-like labor practices with flexible production strategies to stay afloat in a highly volatile market. The
regularity of work for employees depended primarily on the subcontractor's ability
to acquire and retain OEM contracts.

PCB assembly was easily contracted out due to the labor-intensive nature its pin-
hole method of production, which required little capital investment. The customer
typically supplied the components and delivered them directly to the production
sites. Subcontractors simply purchased the worktables, pliers, lamps, and soldering
irons required for in-house assembly (Cho 1987, 126). Labor constituted the only additional production cost. Workers sat either alone at individual worktables (when
working with small PCBs) or alongside other workers at long tables (when working
with large PCBs). Each worker was responsible for assembling an entire board. Refer-
ring to electronics manuals and blueprints for component location, a worker placed
each component, usually no bigger than a thumbnail, through a tiny opening on the
face of the board and then soldered it onto the board.

Cho argues that, although the work was not regulated by "flow lines" or conveyor
belts, the unit-assembly process and the reduction of sequential work interdependence did not undermine labor control. Workers controlled their own work speed and
increased their own work intensity, thereby replacing the need for the regulated,
built-in control of a conveyor belt. They punched a time card before and after finishing each board to keep track of their unit-assembly pace. They also recorded the specific numbers of each component stuffed. Not only did this allow them to monitor
their own quality, but it enabled line leads and supervisors to identify which workers made errors (Cho 1987, 171). Cho (1987, 166) explains that as long as there was
work to be done, "Chinotech workers were never idle. . . . When there was not much
work to do, the company simply announced temporary layoffs or the reduction of
work hours. Often workers at the Loading Section were asked to work only four hours
a day without advance notice. The company usually just announced around 11:00
A.M. that the day's work would end at noon."

The Internal Labor Market

To reproduce a cheap, flexible workforce, employers expended much more energy
finding rather than "creating" certain types of workers. The surplus labor pool of

experienced workers allowed employers to be more selective in their hires. Some firms posted job advertisements in the *San Jose Mercury News*, which advertised for workers who needed "minimum supervision" and already possessed a "self-starter" work ethic (Cho 1987, 141). Cho recalls preparing rigorously the night before for a tryout for an assembly job at Chinotech, studying the electronics manual, components, soldering techniques, and blueprints. The next day she stuffed over fifty tiny components into each PCB for nine straight hours. She explains what happened after she had finished: "Seeing my time card after work, the personnel manager asked me to come to work the following day. At that moment, after being rejected from almost fifteen places, I felt as if the personnel manager were an angel" (142). Highly competitive peripheral firms also relied heavily on ethnic networks to recruit workers, and news of jobs often traveled to immigrant workers by word of mouth and ethnic newspapers (Cho 1987, 152).

After workers were recruited, few opportunities existed for job mobility within the firm. If workers wanted to find better paying and more secure jobs, they had to look outside their workplaces. Although job mobility was also limited in the external labor market, the regional labor market offered some opportunities for movement between firms. Younger, more proficient English-speakers could obtain higher paying, more secure jobs at white American–owned companies, while older, more limited English-speakers were confined to jobs at ethnic-owned subcontracting firms. Cho (1987, 145) describes one instance when an older worker "advised" her to find employment elsewhere:

> Why do you stay here? You are young, can speak English, and have work experience. You can get a job in an American firm. Right now, they probably do not hire because the economy is so bad, but soon they will begin to hire new people. They like young people. I am too old, and don't know English. They would not hire people like me and I have to stay here.

Young women without familial responsibilities were better able to secure higher paying and more stable jobs. However, most of Cho's co-workers believed that "there is no hope in this kind of job" and that they had "no choice but to be stuck" at their jobs (Cho 1987, 145).

The external conditions of the labor market also eliminated the need for firms to train workers and offer systematic job incentives. At Hantronics, the rules and regulations were informally communicated to the workers. After workers were hired, they were simply told that employment was temporary for the first three months and that promotions (limited solely to wage increases) were based on performance. A similar policy existed at Chinotech. Although workers were told that employment was temporary, they were not given formal evaluations after three months nor were they given specific reasons regarding dismissal. Firms linked the possibility of permanent employment with job performance, yet gave no written contractual guarantees. For example, employers promised workers bigger bonuses for better work. Yet the disbursement of bonuses was erratic and arbitrary. The owner of an ethnic-owned subcontracting firm admitted that his company's informal bonus system depended more on the current state of the market than on workers' performance. His intricate system of bonuses, comprised of cash and assorted gift certificates, was theoretically based on "production outputs," but "during a 'soft' labor market, bonuses are phased out; [while] during a tight labor market, they are phased in" (Park 1992, 158). At a Chinese-owned subcontracting firm, bonuses were sporadically changed "without 'rewriting' wage and benefit schedules" (Park 1992, 155). Owners often asked workers not to report these bonuses as part of their real income.

Ambiguous company policies often translated into intensified working conditions. Under the elusive yet scrutinizing eyes of management, workers constantly needed to prove to management that they were good workers. Self-surveillance and surveillance by other co-workers helped management reinforce labor-management cooperation. Co-workers continually advised Cho not to be late or absent from work, for "absence is what the manager likes the least" (Cho 1987, 178). To protect their jobs, Cho (1987, 172–174) explained,

> workers have to assume . . . that they are being watched all the time. So it was not surprising that Mrs. Park at Hantronics warned me on a bus (on the way home) not to talk at work. She said, "Don't talk with other workers while you work. Someone always watches you and reports everything to the boss. . . . It would influence your promotion and pay raise. . . . Many people got fired even before the first three months. When I was hired last August [1985], my employee number was 18, now [January 1986] I am number 8; 10 people left. Almost all of them got fired, including a line lead at our stuffing section. The company thought that she was not tough enough to us. I know that she didn't tell the boss 'everything' about us. Other workers all know about this stuff and feel the same way I do. That's why they usually don't talk at work. . . . Well, I can tell these things to you because we are here [on the bus]. Inside the company you can never talk about this stuff." The anxiety-ridden climate of intense job instability and insecurity was constantly reinforced by frequent turnovers, instant layoffs, "slipped schedules," frantic production schedules, and sporadic income loss. Many assemblers began work early, stayed late, and worked through coffee breaks without ever being paid.

The Organizational Culture

Although managers admitted that the size of workers' bonuses rarely depended on their individual performance, they promoted this idea to workers. Some employers also convinced workers that they were providing a valuable community service to newly arriving immigrants. A Korean American woman supervisor explained that the workers she hires "are usually family members or fellow church members who just came to the U.S. or to San Jose . . . in tough situations and [in] need of work badly. They come to me as a fellow Korean." Because the company often makes generous hires, even "when it does not necessarily make business sense," workers should "feel a personal debt" to the company for "giving them this opportunity" (Park 1992, 95).

However, to factory owners, fostering "community goodwill" often meant appropriating ethnic ties. For example, a Korean American male, who served as a deacon in a Korean Presbyterian church, hired members of his church for a local subcontractor. He tells Park:

I ask the Korean American workers to view this firm as a valuable resource for the Korean American community. By giving Korean Americans jobs, this firm offers a real opportunity for Korean Americans to find the American Dream. I urge the Korean American workers to save the money they earn here to buy their own business and move out of the working class into the middle class. . . . As Korean Americans, we should be grateful to this company for providing us with this tremendous opportunity. . . . Each Korean American worker in this firm must feel a sense of responsibility. (Park 1992, 92)

This supervisor believed workers should take a collective sense of ownership in the firm and avoid acting in individualistic ways that could "jeopardize the [entire] Korean American community" (Park 1992, 93).

Workers themselves often repeated this sentiment, particularly when reminded of the chronic unemployment. One Korean immigrant woman told Cho: "We [employees at Hantronics] are the chosen. There are hundreds of people lined up for this job. Not everyone who wants to work here can get a job" (Cho 1987, 151). By emphasizing workers' and employers' shared ties as members of a common ethnic community, management attempted to mask the coercive character of their despotic labor practices. They tried to convince workers that they offered them material opportunities in a context of very limited resources and jobs, particularly for newly arriving immigrants of color.

Contract Manufacturing Regimes

When I first stepped onto the shop floor of FlexTech, I observed dramatic changes in the character and organization of work as well as the composition of the workforce. Gone were the long worktables filled with older, married women of a single racial-ethnic group doing simple, labor-intensive assembly. Sophisticated technology and segmented workstations along highly automated assembly lines produced more complex PCB boards made by both male and female workers from a diversity of ethnic and racial backgrounds as well as age groups. On the surface, changes in flexible production seemed to result in a significantly different workforce performing a much greater variety of work operations. Yet, as each day passed, I began to notice distinct differences between the subcontracting plants of the 1980s and FlexTech. Increased flexibility in manufacturing, hiring, and the organization of work resulted in new managerial strategies of labor control, qualitatively different relations between the workers, and a different character of insecurity and uncertainty in the workplace.

The Labor Process

Although board-stuffing subcontracting shops still operate throughout the Silicon Valley, FlexTech represents the sleek, technologically upgraded, new face of flexible production in the PCB industry. The introduction of capital intensive surface mount technology (SMT) has dramatically changed the technology of production. SMT machines automatically stuff components onto PCBs using a highly chemical and computerized process. They have effectively reduced an entire workforce devoted to board stuffing to performing a single task on the SMT line, the hand-load position. This has allowed PCB manufacturers to develop more sophisticated boards and systems. Contract manufacturers now offer their customers a wider array of Electronic manufacturing services (EMS), such as product design and engineering, prototype development, marketing trend analysis, and computerized testing.

Contract manufacturers are autonomously managed but connected extensions of OEM product development in the overall production chain. They do not possess any internal product development capacity, nor do they manufacture any visible products that bear their company label. Unlike subcontractors, they do not receive their components directly from customers. As the project engineer for my line explained: "We are strictly an assembly house. We don't make anything from scratch. We buy the boards, the components, screws, metal casings, everything. We simply assemble everything together for our customers." Their customer base is larger, yet their capital costs are much higher (one SMT costs over a million dollars), and they are highly integrated into the global production chain. Thus the risks and uncertainties for firms like FlexTech are an ever-present and often-highlighted concern by management. In their public company literature FlexTech warns potential investors of the highly risky character of their business due to "rapid technological change" and "product obsolescence."

The added dynamic of customers in the employer-employee relationship has complicated the basic paradigm in labor-management industrial relations, much in the same way that the direct involvement of service recipients in the relationship between employers and interactive service workers has complicated the basic struggle between management and labor for control over the production process (Leidner 1993, 3). Although OEMs are formally disconnected from contract manufacturers, they continue to exercise influence in the daily operations of contract manufacturers. Each line is engineered for a specific project for a particular customer. In my building FlexTech assembled boards and systems for two customers, whom I will call OEM[1] and OEM[2].

Expanded EMS services, the role of the customer, and technological advancement in production have also brought cosmetic changes to the organization of production. I worked on the OEM[2] line, which initially assembled PCB systems for a six-modem board. After two weeks, an eight-modem board was added and by the end of six weeks, an eighteen-modem board was added. In the first phase of production, SMT machines stamp components onto the boards. In-circuit test (ICT) workers verify that all the components have been properly inserted and that all electrical circuits are operational. Quality control (QC) workers inspect the boards under large magnifying glasses and bright lights to verify the location of components against the blueprints. Once the boards emerge from the SMT machines, they await additional stuffing, which marks the beginning of the second phase. Hand-loaders manually place a few tiny pieces that resist SMT placement onto the boards. They control the pace of the line, for they determine the number and pace of boards placed onto the conveyor belt, and subsequently, the number of boards that reach the rest of the workers on the line. The boards then pass through wave machines that fuse the additional components onto the boards and sterilize the entire unit. The wave machine operator removes the boards from scorching trays and places them back onto the conveyor belt. During the third phase another ICT tester checks the quality of the PCBs on a sophisticated computer terminal before sending them through mechanical assembly. More complicated PCB systems often entail more sophisticated mechanical assembly. Two different boards came down our line that needed to be screwed together like a sandwich. Then, a metal casing had to be constructed around the board. Finally, the board passes a series of computerized batch tests using customized software for additional quality checks. A final quality assurance (QA) check is conducted in which a worker spot-checks for errors in mechanical assembly. The PCB systems are then packed and shipped to customers.

Throughout the entire production process, sophisticated statistical controls, software-designed quality tests, and manual inspections monitor quality. At every stage the unit is tested on a computer terminal or a manual inspection station. Then the bar code is scanned "pass" or "fail." At certain stations, workers also keep a written log of boards that have passed or failed to double-check inventory and quality control. Color-coded laminated diagrams outlining the tasks for each job are hung at each station. In addition, visible reminders of the "5 Ss"—for the five Japanese words that start with S and mean orderliness, cleanliness, discipline, respect, and self-motivation—are scattered on laminated flyers and computer screen savers throughout the line. The interweaving of computerized testing stations and human quality controls creates the appearance of a smoothly integrated, continuous assembly line.

The layout of the shop floor is also neatly marked and clearly organized. Workers enter the building through a single back door. After they pass the cafeteria, they slide their company identification badges into a slot next to the door to the shop floor. Once inside, workers slide their badges again, but this time into an automated time clock. Then, they step onto a checking station that indicates whether they are wearing their wrist and heel straps properly.[10] Workers proceed to find their names in two binders labeled by customer—one that verifies the time that they punched in and out, and one that documents whether they have actually checked in at the wrist and heel strap station. Along the same wall are rows of moveable office cubicles for supervisors, managers, and engineers. Large, laminated graphs and charts that describe up-to-date productivity information hang from the outer walls of the cubicles. At the very end of the same wall is a door leading to a conference/class room. A chalkboard, an overhead, and a podium are located at the front, and rows of long, thin tables with padded swivel chairs fill the rest of the room.

At first glance, the neat and clean layout of the shop floor and the sophisticated technological equipment create the impression that the actual production of PCBs is just as orderly. However, these flexible manufacturing systems designed to deliver customized, quality-assured, and timely products for customers also can deliver turbulence and uncertainty to workers. Just-in-time manufacturing principles keep the exact supply of materials in stock for daily production. Yet if the day's shipments do not send the appropriate amount of materials to run the assembly line, production is shut down. Fully operational assembly lines depend on fully operational SMT machines and computerized quality control systems. However, if a machine breaks down, the entire line is sent home early. I quickly learned that workers could not always expect to show up to the production site, work a full eight-and-a-half-hour shift, and punch out. They could not always expect to be given advanced notice for canceled shifts. Nor could they expect to be paid for work lost when shifts were canceled.

Amidst the turbulent and irregular conditions of work, the intensification of work seemed to represent the only consistency. Throughout my fieldwork, I felt a mixture of bewilderment, frustration, admiration, and amazement at the extraordinary amount of effort workers exerted and the tremendous lack of autonomy they could exercise in the face of so much uncertainty. When I learned that some workers even held second full-time, wage-earning jobs, in addition to their responsibilities to their families and communities, the following question began to plague me. Why did workers work so hard to promote the company's interest, when most could not even depend on the stability of day-to-day or long-term work? However, after I left Flex-Tech, I quickly realized that the more appropriate question to ask workers is "Why *not* work hard?"[11]

For FlexTech employees, dependence on continued work constitutes a crucial element of labor control. Economic marginalization due to race and ethnicity, gender, familial responsibilities, and immigrant status largely shape workers' struggles on the shop floor. Rosa, a Chicano woman who had been working at FlexTech for ten years told me: "I have had a hard life. I started working when I was twelve years old. I got a fake green card and a fake visa. I worked at a cannery. My friends at the plant helped me get the job. Now, I'm stuck here. I keep telling my sons, 'Work hard in school so you don't have to work like me.'" Robert, the line lead, also felt few good job opportunities existed for him as a young, twenty-two-year-old black male who grew up in a low-income community in East Palo Alto. He heard about FlexTech through a friend and applied for the job. Now that he is permanent and receives a good benefits package, including life, medical, and dental insurance, he would like to work at FlexTech as long as possible since few good job opportunities exist for him as someone who is "young, black, and from the ghetto." Some workers also tried to "score points" because "if they [supervisors] see you work hard, they won't call you first" for a layoff. Every time a production line was shut down or an entire section sent home, it meant an absolute loss in wages.

Each time a shift was canceled because of shipment delays, technical problems, or managerial mix-ups, workers did express feelings of frustration, anger, and bitterness. Yet for most workers, these feelings simply exacerbated the reality that they had very little ability to contest disruptions. Mary, a white single mother with two kids, often could not make ends meet during production shutdowns. When she first started working, she had two jobs. In addition to working the graveyard shift, she worked as a cashier. Two jobs, plus the responsibility of taking care of her children, proved to be too much, and she quit her cashier's job. As a result, she depended solely on her wages from FlexTech. During the last shutdown, she told me:

> I was having a tough time. I had not worked for two weeks. I had two kids, for God's sake. I finally said something to Elvis [her supervisor], and he seemed generally surprised that I was having such a tough time. I said, "C'mon Elvis, I'm a single mother with two kids." He just repeated, "Wow. Are you really having that tough of a time? I didn't know it was so bad for you." He just didn't get it.

Worker consent to despotic work conditions reflected wider acknowledgment of the overall bleak economic state facing most employees. For example, a UPS strike caused a temporary halt of shipments for the OEM[1] line, a characteristic problem of just-in-time manufacturing. Since there were no parts to run assembly lines, production was shut down for two-and-a-half days. Most workers to whom I talked seemed upset that there was no work, feeling that the UPS workers "were ruining it for the rest of [them]." Workers did not seem to identify with the strikers' demands as temporary workers. Instead, workers' frustration toward the UPS workers or general indifference about the strike reinforced the notion that disruptions were not only part of the job, but also part of their lives.

Oftentimes, the extent of workers' marginalization in the larger labor market along lines of gender, race, immigration, and language created stronger conditions of dependence and, subsequently, more virulent forms of labor control. During one shift, I moved to the hand-load section to help Meena, a thirty-year-old South Asian immigrant woman who had moved to the United States seven months ago. This section required two workers; however, she was the only one working there after one worker was fired and another quit (both young women of color). Since this was one of the "dirtier" and more monotonous tasks on the line, older, limited-English-speaking immigrant women of color often were placed in this position. Since these workers handled the boards immediately after they emerged from the SMT lines, they were still laced with harsh, toxic chemicals.[12] Although workers were given the option to wear latex gloves, it was extremely difficult to stuff the tiny components on the boards while wearing gloves and still keep up with output goals. Meena's fingers were bright red and had puffed up to three times their normal size. When she had briefly mentioned her condition to her supervisor, he brushed her off, so she decided to endure the health risks of her job rather than face the possibility of termination. That evening, however, I decided to intervene and try to help get her medical treatment. During the break we walked over to see Michael, our supervisor. He told Meena simply to wash her hands, go back to work, and see a doctor the following day. Meena hesitantly explained to him that she had no health insurance. Michael seemed irritated and just muttered that he would figure something out. Instead of figuring out how to arrange health care for a workplace-related injury, Michael said he wanted "to make sure that it was not something in the air that caused her allergic reaction," because if that were the case, according to the other shift supervisor, "they would have to let her go." He explained: "I have lots of other hand-loads, and their hands are fine. She doesn't wash her hands after she touches the boards." Terrified that she was going to lose her job, Meena adamantly started walking back to the hand-load station. "No, I work. I go back to hand-load," Meena insisted. She told the other Punjabi-speaker that this was the first job that she had been able to get since she had moved here and that she could not afford to lose it. She had a seven-month-old baby, and she desperately needed the work. Michael yelled at her and told her she was crazy. "Go home," he practically shouted. Meena left in tears, and we all watched in utter silence.

Part of the consequences of contract manufacturing's image as a "clean" industry lay in the denial of occupational health and safety violations by management. The OEM[1] supervisor's claim that Meena's health problem was personal, rather than job-related, characterized management's basic perspective on workers' health issues. By emphasizing the generally "clean" nature of SMT production, management could minimize their liability for work-related injuries. They could also rely on workers' desperate need for jobs to effectively eliminate worker complaints.

Most workers could identify with the precariousness of work, having changed jobs in the industry often, uncertain each time of how long the job would last. Robert explained; "When I first moved to this building, people were getting fired by the dozens. Throughout the day, they would point to someone and say, 'Meeting,' and that person would be gone the next day. The supervisors and managers don't yell at you, but they breathe down your neck." This identification helped connect workers' dependence on wages to their efforts to keep their jobs. Lin, a Cambodian American female who worked the graveyard shift, told me: "Someone was fired from my line yesterday too. You know the piece that we have to screw onto the board. I guess it costs like $600. The person kept messing up, so they fired him. I better be hella careful when I screw on those boards."

This message was also delivered through FlexTech's appropriation of feedback as a means to weed out bad workers. Although management said that the reason that worker feedback was solicited during shift meetings was to improve quality standards, in fact it was often used to reprimand individual workers. If a worker at a mechanical assembly station did not fully screw in the boards, he or she was given "feedback" about the quality of the work. As workers became more accustomed to the true purpose of feedback, they learned that giving it could mean getting other workers in trouble or even fired. Failure to incorporate suggestions for improvement could result in employee dismissal. In addition, management translated certain Japanese management principles to intensify the conditions of work. FlexTech's official managerial philosophy, the "5 Ss," did not directly translate across cultures. However, it did not matter what the "5 Ss," stood for, because the literal meaning was secondary to the discursive power. The supervisor also did not know what the "5 Ss," exactly stood for, but he clearly articulated the underlying message—come to work on time, work hard, keep your station clean, or get fired at any moment. Some workers realized the disjuncture between company rhetoric and practice, but still remained with FlexTech. Mary, a temporary worker hoping to become permanent, complained:

They make you all these promises here, but they lie. I have been working here for seven months. I have seen a lot of people go through here. Three months ago, they let go about half the people. My daughter warned me about the electronics industry. She said how they don't care about you and how you're just going to get fucked over.

The relationship between contract manufacturers and their customers is reinforced through on-site visits by customers. Although I never worked while a customer was present on the floor, the night before a customer visit we were always warned to maintain the "5 Ss." The presence of the customer strengthened FlexTech management's claim that they were subject to the same kinds of rigorous quality inspections that they subjected their workers to. Robert explained that sometimes the customers would come around and ask the workers questions. He tried to make a good impression on behalf of FlexTech, even changing his appearance: "I had a real hard time when I started here. Why do you think I wear my hair like this?" Everyday, he slicked his hair back and tied it in a tight knot at the end. "I'm tired of this hairdo," he said. "It takes me a good thirty–forty-five minutes everyday. They don't want to see no long hair, no Afros. They also don't want to see no tattoos." "When I asked him why they are so strict, he replied, "Because, when the OEM[1] bosses come, they don't want to [show the customers] that there's gang shit here." Robert's efforts reveal how the company's need to convey a "good image" to their customers intersects with workers' struggles.

The Internal Labor Market

Much like the contradiction between FlexTech's "hyperclean" and "superorganized" production image and day-to-day production operations, a disparity also exists between the normal, bureaucratic character of FlexTech's internal labor market and its effects on workers' lives. FlexTech expends little direct energy on recruitment. They outsource labor recruiting to several temporary agencies that operate a staffing site at a local shopping center, exclusively for FlexTech. Anyone who is shopping in the mall can drop by the staffing office and fill out an application. The decor resembles the reception area of a sterile office. Framed pictures of happy, hard-working engineers, signs describing FlexTech's commitment to customer satisfaction, and awards commending FlexTech for superior quality and performance hang on the plain, white walls.

My attempts to obtain employment gave me a preliminary glimpse of the many instabilities that accompany temporary work at FlexTech.[13] In front of the staffing site, a sign, like those announcing clearance sales, advertised "immediate temporary positions." I walked up to the reception desk and inquired about the entry-level assembly positions publicized. I told her I was a student looking for summer employment. She immediately informed me that FlexTech did not offer summer employment and turned her attention to the person behind me. Distraught by her abrupt dismissal, I persisted, "But, the sign in front says you are looking for temporary workers." She curtly informed me that FlexTech solely hired full-time workers. "Temporary" did not mean workers could personally tailor their employment schedules. She explained bluntly: "Yes, FlexTech hires temporary workers, but that means that they decide how long they need workers to work, *not* the other way around. If FlexTech only hired people who wanted summer jobs, then what would happen when they all left at the end of the summer? The company would be stuck with all these empty positions and that would be bad for the company." Although she resisted giving me an application, I persisted and applied for a position. After filling out three different forms, I walked out thirty minutes later with a verbal job offer and an appointment to take the required English and math tests. Due to production shutdowns and overhiring by temporary agencies, my start date kept getting delayed. After three weeks, I accepted the first available opening that I was offered—the graveyard position.

Although FlexTech passes the responsibility for recruiting workers onto temporary agencies, they take an active and direct role in molding workers on the shop floor. Their reliance on temporary agencies simply lays the foundation for their formal employment policy. All workers start on a "probationary" status as temporary workers. They are given badges with their names and their temporary agencies written on them. On every shift, temporary workers must wear these badges, which distinguish them from other, permanent workers. Supervisors and temporary agencies tell workers that if they work hard and come to work on time, they will eventually become permanent. By "choosing" to work overtime, often with less than twenty-four hours notice, employees can supplement their low wages and increase their chances of becoming permanent employees. Michael explained the benefits of hard work to his line workers:

> I'm not like other supervisors. I work like a dog just like you guys on the line. I had a badge just like you guys a year ago. I worked really hard and moved up. If you work hard, you can too. If you move up, then the guy behind you can too. After six months, you can become permanent. Follow the "5 Ss." They are Japanese. I don't remember what they stand for, orderliness, cleanliness, that kind of stuff. Just be on time, work hard, and you can become permanent. Once you're permanent, you get sick days, vacation, and holidays.

The intervention of the customer in the employer-employee relationship and in the labor process also informs the reorganization of the internal labor market along customer-specific group lines rather than individual worker lines. Each customer project has its own specific team of workers, including a separate supervisor and separate shift meetings. Workers all identify themselves and each other by the identity of their customer. Although some workers intensify their conditions of work in hopes of becoming permanent employees, FlexTech's temporary-to-permanent employment policy is primarily group-based. "Promotion" to permanent status depends more on the profitability and productivity of a specific customer project than on an individual worker's performance. At the end of my first week, approximately fifteen OEM[1] workers celebrated their conversion into permanent workers by throwing themselves a party during the lunch break (2:30–3:00 A.M.). They were the first group of temporary workers hired on the OEM[1] project, and after eleven months of delays and excuses, they were finally offered permanent employment. Those OEM[1] workers who were hired later and were not granted permanent employment did not partake in the celebration.

Most of the workers on the OEM^2 line were temporary workers.[14] During one of the shift meetings, Michael seemed pleased with our line's productivity and stressed the need to maintain our output levels. He began the meeting by telling us we had a "good shot" at becoming permanent: "We're doing OK. Last night, even though we were missing two people, we still did over 250 boards. We work well as a team. We have to keep it up." But he qualified his appreciation by telling us about the feedback he had received from the day shift: "We did well, but not well enough," he said. "The day shifts reported that their work spaces were left messy by the graveyard shift, and that some of the boards that were left to be tested for the day shift by the graveyard shift had been mislabeled as failed boards."

Michael knew how difficult it was to stay awake and do good work, and he was happy that we were holding our own in comparison to the day and swing shifts. Then he said:

> In 3 months, I think I can try to get everyone permanent. I'll push. I can't guarantee, but I'll try. It is easier to get permanent on the graveyard shift. Day and swing is much harder. Even me, I asked my boss if I could switch to swing shift, but he said no. So, I'm stuck. Once you get permanent, you get paid sick days, you can take a vacation when you want and get paid.

Our reward for good teamwork was the possibility of a group promotion. He emphasized that we—meaning only those of us who worked the graveyard shift on the OEM^2 line—could be granted permanent employment earlier than usual, thus making us eligible for additional "bonuses" such as paid sick days and vacation, but only if we worked hard and maintained our quality. Management thus offered the possibility of permanent work to deepen the entire work team's commitment to the specific goals of the customer's production needs.[15]

Real possibilities for job mobility within the firm also hampered the formation of a collective worker-based rather than a work-team-based solidarity. During a conversation about a worker who was granted permanent work but denied a raise, Jan, a temporary worker on the next line, commented that FlexTech workers were lucky even to have the possibility of getting a raise. Her boyfriend had worked at the Santa Clara post office for over ten years and had only received cost-of-living increases. On another occasion, Robert, who used to work as a mechanical assembler, reprimanded Francis, one of the mechanical assemblers on his line, for working too slow, but later admitted:

> I figured it out. People aren't mean before they come here. This place makes you mean. I'm all stressed out. I see people working too slow and think, "No, I can't have that on my line." I know why now. Yesterday morning, I got yelled at. Lin Nguyen [the day shift supervisor] got mad at me. Michael told me that he got yelled at too. They yelled at him because of me. [They were angry] because SMT shut down early; they thought that I told them to go home or something. Graveyard gets blamed for everything. It's like they think we make mistakes because we're too sleepy or something. I know, because I was one of those people who got graveyard in trouble. In the meetings, I would say that screws were

coming loose and washers were missing. They were always blaming graveyard for something. How do you think I got here? Now, they pay me $10 an hour to just stand there.

Robert's quest for promotions and higher wages changed his worker-based subjectivity. He had begun internalizing the company's interests as his own.[16] Thus although he had started working at FlexTech as a line worker just a few months earlier, his rapid climb up the ladder—from temporary to permanent and from line worker to line lead—overshadowed his identification with other line workers. His desire for more secure and more mobile jobs in the context of limited job opportunities also strengthened the effects of internal labor market incentives.

In addition to the institutionalization of temporary-to-permanent employment and other possibilities for job mobility within the firm, FlexTech's internal labor market also offered monetary incentives—quarterly bonuses. The elaborate bonus system created material links between workers' interests and the firm's interests. Bonuses are graduated in terms of temporary/permanent distinction and job position on the hierarchical occupational ladder. Temporary workers can receive bonuses after three months. This allows the firm to pay workers $6 an hour as the base rate, with the possibility of averaging as much as $16 and hour after the quarterly bonus. Permanent workers receive higher bonuses than temporary workers (although the increase in their base wage is negligible and sometimes nothing), line leads make more than permanent assembly workers, supervisors more than line leads, and managers more than supervisors. Although temporary workers can receive quarterly bonuses, they cannot buy subsidized shares in the company's stocks. This is a benefit reserved for permanent workers. The possibility of moving up the occupational ladder also motivates workers to work harder and be more attentive to quality. Moving up means getting substantially more pay (a $3-an-hour raise versus a $0.50-an-hour raise) and having more responsibilities that are directly tied to the firm's interests.

Like the temporary-to-permanent employment policy, the amount of quarterly bonuses is tied to profitability of specific customer lines. The most profitable lines receive the highest total disbursement of bonuses. This type of reward system pits teams of workers in direct competition with each other. Workers from the OEM[1] line often asked workers from the OEM[2] line how many boards they had assembled for the night. Competition between lines also filters up between line leads and supervisors. I often heard Michael joke with Carl, a line lead from the OEM[1] project line. "I heard you passed a thousand boards the other night. Are you guys cheating?" he asked Carl as he pushed a cart by our line. "Hell, no, we didn't cheat. We have been working our asses off!" he retorted. "I don't believe you!" Michael exclaimed, although he himself had been working double shifts since graveyard production started. Qua, a technician on the OEM[2] line, explained that Michael and the OEM[2] team were working such rigorous overtime because they wanted to make productivity goals and earn bigger quarterly bonuses. During one period, the swing shift had been working extremely long hours. They had worked four straight Saturdays and stayed until 1:00 A.M. every night. Qua had also been working double shifts. His eyes were completely bloodshot, so I asked why he was so tired. He explained that he had been covering for Michael during the nights, so he could go home for a couple hours, sleep, and return before the day shift began. He then added, "Besides, we have to make 40 percent profit for the California side." Since I did not understand the meaning of his comment, I pressed him to explain:

> Our line is the only project and the only building that is making money right now. So, we [OEM²] have to cover everyone else in our building. OEM¹ is not making any money. [We have to cover for everyone because] even though there are a lot more OEM¹ workers, you have to make $280 per person to make a profit. We [OEM²] make more money per board. There are sixteen buildings here, and we are divided into hubs. Buildings A, B, and C are part of one of four hubs in California. Besides, the average bonus is $300 each quarter, but supervisors get more, sometimes $1600. That's why we work so hard. At least you guys [line workers] get overtime pay. Supervisors work for free. Each building wants a bigger bonus, so they sort of compete with one another about quality and profit. Each building even has their own budget and their own roster of workers.

Receiving bonuses meant getting an additional reward, something that was not part of a worker's base wages. Trinh, a young Vietnamese male, was listening to our conversation and asked if temporary workers also could get bonuses. Qua answered that temporary workers also could receive bonuses, but only after they had worked for at least three months. Trinh seemed excited by the news and told us that he hoped to become permanent soon.

The Organizational Culture

The drive for flexibility proliferates the risks involved in production. OEMs possess limited control over the actual production of their technological innovations. Because many layers of abstraction exist between the original product, the technological innovation developed by OEMs, and the worker who produced it, contract manufacturers compensate for additional risks by offering "total customer satisfaction." However, this added emphasis requires an additional component of labor control. Contract manufacturers need workers who will consent to the despotic conditions of production *and* deliver high-quality products. To ensure labor control, contract manufacturers expend their energy *transforming* workers into the kinds of employees who will deliver high-quality products under conditions of flexible despotism. To obtain such a workforce, they cultivate an organizational culture that reinforces the functions of their formal internal labor market. FlexTech also tries to generate a more company-based subjectivity for workers in two ways: (1) by appropriating the notion of "team concept" for the benefit of the "team manager" (i.e., the employer); and (2) by connecting workers' identities as consumers to the firm's identity as a service provider.

FlexTech constantly emphasizes that workers' survival is linked not only to their performance in the workplace but also to the firm's survival in the global market. Unlike subcontractors who elicit worker consent through ethnic and community particularities, FlexTech repeatedly tells workers that the vagaries and demands of an increasingly ruthless market affect all levels of industrial organization, from the stockholders to the line workers, through daily shift meetings that are divided by customer projects. My introduction to shop floor life at FlexTech essentially began during one of these shift meetings. There was no formal orientation; there were no welcoming words about joining FlexTech's "happy family." Instead I was greeted by stressful interrogations and castigating reproofs by Peter, who, I later learned, was the production manager for all the shifts operating in the building during a shift meeting. "Everybody needs to get here on time. Don't be late," Peter reprimanded us. Then he turned on the overhead projector and started lecturing everyone about productivity and quality. "We have good DPM [defects per machine] rates on this board. We're at 99.6. What does 99.6 tell us?" he asked. After a few tense moments of silence, Peter continued, "Nobody knows?" Then, he started writing on the overhead:

$$\text{"}04 = \frac{4}{100} = \frac{40}{1,000}.\text{"}$$

"Is that good?" he asked. Some people nodded. He said: "It's okay. But, it's still 40 out of 1,000 boards that go to the customer with defects. We have to do better. Would you be satisfied if you were the customer?" He began pinpointing individual workers and quizzing people. He held up a board: "Look at this board. It is ugly. I am embarrassed for this board. What should you do if you see this?" He waited for someone to answer. Then he turned to a touch-up worker on SMT and asked, "What should you do if you see a board come out of SMT like this?" This time, he did not wait for the answer. "If you see a board come down the line looking like this, you have the right to shut down the line. If you don't . . . "—he paused, and then pointed to another guy—"then you don't care about this guy's life." I heard a few people chuckle. But, Peter got serious again: "We cannot survive with this kind of quality. Quality is most important. More important than quantity, we have to start getting it right. When you are at a restaurant, how do you feel if you get beef when you order chicken? We cannot afford to make mistakes like this. Our survival depends on it."

Although no one had explained to me that we would begin each shift with a meeting, on my first night of work I quickly learned that Peter was leading a daily ritual: production meetings, divided by OEM project lines, designed to underscore the importance of quality, productivity, customer satisfaction, and most importantly, collective survival. None of us could afford to make mistakes because we were told that each employee's survival at FlexTech depended on producing high-quality products. If the quality slipped, FlexTech could lose their customer contract, which would most likely result in lost contracts and lost jobs for all employees. The notion of job survival became synonymous with performance quality, which became synonymous with the larger mission: collective survival in a highly volatile and fiercely competitive global market.

To buffer their need for high-quality products, FlexTech made explicit parallels between their interests as service providers and workers' interests as service recipients. During one meeting, Michael emphasized the connections between our subjectivities as workers and as consumers:

Quality is very important. When you get a paycheck and you want to buy a TV or VCR, what kind do you buy? [Someone said, Sony."] Cause it's popular . . . right? Because of the name. You trust the name. You like the clear picture. What happens if you buy a Sony TV and you bring it home and it doesn't work. . . . You're pissed . . . right? You're not going to buy Sony again. OEM[1] makes laptops. Maybe later, you will buy the same computer you make. Maybe you will buy it for your kids. You want good quality. You don't want to buy a broken one, same thing with us. We want good quality. We want to keep our customers.

Appealing to workers' subjectivities as consumers replaces a sense of shared subjectivity along work lines to their broad common interests as consumers. It also shifts the focus away from workers' diverse ethnic and community backgrounds to a more universal team-based atmosphere.

The production of high-quality products for consumers is emphasized through the "team concept." Even though the workforce consists of a mixture of temporary and permanent employees from highly diverse cultural and linguistic backgrounds, everyone is part of the FlexTech team. A policy based on worker consent versus direct coercion is critical to the effectiveness of the team concept. Supervisors are reprimanded if they engage in abusive and arbitrary labor practices such as intimidation and dismissal threats. Promoting a team-based model means cultivating an internal value system that encourages workers' to identify with the values of good sportsmanship.

Part of the rules for teamwork meant no ethnic favoritism. Workers who do not already possess a minimal understanding of English are already weeded out during the formal recruiting process, but most FlexTech workers are connected to each through informal neighborhood, familial, or ethnic networks. Michael encouraged workers to let him know if they had a friend or cousin who needed a job, but, as he explained during a shift meeting:

> Today, I had to let someone go from my swing shift. He had been working here a month. Every time I gave him feedback, he didn't really listen. He kept making mistakes, so I had to let him go. I want to be fair and give him another chance, but he wasn't working out. [He paused and explained:] I'm Chinese Vietnamese. I don't speak Chinese. I only speak Vietnamese. On the line, you hear me speak Vietnamese to other workers. Some people think I favor them if you speak my language. They think I give better treatment. But, he speaks my language. I still let him go. Sure, we're friends outside of work, but in here, it's business. . . . It doesn't matter if you speak my language or if you don't. I treat everyone equally.

Thus, unlike the favoritism that owners and supervisors gave to workers of the same ethnic background in subcontracting regimes, management condemned the use of ethnic favoritism on FlexTech's team. Ethnic and racial ties could cause team strife. Instead, FlexTech promoted the importance of the generic hard-working employee.

The representation of generic criteria for work performance masked the exercise of power over workers according to specific lines of difference. During a shift meeting Michael officially told the rest of the line workers that he had fired Sabrina, a Latina in her early thirties, because she did not accept the feedback she received. However, Sabrina hadn't fit the image of a "good" team member before her very first day on the OEM[2] line. After being sexually harassed by her supervisor in another building, she requested and received a transfer. Although Michael did not know why she had been transferred when she arrived, he suspected that she had been a "problem" worker. He was also pressured by his supervisor to get rid of Sabrina:

You know Sabrina, she had long fingernails. I didn't want to let her go, but she was too slow. I told her the first day that she had to cut her fingernails, but she didn't listen. She couldn't pick up washers and screws. My boss . . . Peter . . . even kept pressuring me. He wanted to let her go the first night. He asked me; "She's still here. Why? Let her go." I didn't want to let her go, but she also took long breaks. It's OK if you come in late once, but she took one hour a few too many times.

Although Michael told us that he was understanding when workers came back a little late from breaks as long as we still reached our output goal, when Sabrina did this, Michael used it as an "objective criterion" to justify her termination.

Conclusion: Two Faces of Flexible Despotism

The drive for flexibility has generated two faces of flexible despotism: subcontracting regimes and contract manufacturing regimes. Workers' experiences in despotic conditions of production, such as instant layoffs, compulsory overtime, and production shutdowns, are all facets of flexible despotism, yet they are mediated by the specific characteristics of flexible production.

In subcontracting regimes production is labor-intensive and organized according to unit assembly. Because capital costs are low and competition among subcontractors is fierce, the regularity of work depends mainly on the employers' ability to obtain and retain production contracts. Subcontracting regimes operate informal labor markets that promote individual competition between workers. Most of management's energy is directed toward recruiting specific kinds of workers. A greater emphasis on recruitment rather than training provides the material base upon which employers are able to generate shared connections between workers' interests and their own interests. Since employers often rely on ethnic and community networks to recruit workers, they build upon these networks to create subcontracting organizational cultures that emphasize workers' and management's common membership in a particular ethnic community. They also highlight the personal favors they bestow upon workers who are struggling to adjust to the difficult circumstances of immigrant life in the United States. In this context, workers agree to work overtime, consent to unpredictable changes in work schedules, intensify their own working conditions, and monitor their co-workers, all in the interests of management.

In contract manufacturing regimes, production is extremely capital-intensive and takes place on highly automated, technologically advanced SMT assembly lines. Advanced technology in production is coupled with flexible manufacturing tactics, which dictate the terms of daily production for workers. In addition, the emphasis on customer satisfaction and the role of the customer in employer-employee relationships shapes the reorganization of production into customer-specific assembly lines and work teams. This approach creates a much more formal and bureaucratic internal labor market in which the basis for individual promotion (from temporary to permanent and from line worker to line lead to supervisor) and for quarterly bonuses is measured by group productivity. This reinforces workers' identification with customer-specific work teams and replaces individual competition with intrafirm group competition. Their emphasis on team-based performance is strengthened by the cultivation of contract manufacturing organizational cultures. They frown upon ethnic favoritism and repressive control tactics. Instead, they cloak their labor control tactics behind the rationality of high productivity and profitability. To forge close ties between workers' and management's interests, they emphasize workers' subjectivities as consumers and highlight the "impersonal" nature of the current climate of fierce global competition.

The emergence of subcontracting and contract manufacturing regimes reveals that flexible despotic regimes do not simply have one generic face. Coordinating worker consent to coercive labor conditions is not particular to the lives of highly exploitable immigrant women of color toiling in high-tech sweatshops. It also happens in today's sleek, technologically advanced high performance workplaces. Workers' conditions of extreme dependence on employers make them intimately vulnerable to the daily twists and turns of flexible production. The implementation of flexibility in more and more aspects of day-to-day production leaves very little space for workers to effectively contest the encroachment of flexibility in their daily work lives. Discursive managerial strategies reinforce workers' general experience of insecurity in the labor market and in larger social arenas. The general trend toward contract manufacturing regimes is especially insidious because it masks the systematic coordination of worker consent to the coercive demands of flexible production in a neatly packaged, technologically sophisticated, and extremely organized face.

Notes

1. However, no empirical work demonstrates that flexibility directly translates into increased productivity. Fernando Suarez, Michael Cusamano, and Chris Fine (1995) studied printed circuit board (PCB) manufacturing firms and found that flexibility actually has uneven effects on productivity.

2. Shoshana Zuboff (1984) is somewhat more skeptical of the wholesale benefits of information technology for workers. She views information technology as being able both to automate tasks and increase deskilling in addition to producing new information. This creates a duality: technology that either intensifies the division of conception from execution (Braverman 1974) or creates new "intellective" possibilities for workers (Zuboff 1984).

3. Mauro Guillén (1994. 291–294) explains that the lean production system and total quality management principles, two types of flexible workplace systems, operate on a seemingly visionary ideology: "A better world for everyone involved: the consumer gets low prices, variety, and quality; the worker can enjoy job security, satisfaction, challenging tasks, and even higher wages; the engineer can stretch her imagination to develop new designs and production processes; the manager can enjoy the challenges of being responsive to the customer and playing the global competitive game; and the economy benefits from the counter-cyclical mechanism built into the zero-inventory system."

4. Harley Shaiken, Stephen Herzenberg, and Sarah Kuhn (1986) argue that employers cultivated of an "ideology of competition" that persuaded workers to align themselves with management's desire to retain national competitiveness. Labor-management cooperation strategies were also facilitated by union cooperation. Unions similarly appealed to notions of national competition to convince workers to accept flexibility. Ultimately, labor-management cooperation undermined workers' potential threats to retaliate against the continued imposition of flexibility in work processes, manufacturing systems, and employment relationships.

5. New, democratic workplace principles such as the "team concept" simply coordinate line workers to be in sync with the rigorous demands of flexible production systems by exposing those workers who are the "weak links" on the lines (Parker 1996).

6. As the drive for capital accumulation expanded on a global scale, Karl Marx (1977, 581) argued, the factory system's tremendous capacity for expanding with sudden immense leaps, and its dependence on the world market, necessarily gives rise to the following cycle: feverish production, a consequent glut on the market, then a contraction of the market, which causes production to be crippled. The life of industry becomes a series of periods of moderate activity, prosperity, over-production, crisis, and stagnation. The uncertainty and instability to which machinery subjects the employment, and consequently the living conditions, of the workers become a normal state of affairs, owing to these periodic turns of the industrial cycle.

7. In this respect, flexible despotism is theoretically similar to Burawoy's (1985, 127) notion of hegemonic despotism, a period in which production regimes are able to turn hegemonic regimes against workers by coordinating their consent to despotism. However, I emphasize the importance of theorizing flexibility in current modes of industrial domination.

8. Cho also worked at Microtek, a subsidiary of Asahi International a Japanese multinational company. Although Microtek specializes primarily in research and development, it runs an assembly line for prototype production. It is more highly automated than the production lines at Chinotech or Hantronics, yet it still requires manual assembly for approximately half of its production needs. But for the purposes of this comparison, I am looking specifically at subcontracting enterprises.

9. The empirical evidence is somewhat uneven. Cho's study focuses primarily on how capitalist relations of production are affected by the state of capital mobility and industrial restructuring. Park's theoretical questions specifically address the growing significance of race and ethnicity in a globally restructuring regional economy. Yet because each study refers specifically to Asian-ethnic-owned subcontracting firms and their workforces, they provide empirical data for questions concerning the relationship between flexible production and flexible workers.

10. These straps ensure that electric currents that run through the human body do not corrupt the boards.

11. Once I asked a technician who officially worked the swing shift why he worked all night. He always looked overworked—his eyes were constantly bloodshot and he could barely keep them open—and I often asked him why he didn't stay home and rest or spend some time out in the sunshine. He curtly responded, "If you had been through what I had been through, you would understand. I work this hard to keep from remembering my past." He was an ethnic Chinese refugee from Vietnam who came to the United States during his late childhood.

12. Despite the image of the Silicon Valley as a "clean" industry, occupational health and safety issues still plague workers' day-to-day lives. Injuries such as loss of eyesight, nausea, and repetitive stress injury are the most commonly identified work-related health problems.

Industrial restructuring makes the period of testing required to prove health consequences of toxic chemicals extremely difficult.

13. My thanks extend to Boy Luethje, who gave me the tip about the FlexTech staffing site.

14. Several months prior, the graveyard shift had been shut down because of low productivity. However, the enormous success of the day and swing shifts for the OEM^2 project brought an increase in customer demand. Subsequently, FlexTech decided to try to run a graveyard shift again.

15. The trend toward the institutionalization of temporary-to-permanent employment signals a new type of labor control associated with the drive for flexibility. Today discussions regarding labor and the global economy focus on the steady elimination of industrial work and the shift toward a more service-oriented economy. Yet as more and more temporary workers are hired to perform industrial work, the specific experiences of industrial workers are being subsumed under the category of "service-oriented" employment. Much of the literature on flexible labor, particularly on the rise of temporary workers, focuses exclusively on the financial benefits of outsourcing labor needs for employers. Employers hire workers for short periods and successfully avoid providing benefits, job security, and job mobility (Benner 1996a; Carnoy, Castells, and Benner 1997; Smith 1997). But seeing the increasing reliance on temporary workers solely as a way for employers to reduce costs and minimize responsibility limits our understanding of today's use of temporary employment.

16. According to Richard Edwards (1979, 150), this is the most sophisticated type of control in a bureaucratic firm's reward structure, and "grows out of incentives for workers to identify themselves with the enterprise, to be loyal, committed, and thus self-directed or self-controlled."

References

Appelbaum, Richard. 1996. "Multiculturalism and Flexibility: Some New Directions in Global Capitalism." Pp. 297–316 in *Mapping Multiculturalism,* edited by A. Gordon and C. Newfield. Minneapolis and London: University of Minnesota Press.

Benner, Chris. 1996a. *Shock Absorbers in the Flexible Economy: The Rise of Contingent Employment in Silicon Valley.* San Jose: Working Partnerships USA.

———. 1996b. "Win the Lottery or Organize: Economic Restructuring and Union Organizing in Silicon Valley." Working Paper 5:48 (February). Berkeley: Center for German and European Studies, University of California, Berkeley.

Bookman, Ann, and Sandra Morgen, eds. 1988. *Women and the Politics of Empowerment.* Philadelphia: Temple University Press.

Braverman, Harry. 1974. *Labor and Monopoly Capital: The Degradation of Work in the Twentieth Century.* New York: Monthly Review Press.

Brenner, Chris, Bob Brownstein, and Amy Dean. 1999. "Negotiating the Lifelong Tightrope: Negotiating Working the New Economy. A Status Report on Social and Economic Well-Being in the State of California." San Jose: Working Partnership U.S.A.

Bronson, Po. 1998. "Is the Revolution Over? Report from Ground Zero: Silicon Valley." *WIRED,* January: 1–14.

Burawoy, Michael. 1985. The *Politics of Production: Factory Regimes Under Capitalism and Socialism.* London: Verso.

Carnoy, Martin, Manuel Castells, and Chris Benner. 1997. "Flexible Employment in Silicon Valley." *International Labour Review,* 136 (Spring): 27–48.

Castells, Manuel. 1996. *The Rise of the Network Society*. Cambridge, MA: Blackwell.

Cho, Soon-Kyoung. 1987. "How Cheap Is 'Cheap Labor'? The Dilemmas of Export-Led Industrialization." Ph.D. dissertation, University of California, Berkeley.

Edwards, Richard. 1979. *Contested Terrain: The Transformation of the Workplace in the Twentieth Century*. New York: Basic Books.

Gordon, David. 1996. *Fat and Mean: The Corporate Squeeze of Working Americans and the Myth of Managerial Downsizing*. New York: Free Press.

Guillén, Mauro. 1994. *Models of Management: Work, Authority, and Organization in a Comparative Perspective*. Chicago: University of Chicago Press.

Harrison, Bennett. 1994. *Lean and Mean*. New York: Basic Books.

Hossfeld, Karen. 1988. "Divisions of Labor: Immigrant Women Workers in Silicon Valley." Ph.D. dissertation, Department of Sociology, University of California, Santa Cruz.

———. 1990. "Their Logic Against Them: Contradictions in Sex, Race, and Class in Silicon Valley." Pp. 149–179 in *Women Workers and Global Restructuring*, edited by Kathryn Ward. Ithaca: ILR Press.

———. 1991. "Why Aren't High-Tech Workers Organized?" In *Common Interests: Women Organizing in Global Electronics*, edited by Women Working Worldwide. London: Women Working Worldwide.

———. 1994. "Hiring Immigrant Women: Silicon Valley's Simple Formula." Pp. 65–94 in *Women of Color in U.S. Society*, edited by M.B. Zinn and B.T. Dill. Philadelphia: Temple University Press.

Leidner, Robin. 1993. *Fast Food, Fast Talk: Service Work and the Routinization of Everyday Life*. Berkeley: University of California Press.

Levy, David L. 1997. "Lean Production in an International Supply Chain." *Sloan Management Review*, 38(2): 94–102.

Luethje, Boy. 1997. "Industrial Restructuring, Production Networks, and Labor Relations in the Silicon Valley Electronics Industry." Unpublished paper, Institute for the Study of Social Change, University of California, Berkeley.

Marx, Karl. 1976. *Capital*. New York: Penguin.

"The New Work Order." 1994. *The Economist*, February 9, p. 76.

Olmstead, Barney, and Suzanne Smith. 1997. *Managing the Flexible Workplace*. New York: Amacom.

Park, Edward. 1992. "Asian Americans in Silicon Valley: Race and Ethnicity in the Postindustrial Economy." Ph.D. dissertation, Department of Ethnic Studies, University of California, Berkeley.

Parker, Michael. 1996. "Industrial Relations Myth and Shop-Floor Reality: The 'Team Concept' in the Auto Industry." Pp. 249–274 in *Industrial Democracy in America: The Ambiguous Promise*, edited by N. Lichtenstein and H. J. Harris. New York: Cambridge University Press.

Parker, Michael, and Jane Slaughter. 1993. "Unions and Management-by-Stress." Pp. 41–53 in *Lean Work: Empowerment and Exploitation in the Global Auto Industry*, edited by Steve Babson. Detroit: Wayne State University Press.

Piore, Michael, and Charles Sabel. 1984. *The Second Industrial Divide: Possibilities for Prosperity*. New York: Basic Books.

Saxenian, AnnaLee. 1994. *Regional Advantage: Culture and Competition in Silicon Valley and Route 128*. Cambridge and London: Harvard University Press.

Shaiken, Harley, Stephen Herzenberg, and Sarah Kuhn. 1986. "The Work Process Under More Flexible Production." *Industrial Relations*, 25 (Spring): 167–183.

Smith, Vicki. 1997. "The Fractured World of the Temporary Worker: Cooperation and Ambivalence in a High-Tech Manufacturing Setting." Unpublished paper, Department of Sociology, University of California, Davis.

Suarez, Fernando, Michael Cusumano, and Charles Fine. 1995. "An Empirical Study of Flexibility in Manufacturing." *Sloan Management Review*, 37 (1): 25–32.

Taplin, Ian M. 1996. "Rethinking Flexibility: The Case of the Apparel Industry." *Review of Social Economy*, 54 (June): 191–220.

Womack, James, Daniel Jones, and Daniel Roos. 1990. *The Machine That Changed the World*. New York: Macmillan.

Zuboff, Shoshana. 1998. *In the Age of the Smart Machine: The Future of Work and Power*. New York: Basic Books.

CHAPTER 7

The Challenge of Organizing in a Globalized/Flexible Industry: The Case of the Apparel Industry in Los Angeles

Edna Bonacich

The apparel industry combines some of the most backward production methods with some of the most advanced techniques of labor control in the "new world order" of post–"monopoly capitalism."[1] While basic production still depends on a worker, usually a woman, sitting at a sewing machine, because of advances in computer technology and containerized shipping, the industry has been able to engage in global production to an unprecedented degree. "Globaloney" may apply to some industries, but not to apparel. Garment manufacturers (and retailers) are able to shift production from one region or country to the next in order to seek out the best deal, including, importantly, the lowest labor standards in the world. Since they usually engage in arm's-length transactions, such as contracting and licensing, the level of globalization in this industry cannot be captured by investment figures or data on subsidiary ownership. The lack of fixed capital investment in offshore production increases the ease of mobility of the industry.

Apparel firms contract out labor not only offshore but also locally. The contracting system enables them to maximize "flexibility." Because sectors of the industry, especially women's outerwear, are driven by fashion, they are very risky. Apparel manufacturers are able to externalize the risk by only employing labor as it is needed. Contracting out the labor pushes the risk of production fluctuations onto the contractors, and ultimately onto the garment workers. They are the ones who must bear the instabilities of a boom and bust industry.

In this Chapter I shall describe the system of apparel production in Los Angeles, considering it to be a paradigmatic example of global/flexible production. I shall then briefly ask whether the labor process, as it is found in this industry, represents a return to pre–monopoly capitalist production methods or a new type of post–monopoly capitalist labor regime. Finally, I shall turn to the challenge of organizing workers in this system of global/flexible production (Bonacich 2000, Bonacich and Appelbaum 2000).[2]

The Los Angeles Apparel Industry

The apparel industry in the United States is declining. Every month new reports come out enumerating the loss of jobs, while parallel numbers report the monthly rise in imports. In 1970 the United States only imported $1 billion of clothing. By 1996, of the $95 billion of clothing sold at the wholesale level in the United States, 57 percent was imports (American Apparel Manufacturers Association 1997, 4). Meanwhile U.S. apparel jobs declined from 1.4 million in 1973 to about 800,000 today.

Los Angeles is the one exception to this pattern. Between 1993 and 1997 the LA apparel industry added an estimated 26,000 new jobs (Kyser 1997) and is now the largest apparel employer in the United States. As of December 1997, the industry officially employed 120,600 people, up from 115,300 the previous December. Since there is a large underground economy, the real numbers may be as much as 25 percent higher, making the apparel industry the largest manufacturing employer in LA County.

Why is Los Angeles different from the rest of the country? There are a number of interrelated reasons. The LA apparel industry specializes in the fashion-sensitive women's outerwear sector. Indeed, about one-quarter of all the women's wear made in the United States is now produced in LA. Los Angeles is a fashion center in part because of the presence of the entertainment industry, and in part because of the climate and mystique of "California." As a consequence of the volatility and riskiness of fashion, garment production typically requires the quick sewing of small lots. Local production saves time, and enables greater quality control over constantly changing designs. Moreover, LA has a growing textile industry which enhances the ability to design and produce the clothes quickly.

The character of the local population also encourages garment production in Los Angeles. The city is a center of immigration. Some immigrants come with capital and experience, and they become entrepreneurs in the low-capital garment-contracting business. Others are impoverished and some lack legal documents, and they come to LA seeking work. Garment shops are eager to employ them as a low-wage workforce that the employers hope and expect will be docile. Although the low cost of labor in Los Angeles cannot compete head-on with the wages paid in Mexico or China, its low level relative to the rest of the United States, combined with the other features of the local industry, continue to make Los Angeles an attractive garment production site.

Not all LA apparel manufacturers do their production in Los Angeles. Some have almost all of their clothing produced offshore, while others outsource part of their production. Even if they do produce their garments in Los Angeles, few manufacturers do their own production in-house. They instead make use of contractors, often a fair number of them. There are literally thousands of garment contractors in Los Angeles, spread out across the basin. Most contractors are small businesses, employing an average of 35 workers, but some have over 100 workers and a few range up to 1,000 employees. These firms are typically assembly plants where workers sit at sewing machines and stitch together the cut materials that make up garments.

The contracting system is also a critical aspect of the retention of the industry in Los Angeles. Some regions of the country, notably the South, have large factories that mass-produce standard items. These kinds of factories are not easily adaptable to the production of fashion. Small contracting shops are found in New York and San Francisco, which also produce fashion. But LA has more such shops than anywhere else. Indeed, one can claim that LA has the most advanced system of "flexible production" in apparel manufacturing in the country.

Even though LA garment employment has grown in recent years, there is no guarantee that growth will continue. Industry leaders keep threatening to move production to Mexico, and, since the passage of NAFTA in 1994, there are indications that many have moved at least part of their production there. So far Mexico does not have the capacity to make small lots of highly fashion-sensitive garments sufficiently quickly, but the day may come when Mexican firms can replicate LA firms and more of the industry moves there.

The Benefits of the Contracting System to Manufacturers

The contracting system is touted by manufacturers for the flexibility it provides. Apparel manufacturing is unstable, since it is affected both by seasons and by shifts in fashion. The contracting system enables manufacturers to have work done only when they need it, thereby avoiding the need to maintain a stable labor force that they do not need year-round. The contractors are able to absorb the changing demands of the industry, shifting their work among different manufacturers in an effort to keep their factories running at full capacity.

But there is another side to the contracting system: it also serves as a very effective labor-control mechanism. The contractors typically oversee the sewing or assembly. Some contractors specialize in cutting, laundering, or finishing, but the majority are assembly plants. By contracting out, the manufacturers externalize the labor. The manufacturers never lose title to the goods that the contractors sew; they do not *sell* the cut goods to the contractors. Instead, the contractors supply only the labor. They are essentially labor contractors.

As noted, most contractors are small businesses. They are typically run by immigrant entrepreneurs who do not have much capital. Manufacturers are able to pit contractors against one another as they underbid each other to get the work. Contractors are typically offered a price for the work on a "take it or leave it" basis, because the manufacturer can always find another contractor who would be willing to do the work for less.

The small size and dispersion of apparel contracting firms in Los Angeles also mean that they can fairly easily evade state inspection. The number of state inspectors does not remotely come close to the number that would be needed to police the industry systematically. Moreover, even when firms are caught with violations, they can go out of business and open again in a new location, under a new name.

The contracting system enables labor costs to be kept at rock-bottom levels. Meanwhile, manufacturers can deny any responsibility for conditions in their contractors' factories because they are "independent" businesses. They can place all the blame for conditions in these shops on the contractors, turning a blind eye to the fact that they set the low prices within which the contractors must operate. The fictional aspect of this claim is evident in the fact that manufacturers often send quality-control people to the contractors on a daily basis, and keep a tight control over every aspect of production *except* labor standards.

Another way that contracting serves as a labor control system is by inhibiting unionization. The work of a particular manufacturer is spread out over a number of factories. The workers in each of the factories do not even know of each other's existence. Indeed, since manufacturers are very secretive about the identity of their contractors, even the contractors may not know who else works for "their" manufacturers. The inability to identify and locate one's fellow workers makes organizing extremely difficult, a problem that is exacerbated by the manufacturer's ability to shift production from one contractor to the next. Thus, even if you can find your fellow workers, they may not remain your fellow workers for long. Or you may find that the labels you used to sew no longer are being made in your factory.

Another dilemma for workers is that, given the low margins in the contracting shops, even if they should win a union struggle, it would be very difficult to get the contractor to pay higher wages. Moreover, the very act of trying to organize a factory is likely to lead the manufacturer to shift production away from that factory, a fact that contractors do not hesitate to point out to their employees. Worker militancy at the contractor level ends up being self-defeating, because manufacturers will boycott that contractor, and the workers will lose their jobs. This situation leads contractors to be fiercely anti-union, and it serves as a major inhibitor of worker militancy. The mobility of the industry, not just offshore but, more importantly, within Los Angeles, is a deadly club that can be wielded against worker organizing.

Workers are more likely to be successful if all the workers employed by contractors who work for the same manufacturer are able to find common cause. In other words, workers need to organize the entire production system of a single manufacturer simultaneously if they are to have any chance of success. Only then can they demand that the *manufacturer* face the demands for higher wages and benefits, since it is the manufacturer who profits most from their labor and who has accumulated the surplus from which increases could be drawn. And only then can they insist that the manufacturer not shift production away from unionized shops. But the dispersion of the workforce into multiple, shifting, small factories makes coordination extremely difficult. The contracting system is a well-honed, anti-union device.

The Workforce

Los Angeles's garment workers are almost uniformly immigrants. The majority are Latino, from Mexico and Central America, especially El Salvador and Guatemala. About 10 percent are Asian, mainly from China and Southeast Asia, including Vietnam, Cambodia, and Thailand. The largest group is Mexican. There are clear linkages between the movement of capital offshore and the employment of immigrant workers in the United States. First, the penetration of foreign capital, accompanied by the imposition of neoliberal policies, creates a displaced population that finds it necessary to emigrate for sheer survival. Second, the low wages associated with global production create competition for U.S. producers, who seek the lowest-wage local labor force they can find. Immigrants fit the bill, in part because of their desperation for work, and in part because of their legal status. The result is that garment workers tend to be of the same ethnicities: Mexican, Central American, Chinese, and the like, regardless of whether they are employed in their homelands or in the United States.

A large, unknown number of LA garment workers are undocumented, without papers that legitimize their right to work in the United States. Clearly there is an imbalance in a process of globalization that allows capital to scour the world for the lowest price of labor, but puts severe restrictions on the mobility of labor to seek out the best-paying jobs. Stacking the "free market" in favor of capital and against labor obviously serves as a damper on wages and working conditions everywhere. The garment industry, along with domestic service, construction, agriculture, and, to a lesser extent, the hotel and restaurant business, is a major employer of undocumented workers. Undocumented immigrants are obviously especially vulnerable to exploitation, and their vulnerability is exacerbated in times of public, anti-immigrant fervor. Not only do they not have any of the usual legal recourse of citizens and permanent residents, but they are threatened with the possibility of exposure and deportation.

The majority of garment workers in Los Angeles are women—about 70 percent, according to the 1990 Census. Unlike the workers in the *maquiladoras* of Mexico and the Caribbean, LA's female labor force is not composed of teenagers. They are mainly young women in their twenties and thirties. Many are mothers, and some are the sole supporters of their families. The number of men working at sewing machines has grown in the last decade, probably as a consequence of growing anti-immigrant sentiment and policies in California. As the crackdown on illegal immigration is stepped up, more immigrants are driven to take whatever jobs they can find. The garment industry remains a willing employer of the undocumented. The fact that most garment workers are women adds to the likelihood that they will face domination of various types by their employers.

Conditions in the Shops

There is some variation in the conditions in the garment contracting shops of Los Angeles, but overall conditions are remarkably similar. Garment workers typically work on piece rate, that is, they are paid for each procedure they complete. This is similar to the pay system in agriculture, where farmworkers are paid for the number of pounds they pick. Garment workers are *contingent* labor, which means that they are employed and paid only when their work is needed. If there is no work, they are sent home, or sit around without pay until work arrives. While this arrangement obviously maximizes efficiency and flexibility from the point of view of the manufacturers, it creates great insecurity among the workers. They have no job security from day to day. All the risks associated with fashion and seasons trickle down the system and settle on their shoulders.

Both California and federal laws require that workers be paid minimum wage and overtime, even if they are paid a piece rate. The employer needs to keep time cards and ensure that the hourly minimum wage is covered, and that, when employees work over forty hours a week they must be paid one-and-a-half times their base wage. These regulations are *routinely* violated. Contractors want to pay only the flat piece rate, and they devise every trick in the book to hide the fact that that is what they are doing. They falsify the records, they maintain double books, they use double time cards, they cook up schemes so that overtime is calculated after the fact, they clock out workers after eight hours and pay them in cash thereafter, they have them work off the books on Saturdays, they encourage off-the-books homework, they get workers to kick back excess earnings in cash, and so forth. Thus minimum wage and overtime violations are extremely common in this industry. Using the 1990 Census figures, we calculated that the average garment industry operative in LA earned $7,200 a year, well below the minimum wage of $8,840 for a full-time, year-round worker at the time. Even when workers are paid the legal minimum, garment workers remain among the lowest-paid workers in Los Angeles, and make up an important segment of the working poor.

A baseline survey of sixty-nine California garment firms was conducted in 1994 by California and federal labor enforcement agencies. They found that 61 percent of Southern California garment firms failed to pay minimum wage and that 78 percent failed to pay overtime. In addition, 74 percent had recordkeeping violations and 41 percent paid workers in cash (Targeted Industries Partnership Program 1996, 18). While subsequent surveys have found some diminution in some of these statistics, other areas show an increase in violations. The fact is that violations of the law remain at an excessively high level.

The piece-work system encourages self-exploitation, as workers work very fast and for as many hours as possible in order to make a living. It creates the illusion that workers control their earnings by their own skill level, and makes it difficult for them to feel a sense of common exploitation. The illusion of control is occasionally shattered, when workers are shifted to new tasks and find that their earning levels collapse, or when the contractor lowers the piece rate in a cost-cutting move. These kinds of actions are likely to trigger angry reactions on the part of workers, who feel that the rug has been pulled out from under them.

Homework is a fairly common feature in the LA apparel industry. Some work at home full-time, while others only take work home after hours. While homework may sometimes be attractive to women, who combine work with child care, it is typically associated with the lowest pay when all the workers' costs are added in (Fregoso 1988). Furthermore, none of the usual protections of minimum wage and overtime pay can be ensured because of the underground character of the work.

Garment workers rarely receive any fringe benefits whatsoever. They are typically not given paid vacations or paid sick leave. Medical insurance is virtually nonexistent for the workers themselves and out of the question for their families. In other words, the system is geared toward paying workers their piece rate, and that is that. Thus by not paying for the health care coverage of the workers in their contracting shops, manufacturers, who can own a very profitable enterprise and be very rich themselves, force their workers to rely on the impoverished LA County health care system. Once again, the contracting system, by creating a false distance between the employer and the workers, enables the manufacturer to avoid taking responsibility and forces the taxpayers to pick up what should rightfully be a tab that the owner pays.

Apart from poverty-level wages, garment workers are also subject to other forms of abuse. Since garment-contracting shops are small businesses, they lack bureaucratic rules and are subject to the direct authority of the owner and supervisors. This authority can easily be conducted in an arbitrary fashion, with favoritism and discrimination. Workers who are not favored can be given older, less efficient machines, or can be denied work. They can also be subjected to personal abuse of all kinds, from yelling to sexual harassment. Workers will sometimes say that they can bear the harsh burden of low wages, but cannot endure being treated in an insulting and demeaning manner.

In addition, many garment factories in Los Angeles have serious health and safety violations. In a recent sweep it was found that 96 percent of factories violated the law and that 72 percent had serious violations that could result in injury or death (Targeted Industries Partnership Program 1996). The violations included such things as blocked fire exits, exposed wires, and machines without safety guards. Many of the garment shops of LA could turn into death traps in the event of a fire.

Although I have stressed the role of piece rate in the domination of garment workers, it is not clear that putting an end to this system would ameliorate conditions in the industry. Employers are skillful at developing alternative ways to squeeze workers when they are highly motivated. Thus intense quotas can be introduced as another mechanism for extracting the maximum amount of labor from workers. Indeed, quotas take the place of piece rate in most *maquila* factories without alleviating the oppression of the workers.

The Return of Sweatshops

We are in an era in which many government officials and others speak of a return of the sweatshop (U.S. General Accounting Office 1988, 1994; Ross 1997). In the United States, garment industry sweatshops were more or less eradicated by a combination of the development of powerful garment worker unions and the New Deal, which provided support for basic labor standards. However, since the 1970s, and especially during the 1980s and 1990s, we have seen an erosion of wages and working conditions in the U.S. apparel industry. In 1950, average weekly wages of U.S. garment workers were 76.5 percent of the average manufacturing wage. By 1996, this figure had dropped to 55.3 percent. In women's outerwear, the ratio dropped from 87.3 in 1950 to 50.6 in 1996 (American Apparel Manufacturing Association 1997, 19).

Why are we seeing the return of sweatshops now? There are many reasons. Globalization certainly plays a critical role. Since apparel manufacturers and retailers can move—or threaten to move—offshore, they force local workers to face the grim choice of accepting the jobs as they are or losing the jobs altogether. Manufacturers and retailers can argue that they can get the work done offshore for a fraction of the price that they pay in Los Angeles. Any improvement in wages and working conditions is interpreted as a threat to the continuation of the industry in LA.

Globalization can also be seen as part of a larger set of trends that have led to the return of sweatshops, including the decline of the welfare state and the attack on the labor movement.[3] In general, we have been witnessing an effort on the part of big business to enhance its power and to undermine the power of labor. Workers in the United States (and in other industrial nations) have gradually been stripped of the protections they were able to win in the New Deal era. Various public programs and social assistance have eroded, and real wages have fallen. Meanwhile, business owners, along with the managers and professionals whom they employ, have grown richer and richer. The gap between rich and poor has grown wider. Los Angeles shows these trends even more starkly than the rest of the United States.

The first blast of attack against the labor movement occurred when Ronald Reagan became president and broke the air traffic controllers' strike. Since then, unions have faced the erosion of the legal environment that had been developed to protect workers' rights to organize during the New Deal. Unfair labor practices on the part of employers have become more flagrant as they have learned that the cost of union-busting is minor compared to the cost of having to negotiate a union contract.

Another factor in the growth of garment sweatshops has been the consolidation of retailing. Since the mid-1980s there has been a major merger movement in retailing, as giant retailers have bought each other out, assuming huge debt in the process. Some retailers have gone bankrupt. Others have become billion-dollar giants who can exercise tremendous power over the industry. The United States has far too many stores per consumer, resulting in vicious competition. The retailers now have the power to pressure manufacturers to cut costs, change styles more rapidly, and maintain more inventory (Bird and Bounds 1997). Many retailers themselves now have their own private (or store) label, for which they employ their own contractors directly, bypassing the manufacturers altogether. They undercut the major brands, putting price pressure on them. All of this puts pressure down the line of the garment food chain, and the people most affected are the workers, both in the United States and elsewhere.

Although firms claim they must cut costs to remain competitive, the cost-cutting knife is rarely applied to the owners, managers, and professionals. Executive salaries, advertising costs, profits, and similar rewards that go to the nonlabor part of apparel production are allowed to soar with no outcry that these costs must be kept in check. The largest apparel manufacturers in Los Angeles are multimillionaires. For example, six of the one hundred highest-paid executives in Los Angeles are in the apparel industry, and five of them work for one company: Guess? Inc. (Sullivan 1997). Maurice Marciano, CEO of Guess, received $3.4 million in salary and bonus in 1996. It is estimated that the three Marciano brothers, who own most of the company, personally took home over $400 million between 1992 and 1996, including salaries, bonuses, distributions to stockholders, and the results of an initial public offering.

Ethnicity

In Los Angeles, the apparel industry is structured along ethnic lines. The manufacturers are, for the most part, European in origin, although some are Middle Eastern and Asian. Jews play an important role at this level and, while some are immigrants, many are American-born. The contractors, in contrast, are almost all immigrants, as stated. They are from all over the world, but the plurality are Asian. Although Koreans are not numerically the most important, they run some of the largest shops and are very visible in the garment district.

The workers, as we have seen, are predominantly Latino immigrants. While there are some Latino contractors, the predominant pattern in the industry is for an Asian contractor to hire Latino workers. There are cases where contractor and workers are of the same ethnicity, and where there are paternalistic linkages between employer and employees. But this is the exception rather than the rule in Los Angeles, where the relationship between contractor and worker tends to be strictly business. Exploitation is rarely softened by the bonds of family or ethnicity.

This pattern of ethnic differentiation between contractors and workers makes Los Angeles different from other U.S. cities, and maybe from other garment centers in Europe too. In these places, although garment contractors and workers are also immigrants, they often come from the same country and share certain bonds of obligation. For example, South Asians in Britain employ South Asians, Chinese in New York and San Francisco employ Chinese, and so forth. Obviously, some of this occurs in LA as well, and even when it does occur, it does not prevent exploitation. The infamous Thai "slave shop" of El Monte, uncovered in August 1995, involved Thai contractors employing Thai women.

The pattern found in Los Angeles is increasingly found in Mexico, Central America, and the Caribbean, where Asian entrepreneurs from Korea and Taiwan are going to countries like Guatemala and the Dominican Republic and hiring indigenous workers. These firms serve as contractors for U.S. manufacturers and retailers. This pattern may also be spreading to other U.S. cities, such as New York.

The phenomenon of ethnic difference among the three layers of the LA industry—white manufacturers, Asian contractors, and Latino workers—creates an important dynamic that spills over into the general race relations of the city. Considerable tension is developing between the Asian and Latino communities, since they meet at the front lines of an exploitative system. Meanwhile, the real economic powers—the manufacturers, retailers, real estate owners, bankers, and the like, who are mainly native-born whites—do not have to deal with the antagonisms that arise in the workplace, even though they are primarily responsible for them. They can push the blame onto the immigrant entrepreneurs, making them out to be sleazy business operators who mistreat their workers, unlike the good old, decent, American businessman who would never dream of running a sweatshop. Thus is racism fueled and used to maintain current relations of power and privilege.

Efforts to Eliminate Sweatshops

As the sweatshop scourge has grown, more government attention has been devoted to trying to eliminate it. Both the state of California and the federal government have stepped up enforcement efforts. Together, the California Division of Labor Standards Enforcement (DLSE) and the U.S. Department of Labor (DOL) formed the Targeted Industries Partnership Program (TIPP), which singled out agriculture and apparel as the two most egregious violators of labor standards law. Moreover, in a public hearing held by the Los Angeles Jewish Commission on Sweatshops in late 1997, officials from these agencies acknowledged that, while they were making progress in cleaning up agriculture, the apparel industry was proving much more difficult.

The dilemma for enforcement agents in this industry lies in the fact that catching a contractor often results in that particular firm going out of business, sometimes only to open up again in a new location under a different name. Given the large number of contractors, it is impossible to keep track of them all. In any case, since the manufacturers (and retailers) control the prices that set the conditions under which garment factories operate, the challenge has been to find a method to hold them responsible for what goes on in "their" factories.

The DOL has been especially innovative in trying to untangle this knot. They have used the "hot goods" principle to force manufacturers to pay attention to the conditions under which their clothes are produced. Based on a provision in the Fair Labor Standards Act, this principle states that goods made under illegal conditions cannot be shipped across state borders. In the highly time-sensitive fashion industry, invoking this provision made it imperative for manufacturers to be sure that their contractors were not engaging in illegal practices. The DOL was able to get a number of major manufacturers to sign agreements that have forced the industry to develop compliance programs under which they themselves or specialized private firms investigate their contractors to make sure that they are obeying the law.

Needless to say, questions are raised about the effectiveness of such an approach, which has been described as "the fox guarding the chicken coop." Even when manufacturers undertake the effort seriously, there are several problems. Workers are afraid to reveal violations for fear they will be fired by the contractor. Contractors are faced with the threat that the work will be taken away from them by the manufacturer, a club that they use to get workers not to speak candidly with the manufacturer's inspectors. While the threat of removing work may serve as an inducement for some contractors to clean up their act, given the unchanged economics of the situation, for some it just means being more careful in hiding their misdeeds. The truth is, the only real sanction the manufacturer can use against the contractor is the "death sentence"—to stop shipping work, which will probably drive the contractor out of business. Since neither the contractor nor the workers want that, they both "conspire" to hide illegal practices from manufacturer monitors. Moreover, manufacturers themselves may turn a blind eye to problems among their contractors, since they do not want to disturb their production schedules. After all, their prices and practices created the problem in the first place. Their main motivation is to *look* clean so that the DOL will get off their backs.

New proposals, from the White House Apparel Industry Partnership, for example, suggest the need for *independent* monitoring both within the United States and in the global apparel industry. There is a call to have NGOs and religious groups serve as monitors, so that the problems inherent in self-monitoring are avoided. However, given the years of experience contractors have had in hiding violations, one wonders whether independent organizations will be able to ferret out the problems. Moreover, even if legal violations are uncovered, the poverty and poor working conditions endured by the majority of garment workers would still remain, since the legal requirements are very minimal.

A New Form of Labor Process?

Many observers of the apparel industry speak of a "return" of sweatshops, as we have seen. The implication is that we are witnessing a throwback to an earlier phase of capitalism, one characterized by the coercive control of workers as the primary means of extracting surplus from their labor. During the "social contract" period (from the New Deal to around 1960), it has been argued that, at least in the "monopoly sector," bureaucratic controls took the place of direct coercion and, through a combination of internal labor markets and union-imposed rules, the labor regime depended much more on the consent of the workers (Burawoy 1979). Of course, a "competitive sector" still remained throughout this period, retaining pre-Fordist systems of coercive control.

The Los Angeles apparel industry raises an important question: is global/flexible capitalism producing a new type of labor regime, or is it merely replicating the earlier forms of coercive control? I propose that, while there are some old features in the current labor process, it also has some new elements.

The Old Regime

Paying garment workers a piece rate harks back to the earliest and most primitive forms of wage labor under capitalism. It manipulates workers in obvious ways such that they work rapidly, for long hours, in order to make as much as they can, given the low prices per piece. Piece rate encourages self-exploitation, so that supervisors do not need to motivate workers in a directly coercive way.

In addition, simple coercion is found in LA's garment factories. Workers sometimes face abusive employers who yell at them, insist that they not go to the bathroom, prevent them from talking to other workers, and so on. Direct coercion supplements the motivation provided by the piece-rate system.

Contracting out is also not a new concept. It has been used at least since the beginning of the century in the New York apparel industry. Still, as I shall argue below, contracting out is far more developed today than it was in the pre–New Deal (or monopoly capitalist) period.

Finally, the LA apparel industry has returned to its pre–New Deal extreme anti-unionism. From the 1940s to the 1960s, garment workers' unions played a critical role in the near-elimination of sweatshops. Their activism was supported by a government that endorsed and protected the rights of workers to organize. The new attacks on unionism in this industry represent a throwback of sorts.

The New Regime

There are important differences between the labor regimes of the pre–and post–monopoly capitalist eras. First, the nonproduction sectors of the industry, namely the roles played by manufacturers in designing, grading, pattern-making, sometimes cutting, and merchandising, have all become much more sophisticated. In this industry, the division between conception and execution, between mental and manual labor, is almost total. The mental aspects of the industry have been heavily computerized, and, with the help of such elements as bar coding, it has been able to organize and coordinate production systems that range all over the globe. The computerization of the headquarters means that the ability to disperse and shift production has grown immeasurably. Globalization and flexibility change the way business is conducted.

These new characteristics have had an impact on the labor process. Labor control and anti-unionism are built into the very structure of these dispersed production systems. The manufacturers do not need to be overtly anti-union—though, of course, they will be if it becomes necessary. They can rely on the contracting system itself to keep workers disorganized. As described above, workers are unable to locate their fellow workers for the same manufacturer even in Los Angeles, let alone around the world. The shifting around of work means that workers are unstably linked to a particular manufacturer. Meanwhile, workers know, and their contractors inform them repeatedly, in case they have not gotten the message, that demands for any improvements in their wages and work conditions will result in the manufacturer shifting work away from their contractors. The workers may win a skirmish, but will certainly lose their jobs.

As stated, contracting out is not a new feature of apparel production, but it is far more evolved today than it was before World War II. In Los Angeles today almost all sewing is contracted out. In New York, a distinction is still drawn between a manufacturer and a jobber, with the former producing at least partially in-house, and the latter contracting out all production. In LA this distinction does not exist, since all "manufacturers" contract out. Furthermore, the ability to shift production out of the local area to other states, regions, countries, and even continents makes the current contracting system qualitatively different.

In sum, the very system of global/flexible production creates a new kind of labor regime and labor discipline. Workers are kept under control by the mobility and dispersal of the industry. This system, which constantly threatens job loss and severely inhibits labor struggles, keeps workers toiling at rapid speeds for long hours and low wages. They do not require coercive oversight to achieve the desired effect.

In addition, another element of globalization plays into the "new" labor regime in the apparel industry in Los Angeles, and that is the employment of immigrants, most of whom are undocumented. Their political vulnerability as noncitizens, and the ability of employers to threaten exposure and deportation, add to the disciplining effects of global/flexible capitalism.

Approaches to Unionization

I have worked closely with the Organizing Department in the Union of Needletrades, Industrial, and Textile Employees (UNITE) for about 10 years. During that time I have had a chance to talk with union organizing leaders, and to observe and participate in their activities. I have witnessed periods of optimism and growth, and periods of difficulty and loss. I have also witnessed a major change in regime after the merger of the International Ladies Garment Workers Union (ILG) and the Amalgamated Clothing and Textile Workers Union (ACTWU) into UNITE. The merger brought different leadership to the LA organizing effort as well as some different ideas and approaches to the challenge of organizing the city's garment workers.

I would like to discuss five basic approaches to organizing garment workers in Los Angeles, assessing their strengths and weaknesses: National Labor Relations Board (NLRB) elections, jobbers' agreements, corporate campaigns, community organizing, and workers' centers. In practice, they are not mutually exclusive and, in fact, often overlap and are implemented together.

Elections Under the NLRB

NLRB elections would appear to be the ideal way to organize garment workers. The union would meet with workers to discuss the pros and cons of unionization, and they would decide democratically whether they wanted to be represented by the union. The NLRB would then hold the election, ensuring that democratic rules are followed, and garment workers would either become unionized or not.

As most people probably know by now, this approach is fraught with problems in a number of industries. I feel confident in saying that, in the Los Angeles apparel industry, it is worthless. First, assuming that the workers in a particular contracting factory did successfully vote for a union, what would happen? If they were able to sign a contract with their employer, they would not win very much because the profits of the contractor are low. As stated, the real profit centers of the industry are the manufacturers and retailers. Thus the victory would bring few gains. But more importantly, the contractor with unionized workers would almost certainly be avoided by the manufacturers, who would not be willing to employ a contractor whose price was one penny higher than the others', let alone one known to have "labor problems" that might threaten work schedules. The union contractor would be boycotted by all manufacturers, would receive no work, and would go out of business. The workers would have won the election, but lost their jobs.

Second, knowing that they would be driven out of business if a union election were won in their shops, contractors are highly motivated to do everything they can, legal and illegal, to break the union. This is, in practice, the experience of the union in Los Angeles. Case after case of factories with clear pro-union majorities end up in bitter defeat as the employer fires pro-union workers, threatens the others, calls in the immigration authorities, and so on. While many of these actions are illegal, the machinery of justice is so slow and the sanctions so weak that the organizing drive will be dead and buried years before any kind of redress—usually exceedingly minimal—is proffered. The fired union leaders simply lose their jobs, adding to the fear and intimidation that dominate the industry.

Apparel employers will sometimes call for elections, claiming that this is the only fair and American thing to do, that workers should have a free choice, and that they support a secret ballot. But these calls are completely cynical, arising only after the company has engaged in every union-busting practice in the book, and feeling assured that the workers will vote against the union. I feel safe in saying that no apparel manufacturer or contractor in Los Angeles would simply allow a union election to occur, without interference, in their plant. And even if a contractor did allow such an election, he would end up going out of business, as described above.

Clearly legal and procedural reforms are needed in the NLRB process. However, such reforms would still not crack the nut of the contracting system, which enables manufacturers—the real employers—to shift work away from unionized workers, thereby destroying any organizing effort in the long run, if not at the time of the election.

Jobbers' Agreements

The idea of a jobber's agreement comes out of the ILG's long experiences of organizing in the women's apparel industry in New York. The term "jobber" is still used from the New York context, even though it does not apply to the LA industry. A jobber's agreement is the union's equivalent of joint liability. It holds the manufacturer responsible for conditions in its contracting shops by getting it to sign a contract that ensures that it will only use unionized contractors, and will pay them the union scale and benefits. Under such an agreement, the manufacturer cannot boycott union contractors, but on the contrary, is bound to use them. The result is that the interests of the contractors are completely altered. Now it is advantageous for them to have a unionized shop, because it gives them preferred access to that manufacturer. Indeed, jobbers' agreements tend to stabilize the otherwise highly mobile and fluid garment business, since they lead the manufacturers to stick with a particular group of union contractors.

The organizing challenge posed by a jobber's agreement is to organize the entire production system of a manufacturer at one time, namely, both the workers who are employed in its headquarters (maybe sample-makers or cutters), and the workers in the dispersed contracting shops. If the workers in these various locations can be brought together to unite around the issue of gaining a union contract across the entire system, then they may be able to succeed in getting the manufacturer and the contractors to sign.

The basic strategic approach that has been used to organize such a dispersed production system is to turn the manufacturer's benefits of contracting out into weaknesses. The fact that the manufacturer does not have strong and stable ties with its contractors means that the links between them can be severed. The physical dispersal of production also opens up the possibility of interfering with the flow of garments between various plants. Moreover, because of the time-sensitivity of the fashion business, even temporary interruptions in the flow of production can be very costly, especially if they happen at the peak of the season.

Breaking the ties between the manufacturer and its contractors can be accomplished by a number of means. The workers in key contracting shops may go out on strike. Workers may picket certain shops or the company's warehouse, and may be able to persuade truckers not to cross their picket lines. Contractors, who may work with other manufacturers apart from the one that the union is trying to organize, may decide to opt out of the latter relationship for the period of the labor dispute so as to avoid all the disruption; since the manufacturer has probably not been that loyal to them, the contractors have little reason to see it through these tough times. The union may also be able to get some contractors to sign "me too" agreements with the union such that, if they agree to cease working with the manufacturer temporarily, they will be able to sign the union contract on whatever terms are negotiated later—and thus obtain secure work.

Although the manufacturer may be able to move production to other shops in order to avoid those contractors where workers are organized and engaged in various forms of protest, the fact is that, in the height of a publicized labor dispute it is difficult for the manufacturer to find others who will work with it and risk have a picket line thrown at them. As soon as the union is able to trace the work to a new contractor, they can meet with the contractor and warn it of the consequences of working with a manufacturer that is fighting with the union. Thus the obvious advantage to the manufacturer of being able to shift production can be minimized during an organizing campaign.

The strength of this approach lies in tying the manufacturer to the contractors, so that workers can win significant gains. Moreover, such an organizing drive is usually combined with a corporate campaign and community organizing, so that other aspects of the company's functioning, apart from its production, are also under attack. The purpose of such a multifaceted attack is to drive a firm, which otherwise would fight unionization to the death, to negotiate with the union.

Some may feel that such a "coercive" approach should not be necessary in a democratic society, but given the anti-union animus of the employers, nothing short of forcing them to the bargaining table will succeed. The union has to practically drive them out of business in order to get them to accept the organization of their workers. Conditions in the garment industry are such that nothing else will work. Employers will say that, if the industry is unionized, they will leave the country. To prevent that "necessity," they simply must stop unionization. Needless to say, this state of affairs makes organizing in this industry far more confrontational than in most industries.

I want to only mention a few problems with the jobber's agreement approach. First, it is extremely difficult to coordinate all the parts of the dispersed production system so that they are ready to take action at the same time. The general who is coordinating such a battle has to deal with numerous fronts at one time. Second, the problem of secrecy is intense, since the employer is likely to deploy many resources to kill such an effort before it gets off the ground. The need for secrecy obviously impedes organizing, and it certainly weakens the development of democratic structures among workers as the union is building membership. Third, such an organizing drive is most likely to succeed right away or not at all. The longer the struggle is drawn out, the more is the employer able to engage in evasive action, including devising methods for moving work away from contractors with strong union support. The manufacturer may build up the work load for its core contractors, or it may move some of its production to Mexico, among other options. This ability to shift production is deadly to the morale of the workers, who find their factory closed, at least in the short run, and begin to fear whether they will ever be able to win back their jobs.

A fourth problem with a jobber's agreement is that it lends itself to top-down organizing. In other words, it is possible to put sufficient pressure on the manufacturer so that it agrees to sign with union contractors. As we said, this changes the motivation of the contractors, who now rush to join the union. The contractors may sign with the union, not because of pressure from their workers, but because they know that a union contract will guarantee them stable work. The workers thus become irrelevant to the signing of the union contract. The contractors are motivated to sign whether the workers want a union or not. In sum, the agreement becomes one between the union, the manufacturer, and the contractors, with the workers potentially treated as the mere objects of the agreement.

Now there is nothing inherent in a jobber's agreement that precludes workers' participation in the struggle to win it. Indeed, driving the manufacturer to the bargaining table may depend on strong worker activism of various sorts. Nevertheless, the situation lends itself to top-down agreements whereby workers find themselves as members of a union for which they did not fight. Moreover the fact that their bosses, the contractors, are now eager union members makes the dynamics between workers and contractors a bit weird. The antagonistic relationship between the workers and their immediate employers is muted by the union contract, and the union often ends up dealing directly with the contractor rather than with the workers.

Developing union agreements that deal with the tiers and loose ties of industries like apparel is clearly a major challenge for this period of "flexible" capitalism. Perhaps the old ILG jobber's agreement is no longer the appropriate instrument for tying manufacturers (and retailers) to the shops that actually sew their clothing. Clearly some mechanism is needed to force the manufacturers and retailers to cough up some of the excess surplus they expropriate from the garment workers.

As we pointed out above, the contracting network of a manufacturer need not be limited to a particular city, region, or country. Indeed, many LA manufacturers contract offshore as well. The idea of organizing the entire production system of a particular manufacturer thus lends itself to cross-border organizing. In other words, all the workers in all the contracting shops of a manufacturer, regardless of their geographic location, could, in principle, coordinate their efforts and their demands. This vision is not beyond possibility, although only the first steps have been taken in a few cases to bring it to fruition (Armbruster 1995, 1998).

Corporate Campaigns

Since the use of corporate campaigns in the effort to organize workers is not unique to the apparel industry, I will only touch on it lightly. The labor movement as a whole has become much more sophisticated at researching the companies it is trying to organize, and in finding other points of vulnerability apart from their production systems. Such vulnerabilities lie in the various plans and relationships of a particular company. For example, its stockholders may be dismayed to learn about certain company practices, and may be willing to exert pressure on the company to settle quickly with the union. When unions themselves are among the stockholders, this can be a potent weapon.

The fashion industry would appear to be especially vulnerable to one form of this kind of pressure, namely, an attack on a company's image. Fashion has a kind of "postmodern" quality, since it depends very much on the selling of an image, rather than simply a product. The image-selling aspect of apparel has accelerated in recent years, as certain key brand names, spending millions of dollars in advertising, have managed to create identities with which their consumers relate (Klein, 1999). More people happily wear clothing with the brand name plastered on it, helping them to define themselves to the public. Having a strong brand enables a company to sell its clothing at inflated prices, as people spend much more on the items than they are worth as physical products. Of course, advertising "labor" goes into constructing as well as selling these images, so that the discrepancy between sales price and cost of production is not pure profit.

However, the strength of image in fashion is also its weakness. If an image is tarnished, it can quickly drop out of public favor, leading to plummeting sales. Even without any "outside" interference, most apparel brands have a limited life cycle. Hot brands that cool off usually have a hard time revitalizing themselves, although anything is possible. Unions (and other organizations concerned with labor abuses) can try to take advantage of the vulnerability of a brand's public image by developing negative associations with that name. For example, efforts have been made to link Nike and Disney with sweatshop conditions in their offshore contracting shops. I cannot say whether these efforts have directly affected sales or forced the companies to take actions to improve conditions among their contractors, but it seems likely that they do exert a real pressure on the firms.

Corporate campaigns often attack a firm's sales in some form—by encouraging a consumer boycott, by putting pressure on retailers to drop that brand, by getting consumers to question salespeople about production conditions, and so forth. The idea is that, if a company's sales are hurting, it is more likely to be willing to come to the bargaining table. These campaigns may also affect the value of a company's stock, in turn leading the owners to feel that action must be taken to end the damaging publicity—including possibly settling with the union.

A major weakness of this approach arises if it is not linked to a strong worker-organizing component. Corporate campaign pressure on a company may, indeed, hurt its sales or stock prices, which in turn may lead the company to cut prices, cut wages, and lay off workers. In other words, workers may suffer from the consequences of a boycott (for example), and if they are not actively involved in the campaign, will feel that these efforts by others to "help" them are very unwelcome. Without strong worker participation in the decision to boycott, without their informed consent, with full knowledge that they may suffer some immediate repercussions, the approach can backfire, leading to the alienation of the very workers the union is trying to organize.

Community Organizing

Community organizing can have at least two distinct meanings. First, it can refer to outreach to middle-class supporters and other allies, who can help put pressure on the industry in general or on a particular campaign target. These community supporters can become participants in the corporate campaign, helping to demonstrate against the company, publicize its labor abuses, and spread the word about a boycott. In other words, the community that is mobilized helps to provide the troops that exert community pressure on the company. It may include various left-leaning organizations, other trade unions, religious groups, women's groups, students, artists, politicians, and so forth.

The best community organizing of this type involves not just calling on the union's friends and allies in the face of a union-planned action, but also establishing somewhat independent organizations that plan actions themselves and use their creativity and initiative to contribute new and distinctive energy to the movement. This was the idea behind Common Threads, a group of women that formed in Los Angeles to support garment workers and that helped a little with the Guess campaign in its early phases. Common Threads was an independent organization that included an artists' collective. It developed its own projects in support of garment workers in addition to cooperating with the union on a number of actions.

Semi-autonomous community organizations have their strengths and weaknesses. A weakness, from the union's point of view, is that they cannot be completely controlled. They do not simply do the union's bidding, and may thus not satisfy exactly what the union needs at a particular time. On the other hand, what is lost in control is gained in enthusiasm. People who "own" what they are doing obviously engage in it with a great deal more relish than if they were merely pawns in an organization's plans.

The second type of community organizing involves organizing within the workers' own community. This approach is especially relevant when the workers are part of an oppressed group. In the case of LA garment workers, the majority are Latino immigrants, and the remainder are Asian immigrants. As we have seen, many are undocumented, which opens them up to the special stigmatization of that status. Community organizing in this context involves organizing around the broader issues facing the Latino and Asian immigrant communities, including the political assaults on both legal and illegal immigrants. The goal is to link the exploitation faced by garment workers to the broader agenda of the immigrant communities. Similarly, because most garment workers are women, it is possible to organize around the special needs of immigrant women.

The fact that garment workers are so poorly paid and work under such oppressive conditions contributes to the general impoverishment of the immigrant community, while the political oppression of Latinos in particular makes it much harder for garment workers to protect themselves against economic exploitation. Their positions as workers, as women, and as immigrants under attack reinforce one another in the overall oppression of the group. Latino/a garment workers are oppressed simultaneously as workers, as women, and as immigrants. The struggle to improve their situation thus extends beyond winning a union contract to winning political power for their community in general, and to supporting the rights of women within that community and in the society at large. The various types of struggle are all connected. The union needs to align itself with the political aspirations of the Latino/a community, even as Latino/a leaders need to recognize that the labor struggle is an important part of winning rights and respect for the Latino community. (Similar statements can be made for segments of the Asian communities, although they are more heterogeneous in both class and ethnic terms.)[4]

Organizing around race-ethnicity, immigration status, and gender obviously occurs apart from the union. Each community has developed its own organizations to help oppressed workers and to try to organize them in self-defense. For example, Asian Immigrant Women's Advocates (AIWA) in Oakland tries to link race, class, and gender issues in helping oppressed immigrant women workers fight for their rights. The union and these community organizations overlap to some degree, but they also have different approaches. Although at times they have tried to work together, too often they see each other as opponents and criticize each other for their failings. While there is, no doubt, plenty to criticize on both sides, such criticisms are likely to flourish when the task is very difficult and when all the organizations feel frustrated at their lack of progress.

Regardless of the impediments to cooperation between community groups and the labor movement, it is clearly desirable to forge these coalitions, and to overcome the disputes and disagreements that arise between them. Perhaps I am being naive but, having heard criticisms from both sides, I feel they are overdrawn. The overarching desirability of union-community cooperation in both the economic and political struggles should be paramount.

Workers' Centers

The concept behind workers' centers is that the organizing of garment workers needs to proceed, irrespective of a particular organizing drive. A workers' center can help accomplish this in a number of ways. It can provide services to garment workers, who are generally in great need of help in dealing with wage claims or immigration problems. It can also help to educate workers not only about their rights but also about the political economy in which they find themselves. In other words, it can provide workers with the tools they need to understand their world and to begin to fight back. And it can provide an environment where workers can engage in lower-risk political struggles rather than those presented by a full-fledged organizing drive. The importance of political action cannot be overemphasized, since it is in the course of political struggle that workers are able to learn that victories can be won. The very act of participation is radicalizing because it undermines the strong beliefs that the employers are all-powerful and that change is impossible.[5] In sum, a workers' center can be the training ground for the building of a general movement of garment workers. It involves amassing an army of garment workers, regardless of where they work, who are ready to fight when necessary. It is a form of worker-centered organizing.

UNITE has developed a few workers' centers, called Justice Centers, in New York and Los Angeles. I cannot speak about the condition in New York, but I have seen the ups and downs of the Los Angeles center over the years. Too often it has sunk under the burden of providing basic services to a very needy population, and has been unable to pursue the more long-term goals of developing an educational and political program.

I personally believe that this kind of worker-centered organizing is essential for building a *long-term* garment workers' movement in Los Angeles. The Justice Center can work in tandem with particular organizing drives by helping to prepare workers for participation in such campaigns, by providing worker-supporters for them, and by giving the workers who are engaged in a particular drive a place to go and a support structure, even if their factory has been boycotted by the manufacturer. The Justice Center can also provide a community for garment workers who, too often, live under conditions of social fragmentation (as the newest immigrants) and who need to build social support networks.

Needless to say, this approach has potential weaknesses. In particular, the effort to engage in low-risk political actions is fraught with problems. There is an inherent contradiction between taking low risks and winning struggles, especially when the enemy is so fierce and so determined to crush any resistance. Yet in order to build the courage to take greater risks, small victories must be achieved. Finding winning actions that do not jeopardize the livelihoods of very vulnerable workers is a difficult challenge. A couple of possible approaches are pressing demands with state agencies, and engaging in protests in support of workers at a factory that is not one's own and from which one cannot be fired. Building an arsenal of actions should obviously be done by workers themselves, with the aid of union staff. The very act of developing political actions would be educational in itself.

Efforts to Implement These Ideas

A group has now formed in Los Angeles that wants to work on the three-pronged goals of providing services, developing an educational program, and engaging in lower-risk political actions.[6] The group, tentatively called the Garment Workers Coalition, brings together a number of community groups and the union. The community groups include the Asian Pacific American Legal Center (APALC), the Coalition for Humane Immigrant Rights of Los Angeles (CHIRLA), the Korean Immigrant Worker Advocates (KIWA), the Mexican American Legal Defense and Education Fund (MALDEF), the Legal Aid Foundation of Los Angeles (LAFLA), Beit Tzedek (a Jewish group that offers free legal services), and UNITE. Each of the community groups has engaged in organizing and providing services, and has plenty of experience in working with garment workers. The group is engaged in outreach to garment workers, providing them with legal services (with the assistance of student interns), and will help encourage workers to participate in UNITE's Justice Center with a view to building it as a place where workers can develop a political movement. The coalition, we hope, can devise a division of labor so that the center will be freed of some of its responsibility for services, while all the organizations can help with the development of an educational and political program.

The Potential Flight of the Industry to Mexico

Of course any organizing effort on the part of LA's garment workers may simply speed up the process of the flight of the industry to Mexico. Indeed, although they will not admit it, I suspect that many LA apparel manufacturers are looking at shifting production there as a form of insurance against local organizing. What can be done about this?

First, it is possible that sectors of the LA industry will not leave, regardless of improvements in production methods in Mexico. Small lots in the most fashion-sensitive sectors as well as replenishment stock may always be produced in Los Angeles. The number of garment factory jobs may decline in the future, but may not be disappear totally.

Second, the city and state cannot afford to allow the industry simply to leave, since it is such a major employer. So far their primary strategy for keeping the industry in Los Angeles is to try to bribe firms to stay with tax write-offs. However, alternative approaches are possible, including efforts to provide capital for contractors to upgrade their facilities and improve productivity through technology, rather than by squeezing the workers. Ironically, unionization can actually foster this process by stabilizing the relationships between manufacturers and contractors. In the current environment, contractors will not invest in their factories because they cannot count on receiving work from one week to the next. If the relationships are stabilized under a jobber's agreement, the contractors can depend on steadier work, thus reducing the risk of investment. Of course, given the general riskiness of the fashion business, stability is only likely to be attained for those contractors with the strongest ties to their manufacturers.[7]

Third, in the face of industry flight, it is better for workers to be organized rather than unorganized. If they can win a contract in Los Angeles, for example, they may be able to put clauses into it that limit the movement of capital offshore, or that at least make it more costly. They can also set up severance agreements, such as that which was negotiated by UNITE with Levi's, so that local workers are not simply abandoned when the manufacturer shifts production.

Corporate campaigns and consumer pressure are especially suitable for holding accountable firms that move to Mexico. If an apparel firm has shifted production to escape unionization in Los Angeles, consumer groups can point to the even lower labor standards in Mexico and to the greed of the manufacturer in seeking even higher profits from the exploitation of impoverished workers. Of course, such an approach is much more likely to succeed if the Mexican workers join the struggle against the manufacturer, so that both groups of workers call for consumer support to end the abuses on both sides of the border.

Conclusion

The garment industry in Los Angeles poses a formidable challenge to organizing. This industry can be seen as the wave of the future for "globalized/flexible" organization. It is an immensely efficient engine of exploitation. Numerous efforts to slow down the reemergence of sweatshops have been tried, most with only partial success, if that. To counter this, we need approaches that bring together community and union organizing, and that are centered on developing the workers' own understandings and capacities to fight back. Moreover, we need to develop cross-border organizing programs, where workers in the various countries of production join together in attempting to prevent being pitted against one another. We should recognize that social change in this arena is not going to be won overnight, and that the ground must be laid thoroughly and democratically in order to build a workers' movement that can last through the long, hard fights that lie ahead.

Finally, this entire discussion has taken for granted the capitalist approach to the production of apparel. Obviously this approach can be severely criticized from numerous angles. Eliminating it will require much more than a reactivated labor movement. However, given the current power configurations, worker organizing is definitely a step in the right direction.

Notes

Acknowledgments: I would like to thank Rich Appelbaum, Ralph Arbruster, Carol Bank, Jeff Hermanson, Evely Laser Shlensky, and Cristina Vasquez for their helpful comments on an earlier draft of this essay. I would also like to thank Jeff Hermanson, Rebecca Kessinger, and David Young of UNITE for discussing strategic issues with me over the years.

1. In acknowledgment of the work of Harry Braverman, I am using the term "monopoly capitalism" to denote the economic system that held force from the New Deal to late 1950s or early 1960s; this system has been given other names, including the "social contract" and "Keynsian economics." Post–monopoly capitalist has also been known by a number of different names, including "global capitalism," "flexible capitalism," "neoliberalism," and the "new world order." I shall use these terms interchangeably.

2. My conclusions are based on about ten years of investigating the LA (and Pacific Rim) apparel industry, while simultaneously working as a volunteer with the Union of Needletrades, Industrial and Textile Employees (UNITE) Organizing Department. The research has resulted in the book *Behind the Label: Inequality in the Los Angeles Apparel Industry* (2000), co-authored with Richard Appelbaum.

4. The fact that Asian immigrants are overrepresented in the contractor population makes defining the struggle of Asian garment workers as an Asian community issue somewhat more difficult because it raises more intracommunity contradictions. Nevertheless, Asian community activists have plunged ahead in this difficult arena.

5. The influence of Paulo Freire (1970) should be evident in these ideas.

6. There is always a risk in describing a new group, because one never knows whether it will last. Who knows whether this group will still be in existence by the time this volume is published, or whether it will have died along with so many other good ideas?

7. An underlying question is how much the present "flexible" production system is driven by the needs of manufacturers for flexibility, and how much by the desire to shave labor costs to the bone. To the degree that it is driven by the latter, there will be more room for reconfiguring the industry in a more stable, capital-intensive direction.

References

American Apparel Manufacturers Association. 1997. *Focus: An Economic Profile of the Apparel Industry.* Arlington: Author.

Armbruster, Ralph. 1995. "Cross-National Organizing Strategies." *Critical Sociology*, 21(3): 77–91.

Armbruster, Ralph Joseph. 1998. "Globalization and Cross-Border Labor Organizing in the Garment and Automobile Industries." Ph.D. dissertation, Department of Sociology, University of California, Riverside.

Bird, Laura, and Wendy Bounds. 1997. "Stores' Demands Squeeze Apparel Companies." *Wall Street Journal*, July 15, p. B1.

Bonacich, Edna. 2000. "Intense Challenges, Tentative Possibilities: Organizing Immigrant Garment Workers in Los Angeles." Pp. 130–149 in *Organizing Immigrants: The Challenge for Unions in Contemporary California*, edited by Ruth Mikman. Ithaca: ILR Press.

Bonacich, Edna, and Richard Appelbaum. 2000. *Behind the Label: Inequality in the Los Angeles Apparel Industry*. Berkeley: University of California Press.

Braverman, Harry. 1974. *Labor and Monopoly Capital: The Degradation of Work in the Twentieth Century*. New York: Monthly Review Press.

Burawoy, Michael. 1979. *Manufacturing Consent: Changes in the Labor Process Under Monopoly Capitalism*. Chicago: University of Chicago Press.

Fregoso, Rosa Marta. 1988. "The Invisible Workforce: Immigrant Home Workers in the Garment Industry of Los Angeles." Master's thesis, University of California, Berkeley.

Freire, Paulo. 1970. *The Pedagogy of the Oppressed*. New York: Seabury Press.

Harvey, David. 1989. *The Condition of Postmodernity*. Oxford: Basil Blackwell.

Klein, Naomi. 1999. *No Logo: Taking Aim at the Brand Bullies*. New York: Picador.

Kyser, Jack. 1997. *Manufacturing in Los Angeles*. Los Angeles: Economic Development Corporation.

Moody, Kim. 1997. *Workers in a Lean World*. London: Verso.

Ross, Andrew, ed. 1997. *No Sweat: Fashion, Free Trade, and the Rights of Garment Workers*. London: Verso.

Sullivan, Ben. 1997. "Bankers, Financiers Dominate Ranks of L.A.'s Highest Paid." *Los Angeles Business Journal*, June 23, p. 1.

Targeted Industries Partnership Program (TIPP). 1996. *Fourth Annual Report, 1996*. Sacramento: Author.

U.S. General Accounting Office. 1988. *"Sweatshops" in the U.S.: Opinions on Their Extent and Possible Enforcement Options*. Washington, DC: U.S. Government Printing Office.

———. 1994. *The Garment Industry: Efforts to Address the Prevalence and Conditions of Sweatshops*. Washington, DC: U.S. Government Printing Office.

CHAPTER 8

Transcending Taylorism and Fordism? Three Decades of Work Restructuring

James Rinehart

In this chapter I describe and critically evaluate a number of work-restructuring initiatives that appeared over the last three decades of the twentieth century. I concentrate on changes that ostensibly relax, dismantle, or transcend Fordist and Taylorist modes of organizing work, and, consequently, that allegedly benefit workers as well as employers. Developments in the auto industry, from the onset of concession bargaining to lean production and the Saturn model, receive special attention.

The 1970s

In the early 1970s workplace reform ranked among the most pressing issues of the day. Increasing manifestations of worker discontent, most notably the widely publicized 1972 strike at the General Motors (GM) plant in Lordstown, Ohio, led some alarmed observers to warn that the campus ferment of the 1960s was rapidly spreading to the much more dangerous terrain of industry. Governments generously funded research on and set up institutes for improving productivity, labor-management cooperation, and the quality of work life. Criticisms of the way in which work was organized regularly were aired not just in left-wing publications but in the business press as well. Three notable books on the subject found a large audience and, taken together, constituted a powerful indictment of the world of work.

If there was one word that captured the essence of Studs Terkel's 1974 best-seller, *Working,* it was alienation. The profound discontent expressed in his interviews of people in a wide range of occupations led Terkel to conclude that work was organized in ways that do violence to the spirit and the body.

In his 1974 classic, *Labor and Monopoly Capital,* Harry Braverman argued that the advance of technology in the twentieth century has not been accompanied by a net growth of complex jobs and new skills. He asserted that, in tandem with scientific management, technology's inexorable consequence in all sectors of the economy is labor degradation—or the dilution of workers' skill and discretion.

The third book, the 1972 report of a special task force to the Secretary of Health, Education, and Welfare called *Work in America* (*WIA*), concluded that "dull, repetitive, seemingly meaningless tasks, offering little challenge or autonomy, are causing discontent among workers at all occupational levels" (U.S. Department of Health, Education, and Welfare 1972, p. xv). Worker alienation (a term much in vogue in those days) was attributed to the mix of Fordist-Taylorist job designs, diminishing opportunities to be one's own boss, and the rising expectations of an increasingly well-educated workforce.

WIA advocated two types of workplace reform—job redesign and worker participation. If they are more than half-hearted efforts, the authors claimed, these reforms will demonstrably increase productivity anywhere from 5 to 40 percent. For both types of reforms, *WIA* attributed productivity gains and cost reduction to the improved morale and commitment of workers, which result from challenging jobs and/or the satisfaction they derive from participating in the decision-making process.

Braverman did not have much to say about such reforms, known then as quality of worklife (QWL) programs, but it was clear that he viewed them as cosmetic and manipulative. If they did spur workers to greater effort and boost productivity and profits, it was only because workers had been successfully conned.

In a paper I presented to the 1978 Binghamton conference on "New Directions in the Labor Process" (Rinehart 1978) I followed Braverman's lead, but in some important respects my argument was different from his and even more different from that of *WIA*. I argued that worker participation programs—joint committees and task forces, problem-solving groups (e.g., quality control circles), and other forms of employee involvement—could realize corporate objectives by altering workers' attitudes and behaviors and circumventing or weakening unions. However, corporate benefits derived from job redesign had little to do with conning workers or changing their consciousness. When redesign efforts like job enrichment or enlargement did achieve corporate objectives, they did so not by fostering the motivating effects of complex jobs and greater worker discretion but by improving ineffective work designs and processes; introducing more sophisticated management controls over worker performance; combining several fragmented jobs into one, thus intensifying the work process, usually without added compensation; and eliminating certain categories of workers, especially verifiers, inspectors, and first-line supervisors. Job redesign, then, did entail some degree of despecialization and increased worker discretion, but these departures from Taylorism cut labor costs and reduced the time required to produce an item or deliver a service because they were replaced by more sophisticated forms of scientific management and entailed outcomes such as work intensification and labor elimination (Kelley 1982; Rinehart 1986).

The authors of *WIA* had nothing to say about these Taylorist components of QWL reforms. Whether this was a matter of selective reporting or self-deception is difficult to say. In the event, there was a jarring discrepancy between the seemingly genuine concern for workers' well-being expressed in the report and the anti-labor elements of the reforms it endorsed. Much the same can be said about most scholars and management consultants who championed job redesign, including the foremost proponent of job enrichment—Frederick Herzberg (1966, 1968).

The 1980s

In the mid-1970s heightened international competition, declining profits, and fiscal crises prompted corporations and governments to undertake major restructuring. These initiatives were in full swing in the 1980s. As neoliberal economics replaced Keynesian policies and as companies embarked on determined efforts to lower labor costs, unemployment and underemployment grew, and real wages stagnated and then fell. Union membership and bargaining leverage declined, and companies were able to more effectively contain worker resistance. Under these conditions, the term "alienation" lost its bite. It was, in fact, hard to worry about alienated labor when so many people were desperately clinging to or seeking jobs that would alienate them full-time. Increasingly, workplace restructuring was justified by the need to improve the competitiveness of companies and the national economy. The term "QWL" disappeared from the lexicon of management consultants and human resource specialists. Work restructuring now was sold to workers not so much as a means of creating challenging jobs and empowerment, but as a necessary condition for the avoidance of job loss.

The End of Job Enrichment

In the 1980s technologically driven work restructuring escalated with the introduction and spread of microtechnology. Over the decade, companies spent over a trillion dollars on computers, robots, and other types of automated equipment. Computerization was applied not only in manufacturing but also in the service sector, which heretofore had been relatively impervious to productivity gains from technological advances (Rifkin 1996).

Job enrichment programs, whose most common targets were large offices and banks, virtually disappeared in the 1980s. In the heyday of job enrichment, there rarely was more than one computer in any organization or any division of a large organization. These mainframe computers were large, expensive, and slow (Greenbaum 1995). Cheaper and faster personal computers allowed management to achieve more effectively the same objectives as job enrichment—to monitor workers' performance, increase productivity, and cut payroll costs.

Concessions

Because of recession, increased imports, implementation of labor-replacing technology, and plant relocations to low-wage regions of the world, nearly two million manufacturing workers lost their jobs in the late 1970s and early 1980s (Bluestone and Harrison 1982; Raines, Berson, and Gracie 1982). In the depths of the 1982 recession, and with postwar unemployment at an all-time high, a wave of concession bargaining swept the nation. Now it was the company rather than the union that set the collective bargaining agenda. While concession bargaining emerged in a period of economic crisis, the practice was not restricted to money-losing firms, nor did it decline as the economy recovered (Capelli and McKersie 1987). Concessions, which initially were restricted to wages, later included participatory mechanisms, labor-management cooperation, team concept, contingent compensation, outsourcing, decentralization of quality responsibilities, collapsed job classifications, increased flexibility of worker deployment, and the elimination of work rules won in more prosperous years. That labor-management cooperation, team concept, and worker participation became part of the concessionary package demanded by companies reveals a great deal about their purposes and dimensions.

According to scholars at the Massachusetts Institute of Technology (MIT), these changes, especially in team concept, fewer job classifications, and production workers' quality responsibilities, benefited workers because they represented a retreat from the design principles of scientific management. Workers now would escape a detailed division of labor and enjoy greater task variety, job complexity, and empowerment (Kochan, Cutcher-Gershenfeld, and MacDuffie 1989). Even if this claim were true, it is clear that: (1) the companies were interested not in placating workers but in reducing labor costs (Capelli and McKersie 1987); and (2) workers lost far more than they gained.

Elaborate job classifications were associated with seniority rights on job transfers, restricted management capacity to deploy workers, limited workloads, and maintained employment levels (since fewer workers are required to do a given amount of work in the absence of narrowly defined jobs). Concessions on work rules, most notably those governing crew size, effort levels, and work pace, had the (intended) effect of intensifying work. Forms of contingent compensation, such as productivity bonuses, pay-for-knowledge, and merit pay, put workers in competition not only with their co-workers in a plant but with their counterparts in other plants (Capelli and McKersie 1987). Finally, within a given industry concession bargaining "introduced a significant degree of variation across plants in contract terms and work practices" (Katz 1985, 64). As a result of this break in pattern, during negotiations companies were able to use plants with the lowest compensation and most work-intensive operations as standards (the whipsawing strategy).

Worker Participation

During the 1980s there was a "big leap" to worker participation programs, or what *Business Week* called "The New Industrial Relations" (1981) (see also Parker 1985, 77;

Kochan, Cutcher-Gershenfeld, and MacDuffie 1989). One survey found that, by the end of the 1980s, over 80 percent of Fortune 1000 firms had implemented at least one employee involvement (IE) practice (Applebaum and Batt 1994).

Participatory programs did have a certain appeal to workers, especially if they were not accompanied by major changes in the labor process and work rules. However, participation often was jammed down workers' throats with the threat that rejection would put their jobs at risk. As Mike Parker (1985, 7) remarked, "the new programs resembled shotgun weddings, with the company holding the shotgun."

The concept of total quality management (TQM) emerged in the deep recession of the early 1980s (Cole 1995, v). Regarded in some quarters as the most influential management fad of this decade (Micklethwait and Wooldridge 1996, 278), TQM was pioneered by W. Edwards Deming, whose ideas initially were ignored in North America but enthusiastically embraced in Japan. Not surprisingly, it was manufacturing companies facing stiff Japanese competition that were the first to adopt TQM programs (Easton 1995). In 1987 the U.S. government established the Baldridge award—an equivalent to Japan's Deming prize—which was given to the company that had most successfully implemented TQM practices. TQM soon spread to public sector organizations, which were faced with shrinking budgets and the need to rationalize operations. In 1988 the U.S. government by executive order called for TQM to be introduced in federal public services (Micklethwait and Wooldridge 1996).

TQM has been variously defined and takes a variety of forms. To its advocates it is equated with quality assurance, and means "getting products and services right the first time, rather than waiting for them to be finished before checking them for errors" (Micklethwait and Wooldridge 1996, 30). To its critics it is "a cost-containment strategy with a strong anti-labor bias" (Price 1994, 197). There are elements of worker participation in TQM. Project teams are formed to streamline work processes. Employees are urged to use their "trade secrets" to minimize defects and eliminate "waste" (i.e., nonvalue-added labor). Consequently, the "quality" in TQM has less to do with promoting quality in the usual sense of the word—meaning durability, effectiveness, usefulness, and so on—than with raising productivity (Kraft 1999).

Work Restructuring in the Auto Industry

Developments in the auto industry in the 1980s exemplify trends in work restructuring and participation and the conditions under which they were introduced. In 1978 automakers were operating with master agreements and pattern bargaining. A nearly bankrupt American Motors departed from the pattern settlements in 1977, but this was an exception. It was the 1979 Chrysler bailout by the U.S. government that marked the beginning of an era of concessions in the industry. Workers generally opposed such changes, but their resistance often was broken by the auto companies' threats of plant shutdown. "At many [Big Three] companies, the management philosophy for older plants is to attempt major overhauls of work practices only when there will be a 'significant emotional event' (GM's term)—generally a corporate decision about investment and product placement that will shake up employees and ready them for change" (MacDuffie and Pil 1997, 35). In other words, accept our changes or say good-bye to your jobs. Workers had to take these threats seriously. In 1978 there were over one million people employed in the U.S. auto industry. By 1983 there were only about 750,000, a loss of one-quarter of a million jobs.

Faced with a crisis of overcapacity in the early 1980s, GM begin playing off workers in one plant against those in another plant. With the threat of plant closure hanging over their heads, workers were forced into a bidding game to see which union local could hand over the most concessions. The company also used the threat of plant closure to persuade workers to accept participatory mechanisms and work restructuring. For example, in 1984 GM spent $300 million to modernize its Linden, New Jersey, assembly plant, installing computer-based technology, robots, and just-in-time (JIT) procedures. The company also reduced job classifications and introduced problem-solving groups. These changes were "accepted" by the union local because the plant had already experienced severe employment cutbacks and was facing closure (Milkman 1997).

Following major losses in the recession of the early 1980s, Ford initiated EI programs in an attempt to improve productivity. The return of profitability did not deter automakers' pursuit of labor-management cooperation and concessions. In the mid-1980s Chrysler, whose profits were surging, introduced modern operating agreements (MOAs) in many of its plants. These agreements were geared more to transforming labor relations than to restructuring production. They entailed the implementation of teams, pay-for-knowledge, and decentralization of quality responsibilities (MacDuffie and Pil 1997). By the end of the 1980s few union locals had managed to avoid restructuring, and "virtually every auto assembly plant in the United States had institutionalized some form of participation" (Milkman 1997, 139).

The national office of the United Auto Workers (UAW) was hardly an innocent party to these developments, as it caved in on concessions and embraced labor-management cooperation. By endorsing concessions, the union reinforced the view that workers were to blame for the problems of the auto companies. The UAW justified its retreat by arguing it would contribute to Big Three competitiveness, which would insulate workers from further job loss. Ultimately, in exchange for concessions the auto companies agreed to establish a job bank, which cushioned worker dislocation but provided no job security guarantees (Indergaard and Cushion 1987).

That many auto workers found the idea of participation appealing is undeniable. (That many auto workers found the actual experience of participation disappointing also is undeniable.) However, like agreements to concessions in general, workers' consent to participation was conditioned by their insecurity. For example, workers' acceptance of Ford's EI programs hardly signified a burning desire to participate. As former Ford president Donald Peterson said at the time, workers "understood that their jobs were at stake" (Gordon 1996, 63). The point is underscored by cases where jobs were secure. At Chrysler plants where popular vehicles were built and where overtime demands were heavy, union locals "were able to resist nearly all management efforts to make changes in the traditional system" (MacDuffie and Pil 1997, 27). For example, Chrysler's St. Louis plant, which makes the hot-selling minivans, repeatedly voted down MOAs.

The most significant mode of work restructuring in the 1980s appeared with the arrival in North America of Japanese auto assembly transplants. Whereas in 1978 there were no Asian transplants in North America, between 1982 and 1990 seven transplants or joint ventures opened in the United States and four in Canada. (One, Hyundai, is now closed.) All of these plants used Japanese management and production techniques, or what now is known as lean production. The Big Three automakers quickly hopped on the Japanese bandwagon. By 1990 most auto plants in North America had introduced at least some of the practices of lean production. Today, most North American plants can be considered lean production–mass production hybrids, but there are large operational and management differences across companies and across plants owned by the same company (Kochan, Lansbury, and MacDuffie 1997). (I will discuss lean production more fully in the next section.)

The 1990s

The conditions and ideologies that put workers and unions on the defensive in the 1980s became more powerful in the 1990s. Government deficits and debt were used to justify public sector cutbacks, privatization, and work rationalization. Globalization and the need for competitiveness, so it was claimed, left corporate chieftains no choice but to introduce drastic cost-cutting measures. Outsourcing and subcontracting, part-time and temporary jobs, and two-tiered wage systems increased. There was no need to amplify these developments. Companies simply slashed their workforces and restructured without much, if any, sugarcoating. Corporate leaders apparently believed that invoking the mantra of competitiveness was sufficient to persuade workers (and the general public) that they must pull together with management to beat the competition—not only workers in other countries but also workers in their own country, industry, or company—in a dog-eat-dog race to the bottom.

The 1989 Free Trade Agreement and the 1993 North American Free Trade Agreement (NAFTA) strengthened capital's hand at the expense of workers and unions. Employers' threats of plant relocation have escalated significantly since NAFTA. Such threats have been especially effective as a union avoidance strategy and as a means of enabling companies to delay indefinitely signing first contracts (Bronfenbrenner 1996).

Reengineering

An emergent approach to restructuring is known as reengineering. According to Micklethwait and Wooldridge (1996, 29), "reengineering . . . established itself as the first great management fad of the 1990s, contributing to millions of people losing their jobs and millions more working in entirely new ways." In other words, reengineering has become a polite term for downsizing. The founders and major promoters of reengineering, Michael Hammer and James Champy (1993, 48), deny this claim. Downsizing, they say, involves workers doing less with less, while "reengineering, by contrast, means doing more with less."

Hammer and Champy criticize Henry Ford, Adam Smith, and Alfred Sloan (who assumed the presidency of GM in 1923). Ford and Smith were singled out because they extolled the advantages of a highly specialized division of labor on the shop floor, and Sloan because he applied the division of labor to management and the organization as a whole.

While Hammer and Champy never once cite Herzberg, what they advocate is shamelessly similar to job enrichment, but without all the bows to workers' interests. They argue that reengineering empowers workers, but this empowerment is not used to sell their ideas to workers, nor do they view empowerment as a link between job redesign and increased productivity. Worker motivation figures very little in their theory and sales pitch. There is, however, one significant difference between reengineering and job enrichment, namely that reengineering is integrated with the use of the latest technological innovations. In fact, reengineering "arguably is the first management theory to use computers as a starting [point] rather than a neat addition [to work redesign]" (Micklethwait and Wooldridge 1996, 32).

Like job enrichment, reengineering compresses several specialized jobs into one. By doing this, "much of the checking, reconciling, waiting, monitoring, and tracking . . . is eliminated . . . , which means that people will spend more time doing real [i.e., value-added] work" (Hammer and Champy 1993, 69). At IBM Credit, for example, the tasks of credit checkers, pricers, clerks, and administrators were rolled into one and assigned to one person. Hammer and Champy (1993, 39) claimed this led to reduced staff, a 90 percent reduction in cycle time, and a hundredfold increase in productivity.

Benchmarking

An increasingly popular restructuring approach is known as benchmarking. The first benchmarking studies appeared in the 1980s, but they tended to be based on narrative accounts of successful firms. The early works, especially Thomas Peters and Robert Waterman's best-selling 1982 book, *In Search of Excellence,* were typical of this qualitative approach. The authors identified forty-three excellent American companies and summarized the sources of their success. Today, led by Andersen Consulting Inc., the largest management consulting business in the world, benchmarking has become even more prevalent. According to this company, "benchmarking is the most powerful tool for assessing industrial competitiveness and for triggering the change process in companies striving for world class performance" (Andersen Consulting, Inc. 1993, 19).

Recent benchmarking studies rely on quantitative data. They measure and compare a company's operations with those of its competitors in order to identify those practices that distinguish the top-performing companies. This is done by measuring such factors as productivity, work-in-process, defects, space utilization, amount of inventory, setup times, and so on. Armed with these data, consultants sell their "secrets" to less successful companies. What is almost always missing from benchmarking is any measurement of best-practice working conditions or of the effect of recommended changes in the labor process on workers. There are no indices of best practice, for example, in the areas of health and safety, work loads or work pace, skills development, overtime demands, and job complexity.

Lean Production

Spurred by the success of Japanese manufacturers as well as by the evangelical promotion of lean production by James Womack, Daniel Jones, and Daniel Roos in their 1990 book, *The Machine That Changed the World*, lean production methods are being rapidly adopted not just by the Big Three automakers but by a growing number of manufacturing companies of all stripes.

Allegedly, lean production represented a shift from traditional mass production to post-Fordism. Early proponents stressed its advantages, such as precision and flexibility, tight inventories, quick die changes, and low per-unit assembly hours. But they also made exaggerated claims about its benefits for workers—extensive training, multiskilling, challenging work, empowerment, and harmonious labor-management relations. However, these "humane" arrangements arise not just from enlightened management's employment of sound human resources policies. The fragility of a lean system, especially its JIT deliveries and production processes and workers' quality responsibilities, obligates management to use practices that commit workers to the company and its objectives (MacDuffie 1995, 60). Like it or not, lean companies must be nice to their workers.

More recently, Thomas Kochan, Russell Lansbury, and John Paul MacDuffie (1997) retreated from the unsubstantiated argument advanced by their International Motor Vehicle Program (IMVP) colleagues, namely that lean production provides challenging jobs performed by multiskilled workers in a high-trust, participatory environment. Now IMVP simply maintains that the optimal efficiency of lean manufacturing techniques requires "high-involvement" work practices and human resource policies, including teams, extensive job rotation, problem-solving groups, suggestion programs, inspection by production workers, hiring criteria that stress willingness to learn and get along with others rather than prior manufacturing experience, long hours of training, contingent compensation (merit pay, profit-sharing, bonuses), and few status differentials (no special cafeterias, parking lots, and the like). While IMVP's retreat from its earlier position on lean production's impact on workers is welcome, it is open to criticism.

First, many of IMVP's involvement criteria give no substantive indication of the level of involvement. For example, plants get high-involvement scores on the team criterion solely on the basis of having a large percentage of their workforce organized in teams. There is no measure of the degree of team autonomy. We concluded from our longitudinal, in-plant study of CAMI, a GM-Suzuki auto assembly plant heralded as a lean production showcase, that there was little scope for team autonomy. Standardized, short-cycled, line-paced work; JIT pull processes and low inventory; and several layers of production management precluded any but the most routine kinds of team discretion (Rinehart, Huxley, and Robertson 1997). CAMI is not exceptional in this regard. Teams in most of the world's auto plants, including the leanest, have only a fraction of the discretion enjoyed by workers in some Scandinavian factories. The same criticism applies to training. Ratings are based on hours rather than content, and we know much of the training in lean plants is ideological and pertains to "soft skills." The same is true for job rotation. For IMVP, the more extensive the job rotation, the higher the involvement score, but there is no measure of the complexity of the jobs or the skills demanded of the jobs through which workers rotate. As in traditional mass-production plants, some jobs at CAMI were better than others, but workers certainly could not be considered multiskilled. Rather, rotation involved routine variety and workers who were multitasked, not multiskilled. Nowhere in the literature is there evidence of multiskilled production workers in lean plants.

Second, the existence of IMVP's high-involvement practices does not preclude a stressful work environment. Like benchmarking studies, IMVP does not measure workloads, work intensity, job complexity, overtime demands, and health and safety problems, especially repetitive strain injuries (RSIs). Recently the union of Canadian Auto Workers (CAW) conducted its own benchmarking study, which reflected worker, not corporate, interests (Robertson et al. 1996).

The CAW survey was based on the responses of nearly 2,500 workers in GM, Chrysler, Ford, and CAMI auto assembly plants in Canada. It found every plant had become leaner over the past five or six years, but that GM had moved the fastest and the farthest, followed by Ford and Chrysler; CAMI was lean to begin with. JIT procedures were implemented, buffers were reduced, work-in-process was maximized, job content was increased, workers' performance was electronically monitored, and there was a continuous effort to reduce waste (nonvalue-added labor).

Slightly over 70 percent of the respondents said their workload had increased in the last two years. Workers in the leanest plants, GM and CAMI, said they had the heaviest and fastest work, and they reported the highest degree of physical health risks, exhaustion, and stress. Workers at GM, followed by those at CAMI, were substantially more likely than their counterparts at Chrysler and Ford to report low levels of autonomy and control. So much for the empowered workers of lean production.

The CAW also surveyed 1,670 workers employed in the independent auto parts sector in Canada. The companies were placed in one of four categories, ranging from traditional Fordist to lean. It is worth quoting at length the study's conclusions:

Compared with workers in traditional Fordist-style plants, those at lean companies reported their workload was heavier and faster. They reported workloads were increasing and becoming even faster. They did not report it was easier to change things they did not like about their job. They did report that it was becoming more difficult to get time off and were more likely to have to find a replacement worker before they could go to the washroom. They were more likely to report that they would be unable to maintain their current work pace until age 60. (Lewchuk and Robertson 1996, 79)

Conditions like these have been observed in lean plants throughout the world (Babson 1993; Berggren 1992; Fucini and Fucini 1990; Graham 1995; Junkerman 1987; Kendall 1987; Parker and Slaughter 1994; Sandoval Godoy and Gonzales 1994; Watanabe 1993; Price 1995; Garrahan and Stewart 1992). The leanest auto plant in Germany, GM Opel, has the most narrowly defined jobs and allows workers the least discretion (Roth 1997). There is no more revealing evidence of lean production's negative impact on workers than recent developments at Toyota in Japan. Due to tight labor markets and worker discontent, Toyota modified key elements of lean by relaxing JIT procedures, moving tasks from the main to subassembly lines, and adding buffers between the main lines (Ishida 1997).

Independent of the extent to which enlightened human resource practices exist, lean production manufacturing techniques such as JIT; the reduction of buffers; the elimination of off-line subassembly stations; highly standardized, short-cycled jobs; and the continuous reduction of nonvalue-added labor invariably increase the pace and intensity of work. CAMI has a full complement of high-involvement work practices and human resource policies, but most job cycles range from one to three minutes, and some of the most contentious issues are time study, job standards, and workloads.

It is difficult to see how even the most enlightened human resource policies might ease workers' daily burdens in lean factories, for

> wherever it operates, lean production strives to operate with minimal labor. It is a system that aspires to eliminate all buffers save one—an understaffed workforce that is expected to make up for production glitches, line stoppages, unbalanced production scheduling, and injured or absent workers through intensified effort and overtime. The true buffers in this system are workers. (Rinehart, Huxley, and Robertson 1997,195)

Third, the high-involvement practices specified by IMVP do not ensure, let alone correlate strongly with, optimal efficiency. At Toyota in Japan—the undisputed champion of lean production—job design is Taylorist, production is planned and managed from the top, and all employees experience relentless pressure. Improvement activity (*kaizen*) is done mainly by production managers, engineers, and team leaders, as workers are too busy with their jobs to be heavily involved (Ishida 1997). Conversely, efficiency can be achieved without enlightened human resource policies. Big Three plants in Canada, for example, rank high on productivity and quality without using many of the high-involvement practices specified by IMVP (Kumar and Holmes 1997). IMVP also gave high marks on efficiency and quality to the Ford plant in Hermosillo, Mexico. In fact, Womack, Jones, and Roos (1990, 87) stated that this plant's quality topped that of the best Japanese plants and North American transplants. However, there is little evidence of enlightened human resource policies at the

Hermosillo plant, and labor-management relations are highly conflictual. The plant has been hit by strikes, boycotts, and line stoppages, and labor turnover ranges between 25 and 44 percent (Sandoval Godoy and Wong 1994; Shaiken 1993).

Evidence from around the world indicates that lean production is most advanced in so-called greenfield sites (where plant location and new workers are carefully screened), and where companies face heightened competition, shrinking markets, overcapacity, and falling profits—or in other words, where companies' threats of employment cutbacks and/or plant closure are not idle. Relatedly, lean production is least advanced where threats to jobs do not exist and where the union movement or local is strong and militant (Kochan, Lansbury, and MacDuffie 1997). Unless we believe unions are misguided and ignorant of the true character of lean production, their skepticism of and opposition to this system suggest that it contains elements detrimental to workers' interests.

Given this critical evidence, it is surprising that even some left-leaning academics hold out NUMMI in Fremont, California, as a model plant. In her recent book, for example, Ruth Milkman (1997) unfavorably contrasts Big Three plants with NUMMI, attributing NUMMI's efficiency and high-quality products to shop-floor harmony and a participatory environment. However, there are several problems with this argument.

First, it ignores that NUMMI's efficiency is due largely to Toyota's acknowledged superior capacity to produce vehicles that are easy to manufacture. Ease of manufacture means vehicles have a minimum number of components to be assembled, which translates into low assembly hours required to build a vehicle. Second, Milkman ignores the long period of joblessness experienced by NUMMI workers, most of whom were thrown out of work for several years by the closure of the GM plant that now houses NUMMI. It is unrealistic to think that workers' "cooperation" is not influenced by this experience and fears of another plant shutdown. Third, Milkman's enthusiasm for participation (even supposing NUMMI's brand is the genuine article) is puzzling in that she cites much evidence showing at best a weak relationship between participation and productivity. Fourth, labor-management cooperation is less than perfect at NUMMI. Petitions have protested understaffing and the company's strict absenteeism policy. The rank and file have elected union candidates who ran on slates criticizing NUMMI's heavy workloads, speedup, a high rate of RSIs, and management favoritism. The plant was hit by a walkout in 1994. Finally, almost everything written on NUMMI has come from one enthusiastic source—Paul Adler (Adler 1993a; 1993b; 1995; Adler and Cole 1993)—a professor in the Department of Management and Organization at the University of Southern California.

The Saturn Model: Beyond Lean Production?

Liberal academics, in particular MIT professors associated with IMVP, are promoting the Saturn plant in Spring Hill, Tennessee, as a "post-lean" model of efficiency and organizational governance. Saturn is a team-concept plant that uses lean manufacturing processes, but its most unusual feature is the extensive web of collaboration between the company and the union (Rubinstein, Bennett, and Kochan 1993). Proponents call it "the boldest experiment in comanagement in the United States today" (Adler et al. 1997, 62). The company operates with joint union-management decision-making bodies at various organizational levels, and the union is involved in decisions concerning supplier and dealer selection, choice of technology, and product development. At the departmental level, managerial responsibilities are handled not by foreman and general foremen, but by "partnered" union representatives and managers. That one-half of middle managers are union members "challenges long-held beliefs about the separation of management and labor" (Adler et al. 1997, 63).

Many of the problems associated with and criticisms leveled against the labor-management cooperative agreements of the 1920s apply equally well to Saturn (Nyman 1934; Slichter 1941). How can a union represent and promote the independent interests of workers when it is so heavily involved in managing workers and supporting whatever it takes to increase output and keep labor costs low? To the extent that union representatives are compromised by management and adopt managerial attitudes, workers' interests will be subordinated to the achievement of goals set by the company. Under these circumstances, what can a union do to justify dues payments by its members?

This is not a hypothetical dilemma. Surveys and focus-group interviews of Saturn workers revealed a buildup of dissatisfaction with the union's capacity to adequately represent its membership. This rank-and-file dissatisfaction is reflected by the presence of oppositional caucuses and hotly contested union elections. Moreover, shop-floor pressure was successful in changing the process of union crew leader selection from appointment to election and in empowering these crew leaders to file members' grievances. Solidarity House, the UAW headquarters, now questions the Saturn union local's ability to effectively address members' problems and is opposed to extending this kind of union-management partnership arrangement to other plants (Adler et al. 1997).

With Saturn sales slipping and workers' bonuses falling, the union local held a referendum in March 1998 that could have abolished the collaborative agreement in favor of a traditional UAW-GM contract. Workers voted two-to-one in favor of maintaining the special arrangements. However, the vote, it appears, was not an endorsement of labor-management cooperation. Rather, it reflected workers' fears about job security. The president of the local warned that changing the contract, which guarantees no layoffs except for cataclysmic events or severe economic conditions, would result in 2,700 workers being laid off (Slaughter 1998).

Conclusions

What conclusions can be drawn from this overview of work restructuring over the past three decades? First, work restructuring increasingly is being introduced in conjunction with the implementation of advanced technology. Second, corporations and management consultants are less prone than in previous decades to claim or promise that restructured work will improve the quality of worklife. The need for competitiveness and/or the avoidance of job loss now are the operative justifications. This represents a more candid appraisal of the true dimensions and consequences of workplace reorganization. It also reflects a rather decisive shift in the balance of power between labor and capital and a related capacity of companies to limit and contain worker resistance and neutralize or weaken union power. Third, despite the vigorous efforts of IMVP to promote lean production as mutually beneficial to labor and capital, rapidly accumulating evidence from around the world indicates otherwise. Lean production has failed miserably to live up to its promise of humanizing the workplace. This has become so obvious that IMVP has had to retreat from its original claim of an invariable connection between lean manufacturing techniques and enlightened human resource policies and work practices. Now IMVP proponents simply argue that the full advantages of lean manufacturing procedures can only be realized under enlightened management policies, but their definition of "enlightened" is highly questionable. Finally, the current sorry state of industrial relations is revealed by the fact that companies like NUMMI and Saturn are portrayed as models not only of efficiency but also of worker-friendly environments and harmonious labor-management relations.

References

Adler, Paul. 1993a. "The Learning Bureaucracy: New United Motor Manufacturing, Inc." *Research in Organizational Behavior*, 15: 111–94.

———. 1993b. "Time and Motion Regained." *Harvard Business Review*, January–February: 97–108.

———. 1995. "'Democratic Taylorism': The Toyota Production System at NUMMI." Pp. 207–219 in *Lean Work: Empowerment and Exploritation in the Global Auto Industry*. Detroit: Wayne State University Press.

Adler, Paul, and Robert Cole. 1993. "Designed for Learning: A Tale of Two Auto Plants." *Sloan Management Review*, Spring: 85–94.

Adler, Paul, Thomas Kochan, John Paul MacDuffie, Frits Pil, and Saul Rubenstein. 1997. "United States: Variations on a Theme." Pp. 61–83 in *After Lean Production: Evolving Employment Practices in the World Auto Industry*, edited by T. Kochan, R. Lansbury, and J. P. MacDuffie. Ithaca: ILR–Cornell University Press.

Andersen Consulting, Inc. 1993. *The Lean Enterprise Benchmarking Project*. London: Author.

Applebaum, Eileen, and R. Batt. 1994. *The New American Workplace: Transforming Work Systems in the United States*. Ithaca: ILR Press.

Babson, Steve. 1993. "Lean or Mean: The MIT Model and Lean Production at Mazda." *Labor Studies Journal*, 18(2): 3–24.

Berggren, Christian. 1992. *Alternatives to Lean Production*. Ithaca: ILR Press.

Bluestone, Barry, and Bennett Harrison. 1982. *The Deindustrialization of America*. New York: Basic Books.

Braverman, Harry. 1974. *Labor and Monopoly Capital: The Degradation of Work in the Twentieth Century.* New York: Monthly Review Press.

Bronfenbrenner, Kate. 1996. *The Effects of Plant Closing or Threat of Plant Closing on the Right of Workers to Organize.* Final report submitted to the Labor Secretariat of the North American Commission for Labor Cooperation, September 30. Ithaca: Cornell University.

Capelli, Peter, and Robert McKersie. 1987. "Management Strategy and the Redesign of Work Rules." *Journal of Management Studies,* 24(5): 441–462.

Cole, Robert. ed. 1995. *The Death and Life of the American Quality Movement.* New York: Oxford University Press.

Easton, George. 1995. "A Baldridge Examiner's Assessment of U.S. Total Quality Management." Pp. 11–41 in *The Death and Life of the American Quality Movement,* edited by R. Cole. New York: Oxford University Press.

Fucini, Joseph, and Suzy Fucini. 1990. *Working for the Japanese: Inside Mazda's American Auto Plant.* New York: Free Press.

Garrahan, Philip, and Paul Stewart. 1992. *The Nissan Enigma.* London: Mansell Publishing.

Gindin, Sam. 1989. "Breaking Away: The Formation of the Canadian Auto Workers Union." *Studies in Political Economy,* 29: 63–89.

Gordon, David. 1996. *Fat and Mean: The Corporate Squeeze of Working Americans and the Myth of Managerial Downsizing.* New York: Free Press.

Graham, Laurie. 1995. *On the Line at Subaru-Isuzu: The Japanese Model and the American Worker.* Ithaca: ILR Press.

Greenbaum, Joan. 1995. *Windows on the Workplace: Computers, Jobs, and the Organization of Work in the Late Twentieth Century.* New York: Monthly Review Press.

Hammer, Michael, and James Champy. 1993. *Reengineering the Corporation: A Manifesto for Business Revolution.* New York: HarperBusiness.

Herzberg, Frederick. 1966. *Work and the Nature of Man.* New York: Mentor Books.

———. 1968. "One More Time: How Do You Motivate Your Employees?" *Harvard Business Review,* September–October: 53–62.

Indergaard, Michael, and Michael Cushion. 1987. "Conflict, Cooperation, and the Global Auto Factory." Pp. 203–228 in *Workers, Managers, and Technological Change,* edited by D. Cornfield. New York: Plenum Press.

Ishida, Mitsuo. 1997. "Beyond the Model for Lean Production." Pp. 45–60 in *After Lean Production: Evolving Employment Practices in the World Auto Industry,* edited by T. Kochan, R. Lansbury, and J. P. MacDuffie. Ithaca: ILR–Cornell University Press.

Junkerman, John. 1987. "Nissan, Tennessee." *The Progressive,* 51 (6): 17–20.

Katz, Harry. 1985. *Shifting Gears: Changing Labor Relations in the U.S. Automobile Industry.* Cambridge: The MIT Press.

Kelly, James. 1982. *Scientific Management, Job Redesign, and Work Performance.* New York: Academic Press.

Kendall, R. 1987. "Safety Management: Japanese Style." *Occupational Hazards,* 49: 248–251.

Kochan, Thomas, Joel Cutcher-Gershenfeld, and John Paul MacDuffie. 1989. *Employee Participation, Work Redesign, and New Technology.* Washington, DC: U.S. Department of Labor.

Kochan, Thomas, Russell Lansbury, and John Paul MacDuffie, eds. 1997. *After Lean Production: Evolving Employment Practices in the World Auto Industry.* Ithaca: ILR–Cornell University Press.

Kraft, Philip. 1999. "To Control and Inspire." Pp. 17–36 in *Rethinking the Labor Process,* edited by M. Wardell, T. Steiger, and P. Meiksins. Albany: SUNY Press.

Kumar, Pradeep, and John Holmes. 1997. "Canada: Continuity and Change." Pp. 85–108 in *After Lean Production: Evolving Employment Practices in the World Auto Industry*, edited by T. Kochan, R. Lansbury, and J. P. MacDuffie. Ithaca: ILR–Cornell University Press.

Lewchuk, Wayne, and David Robertson. 1996. "Working Conditions Under Lean Production: A Worker-Based Benchmarking Study." *Asia Pacific Business Review*, 2(4): 60–81.

MacDuffie, John Paul. 1995. "Workers' Roles in Lean Production: The Implications for Worker Representation." Pp. 54–69 in *Lean Work: Empowerment and Exploitation in the Global Auto Industry*, edited by S. Babson. Detroit: Wayne State University Press.

MacDuffie, John Paul, and Fritz Pil. 1997. "Changes in Auto Industry Employment Practices: An International Overview." Pp. 9–42 in *After Lean Production: Evolving Employment Practices in the World Auto Industry*, edited by T. Kochan, R. Lansbury, and J. P. MacDuffie. Ithaca: ILR–Cornell University Press.

Micklethwait, John, and Adrian Wooldridge. 1996. *The Witch Doctors*. London: Heinemann.

Milkman, Ruth. 1997. *Farewell to the Factory: Auto Workers in the Late Twentieth Century*. Berkeley: University of California Press.

Mishel, Lawrence, and Jared Bernstein. 1994. *The State of Working America, 1994–1995*. New York: M. E. Sharpe.

Murakami, Tetsuo. 1997. "The Autonomy of Teams in the Car Industry—A Cross-National Comparison." *Work, Employment, and Society*, 11(4): 749–758.

———. 1998. "Work Organization: Taylorism and Teamwork." *Perspectives on Work*, April: 69–70.

"The New Industrial Relations." 1981. *Business Week*, 11 May, pp. 85–98.

Nyman, Richmond. 1934. *Union-Management Cooperation in the "Stretch-Out."* New Haven: Yale University Press.

Parker, Michael. 1985. *Inside the Circle: A Union Guide to QWL*. Detroit: Labor Notes/South End Press.

Parker, Michael, and Jane Slaughter, eds. 1994. *Working Smart: A Union Guide to Participation Programs and Reengineering*. Detroit: Labor Notes.

Peters, Thomas, and Robert Waterman. 1982. *In Search of Excellence: Lessons from America's Best-Run Companies*. New York: Warner Books.

Price, John. 1994. "Total Quality Management in Health Care: Wonder Drug or Snake Oil?" Pp. 196–199 in *Working Smart: A Union Guide to Participation Programs and Reengineering*, edited by M. Parker and J. Slaughter. Detroit: Labor Notes.

———. 1995. "Lean Production at Suzuki and Toyota: A Historical Perspective." Pp. 81–107 in *Lean Work: Empowerment and Exploitation in the Global Auto Industry*, edited by S. Babson. Detroit: Wayne State University Press.

Price, Michael, and Eva Chen. 1995. "Total Quality Management in a Small, High Technology Company." Pp. 115–37 in *The Death and Life of the American Quality Movement*, edited by R. Cole. New York: Oxford University Press.

Raines, John, Lenora Berson, and David Gracie. 1982. *Community and Capital in Conflict: Plant Closings and Job Loss*. Philadelphia: Temple University Press.

Rifkin, Jeremy. 1996. *The End of Work*. New York: G. P. Putnam's Sons.

Rinehart, James. 1978. *Job Enrichment and the Labor Process*. Paper presented at the conference "New Directions in the Labor Process," State University of New York, Binghamton, May.

———. 1986. "Improving the Quality of Working Life Through Job Redesign: Work Humanization or Work Rationalization?" *Canadian Review of Sociology and Anthropology*, 13(4): 507–530.

Rinehart, James, Christopher Huxley, and David Robertson. 1997. *Just Another Car Factory? Lean Production and Its Discontents*. Ithaca: Cornell University Press.

Robertson, David, Wayne Lewchuk, B. Roberts, and C. McDonald. 1996. *The CAW Workers Conditions Study: Benchmarking Auto Assembly Plants*. North York, Ontario: CAW-Canada.

Roth, Siegfried. 1997. "Germany: Labor's Perspective on Lean Production." Pp. 117–36 in *After Lean Production: Evolving Employment Practices in the World Auto Industry*, edited by T. Kochan, R. Lansbury, and J. P. MacDuffie. Ithaca: ILR–Cornell University Press.

Rubinstein, Saul, S. Bennett, and Thomas Kochan. 1993. "The Saturn Partnership: Co-Management and the Reincarnation of the Local Union." Pp. 339–370 in *Employee Participation*, edited by E. Kaufman and M. Klewer. Madison: Industrial Relations Research Association.

Sandoval Godoy, S., and P. Wong. 1994. "Labor Relations and Trade Union Action in Hermosillo's Ford Plant, 1986–1994." Paper presented at the Cars and Continentalism Conference, University of Toronto, May.

Shaiken, Harley. 1993. "The New International Division of Labor and Its Impact on Unions: A Case Study of High-Tech Mexican Export Production." Pp. 224–239 in *Workplace Industrial Relations and the Global Challenge*, edited by J. Belanger, P. K. Edwards, and L. Haiven. Ithaca: ILR Press.

Slaughter, Jane. 1998. "Car Sales Slip, Saturn Workers Worry About Job Security Under 'Cooperation' Regime." *Labor Notes*, April: 16.

Slichter, Sumner. 1941. *Union Policies and Industrial Management*. Washington, DC: The Brookings Institute.

Terkel, Studs. 1974. *Working*. New York: Pantheon Books.

U.S. Department of Health, Education, and Welfare. 1972. *Work in America: Report of a Special Task Force to the Secretary of Health, Education, and Welfare*. Cambridge: MIT Press.

Watanabe, Ben. 1993. "The Japanese Auto Industry: Is Lean Production on the Way Out?" Paper presented at the Lean Workplace Conference, Port Elgin, Ontario.

Womack, James, Daniel Jones, and Daniel Roos. 1990. *The Machine That Changed the World*. New York: Rawson and Associates.

CHAPTER 9

Manufacturing Compromise: The Dynamics of Race and Class Among South African Shop Stewards in the 1990s

Edward Webster

During the 1970s and 1980s a powerful shop-floor-based trade union movement took root in South Africa. Shop stewards emerged as crucial leaders in the struggles that began in the 1980s in the townships over rent, shack removals, education, and the occupation by the South African Defense Force. Their involvement in issues beyond the factory distinguishes the South African shop stewards from their European and North American counterparts. It also distinguishes South Africa from the rest of Africa, where the struggle against colonial rule did not involve the mobilization of a grassroots working-class movement. Instead independence was won either by nationalist movements led largely by the professional middle classes or by peasant-based guerrilla movements that did not address the concerns of an industrial working class.

At the center of this grassroots movement was the Congress of South African Trade Unions (COSATU), a federation of industrial unions. Its membership was overwhelmingly drawn from semiskilled and unskilled black workers. At the base of this movement was the shop steward, a worker representative directly accountable to the shop floor. Little was known of the shop steward, whose popular stereotype was that of a political activist aggressively challenging managerial prerogative in the workplace.

In the early 1990s the author was approached by COSATU to identify the social background and attitudes of the more than twenty-five thousand shop stewards. In the first half of 1991, an extensive survey of COSATU shop stewards was conducted. The findings of this survey challenged the simplistic view of the shop steward as an aggressive and disruptive activist and revealed a more complex and ambivalent picture.

In particular, the shop stewards appeared to personify a paradox. On the one hand, they were at the center of political resistance to apartheid and expressed a desire for a thorough transformation of capitalist society in the direction of greater worker control; on the other hand, the respondents exhibited a high degree of cooperation toward management and a willingness to agree at times with management rather than their members. The survey revealed that shop stewards were often involved in preventing strike action and persuading workers to accept industry-level agreements. In fact, they sometimes even disciplined their members in the interests of higher productivity. At the center of the shop steward's role then, was the manufacture of compromise.

Of course this characterization of the shop stewards is not new, for they are described in the literature as "men in the middle" or "men with two masters," caught between the employer who pays his or her salary and the members she or he represents (Lane 1974). An important characteristic of the shop stewards is that they are not simply "stirring up" trouble; they often perform a managerial function of settling grievances. As the Donovan Commission, set up to examine British industrial relations in the 1960s, argued, shop stewards have an interest in maintaining "orderly" industrial relations: "it is often wide off the mark to describe shop stewards as 'troublemakers.' Trouble is thrust upon them. . . . Quite commonly they are supporters of order exercising a restraining influence on their members in conditions which promote disorder" (Hyman 1975, 103).

This essay evolved out of an attempt to explain the paradoxical results of the COSATU shop steward survey. The first attempt at an explanation drew on class theory and Erik Olin Wright's (1978) notion of contradictory class location. Revisiting the question five years later, and observing the impact on the shop steward of "deracialization" at work and in society during the period of transition from apartheid to democracy, the racial context of class relations emerged as central in any understanding of the changing role of the shop steward.

This chapter is divided into three parts. The first traces the emergence of a new research program in industrial sociology in South Africa in the 1970s and 1980s that had at its core Karl Marx's theory of the capitalist labor process. Drawing on the COSATU survey of shop stewards, the second part illustrates their paradoxical role in workplace industrial relations. The final section attempts to explain the paradox in terms of the ambivalent function performed by the shop steward in the workplace, informed by changes that have occurred over the past five years.

I conclude by arguing that the behavior of shop stewards in South Africa cannot be fully understood without exploring how their identity in the workplace is shaped by the changing political context. The apartheid workplace nurtured strong, oppositional shop-floor structures and blocked the promotion of shop stewards; the abolition of political apartheid has led to a decline in shop-floor structures and the rapid promotion of key shop stewards.[1]

The implications of the argument are that the mobilizing power of class discourse under apartheid seems to have been derived to a large extent from its association with race. The removal of political apartheid has disarticulated the nexus between race and class, leading to an erosion of the power of the shop steward. The impact these changes are having on the role of the shop steward will be explored in the conclusion.

From Marx to Mayo

It became commonplace in the 1950s and 1960s to argue that much of industrial sociology, shaped as it was by Elton Mayo, was "managerial sociology." By labeling industrial sociology as managerial, it was being suggested that sociology was being used, to put it simply, to facilitate management's task of increasing the profitability of the enterprise. For Robert Merton (1957, 625) "of the limited body of social research in industry, the greater part has been oriented towards the needs of management." Allan Flanders (1970, 60) summing up the literature in industrial sociology, wrote that it did not study how "to make management formally more accountable to the managed" but rather how to make the "employees more accountable to management." Loren Baritz (1965) entitled his comprehensive history of the use of social science in American industry *The "Servants of Power."* C. Wright Mills (1959, 58) summarizing the work of managerial sociology, in particular that of Mayo, argued that these scholars had discovered,

> one, that within the authority structure of modern industry there are status formations (informal organization), two, that often these operate to protect the workers against the exercise of authority, three, and that, therefore, for the sake of efficiency and to ward off uncollaborative tendencies (union and worker solidarity), managers should not try and break up these formations but should rather try to exploit them for their own ends. And four, that this might be done by recognizing and studying them, in order to manipulate the workers involved in them rather than merely authoritatively order them.

The breakdown of industrial consensus in the wake of economic crisis in the late sixties was to bring into question the theoretical presuppositions of industrial sociology. Richard Hyman (1981) distinguishes between two moments in the assault on traditional industrial sociology in the 1960s and 1970s. The first moment saw the acceptance of Marx as a central figure among the "founding fathers" of sociology, signaling a critical and humanistic dimension to industrial sociology in the 1970s, or what some have called "left Weberian" sociology (Giddens 1971). The rapid impact of this radicalization process created in its turn a second moment in the assault on industrial sociology, when, by the late 1970s, there were increasing signs of the Marxist challenge to the adequacy of the "radical approach." Some whose initial orientation to Marx was as a complement to the sociological classics came, Hyman argues, to reverse the emphasis: no longer subsuming Marx within industrial sociology, but subordinating sociology to Marxian political economy.

This was most evident in the rediscovery of Marx's account of the capitalist labor process in Harry Braverman's *Labor and Monopoly Capital: The Degradation of Work in the*

Twentieth Century (1974). In particular, Braverman highlighted Marx's discussion of the capitalist labor process, which posed an overwhelming challenge to the sociological orthodox (Hyman 1981). The recovery of Marx's theory of the labor process acquired a particular relevance in South Africa because of the rise of a militant labor movement in the 1970s and 1980s. It generated a number of substantive studies of the labor process that were to transform the sociological study of work in South Africa (Lever 1983).

The rapid growth of the new shop-floor-based unions, facilitated in 1979 when the Wiehan Commission (set up in 1977 to investigate the industrial relations system) recommended that unions among black workers be recognized, led sociologists to examine the origins and nature of the labor movement. How does one explain, sociologists began to ask, the emergence of mass based industrial unions among black workers at this time? What accounted for the emergence of strong shop steward structures and their extension into radical social movements in the townships?

As a starting point, the new industrial sociology sought answers in the labor process. The transition to monopoly capitalism in the post–World War II period had, it was argued, deskilled craftwork, extending the use of mass production methods, or what is called Fordism. This concentration of workers in crowded assembly lines provided the basis for their unity and organization on a mass scale. In a large, integrated manufacturing operation such as the auto industry, a relatively small group of workers can cripple an entire system by shutting down a part of the line. This, as has been argued elsewhere, provided the conditions for the rapid growth of militant shop-floor-based industrial unionism (Edwards 1979).

A number of studies have demonstrated the link between changes in the labor process and the growth of workplace bargaining, although racism complicated any simple transfer of Fordism to South Africa (Lewis 1984; Webster 1985; Innes 1983; Southall 1985; Maree 1985; Ewert 1988; Maller 1992). The spread of unionism in South Africa differed from that in the United States or Europe. Research on the process of deskilling showed how white craft workers were able to maintain control over the job by resorting, through craft unions, to explicitly racist forms of job protection. This has been called "racial despotism": racial, because one racial group dominated through political, legal, and economic rights denied to others; and despotic, because coercion, both physical and economic, prevailed over consent (Burawoy 1985).

Fordism involves more than a production process, or a particular way of building cars; it is an ideal type that describes the process of accumulation within the whole economy. Put simply, Fordism is mass production plus mass consumption. What emerged in South Africa after 1945 was not Fordism but a caricature of Fordism; partial mass production was introduced, given the limited and racially skewed nature of the local market. Whites monopolized the skilled and supervisory positions in the labor process. The wages of white workers rose steadily, making possible the spread of mass consumption of housing and locally produced consumer durables, while blacks were excluded from the mass consumption norms that applied to whites and, at a later stage, were extended to the Indian and colored groups. This Fordist caricature has been described as "racial Fordism" (Gelb 1991).

The hostels of migrant workers served the same function in South Africa as large man-ufacturing firms in the advanced economies; by bringing together large numbers of the industrial workforce who had a shared sense of grievance, they facilitated communica-tion between workers and facilitated the spread of unionism. In the early days of the new unions, a high proportion of their members came from the migrant workers in these hostels. In many respects, they built the South African union movement (Sitas 1983).

While research on the labor process provided the starting point for the new indus-trial sociology, many found labor process theory restrictive in two ways. First, the involvement of workers and their shop stewards in community politics drew sociol-ogists away from the workplace to explore the distinct cultural formations created by workers. To understand worker leaders, sociologists followed them into their rooms in the hostels and their shacks in the townships, to identify the associations to which they belonged, their ties of kinship, and their village origins. Using the biographical method, the "defensive combinations" that were beginning to provide the basis for collective mobilization of migrant workers were identified (Sitas 1983). One of these biographical studies was of Mandlenkosi Mokoba, a migrant worker from Zululand (Stewart 1981; Webster 1991). This study established the many identities of this "ordi-nary" shop steward: furnace "boy," worker leader, Zulu patriarch, subsistence farmer, preacher, and a member of the Inkatha Freedom Party (IFP).

These nonclass identities raise complex theoretical questions for class theory and have generated a number of studies of culture and working life (Sitas 1983; Bonnin 1987). They have also led to studies on the relationship of the unions to the new social movements—what has been called social movement unionism (Munck 1987; Lambert and Webster 1988). More importantly, sociologists began to see workers not simply as abstract categories, but as women and men with lives outside of work and with the creative energy to participate fully in cultural and political life. What has not yet been systematically explored is how nonclass factors influence the identity and actions of workers inside the workplace (Leroke 1993).

The second area in which labor process theory proved too restrictive is in its assumptions that work is always coercive and that workers are the passive recipients of managerial authority. I argued that most studies of the labor process neglected worker resistance (Webster 1985). I challenged Braverman's depiction of mass pro-duction as a juggernaut, that inherently imposed tighter controls on workers, and instead pointed toward two forms of worker resistance that have been important in the history of the workplace in South Africa: (1) the resistance of craft workers to deskilling; and (2) the increase in bargaining power conferred on semiskilled work-ers by mass production. There is considerable evidence that the transition to mass production linked together workers in the production process and increased capital's vulnerability to workers' direct action at the point of production, creating favorable conditions for workplace bargaining.

I have argued that Marx's theory of the labor process emerged as the core theory of the new industrial sociology in the late 1970s. At the center of this theory was the assumption that work is always coercive and antagonistic. However, it is in this area that the most substantial modification to the existing theory must be made, as capital cannot rely wholly on coercion. At some level, workers' cooperation, productive powers, and consent must be engaged and mobilized.

The findings of the study on shop stewards confirm this approach. They challenge the simplistic view of the workplace as coercive and reveal a more complex picture. These results will be explored in the second part of this chapter.

The Workplace: Conflict and Cooperation

Shop stewards were introduced into trade unions in South Africa in the late nineteenth century by British craft workers. However, they operated rather weakly until the early 1970s when, influenced by the growth of the shop steward movement in Britain, the emerging industrial unions placed central emphasis on building a working-class leadership on the shop floor in South Africa. The shop stewards and their committees rapidly emerged at the center of the organizational structure of these new unions. The "shop-floor" unions that first developed in 1973 avoided political action outside the workplace. They emphasized instead the building of democratic shop-floor structures around the principles of worker control, accountability, and mandating of worker representatives.

In spite of the shop stewards' importance in the emerging industrial relations system, their role remained unexamined during the 1970s. The Wiehan Commission made no reference at all to their existence in South African workplaces. Between 1983 and 1984, the number of shop stewards doubled from 6,000 to over 12,000, thereby consolidating union power at the shop-floor level. By 1984, these unions had an organizing presence in over 3,400 workplaces, with formal agreements in 450 (Lewis and Randall 1985). The recognition agreements contained significant rights for shop stewards, including time off for meetings and training and the right to represent their members in grievances and disciplinary matters. Unionization could no longer mean a simple process of recognition and annual bargaining of wages; instead the union was now situated within the workplace, had changed the nature of workplace relations profoundly, and had challenged the unilateral exercise of power by management.

Shop stewards became the pivot of the organizational structure of the new unions. They performed an important role in recruiting new members, particularly where access for union officials was a problem. They also created a structure of workplace representation that ensured the unions remained democratic and sensitive to their members' needs and interests. The shop stewards ensured that power was devolved within the system of industrial relations to the workplace and did not become a bureaucratic exercise between representatives of management and labor.

The role of the shop stewards is multifaceted. Firstly, it is to represent the interests of union members in their department and to protect their interests against management. Each department elects its own shop steward; on average, there was one steward for every sixty members in the early 1980s (Webster 1985). The shop stewards collectively constitute a shop stewards' committee, which is instrumental in plant-level negotiations over wages and working conditions (in the absence of industrial councils). It is also the job of the stewards to ensure that agreements are implemented correctly.

Even at the early stage of development of the shop stewards movement, the ambivalence in their role was apparent. They were representatives of their constituency in a situation in which class interests were antagonistic. But they were also charged with the resolution of grievances and the maintenance of discipline among the workers under them (Webster 1985, 82). A crucial characteristic of the South African shop stewards, and one that differentiates them from their British counterparts, is that their leadership activities are not confined to the workplace, but extend into the township struggles over housing and local politics (Webster 1985).

Nowadays, the legitimacy of the shop steward as a significant actor in the industrial relations system is widely accepted. The vast majority of stewards (97 percent) interviewed in the sample had formal recognition from management. Interestingly, 31 percent said they were full-time shop stewards, which we assume meant that they spend their entire working day, with or without the permission or knowledge of management, performing shop steward duties.

The social background of COSATU shop stewards shows that they are relatively young: a third are under twenty-nine, and a half are in their thirties. Most shop stewards are men: only 14 percent are women, although COSATU's membership consists of 36 percent women (Baskin 1992). They reflect the ethnic diversity present in South Africa, yet the vast majority consider themselves to have a mainly South African identity (86 percent) rather than an ethnic one (5 percent). The overwhelming majority of shop stewards are affiliated to a religious faith or denomination and attend services regularly, particularly the women. Slightly more than half are married or live with a partner and most have children (89 percent). It is clear from the survey that their shop steward duties considerably disrupt family life.

Shop stewards are, on the whole, stable and long-serving employees. Half (49 percent) have worked more than eight years in the same company. Of these, 40 percent have in fact worked in the same job for over seven years, suggesting a lack of job mobility and possible job frustration. It also implies close connections with fellow workers who experience the same lack of mobility. Their wages show that they are firmly located within the working class, as half earn less than R250 per week. This puts their earnings on a par with those of unionized workers in unskilled and semiskilled positions in the manufacturing and retail sectors. Only 10 percent of the shop stewards earn more than R400 per week, and the jobs of this group are classified as either clerical or supervisory.

All stewards are subject to formal and regular elections by their constituents, either through a show of hands (52 percent) or secret ballot (48 percent). The vast majority are relatively new in their role. Sixty-six percent had served as stewards for three years or less. Only 1 percent had served for ten years or longer, suggesting that there is little entrenchment of power at the shop-floor level.

Shop stewards are a deeply committed group of activists who take their responsibilities seriously. Forty-six percent reported attending shop-steward meetings several times a week. In some unions, over 60 percent attendance was recorded. Shop stewards on the whole are drawn from the traditional, industrial working class, and are predominantly in the unskilled and semiskilled categories (55 percent). This underlines the fact that they are representatives of their constituency, working side-by-side with their members. However, a significant number of stewards are now drawn from the middle strata—the higher skilled, supervisory, and clerical levels—especially in public sector unions, such as NEHAWU, SAMWU, and POTWA.

Table 9-1 shows clearly that the shop stewards in industrial unions are mostly concentrated among semiskilled and unskilled workers, although the number of skilled stewards is clearly expanding in line with the changing demographics of skill (Crankshaw and Hindson 1991). As noted, it is the nonindustrial unions, mainly in the public sector, that have significant concentrations of shop stewards in the middle strata. For example, in POTWA, 43 percent of shop stewards are technicians. In NEHAWU, 30 percent are semiprofessionals and 32 percent are clerical workers. SAMWU also has a relatively high proportion of shop stewards in the semiprofessional and clerical categories.

Shop stewards are often elected because of their relatively higher level of skills or education, as this will place them in a better position to represent the interests of their members to management. The stewards, on the whole, tend to be more educated and better paid than their constituents. Twenty-four percent have some form of postsecondary education, and 60 percent have gone beyond primary school. This is in stark contrast to the black population as a whole, of whom 59 percent have not completed primary school (National Manpower Commission 1989).

Although the co-optation of this layer of worker leadership is a possibility, there is nothing in the evidence from the survey to suggest that this is inevitable. Although stewards are found in relatively higher job grades (for example, 11 percent of the subjects are supervisors), respondents overwhelmingly (75 percent) supported the idea

TABLE 9-1. Job Classifications of South African Shop Stewards (percentage)

Union	Semiprofessional	Clerical	Supervisory	Techical	Skilled	Semiskilled	Unskilled
CAWU	3	—	—	—	29	34	34
CWIU	2	8	11	5	26	37	11
FAWU	—	7	12	3	19	33	26
NEHAWU	30	32	—	2	8	8	20
NUM	5	10	10	1	14	38	22
NUMSA	3	10	5	1	17	46	18
POTWA	—	8	4	43	15	15	15
PPWAWU	—	7	—	7	23	39	24
SACCAWU	7	20	15	2	18	19	21
SACTWU	6	6	6	1	29	41	11
SAMWU	15	15	11	—	4	22	33
SARWHU	—	3	—	14	3	38	42
TGWU	2	—	1	—	29	34	34

of workers' committees running factories. Part of the explanation for this apparent paradox is the existence of important mechanisms that keep the stewards in touch with their constituents. In the first place, a strong democratic political culture has been built up inside the labor movement. An overwhelming majority of respondents (95 percent) agreed with the statement that stewards are bound by workers' mandates. Secondly, stewards have internalized the idea that they must represent the interests of workers. In the survey they defined their chief duties as representing workers (47 percent) and promoting worker rights (19 percent).

However, this role contains many tensions. Stewards are faced with constituents whose expectations are greater than the stewards' capacity to deliver. Consequently, 80 percent of our respondents felt that they may be in conflict with their constituents, and they admitted that occasionally they were required to discipline their members. This points to the ambiguous nature of the role of the shop stewards: on the one hand, it involves representing their constituents' grievances and defending their interests. On the other hand, stewards have to operate within the constraints of the industrial relations system. This involves, at times, agreeing with management rather than their members (59 percent), preventing strike action (52 percent), and persuading workers to accept industry-level agreements (65 percent). In addition, shop stewards have to reconcile individual and sectional interests with the interests of workers as a whole.

Contrary to popular stereotypes, not all shop stewards see themselves in permanent opposition to management. Thirty percent of our respondents agreed with the statement that management and workers have the same aims and objectives. This is a surprising finding, given the high levels of conflict within our industrial relations system. These results were confirmed by 77 percent of our respondents, who believe that management is becoming less confrontational. Older workers (i.e., those over forty) more readily agreed with this statement than younger workers.

In spite of the high degree of cooperation between management and labor identified in our survey, the idea of workers' control is deeply entrenched in the labor movement. Shop stewards believe that workers' committees should run the companies. This opinion is particularly strong among stewards in those unions that have incorporated the concept of workers' control in their educational programs, such as NUM (89 percent) and NUMSA (76 percent). Contrary to the apparent shift at leadership level against nationalization of unions, 67 percent of our respondents supported nationalization.

At the core of the concept of workers' control is the independence of the trade union and the right to strike. Ninety-three percent of those interviewed believed in retaining this right. Stewards' responses seemed to indicate a tension between their strategic need to cooperate with management in their day-to-day work and their long-term objective of establishing greater worker control. Their responses leave open the form of worker control that should be implemented. Worker control is an ambiguous concept, and it is not clear whether our respondents' conception of it is a radical one. They could mean a system of worker participation along the lines of the German system of codetermination, or a more thoroughgoing transformation of ownership, control, and indeed society.[2] Ninety-five percent of the stewards believed that workers should share in company profits—a practice readily consistent with capitalist ownership of the means of production and one often adopted by management to undermine independent trade unionism.[3] This aspiration could easily be accommodated within a system of co-determination.

But 70 percent of stewards also believe that workers' overall interests are best represented by COSATU, compared to 21 percent who instead support the African National Congress (ANC) and 9 percent who favor the South African Communist Party (SACP), suggesting that the consciousness of shop stewards goes well beyond the factory. Their politics is working-class politics.[4] This response points toward the desire for a radical social transformation in which workers and their unions play a far more assertive role in the control of work. It is this ambiguity that I will now attempt to explain.

The Shop Steward: In Between Management and Labor

Cooperation and the generation of consent are, as Michael Burawoy (1979) has made clear, systematically built into the capitalist labor process. Paul Thompson (in Thompson and Bannon 1985, 58) has summed up the dual relation between conflict and cooperation:

> Workers are compelled into acts of resistance while actively participating in the workings of the capitalist labor process. Conflict and cooperation are not entirely separate phenomena, one inherent in capitalist production, the other externally induced false consciousness. They are produced, in part, by the same process. The result is a continuum of possible and overlapping worker responses, from resistance, to accommodation on temporary common objectives, to compliance with the greater power of capital, and consent to production processes.

The contradictory nature of the capitalist labor process underlies the specificity of the shop stewards' role within the workplace. The stewards' essential role is to coordinate the broad interests of labor and represent these interests in interactions with management. If we understand the social relations between management and labor to consist of a continuum ranging from conflict to cooperation, then it is clear that the shop stewards' representation of workers' interests will simultaneously include a range of strategies from resistance to consent. The stewards find themselves in a contradictory position that is not part of management yet is also different from that of the workers. This has been captured in a study of labor relations in the motor industry by Herbert Turner, Garfield Clack, and Geoffrey Roberts (1967, 222):

> In a sense, the leading stewards . . . [perform] a managerial function, of grievance settlement, welfare arrangement, and human adjustment. . . . The stewards' organization is under pressures that compel it towards certain responsible patterns of institutional behavior "responsible" at least in the sense that its leaders are obliged to balance a variety of group interests against the particular sectional claims with which they are confronted, and to bear in mind the long-term desirability of maintaining good negotiating relations with management.

It is an essentially ambivalent function that the shop stewards perform, reflecting the convergence of relations of conflict and cooperation in the workplace. They are thus propelled into a contradictory role, as described by C. Wright Mills' (1948, 222) classic study of union leaders: "Yet even as the labor leader rebels, he holds back rebellion. He organizes discontent and then sits on it, exploiting it in order to maintain a continuous organization; the labor leader is a manager of discontent."

The veteran black South African trade unionist Emma Mashinini (1991, 22) described her ambivalent role as a shop steward in these words:

> They could have sacked me if they had wanted. I was a shop steward, but if they wanted to sack you they could still sack you. Instead, they would try and use me to stop the trouble. They would use me like a fire extinguisher, always there to stop trouble. I would have to go to meet with the workers and ask, "Now what is actually going on?" And they would tell me they wanted money, or they wanted that person who had been shouting and yelling at us to behave him- or herself. I would listen to all that, and then I would convey it to the employers. They would be adamant, and so the workers would stay outside and not come in. Often the police would arrive with dogs and surround the workers. Many times with the help of the union we would eventually receive assistance, and perhaps the people would achieve a part of what they wanted and go back to work.

The simple fact is that union leaders, including the shop stewards, perform a different kind of job from that of the members they represent. They perform, in part, a managerial function but they are not managers: they do not derive their authority from the control of the means of production, as do managers; instead their authority comes from below. They wield power by virtue of their representation of the collective worker. This feature of the shop steward is captured best by this comment by Mashinini (1991, 62): "I had a dual role in the factory, but I was very clear where my first loyalty lay. I was appointed a supervisor, but I was elected to be a shop steward by my fellow workers."

But election to the position of shop steward opens up to the individual the possibility of a career track that is different from that of an ordinary worker.[5] Promotion is a common device for dividing shop stewards' loyalties. In many firms it is well understood that service as a shop steward could be a prelude to a position as foreman, supervisor, or personnel officer. As Huw Beynon (1973, 47) describe in his classic study of shop stewards in Liverpool:

> The promotion of the steward to the foreman's job is one of the oldest tricks in the book, and many of the stewards would get worked up about anyone who turned coat. . . . Those supervisors who had once been stewards were pointed out to me like lepers. "Did you see that bloke in a white coat we just passed? He used to be a shop steward . . . the bastard. The lads gave him hell for a bit though."

When the new South African unions were still struggling for recognition, the possibilities for a shop steward to be promoted to management were limited. Those who were thought to have been "bought" by management triggered stoppages on the East Rand in 1981 and 1982 (Webster 1985, 243). But once these unions start to institutionalize their relationship with management, the opportunities for promotion grow rapidly. Management need staff who have the confidence of workers and a knowledge of production; who better to play the role of manager than the leading worker representative in the plant?

The COSATU shop steward survey shows that worker leadership is increasingly drawn from the better educated and more skilled urban-based stratum of the working class. In the early days of the new unions, a high proportion of union leadership came from migrant hostel dwellers on the East Rand. But the situation had changed by 1992, when Jeremy Baskin wrote that "it is unusual to find such people (often semi-literate, unskilled laborers) in senior positions within COSATU and its affiliates today. In 1986 and 1987 meetings of COSATU's Central Executive Committee [CEC] were still conducted in a mixture of English, Zulu, and Sotho. Today English is almost the only language heard at CEC meetings" (Baskin 1991, 44).

The fact that shop stewards are drawn mainly from the relatively better educated members of the workforce makes it materially possible for management to co-opt them. In an increasingly stratified employment situation, this may take the form of accelerating the occupational mobility of the shop stewards; for example, by promoting them to supervisory roles. This, combined with their high levels of cooperation with management, increases the chances for co-optation.

Although the promotion of this section of the workers' leadership is beginning to take place, there is nothing to suggest, as we argued above, that co-optation is inevitable.[6] Eleven percent of the shop stewards are already supervisors, yet respondents overwhelmingly expressed a preference for factories to be run by workers' committees and for workers' to share in the profits.

The shop stewards' ability to withstand these counteracting pressures and contradictions is enhanced by their strong sense of collectivism, the support they enjoy from the union, and, most importantly, their racial identity. The survey demonstrates the active role stewards play in national and community politics: the vast majority are members of political organizations and believe that unions should also get involved in politics. Furthermore, 94 percent said they intend to vote for the ANC in a future election, and 78 percent believe that workers can influence the political system.

The internal structures of trade unions also promote a common sense of identity between all members, regardless of their skill and job grade. Those in supervisory positions have not been excluded from union membership and can even assume leadership roles, including shop steward (although this is expressly prohibited in some unions). In this important respect the South African shop stewards differ from those in other countries; black supervisors continue to identify themselves with black workers, as they share similar living conditions and a common racial identity (Sarakinsky and Crankshaw 1985). These political and racial identities are crucial in explaining why South African shop stewards are not, in general, prone to cooptation, despite their upward occupational mobility. However, this identification downward depends crucially on the continuation of a strong tradition of shop-floor democracy and a common racial identity with fellow union members.

Conclusions

South African shop stewards, like their counterparts elsewhere, are primarily representatives of their members in the workplace. They are directly accountable to them and reflect their aspirations in negotiation with management, within union structures, and beyond the workplace. They draw on this system of direct democracy to articulate and represent their specific class interests in the national polity and within the Triple Alliance (COSATU, ANC, and SACP).

They form the pivotal part of what has been called social movement unionism, which is a product of the specific South African struggle for liberation. They have had political roles imposed on them by the specific historical circumstances of that struggle. Because of their strong shop-floor base and their active community involvement, shop stewards were the most organized cadres of the liberation movement.

But South African shop stewards have not escaped the dilemma of being sandwiched between two opposing sides, where they play a mediating role, simultaneously seeking to promote the particular interests of their members and to encourage cooperation between management and workers. They stand apart from the membership in as much as they are called upon, at times, to perform a managerial function.

This opens up the possibility of their promotion into the ranks of supervisor or even manager. However, in the past the strong tradition of accountability, mandates, and report-back processes, as well as their shared racial and political identity, has given the labor movement a degree of control over those shop stewards who are promoted that has often led to a widening of workers' control over production.

But traditions of worker control and strong shop-floor structures have been in decline in recent years. "What seems to have held the union movement together in the past," wrote Sakhela Buhlungu (1997, 42):

> was a clear sense of purpose, clear political objectives and an associated value system. . . . Today there is a pervasive sense of a lack of political direction accompanied by confusion regarding the future of the workers' struggle. Old value systems and bonds of solidarity have virtually disintegrated. The context for this is that in the broader society, notions of sacrifice and the collective ethos of the struggle days have been replaced by individualism and a quest for wealth accumulation.

The opportunities for black advancement have opened up career trajectories that were unthinkable six years ago. The increasing significance of occupational and income divisions among black workers means that it no longer makes sense to conceptualize black workers as a homogenous group. This is particularly true now that these differences are manifesting themselves residentially, with better paid black workers moving into "white" suburbs (Crankshaw 1997).

To explain this decline in mobilization among workers, it is necessary to return to the relations between race and class in South Africa. As Ran Greenstein (1993) has argued, the mobilizing power of class discourse is derived to a large extent from its association with race and more specifically with African racial identity. The transition to a different political system is beginning to sever these associations. The removal of political apartheid has broken the link between the state and racial despotism in the workplace, dissolving the specific articulation of class in that setting.

This does not mean that class will disappear as an important basis for mobilization, but that its meaning will change. "Mobilization," wrote Greenstein (1993, 19) on the eve of the first democratic election in South Africa,

> will no longer be marked by the highly charged and powerful notions of the liberation struggle. . . . A confrontation with the democratically elected government, representing the African majority, will be invested with a very different meaning than a clash with the illegitimate apartheid state.

The precise outcome of this disarticulation of the racial-national-class-political nexus is not yet clear. What is clear is that shop stewards are not simply a product of their class location and do not only have a class identity. The power they exercised under apartheid was not a pure class phenomenon but rather was contingent on a specific political artic-ulation. The transition to a political democracy has eroded that power. It has made the shop steward a less militant and powerful figure. Whereas under apartheid the stewards were caught between an intransigent management and their militant members; today militant actions appear to be directed against the shop stewards as much as against man-agement. While politically speaking apartheid is no more, in the workplace its legacy continues in low pay, racist differentials, authoritarian management, and racism (Von Holdt 1999). Ironically, the transition to democracy has eroded the power and militancy of the shop steward while leaving the pillars of the apartheid workplace largely intact.

Notes

Acknowledgment: I would like to thank Judy Maller for permission to publish this version, which is based on an earlier, unpublished paper we wrote together.

1. Apartheid consisted of four pillars: (1) the denial of political rights to black people—polit-ical apartheid; (2) the enforced segregation of peoples both residentially and socially—social apartheid; (3) separate and unequal education, health, and welfare services—welfare apartheid; and (4) racism in the workplace and racial restrictions on occupational mobility—economic apartheid. While political apartheid has been removed, apartheid's legacy—social, welfare, and economic—has only been partially removed.

2. In 1995 the Labor Relations Act was amended to allow for the introduction of workers' committees in all workplaces with more than one hundred employees. These committees—known as Workplace Forums—have rights to information, consultation, and, in some areas of decision-making, co-determination. Only a dozen of these Workplace Forums have been estab-lished, and COSATU remains divided on how to respond to them. A significant number of worker leaders fear that they will lead to the co-optation of worker representatives and an undermining of the union on the shop floor.

3. Indeed, since this survey was conducted, most of the COSATU affiliates have set up investment companies with the intention of developing sufficient funds to be able to provide

benefits for their members from the returns on the investments in the stock market. The union investment companies have triggered a debate within the union and allegations of corruption against many of the senior union leaders who now work for these investment companies on a full-time basis, becoming very wealthy in the process.

4. The survey reflects the attitude of shop stewards before the ANC had asserted its hegemony within the Triple Alliance, which brings together the leading force of liberation struggle, the ANC, with the SACP and the major trade union federation, the COSATU. In 1993 COSATU decided to support the key leadership of the ANC and to campaign for the ANC in the April 1994 elections. COSATU shop stewards overwhelmingly voted for the ANC in 1994 and 1999 (for surveys of workers voting patterns, see Ginsburg and Webster 1995 and Buhlungu and Poulis 1999).

5. In the earlier formulation of this essay, an attempt was made to understand the shop steward as being in a "contradictory class location" between management and workers, and the concept of temporal class relations was used to explain the upward mobility of shop stewards (see Wright 1978, 1993). While this concept remains useful, I have left it out of this essay because the rapid upward mobility of shop stewards since the end of apartheid suggests that the contradiction was related as much to race as to class.

6. The advent of US-style affirmative action under the Employment Equality Act has accelerated "brain drain," as shop stewards leave union leadership to become supervisors and managers in personnel and human resources departments (Buhlungu, 1994).

References

Baritz, Loren. 1965. The "Servants of Power." New York: Wiley and Sons.

Baskin, Jeremy. 1992. Striking Back: A History of COSATU. Johannesburg: Ravan Press.

Beynon, Huw. 1973. Working for Ford. London: Penguin Education.

Bonnin, Deborah. 1987. Class, Consciousness, and Conflict in the Natal Midlands: The Case of BTR Sarmcoll. Master's thesis, University of Natal, Durban.

Braverman, Harry. 1974. Labor and Monopoly Capital: The Degradation of Work in the Twentieth Century. New York: Monthly Review Press.

Buhlungu, Sakhela. 1994. "The Big Brain Drain: Union Officials in the 1990s." South African Labour Bulletin, 18(3): 24–43.

———. 1997. Working for the Union: A Profile of Union Officials in COSATU. Sociology of Work Unit, Labor Studies Research Report 8. Johannesburg: University of the Witwatersrand.

Buhlungu, Sakhela, and Christine Psoulis. 1999, "Enduring Solidarities: Accounting for the Continuity of Support of the Alliance Amongst Cosatu Members." Society in Transition, 30(2).

Burawoy, Michael. 1979. Manufacturing Consent: Changes in the Labor Process Under Monopoly Capitalism. Chicago: University of Chicago Press.

———. 1985. The Politics of Production. London: Verso.

Crankshaw, Owen. 1997. Race, Class, and the Changing Division of Labour Under Apartheid. London: Routledge.

———, and Doug Hindson. 1991. "New jobs, new skills, new divisions: The changing structure of the South African Workforce." South African Labour Bulletin, 15(1): 23–31.

Cressey, Peter, and James MacInnes. 1980. "Voting for Ford: Industrial Democracy and the Control of Labor." Capital and Class, 11: 5–33.

Edwards, Richard. 1979. Contested Terrain: The Transformation of the Workplace in the Twentieth Century. New York: Basic Books.

Ewert, Jochim. W. 1988. "Changing Labor Processes and Worker Responses in the South African Newspaper Industry and Printing Industry." Ph.D. diss., University of Stellenbosch, South Africa.

Fizikolo, Tembalethu. 1993. Letter. *South African Labour Bulletin,* 17 (January/February).

Flanders, Allan. 1970. *Management and Unions.* London: Faber and Faber.

Gelb, Stephen. 1991. "South Africa's Economic Crisis: an Overview." Pp. 1–32 in *South Africa's Economic Crisis,* edited by S. Gelb. Cape Town: David Philip.

Giddens, Anthony. 1971. *Capitalism and Modern Social Theory: An Analysis of the Writings of Marx, Durkheim, and Max Weber.* Cambridge: Cambridge University Press.

Ginsburg, David, and Edward Webster. 1995. *Taking Democracy Seriously: Worker Expectations and Parliamentary Democracy.* Durban: Indicator Press.

Greenstein, Ran. 1993. "From Class Analysis to the Analysis of Class." Paper presented at the symposium "Work, Class, and Culture," University of the Witwatersrand, Johannesburg.

———. 1996. *Genealogies of Conflict: Class, Identity, and State in Palestine/Israel and South Africa.* Hanover and London: Wesleyan University Press.

Hyman, Richard. 1975. *Industrial Relations: A Marxist Introduction.* London: Macmillan.

———. 1981. "Whatever Happened to Industrial Sociology?" Pp. 213–262 in *International Yearbook of Organizational Studies,* edited by D. Dunkerely and G. Salaman. London: Routledge Kegan Paul.

Innes, Duncan. 1983. "Monopoly Capitalism in South Africa." Pp. 171–183 in *South African Review One: Same Foundations, New Facades,* edited by South African Research Service. Johannesburg: Ravan Press.

Lambert, Robert, and Edward Webster. 1988. "The Reemergence of Political Unionism in Contemporary South Africa." Pp. 20–41. in *Popular Struggles in South Africa,* edited by W. Cobbett and R. Cohen. London: Africa World Press.

Lane, Tony. 1974. *The Union Makes Us Strong: The British Working Class, Its Policy, and Trade Unionism.* London: Arrow Books.

Leroke, Windsor. 1993. "The Politics of Identity and the History of the South African Labor Movement." Paper presented at the African Studies Seminar, John Hopkins University, Baltimore.

Lever, Jeffrey. 1983. "Labor Process Studies in South Africa." Paper presented at the Association for Sociology in South Africa Conference, University of the Witwatersrand, Johannesburg.

Lewis, Jon. 1984. *Industrialisation and Trade Union Organization in South Africa, 1924–55: The Rise and Fall of the South African Trades and Labor Council.* Cambridge: Cambridge University Press.

Lewis, Jon, and Estelle Randall. 1985. "Survey: The State of the Unions." *South African Labor Bulletin,* 11 (October–December): 60–88

Maller, Judy. 1992. *Conflict and Cooperation: Case Studies in Worker Participation.* Johannesburg: Ravan Press.

Maree, Johann. 1985. "The Emergence, Struggles, and Achievements of Black Trade Unions in South Africa." *Labor, Capital, and Society,* 8 (November): 278–303.

Mashinini, Emma. 1991. *Strikes Have Followed Me All My Life: A South African Autobiography.* New York: Routledge, Chapman, and Hall.

Merton, Robert. 1957. *Social Theory and Social Structure.* Chicago: Chicago Free Press.

Mills, C. Wright. 1948. *The New Men of Power: America's Labor Leaders.* New York: Harcourt Brace.

———. 1959. *The Sociological Imagination.* London: Penguin.

Munck, Ronaldo. 1987. *The New International Labour Studies.* London: Zed Press.

National Manpower Commission. 1999. *Annual Report*. Pretoria: Author.

Pityana, Sipho, and Mark Orkin. 1992. *Beyond the Factory Floor: A Survey of COSATU Shop Stewards*. Johannesburg: Ravan Press.

Sarakinsky, Michael, and Paul Crankshaw. 1985. "Supervisors: Workers or Managers?" *South African Labour Bulletin*, 10 (January–February): 107–118.

Sitas, Aristedes. 1983. "African Worker Responses on the East Rand to Changes in the Metal Industry, 1960–1980." Ph.D. dissertation, University of the Witwatersrand, Johannesburg.

Southall, R. 1985. "Monopoly, Capital, and Industrial Unionism in the South African Motor Industry." *Labor, Capital, and Society* 18 (2): 304–342

Stewart, Paul. 1981. "A Worker Has a Human Face." Honor's dissertation, University of the Witwatersrand, Johannesburg.

Thompson, Paul, and Edward Bannon. 1985. *Working the System: The Shop Floor and New Technology*. London: Pluto Press.

Turner, Herbert A., Garfield Clack, and Geoffrey Roberts. 1967. *Labour Relations in the Motor Industry*. London: Allen and Unwin.

Von Holdt, Karl. 1999. "From the Politics of Resistance to the Politics of Reconstruction: The Union and 'Ungovernability in the Workplace.'" In *Trade Unions and Democratization in South Africa, 1985–1997*, edited by G. Adler and E. Webster. New York: St. Martin's Press.

Webster, Edward. 1985. *Cast in a Racial Mold: Labor Process and Trade Unionism in the Foundries*. Johannesburg: Ravan Press.

———. 1991. "Taking Labor Seriously: Sociology and Labor." *South African Sociological Review*, 4(1): 50–72.

Wright, Erik Olin. 1978. *Class, Crisis, and the State*. London: Verso.

———. 1993. *Reconstructing Class Analysis*. Paper presented at the symposium "Work, Class, and Culture," University of the Witwatersrand, Johannesburg, June.

Part IV

Professional and Technical Workers

CHAPTER 10

"Globalization": The Next Tactic in the Fifty-Year Struggle of Labor and Capital in Software Production

Richard Sharpe

The making of software is a high-value-added production process that is concentrated in a handful of locations worldwide. On the surface, virtually none of the conventional forms of struggle between labor and capital seem to be employed. With software production, we cannot see the production line of, say, a car plant; we cannot put our finger on piles of primary or secondary goods going out of a factory door. But the seemingly intangible nature of software production does not mean there is no continued struggle between labor and capital in the process, for the underlying struggle for control is masked by a technical ideology and vocabulary. This technical ideology and vocabulary are in turn overlayed by simultaneous strategies of "control and inspire" (Kraft 1999) that mark the forefront of capital's continued initiative to extract more work and more value from labor. As we analyze software production, the current state of the struggle will become more evident.

We will use a three-fold categorization of software production:

1. *Primary software products,* which are produced in centralized locations and sold as software commodities to enterprises, governments, and individual consumers for further exploitation. Examples include operating systems, word-processing packages, development tools, and accounting suites.
2. *Secondary software products,* which are built using primary software products. Secondary products are the custom-made applications or amended standardized packages employed in enterprises and governments for their information systems applications. Examples include public service command and control systems; utility billing systems; airline reservation systems; manufacturing control systems; online analytical processing systems; and human resources applications.

3. *Tertiary software products,* which are produced by individual users for their own personal or small-scale application. These include scripts for handling e-mail; macros for spreadsheet applications; stored analysis queries; preferred web site addresses; and settings for graphical users interfaces. (In this essay, I shall be concerned with only primary and secondary software.)

This categorization allows us to divide the forms of software production according to the role that particular capital plays in the development of the value chain. We will see that this is not an arbitrary division. Different forms of production are used by capital to produce different types of software products. We can clearly distinguish the forms of software production used in the metropolitan center of primary software production at Microsoft in the United States from, for example, that used in a semimetropolitian location of secondary software production in the United Kingdom.

As the relationships between labor and capital are analyzed, we will show that both the form of software production and its location are determined by the options capital has in its struggle with software workers. In particular, the current form of the struggle over primary software production creates the circumstances with which labor and capital have to deal in secondary and tertiary software production. We will first focus on the production of primary software products by Microsoft and others. We will then show how this production triggers changes to the form of production of secondary products. We will see that the production of secondary software and the struggle between capital and labor are very much determined by the state of struggle in primary software.

A Cycle of Struggle

Attempts by management to retain or regain control production processes that are centered on new technologies have often relied on conventional strategies to "deskill" the workforce (Kraft 1977; Noble 1984). Critics such as Paul Adler (1992) have pointed to the reemergence of other technologies and production techniques to counter the tendencies toward deskilling. But instead of offering such one-sided analyses, we see a cycle of struggle between capital and labor played out over a wide terrain and involving the use of different tactics on different sides. It is a long-term struggle that has lasted over fifty years.

We will first describe this long-term cycle of struggle between labor and capital within software production. The struggle does not develop in a uniform and rigid manner. Some parts of the labor side are in one phase while others are in another. All is determined by the balance of forces between different and identifiable sets of software producers and capital at any one time. Furthermore, actors within this struggle are frequently not aware of their roles. Software workers, for example, often focus on the technical aspects and personal opportunities of their jobs (Lammers 1986). Sometimes, as our narrative will show, the clearest statements of strategy come from the capital side. In particular, we will use Microsoft as a prime example of this self-conscious organization of the production of primary software. Microsoft has so often been used to represent resurgent capital within a period of "free markets" that it deserves another and rather different focus of analysis.

Software Production's Dependence on Tools

The job of producing software, like the job of producing cars, is in large part dependent upon the technical tools of production. Software, however, is produced by the symbolic transformation of the means of production itself—software development tools—through the use of raw materials—utilities and other inputs. These tools of production are similar to the capital goods generated by primary manufacturing and used in secondary manufacturing processes: lathes, plastic moulding equipment, and the like. These capital goods, in other words, are the output of a previous cycle of production. Once produced, these products confront the labor of secondary production processes in the next phase of production as givens. They are artifacts of production that capital wished to introduce in order to reorganize production. The primary tools of production in our narrative include software compilers, operating systems, hardware platforms, databases, and programming languages.

The first phase of the production of primary tools occurs when software tools are fashioned in response to induced innovation, evolutionary theory, and path dependence (Ruttan 1997). The start of Microsoft's interest in the production of operating systems—a key primary software product—is a clear case of induced innovation. At first, when contacted by IBM in 1980, Microsoft's proposed role was to produce a version of the BASIC programming tool and three other programming languages for IBM's emerging personal computer (PC) design. As other avenues for an operating system closed down while the scheduled launch date of the PC loomed, IBM's negotiators turned to Microsoft's Bill Gates. "We [IBM] wanted this [the lack of an operating system] to be their [Microsoft's] problem, to find us the right operating system, the one that we could integrate successfully on our schedule," a member of the IBM team later told researchers (Wallace and Erickson 1992, 185). Microsoft took the bait:

> IBM had told Gates it wanted a final proposal from Microsoft [for an operating system] in October [1980], and time was running out. Gates faced a critical decision. Could Microsoft deliver languages and an operating system and still meet the demanding schedule IBM had set to have a computer ready for market within a year? The software would have to be finished before that, probably in about six or seven months. The four languages IBM wanted—BASIC, COBOL, FORTRAN, and Pascal—would require writing about 40,000 bytes of [complied] code. An operating system would likely mean another 2,000 bytes of code. According to Microsoft, on September 28, 1980, Gates, [Paul] Allen, and [Kay] Nishi were in Gates's eighth-floor corner office in the downtown bank building, brainstorming about the operating system. Should they commit to it? Suddenly, Nishi jumped to his feet, waved his short little arms in the air and shouted, "Gotta do it! Gotta do it!"
>
> That's when it became obvious to Gates that 2,000 more bytes of code for an operating system was no big deal. Of course they had to do it. "Kay's kind of a flamboyant guy, and

when he believes in something, he believes in it very strongly," Gates would say later. "He stood up, made his case and we just said 'Yeah!'" (Wallace and Erickson 1992, 185–186)

Whatever the technical debate about the quality or real origins of the operating system they developed (DOS), it was, nonetheless, an innovation in primary software clearly induced by the demand of the hardware supplier.

The production of Microsoft's operating systems from then on developed according to the path-dependence model of innovation. This model expects that developments will be dependent on the qualities and characteristics of previous innovation, and that incremental steps will continually integrate other features into it. Some steps Microsoft took along this development path, such as IBM's OS/2 and versions 1 to 3 of Windows, were not successful, whereas Windows 3.1 and NT clearly were.

Microsoft's decision to start production of what would become the cornerstone of its dominance of the worldwide desktop software market also shows the company's decision-making method at that time. Microsoft then had fewer than twenty employees. The decision-making process was casual, confrontational, male-dominated, youth-oriented, and focused in the hands of a small coterie of highly educated elite owners and decision-makers. It was also located in what was and remains the metropolitan center of primary software production, the United States.

Whatever the particular reasons for the development of the new tools and hardware platforms, they are produced by one set of capital and offered to other sets as a tool for further, secondary software production. Once this primary tool for software production becomes available, a workforce with expertise in that tool is assembled. The assembly of this workforce is the second phase of the cycle.

Skills Authenticated by Capital

The development of the new tools for software production creates a demand for expertise in this tool if it is to be exploited. To this extent, capital ushers in a new set of skills. Then the demand for these skills authenticates them in the labor market.

But it is not enough to merely possess the skill; it has to be deployed in the way best fitted at that moment to the exploitation of labor in a particular software production process. The appropriate combination of skills and mode of production is central to the assembling of a workforce. If workers with the right combination of skills and experience can be found, they can be rapidly productive. Capital can assemble its workforce in several ways:

- Recruit
- Train
- Poach
- Transfer from another area of expertise

Numerous examples can be given of each tactic of assembly. The recruitment during World War Two of "computers"—women with mathematical skills—as the first elite of programming in the United States is well documented (see, e.g., Slater 1987).

Their replacement in the 1950s by a new male elite of coders and programmers forms part of the narrative of the "heroic," or "pioneering," stage of the formation of the computer industry. The skills authenticated by the growing Microsoft in the 1980s, however, were different from those sought in other areas of software production. Microsoft authenticated the skills of "nerdy" software production, production methods that would have horrified the "professional" software production shops down the coast in the defense industry of California or across the country in the strongholds of IBM's large-systems software production in New York State. The skills Microsoft authenticated in this growing workforce and the modes of production the company planned to use are encapsulated in the term used for early recruits: "Microkids." The focus was on extensive exploitation of youthful talent from a handful of elite educational establishments. The system of production they were to use was:

- *Process-centered,* focusing on the actions of developing software and not just on the output itself
- *Team-oriented,* placing the individual within a team rather than as the single focus of Taylorist methods and allowing the team a degree of self-direction
- *Empowered,* being flexible in the choice of production tools and internal organization, including hours and dress codes
- *Inspired,* hiring middle and senior managers who are coaches, leaders, facilitators, and resources "who inspire rather than flog" (Kraft 1999, 29)

Microkids were strongly challenged by their management not through regular management techniques but, more effectively, by management's own expertise in software production. Gates explained the process in 1986. "I do two key things," he said. "One is to choose features to put into programmes. . . . I also work on the best way to implement that feature, so that it will be small and fast. For example, I wrote a memo on how to design and implement a feature we used on Excel to make the program recalculate the formulas every time the screen changes" (Lammers 1986, 72). Gates has also partially collapsed design and production so as to shorten the production cycle. A programmer expressed what this control mechanism felt like: " 'Bill was always pushing,' said one programmer. 'We'd do something I thought was very clever, and he would say, "Why don't you do this, or why didn't you do that two days ago?" That would get frustrating sometimes' " (Wallace and Erickson 1992, 128).

The work ethic did not have to be imposed: it came straight from the Microkids, who transferred their lifestyle from academia into the workplace, without the workplace seeming to discipline them into the regimented ways of conventional work. They could keep the same clothes, hours, leisure activities, work tools, and consumption patterns as in their recent academic lives. Many work practices that would have been collaborative in other environments were turned into competitions within the growing Microsoft. Competitions are probably the most-used method of socialization and character creation among young males in Western society. And "superbright" young males—clones of Bill Gates—were what Microsoft aimed to recruit for its software production workforce.

Waves of Elites

As a new elite workforce is assembled by capital, new terms and conditions are coined for it. These new terms include job titles, which may be formal, as in "programmer" or "software engineer," or informal, as in "Microkids." They may seem to be a superficial detail, yet the names given to these elites are an important part of the identity of individuals within the workforce. They signal to those both within and outside the group issues of status, that is, of their relationships with other parts of the workforce in software production, the company, or the total workforce. They also signal the terms of relationships to technology and capital. Capital will forge new terms for the new software production workforce it assembles to differentiate it from existing software production workforces. For example, how could the Microkids see or feel an affinity with software production workers in the traditional COBOL shops, when they were given so much opportunity? Why, the boss even reads their code! They are given free Cokes and pizza. They can play frisbee in the halls. Sections of labor will comply with this fragmentation of the workforce so as to differentiate themselves from labor as a whole. The workforce may even coin its own labels. This sense of empowerment in naming itself is part of the pact this labor force forges with capital.

As the Microsoft elite expanded, by the late 1980s its form of organization had also matured to the current pattern of software production in Seattle, which reflects a particular relationship between employees, their tools, and the capital employing and directing it in a defined social setting. It has been dubbed a pattern of "institutionalized tiger teams," one of ten different patterns of software production (Boehm 1996). These tiger teams were the early groups of "Microkids" assembled and let loose on primary software production. The frenzied, intense exploitation of this small elite was institutionalized by Microsoft as its demands for software production grew. The characteristics are the continued recruitment of the brightest as a specific objective. They become institutionalized tiger teams when Microsoft consciously assembles a large workforce along these lines *only* for its metropolitan center of production.

Microsoft teams are assembled for projects and given specifications that may be in text, in dummy screen layouts, or in prototypes encapsulated in code. Functions within the team are split between the three roles of developer, tester, and others with the latter including documentors of the process and writers of support material for eventual users. Numbers are allocated almost evenly between these roles. Managers of each team are tasked to deliver within the schedule two targets: (1) the software products, documented and running to specification; and (2) the team members ready and able to work on another project.

The tools of production are largely chosen by the team itself under the guidance of management. Hence, Microsoft has never become a center for the advocacy of any one of the key software development tools that have characterized some other production teams. It was not, for example, a heavy and uniform user of either object-oriented software production and formal methods-based software production, which are two of the 10 patterns for the organization of software engineering identified by Barry Boehm

(1996). Management has not selected a single tool set for production. It has instead given teams the "bounded rationality" of choice about tools, but not about process.

The main discipline exerted on the institutionalized tiger teams is the "daily build," a daily assembly and test run of all the software so far produced in the project. This is implemented as an iterative process of building more working functions into a growing base of software; it is a highly disciplined and process-oriented application of Boehm's (1996) spiral method of software production. As the software is developed day-by-day, it is put together and run to see what functions work and what problems exist; as Michael Cusumano and Richard Selby (1996, 268) tellingly describe, "This rule is analogous to telling children that they can do whatever they want all day, but they must go to bed at nine o'clock."

The daily build process is supported by an eleven-step regime for each project. The goal is a completely successful compilation that incorporates all of the code so far generated with some linking code for modules not yet developed. This compiled object program is then run with test data by a "build master," a team member who acts as the coordinator of the build for that team that day. In one part of the Microsoft production process, the master builder is often the developer whose code caused the previous build to "break," in effect, the programmer who wrote a defective code. In other parts of Microsoft, two people serve as the permanent build masters. All the items that "broke" the build have to be fixed before the team can incorporate any more code into the code base.

The daily build acts as a technical target to uncover unsatisfactory work while the project is in progress, rather than at the end. This process can be seen as analogous to the total quality management (TQM) movement, whose slogan is that quality has to be built in and cannot be added at the end. More traditional software production processes, described in the "waterfall" technique, attempt to create discipline by functional specialization among the design, programming, testing, and maintenance stages. In contrast, the iterative software production method employs the daily build as a checkpoint and imposes discipline every day, not just when deadlines loom on a preconceived schedule. If we substitute "the daily build" for "satisfying the customer" in the following, we have an ample description of the impact of the daily build:

> The unrelenting pressure of "satisfying the customer"—that is, to work faster and produce more—combined with the social pressures of team membership can get team members to reveal their attitudes and opinions, to confess their individual sins, and seek forgiveness from the group. In other words, teams make it easier for managers to apply group pressure to slackers. (Kraft 1999, 29)

Not only does the discipline of the daily build work as a production target for all team members, it also acts as a focus for commercial development. From almost the first day of the project, Microsoft can ship some code as a test prototype to customers willing to take the risk. Thus

> a major benefit resulting from the daily build is that a project constantly has a stable yet evolving product with a flexible set of features. The incremental feature development,

frequent synchronisation, and continuous testing help force the project to try to establish and maintain a version of the product that is always at or near the level of quality needed for shipment to customers. (Cusumano and Selby 1996, 276)

It is rather like the writer who sketches out a whole report on the first day. Readers who ask for the report after the first day will receive the complete outline. On successive days more detail is added to each part of the report in a disciplined fashion, so that the same level of detail is generated for each section each day. And this continues until the final, acceptable report has been written. This is a key characteristic that distinguishes the iterative from the waterflow approach to software development.

Microsoft management then employs the "good enough" triangle to decide when the project is ready for the outside world. It may be sent as either a beta version or as a complete, shrink-wrapped product. Factors that are considered are:

- The original schedule for the project
- What the software actually does (called "feature richness")
- The quality of the software, probably calculated by the absence of bugs

For example, one piece of systems software, version 3.1 of Windows, was shipped as a commercial product even though the development team knew that it had five thousand bugs. Other, unknown bugs will be identified as customers start to use the software in configurations and sequences not yet tested by the Microsoft team (Yourdon 1995). The customer, in effect, acts as the quality control inspector for the company.

Clawing Back Control

The most recent phase in the cycle of struggle in software production is capital's long, drawn-out effort to take back the control over software production that it has temporarily ceded in the early phases of workforce assembly and skills legitimation. Capital has created a software production elite, which often works with the latest technologies, is often paid the highest salaries, and has the fastest mobility between employers, while also providing the opportunity for capital to exploit the latest technology to its advantage. The more capital needs to exploit this technology to survive in the market, the more it ushers an elite workforce into the market. This quickly poses a problem for capital.

Central to the balance of forces in software production is the issue of control. Are managers in control of the software production process? Can the control mechanisms in other sectors of employment be used in this new kind of relationship in software production labor? Or does the current control exercised by different sectors of the software production labor force negate the control that capital tries to impose on this section of the software workforce?

In the first phases of this struggle, capital exercises its historical control by creating the workforce. Expertise in a labor force that is not authenticated by capital remains a hobby, not a skill. Social relations that cannot form part of the pattern of exploitation become private life. This private life, in turn, is made into the target of capitalist exploitation. Indeed, so total is the level of exploitation of the Microkids that they or their partners often complain that they have no private life: work has squeezed out all other activities. One of the earliest Microkids, Steve Woods, recruited in 1976, described this pattern:

> There were times, not that infrequently, that I'd be going home for a few hours sleep about the time Marla [his wife] was getting up. . . . We'd often be there 24 hours a day trying to meet a deadline for another OEM [original equipment manufacturer] or getting a new product out. We noticed the long hours, but it wasn't a burden. It was fun. . . . We were doing it because we had stuff to do and we had to get it done. (Wallace and Erickson 1992, 129)

When a software production labor force is consolidated as an elite, it becomes a target for attack, since control over production processes by the workforce is a direct threat to the ability of capital to re-create the relationship in which labor is forced, every day, to sell the product of its labor for less than it is worth. Hence the search for methods by which capital can regain control.

In this phase capital has been forced to exploit the technology generated by other sectors of capital. Now it seeks to reimpose control over the elite sector of the workforce it has created. As it does so, capital may choose a single or mixed set of the five tactics historically open to it:

1. The continued application of management control to deskill software production
2. The adoption of packaged software products to replace the demand for custom software development
3. The attempted automation of software production with more software production tools
4. The reformation of the contractual relationship between capital and labor from employer/employee to customer/contractor
5. The creation of another location for software production in an area where the current restrictions implicitly imposed by the elite do not operate, also known as "globalization"

Each of these tactics will be considered below.

The Application of Management Control

The attempted control of elite sectors of software production workers through their integration into standard control patterns has been well documented (Kraft 1977; Greenbaum 1979). This tactic was heavily used in the 1970s in an attempt to regain the control lost to the generation of programmers recruited in the late 1960s. "The problem is as much one of organisation as of technology," argued two leading proponents of the tactic of management control of software production workers in the early 1970s:

> To address this [in the early 1970s], IBM has developed a programming organisation called a chief programmer team. This represents a new managerial approach to production

programming. While the approach is made possible by recent technical advances in programming [structured programming, HIPO charts, etc.,] it also incorporates a fundamental change in the managerial framework which includes restructuring the work of programming into specialised jobs, defining relationships among specialists, developing new tools to permit these specialists to interface effectively with a developing visible project; and providing for training and career development of personnel within these specialities. (Yourdon 1979, 195–196)

The Adoption of Packaged Software

The tactic of using packaged software for taking back control is best illustrated by the discussion of secondary software production below.

The Automation of Software Production

Waves of attempts have been made to automate software production. The most successful have been based on incremental changes, as in the introduction of third-generation languages (3GLs) in the late 1950s and 1960s and of fourth-generation languages (4GLs) in the 1980s. Each step up in automation has been accompanied by the creation of another tier of elite in the software production workforce.

The least successful, from the point of view of capital, have been attempts to make radical changes in automating software production, such as efforts to implement computer-aided software engineering (CASE). Its adoption generated many jobs for a new elite but only because the technology was not able to deliver the necessary levels of productivity. More labor was employed until employers generally decommitted from the project and adopted more tactical approaches than CASE.

The Reformation of the Contractual Relationship Between Capital and Labor

When the relationship between capital and the labor for software production assumes the form of employer and employee, capital has to take on a range of extra costs beyond the salaries of the employees. These extra costs, the overheads and social costs of labor, are historically defined by the strength of the opposing forces within each labor market. For example, in the United Kingdom in the late 1990s, labor directly employed in software production could cost employers any or all of the following:

- Contributions to state health and welfare schemes
- Contributions to pension schemes
- Infrastructure and information technology (IT) overheads
- Use of infrastructure and IT overheads by employees for nonwork functions
- Subsidized transport or the provision of cars for select staff
- Subsidized sports and leisure facilities
- Paid holidays
- Sick pay

- Maternity and paternity pay
- Costs of administering the employee relationship through human resources and payroll departments
- Subsidized products or services from the employer
- Stock options
- Profit-sharing or bonus schemes

To avoid or reduce these costs, the relationship of employer and employee is replaced by that of customer and contractor. This may take the form of a single contract between a self-employed software producer or, more likely, a group contract between a specialist software producer and a customer. The state, acting as the agent of the community and collecting for community-delivered services, receives less from the self-employed than from the directly employed. And the software user has no corporate concern for the conditions of employment or levels of profit of their suppliers. They focus on control, not employer obligations. This is the IT sector's version of outsourcing, and involves the transfer of IT functions from internal departments with employment contracts to external specialist suppliers under contract. Internal IT staff are transferred or made redundant when the transfer occurs. The software production workforce is now increasingly concentrated into specialist companies rather than spread through the IT departments of users.

The trend toward outsourcing does not eliminate the question of control as much as shift it. The issues of control move, for example, from the public sector, with its higher incidence of trade union membership and collective bargaining and thus its higher social costs, to private sector enterprises, with their anti-union management, fragmented bargaining, and hence lower social costs. Because of the more "flexible" labor practices of these contracted providers of software production, capital gains an overall advantage. Many of the employees within these outsourced software-production centers are on short-term employment contracts. At the same time, economies of scale are achieved by specialization such that the total numbers needed for software production in a software house are fewer than those needed in the dispersed IT centers of their customers before outsourcing; hence the role of layoffs in the shift to outsourcing.

As the relationship is changed to one of a contract, through either outsourcing or the heavier use of packaged software, capital can use new tools to extract control. It can withhold payment from a supplier or use various forms of litigation, including breach of contract suits. Withholding payment from a contractor was precisely the solution tried by over a third of U.S. organizations faced with a "runaway" software project, which is one that "goes out of control primarily because of the difficulty of building the software needed by the system" (Glass 1998, 3). Withholding payments from employees or paying them with the employer's own currency was a tactic of early nineteenth-century manufacturers in metropolitan centers but is not generally acceptable at the beginning of the twenty-first century, at least outside Russia. Yet in the case of software production, capital can exert more control precisely because it has found a way to avoid direct employment of software labor.

The Creation of Another Location for Software Production, or "Globalization"

Once the process of software production has been taken out of the organization and placed in a specialist location, it can then be moved to different locations outside the nation-state, as we will see in the discussion of secondary software production below. This shift of production is called "globalization," yet it is not global. It is the selective adoption of new locations for software production that will provide capital with the highest benefits. These benefits can be supplied by various settings only in certain, specific historic phases of their national economic and social development. Hence, the locations that capital finds attractive are not "globalized." They do not by any means cover the full spectrum of the over two hundred nations in the world. Who is proposing to assemble a fresh elite of software production labor in Somalia, Ethiopia, Iraq, North Korea, Fiji, Argentina, South Africa, Sweden, Germany, or Turkey? The locations chosen for "globalization" are highly concentrated in those nations with appropriate political and economic circumstances.

For example, today a compliant political leadership in India has been able to attract increasing attention for outsourced software production under terms that are highly favorable to foreign customers. Since 1990 the value of software produced for export from India has risen 52 percent a year to over $600 million in 1996. The Indian National Association of Software and Service Companies expects this to grow to $4 billion by 2002. This demand for outsourced software production has generated 160,000 jobs in the sector. India has established a network of software technology parks, the largest of which is in Bangalore. The Software Technology Parks of India (STPI) initiative is clear about the advantages it can offer metropolitan capital when software is produced in India:

- Low-cost–high-quality
- Mathematical and logical expertise
- Adaptability to new technologies
- Virtual software organizations
- Increased quality consciousness
- Tough IPR [intellectual property rights] laws

In the late 1990s foreign companies enticed by these features to locate branch plants to produce software in India included IBM, Oracle, Digital Equipment, Novell, Texas Instruments, Unisys, Hewlett-Packard, Apple Computer, Honeywell, Citibank, Alcatel, and Motorola.

In stark contrast to the institutionalized tiger teams used in the metropolitan software production centers, such as Microsoft, STPI offers a standardized software production pattern that incorporates the "progressive maturity model" of the U.S. Software Engineering Institute (SEI). Motorola software production at Bangalore has achieved the highest level of this process and is claimed to be "a world-class achievement" by STPI. Motorola employs some two hundred Indian software engineers on about thirty projects involving cellular phones and network control. The production process was started in 1991 under U.S. leadership. It was considered a "greenfield" site, where capital could pick and choose who it employed, under what terms and conditions. This U.S. leadership committed the whole operation to working with the SEI's methods of software patterns. Each employee is initially given a 48-day training period, and then an additional 80 to 100 hours of training each year. Personality profiling is used to select the recruits that will fit best with the company. Code is written on C and C++ on Unix platforms—highly standardized tools and systems. Teams are encouraged to reuse code modules, and reuse can account for 10 to 80 percent of a project's code. The higher the reuse, the faster the development process, and the more the code will have been tested.

The advantage of the SEI pattern of software production as implemented by Motorola in Bangalore is that it focuses on repeating standardized routine tasks. Instead of writing fresh code, software engineers are trained to browse through the base of existing code and select what they need, rather like selecting engineering components from a catalogue.

The whole pattern of software production climbs a five-rung ladder of maturity in the SEI model, which the SEI describes as follows:

1. *Initial:* The software process is characterized as ad hoc, and occasionally even chaotic. Few processes are defined, and success depends on individual efforts and heroics.
2. *Repeatable:* Basic project management processes are established to track cost, schedule, and functionality. The necessary process discipline is in place to repeat earlier successes on projects with similar applications.
3. *Defined:* The software process for both management and engineering activities is documented, standardized, and integrated into a standard software process for the organization. All projects use an approved, tailored version of the organization's standard software process for developing and maintaining software.
4. *Managed:* Detailed measures of the software process and product quality are collected. Both the software process and products are quantitatively understood and controlled.
5. *Optimizing:* Continuous process improvement is enabled by quantitative feedback from the process and from piloting innovative ideas and technologies (Paulk et al. 1993).

As of late 1997, fourteen companies on STPI sites had achieved level two, five had achieved levels four and three, but only Motorola had achieved level five.

Downstream: Secondary Software Production

We have described in some detail two locations for the production of primary software—a metropolitan center and an outsourcing site. The products of these two locations are then employed in the next step of the value chain: the exploitation of primary software to create secondary software for enterprises, governments, and individual consumers. The introduction of these secondary products by capital "downstream" is the start of another cycle of the struggle between labor and capital in software production. New software products employed in enterprises and government initiate the creation of another software production elite. Once assembled, this labor force will form its historic contract with capital. All of the naming and norming issues seen in the third phase of the formation of Microsoft's software production labor force will also surface and have to be resolved. Then capital will once again seek to reclaim the control it has ceded to labor by using one or a combination of the tactics outlined above.

We will take a snapshot of the U.K. secondary software production scene in the late 1990s. The United Kingdom is a semimetropolitan location of software production; it has not been a fully metropolitan center since the collapse of its indigenous computer industry in the late 1980s. Some production of primary software is undertaken in the United Kingdom, but it is part of the same process of "globalization" that leads capital to view India in such a favorable light. This work includes IBM's production of systems software and the role the British computer company ICL plays in the "global" strategy of its owner, Fujitsu. There is also a scattering of small, independent software vendors generating primary software for selected industries or applications. But for reasons that continuously disappoint the supporters of indigenous capital, these independent vendors do not make the transition into larger-scale production at anything like the rate achieved by capital in the United States.

The collapse of the indigenous IT supply sector and the low use of the United Kingdom as an offshore software production center has depressed job-creation levels in the U.K. computer and communications industry as a whole. The 1990s profile of employment was one of strong job cuts when the gross domestic product (GDP) slackened or stagnated; continued cuts in the succeeding year of GDP growth; strong employment increases in the second year of GDP growth; and only modest employment increases in successive years of growth (Sharpe 1997a). From this pattern we can see that economies of scale, increased capital intensity, and other factors continued to hold down prospects of job creation even in periods of general GDP expansion. The computer and communications sector ended 1996 with 241,800 employed, compared with 290,700 at the end of 1991, according to U.K. government employment statistics ("Labour Market Trends"). This decline occurred when the overall GDP had increased by just over 10 percent.

The majority of software production in the United Kingdom is, therefore, focused on secondary software. This is the stage at which an organization exploits the products of the first tier of software production by combining systems software and applications software into custom or tailored applications software.

The commercial exploitation of software started early in the United Kingdom; indeed, some would argue that it had its origins there, with the development of the Leo computer by Lyons in the 1950s. We shall start our discussion at the phase when the primary software producers had developed third-generation programming languages, notably FORTRAN, which was shipped initially in 1957. The third-generation tools soon included COBOL, which was available on IBM 1401, 705 and 7070 systems by the first quarter of 1962 (Bashe et al. 1986).

The first U.K. workforce that was assembled in the late 1950s and early 1960s to exploit these third-generation languages was called "programmers." They were supplemented with "systems analysts" in a classic functional specialization that reflected capital's adoption of more Taylorist methods of software production in the 1960s.

The next primary software to be widely adopted in secondary software production in the United Kingdom was the process- and data-oriented fourth-generation tools of the late 1970s and early 1980s. The focus here was on the higher levels of price and performance available from minicomputers used for commercial rather than scientific purposes. The primary software employed included Synon for IBM's System/38 minicomputer, and Pick and Mumps for Digital Equipment and other minicomputers.

From the mid-1980s on, the workforce was called "analyst/programmers" (Sharpe 1997b), which clearly signifies the attempt by employers to reintegrate the two roles into a single hybrid. Technical expertise had to be mixed with business knowledge. Managers needed to win back control of software production from programmers who had turned it into a "black art"—that is, one that capital could not control. Management used anecdotal evidence of long delays in the delivery of secondary software, technical complications, and poor labor habits of software workers in its initiative.

The third wave of labor assembled in the production of secondary software in the United Kingdom focused on the exploitation of tools for the development of client/server systems. The primary software tools were third-generation relational databases such as Oracle and its associated development tools on the one hand, and more desktop-oriented tools such as Visual Basic on the other. This workforce was assembled to exploit the rapid application development (RAD) mode of software production through the use of iterative software development techniques. The term coined for these workers was "systems developer."

As these three workforces were being assembled, another, involved mostly in software production for defense and telecommunications, was formed and titled "software engineer." The title "was deliberately chosen as being provocative, in implying the need for software manufacture to be based on the types of theoretical foundations and practical disciplines that are traditional in established branches of engineering" (Naur and Randall 1969).

The IT sector is highly fragmented, despite its use of common digital technologies. It is segmented into different cults with strong barriers against communication and job movement (Sharpe 1997b). As these job titles and definitions are commonly accepted in the third phase of the cycle, individuals in the new area will be treated as a privileged group of workers, another elite. Employers will pay more for their services and also offer special incentives to recruit members of this new workforce. In the U.K. market in 1994, these differentials were reflected in the median salaries for the four main job titles for software production labor employed in inner London ("Survey of Appointments" 1997):

- Systems developer: £30,000
- Software engineer: £28,000
- Analyst/programmer: £26,000
- Programmer: £21,000

A hierarchy of labor is created within each of the workforces. With the first generation of programmer, the hierarchy is junior programmer, programmer, senior programmer, and programming/software team leader. With the second generation of analyst/programmer, the hierarchy is much the same: analyst programmer, senior analyst programmer, and team leader. The third generation has a flatter structure: systems developer and senior systems developer. The junior post disappears because the higher level of supervision inherent within it can no longer be afforded. Again, the description of the structural bases of "inspirational" control fully applies to this fourth phase of software production organization: "the ideology of 'empowerment' reflects the new management conviction that 'delayered' or flattened organizations—organizations in which work teams monitor and intensify their own labor—can extract value more quickly than traditional systems of fragment and flog" (Kraft 1999, 29).

When we look at the whole market for software-production labor in the United Kingdom from 1993, we see the position of the programmer being eaten away. From 7.1 percent of the top ten job titles required in 1993, it dropped to 5.6 percent in 1997 and is projected to be 4 percent or less by 2003. We also see the lead that analyst/programmer had over all other job titles being whittled away from its 1995 peak of 23.2 percent to 19.6 percent in 1997 and, potentially, to 14.5 percent in 2003 (Sharpe 1997a). Demand for developers was already at 11.4 percent of the top ten jobs requested in 1997, a proportion that had doubled since 1995. In short, the U.K. labor market in secondary software production shows capital gradually squeezing out the older programmer workforce and the newer analyst/programmer workforce in favor of the newest systems developer workforce.

The Struggle in Secondary Software Production

The tactics available to capital in the sphere of primary software production—deskilling, adoption of packages, automation, change in contractual relations, and "globalization"—are equally employed in the sphere of secondary software production. In the United Kingdom in the late 1990s, corporate IT users spent more on bought-in application software packages than they did on development tools or systems software products. The total U.K. expenditure on external applications in the U.K. market in 1997 was expected to turn out at £2 billion. Corporate users would spend £843 million on development tools and £1.2 billion on system software ("Kew UK IT Expenditure Survey" 1997). The current trend shows that this expenditure on packaged software will soon overtake the expenditure on the other two types of software: growth in 1996 was projected to be 16.2 percent for application software compared with 13.4 percent for system software and a drop of 2.7 percent for development software.

Larger corporate users are increasingly replacing their own custom software for core business applications, which require continued maintenance and development, with suites from vendors such as SAP, Oracle, and Baan. This tactic claws back control from the software production sectors engaged in developing and maintaining custom applications. It does not, however, fully obliterate the question of control: it only shifts it. As a result of adopting these packages in large numbers, two other software elites are ushered in: centralized producers of the package (primary software production), and local specialists in implementing and maintaining these packages (secondary software production).

A software elite is created at the central location where the package itself is produced and maintained. For example, the products made by the German software firm SAP had been installed in 7,500 sites worldwide to the middle of 1997. This changed the role and numbers of software production workforce needed by these 7,500 employers, as the focus shifted to the 11,000 people within SAP, only a minority of whom produce software.

The elite of the software producers of custom systems is, therefore, replaced by two elites: the local implementers of the package and the original developers of the package. But fewer people will be needed for the central development and the local implementation of a package than will be needed for the dispersed development of many custom applications.

This adoption of software application packages shifts the skills necessary from generic languages, which are somewhat standardized, to closed and proprietary packages, which are not standardized. A programmer may have knowledge of third-generation COBOL and be able to convert from one implementation of COBOL to another. However, a software production worker versed in the internal workings of Oracle would find the transition to DB/2 or another relational database far more difficult.

The adoption of a package also requires the creation and assembly of a workforce able to implement it. This has the local effect of creating another elite to complement the one recruited in the central location of package production. Consider the effect of the adoption of SAP's R/3 as a replacement for custom accounting suites among larger U.K. information systems users. By April 1997, 2,114 jobs for those skilled in SAP's R range of packages had been advertised in the United Kingdom in the preceding twelve months ("Survey of Appointments" 1997). In the first quarter of 1997, the systems developer with SAP skills was being enticed by the highest salaries offered for all other skill sets among systems developers: £32,288 a year compared with, for example, £29,178 for skills in Windows NT or £28,903 for skills in Java running on Unix.

Hence, as capital uses the packaged tactic, the skills required and rewarded are less general and more restrictive. As capital tries to turn a general software technology into a particular product, it reduces the general applicability of software production labor. Labor faces the prospect, therefore, of its skill base disappearing as the vendor of the prime software product twists and turns the technology in competition with other capitals. We can see this trend in the packaged database market. SQL is the standard language for accessing relational databases. But primary software vendors have added their own features and functions to it in order to distinguish their products from those of competitors. The result, in the U.K. secondary software production market, was that in 1997 19,806 jobs requiring Oracle skills were advertised in the eleven specialist and national recruitment media, whereas only 10,142 advertised jobs required SQL in the same period. In addition, the jobs requiring DB/2, Sybase, Informix, and Ingres—other relational databases—totaled 20,739. Thus the number of jobs requiring particular package skills was four times greater than the number requiring general relational database skills.

Rather than reskilling the workforce it has assembled, capital in secondary software production often decides to recruit when it changes from one primary software product to another. Hence the heavy churn in the secondary software production labor market as exhibited by the high amount of recruitment advertising. Labor fresh to the workforce is employed for its understanding of more generalized technology, such as C, C++, and object software techniques.

The Contractor-Customer Relationship in Secondary Software Production

The shift from an employer-employee relationship to a customer-contractor relationship in the U.K. secondary software production market is called "outsourcing." The outsourcing tactic grew as a method of consolidating and reducing labor in IT operations. By the later 1990s it had clearly spread to software production. As early as the mid-1990s, employers could see outsourcing of operations and software production as part of the same overall strategy of replacing employer-employee relationships with customer-contractor relationships. Take this classic description from BP, the oil exploration, refining, and retailing company:

> Outsourcing was not an end in itself but part of a broader initiative to reshape our IT department. At BP Exploration, information technology was for many years an operations utility: five years ago [1990], we employed 1,400 people to supply processing power to business managers, develop the applications that managers requested, and provide help-desk service and other technology support. Today [1995] the operations are gone—delegated to outsourcing providers. We develop few applications ourselves and instead either buy generic applications or contract the work. We reduced our staff to 150 employees; and, over time, they will become increasingly engaged in activities that create real value for the organisation, such as working directly with business managers to suggest technologies that will improve business processes, cut costs, or create business opportunities. We want the IT department to improve business, not to be an internal group whose mission is to respond and supply. (Cross 1995, 94–95)

So, not only is the relationship between the previous labor used for software production turned into a contractual relationship, but the mode of operation and role of the surviving IT department are refocused along business lines. The contractual relationship is not only one of costs; it also includes other issues of control that were hard to implement when labor was part of the employee/employer relationship. As John

Cross (1995, 100) said when commenting upon some of the less favorable outcomes of the early phases of the program:

> Some of the blame for these early challenges rested with us. We mistakenly set cost reduction as the most important target for our suppliers to achieve during the first year. The provider that added too few of his own staff to our former IT site, for example, was working under particularly stringent cost targets. In 1994 we shifted the emphasis from costs to service responsiveness, quality, and customer satisfaction. And this is better controlled through contracts than through direct employment.

By the late 1990s IT was so essential for capital, and capital was so dependent on IT, that changes in the commercial, political, or economic structure had immediate implications for the producer of secondary software, which gave rise to the talk of the software skills crisis.[11] The two largest recent software skills crises in the United Kingdom have been the year 2000 (Y2K) problem and the European Monetary Union. The major previous crisis occurred when the United Kingdom moved to a decimal-based currency in the early 1970s, and was "solved" largely by direct employment. Such changes no longer can be implemented by direct employment because of the tactic of outsourcing.

If capital were to adopt the direct employment strategy today, it would have to break the dominant form of direct employment in secondary software production: full-time employment of males. This would give capital access to a much wider pool of labor, both part-time and female. Many have advocated such a move. Indeed, a small number of software production suppliers do rely largely on this section of the workforce. Some, like F International, make it a highly visible policy. But a look at the employment patterns shows that the proportion of women employed in the crucial computer services sector steadily fell to 28 percent in the fourth quarter of 1996, down from 30 percent in the fourth quarter of 1995 and from 33 percent in the fourth quarter of 1994. In comparison, the proportion of women in the whole workforce in 1995 was 43.9 percent ("Labour Market Trends"). At the same time, part-time employment is being squeezed. Part-time work was down from 9 percent of all those employed in the computer services sector at the end of 1994 to 7 percent at the end of 1996.

Capital is clearly, at least in the short term, rejecting a strategy of assembling a new flextime, mixed-gender elite of secondary software producers in response to its requirements in the early twenty-first century. Instead, the favored strategy is "globalization."

"Globalization" of Secondary Software Production from the United Kingdom

"Globalization" of secondary software production is a key strategy for capital because it has already shifted much of this work into an indirect relationship with labor. Once the process of using indirect employment has been established, it is a relatively simple matter, given both the technology and the product, to shift production around the globe to the best sites available. U.K. secondary software producers, such as the larger oil, transport, and even public sector employers, are developing a layered strategy with clear preferences. Preference one is to implement a package tailored for them outside the United Kingdom; preference two is to commission a custom application, also outside the United Kingdom. The common theme in both is to do all of this outside the United Kingdom. Such enterprises have shifted their focus from their "domestic" to "global" markets. As they do so, they shift their purchasing of services, including those of secondary software production. The attitude is that if an elite for secondary software production has to be assembled, it is more advantageous for capital if this is done by another capital and, certainly, in another location.

Conclusion

Capital and location are the watchwords of the "globalization" of software production, yet in this process labor again has become the object of history and not its determining force. Capital in the late 1990s was able to choose the location of production so as to continue its struggle for control over fragmented workforces in software production. When capital demands more labor for software production, this labor will be sucked in, labeled, and worked. This labor may feel privileged; it may act as an elite that is given special powers and incentives to perform. But when capital demands less labor, labor will be expelled from the production process. When capital demands a different type of labor, it will be assembled from a different workforce and, increasingly, in a different location. Millions of individual labor-market transactions thus again resolve themselves into a pattern of the continued struggle over control of skills and work.

References

Adler, Paul 1993. "Time and Motion Regained." *Harvard Business Review* 71(1): 97–108.

Bashe, Charles, Lyle Johnson, John Palmer, and Emerson Pugh. 1986. *IBM's Early Computers.* Cambridge: MIT Press.

Boehm, Barry. 1996. "Software Engineering: Role of Focused Agendas." Report from the History of Software Engineering Seminar, Schloss Dagstuhl, Wadern, Germany.

Cross, John. 1995. "IT Outsourcing." *Harvard Business Review,* May–June: 94–102.

Cusumano, Michael A., and Richard W. Selby. 1996. *Microsoft Secrets.* London: HarperCollins.

Glass, Robert L. 1998. *Software Runaways.* Upper Saddle River, NJ: Prentice Hall PTR.

Greenbaum, Joan M. 1979. *In the Name of Efficiency.* Philadelphia: Temple University Press.

"Kew UK IT Expenditure Survey." 1997. *Computer Weekly/Kew Associates,* Spring: Table 3-4.

Kraft, Philip. 1977. *Programmers and Managers: The Routinization of Computer Programming in the United States.* New York: Springer.

———. 1999. "To Control and Inspire." Pp. 17–36 in *Rethinking the Labor Process,* edited by M. Wardell, T. Steiger, and P. Meiksins. Albany: SUNY Press.

"Labour Market Trends." 1995–97. *Labour Trends* (various issues), London (known as *Employment Gazette* before 1996).

Lammers, Susan. 1986. *Programmers at Work.* Redmond, WA: Microsoft Press.

Naur, P., and B. Randall, eds. 1969. *Proceedings of the First NATO Software Engineering Conference.* Brussels: NATO.

Noble, David. 1984. *Forces of Production.* New York: Knopf.

Paulk, Marc C., Bill Curtis, Mary Beth Chrisis, and Charles V. Weber. 1993. "Capability Maturity Model, Version 1.1." *IEEE Software,* 10(4): 18–27.

Ruttan, Vernon. 1997. "Induced Innovation, Evolutionary Theory, and Path Dependence: Sources of Technical Change." *Economic Journal* (UK), 107 (September): 1520–1529.

Sharpe, Richard. 1990. *The Computer World.* London: TVC and Computing.

———. 1995. "Expectations and Cults." *Itext,* 1(1): 5–9.

———. 1997a. "A Rose by Any Other Name." *Computer Weekly,* November 13, p. 13.

———. 1997b. The UK IT Skills Market in 2003: Future Proof." *Computer Weekly,* November 6, p. 17.

Slater, Robert. 1987. *Portraits in Silicon.* Boston: MIT Press.

Software Engineering Institute at Carnegie Mellon University: Available at http://www.sei.cmu.edu.

"The Survey of Appointments and Data Trends Quarterly Survey." 1997. *Red Book,* April: 74, 80, 88, 116.

Thompson, E. P. 1968. *The Making of the English Working Class.* London: Pelican.

Wallace, James and Jim Erickson. 1992. *Hard Drive.* New York: Wiley.

Yourdon, Edward. 1994. *The Dawn of the Guerrilla Programmer.* Philadelphia: Cutter Information Corp.

———. 1995. *Guerrilla Programmer Newsletter,* 2(4):3–6.

CHAPTER 11

Controlling Technical Workers in Alternative Work Arrangements: Rethinking the Work Contract

Peter Meiksins and Peter Whalley

Managing technical workers presents a continual dilemma for employers. Routinizing it, deskilling it, and using other conventional strategies for controlling labor threaten to minimize the application of knowledge and creativity for which these employees are nominally hired. Similarly, purchasing such expertise from external sources has usually been regarded as impractical or inefficient because of the transaction costs involved.

Although there are a variety of national and firm-specific differences in the responses to this dilemma (Meiksins and Smith 1996), the general practice has been to employ a variety of mechanisms that bind the technical expert to the organization without compromising autonomous work conditions. These generally involve: (1) recruitment mechanisms that have been selected or developed as reliable providers of technical professionals willing to apply their skills to employers' objectives; (2) forms of work organization that allow for autonomy and creativity but that include mechanisms of unobtrusive control (such as the formation of highly interdependent work teams); (3) a package of relatively high salaries and benefits that purchase loyalty; (4) the use of time demands to encourage employees to focus on corporate activities; and, arguably most importantly, (5) the provision of career promotion ladders into middle- (and occasionally upper) management positions that select, motivate, and reward. Indeed, the development of internal labor markets has been so much a part of technical labor markets that the existence of such "careers" has traditionally served as one means of demarcating technical work from skilled manual positions (Whalley 1991).

This approach to the management of technical professionals worked well in a world in which companies felt they could afford to have large, in-house technical staffs, one in which employees were willing to commit themselves to long hours and a long-term relationship with a single employer. But what happens when, as is increasingly the case, neither of these conditions is consistently present? It is becoming apparent that corporate downsizing and restructuring are eliminating many of the middle-management positions once held out as incentives. Midcareer layoffs have undermined expectations about employment security and organizational loyalty, and have combined with flatter corporate hierarchies to weaken the internal labor markets that once characterized technical employment. Flexible manufacturing (whatever its structural origins) is leading to a growing demand for "just-in-time" expertise (i.e., outside contractors). This, in turn, has expanded the numbers of independent technical consultants (and consulting firms that employee technical experts), whose connection to the client organization is often both temporary and weak. All of this raises the question of whether new mechanisms will replace career ladders as the central feature of the management and control of technical work (Osterman 1988, 1996; Hecksher 1995).

The impetus for change has not come entirely from the actions of employers, however. A significant number of technical professionals, particularly among the growing number of women in these occupations, have also made choices that challenge traditional patterns of commitment at work. Chris Tilly (1992) argues that a significant number of employees seek "retention" part-time jobs, that is, good jobs with reduced work hours; the technical professions are one area where one can begin to see examples of a successful pursuit of such employment. Similarly, at least some of the growing numbers of independent consultants have chosen this form of economic activity because it seemed better suited than organizational employment (or "captive employment," as one of our respondents called it) to their individual needs. Technical professionals are particularly likely to be voluntary part-timers or consultants; because they have scarce marketable skills, they are more likely to be able to arrange part-time employment and/or to "hang up a shingle" as an independent technical consultant. The growing demand by women, and by some men, for more flexible, part-time, or home-based work is also opening a space between the on-site display of commitment and loyalty and the practice of expertise.

One could argue that there is a degree of fit between the pressures on companies to reduce their workforces and develop greater flexibility and some of their employees' desires to reduce their work time and/or to strike out on their own as contractors. Indeed this is the basis for many of the popular arguments that we are in a period of transition to a new, less bureaucratized economy. But there remains the fundamental problem of control. If a greater percentage of technical work is done by part-timers and contractors, not tied to organizations by traditional career mechanisms and time demands, how can employers assure that they have control over the ways in which the work is done?

In this chapter, we explore the impact of control issues with a sample of newly "flexible" technical professionals in the United States, including some part-timers who are salaried employees and others who are forging flexible schedules through independent contracting. Employees attempting to renegotiate the traditional extended time commitment of corporate professionals to their employers—whether in terms of hours worked or of career commitments—offer an excellent opportunity for examining such issues of control. Does, for example, less than full-time employment lead to the use of novel methods of control? Does the growth of independent technical contracting and home work undermine traditional methods of managing technical professionals? What can we learn about the future evolution of the technical labor process from an examination of the experiences of these kinds of technical professionals? We argue that questions about control lie at the heart of employers' complex response to part-time and contract technical employment. Managers' behavior suggests that part-time technical employment raises troublesome control issues and that acceptance of the idea of part-time work increases if it takes forms that do not require a radical rethinking of relatively familiar control mechanisms.

We shall report results from our two-city study of voluntary part-time work among engineers, computer professionals, and technical writers in the United States. It draws on 120 interviews conducted in 1995–96 with employed members of these occupations. Respondents were located through a snowball sampling process. The principal investigators contacted major professional associations, employers, employment agencies, and universities in the two metropolitan areas and were referred to potential respondents. We then conducted an unstructured, conversational interview with each respondent. The interviews lasted from one to two hours; they took place in a variety of locations, ranging from places of employment to residences. In most cases, the interviews were tape-recorded; in some cases, only field notes were possible. The sample represents a wide variety of employment situations: it includes independent contractors and consultants, employees of small firms, and employees of large, multinational corporations. And, while the modal respondent is a married mother between the ages of twenty-five and forty, we have made an effort to include other types of respondents, including older workers and fathers. We make no claim that the issues raised by our respondents necessarily are typical of all part-time technical professionals, still less of part-time workers in other settings. Ours is in many ways a privileged group, not simply because of their class and occupational privilege, but because they were operating in a favorable labor market and because many, though not all, had family support that helped them make choices and take risks not available to other, less privileged workers. Nonetheless, we interviewed a diverse group of workers, and their responses do shed light on a range of employment situations and life experiences among technical professionals seeking to renegotiate the conventional time contract with employers.

The Labor Process of Technical Professionals

The work done by most technical professionals has traditionally been highly resistant to routinization and deskilling. While few technical professionals perform tasks that require pioneering activities or the development of entirely new knowledge, most work in nonrepetitive jobs that require considerable creativity, discretion, and the ability to respond to a wide variety of demands. In Charles Perrow's (1967) terms, then, they perform jobs that involve limited uncertainty but are clearly nonroutine.

Technical writers, for example, document technical devices and systems, and may also prepare instructional materials and help train potential users. This work requires considerable creativity and involves a great deal of variety because, by definition, technical writers are always documenting new or customized technologies. Documentation must be specific to each new technology and/or to the particular set of users for which it is being prepared. Preparing it involves a wide variety of skills. It requires both a degree of comprehension of the technology itself and the ability to explain technical matters to lay users who may not possess such understanding. It also frequently requires considerable interpersonal skill and initiative. Companies and engineers who produce new technologies may not know much about or even think about how to document their products. Technical writers often find that they have to anticipate user needs and to develop the ability to help the producers of technologies sharpen their understanding of their own documentation needs. Since producers often do not know what they want, and since, even when they do, what they want is never exactly like previous requests for documentation, technical writing involves a substantial level of variety and unpredictability.

Computer professionals are in a similar situation. These technical workers perform a wide variety of computer-related tasks, from designing or customizing software or computer systems to trouble-shooting hardware to servicing computer networks. While it is difficult to generalize about so diverse a group of occupations, the nonroutine character of most of these jobs should be apparent. Computer professionals rarely are called upon to be inventors or pioneers; but their work typically involves variety and creativity, because they are asked either to respond to unpredictable problems that arise in computerized technologies or to produce unique or customized products.

Finally, engineers are also a diverse group, but one that, like computer professionals, typically has traditionally been insulated from routinization and deskilling. While there are some relatively repetitive jobs at the fringes of engineering (such as testing), most engineering work is far from routine. Some students of the engineering profession even claim that there is a distinctive form of engineering knowledge—called "design" or "engineering science"—that they alone possess and apply within the production process (Vincenti 1990). This latter claim may be challenged, but the available evidence clearly indicates that most engineers work in jobs that involve considerable variety, skill, and autonomy (Meiksins and Watson 1989).

There is little evidence that this situation is changing in fundamental ways. Recent analyses of engineering employment, for example, emphasize shrinking opportunities for engineers, and envisage a growing polarization between secure and insecure employment; but they do not anticipate the imminent routinization of the engineering jobs that remain. Even the more pessimistic assessments foresee the development of a hierarchy of technical skill, rather than the actual routinization of engineering

(Bell 1993; Schoenberger 1988). New technologies, such as CAD-CAM, have affected engineers, but they have tended to eliminate, rather than create, routine engineering tasks such as drafting or testing. Even in the computer field, where one can point to evidence of the routinization of programming and of firms exporting portions of software production to low-wage countries such as India, much highly skilled, nonroutine work remains. If anything, the most notable trend has been the shift from mainframe computers to networks of personal computers. This has been accompanied by the externalization of much computer work to software design companies and consultants. But the work these companies and consultants do remains quite varied, and involves a substantial amount of creative work in both designing and adapting computer systems (Salzman and Rosenthal 1993). Remarkably, our interviews with part-time technical professionals revealed little evidence of growing routinization or deskilling. On the contrary, our respondents, who, because they are part-timers and/or consultants, one might have regarded as particularly likely to be given the least desirable kinds of work, were virtually unanimous in emphasizing that their jobs were technically interesting, varied, and challenging.

Part-timers, for example, whom we questioned extensively about the kind of work they were given after their change in status from full-time employees, were nearly unanimous in arguing that the work continued to be intellectually challenging and interesting. Most argued that their work had not changed significantly as a result of their change in work schedules, and many even sounded surprised by the degree to which their jobs remained challenging. A chemical engineer provides a good example; although her employer required her to work through a contractor to obtain part-time status, she found that her work had been largely unaffected:

Q. Do you think that you wind up doing different kinds of work than you might had you been full-time?

A. No, I don't think so. I feel very good about the way I'm being treated at [a petrochemical company]. I feel like I'm really part of the team, and they value my work and stuff like that. There are some things that we've talked about. I can think of one example in particular where I . . . somebody had to take on a role as a quality assurance for the software, and I was willing to do that, but they felt that since I wasn't there eight hours a day, that I might not be the person to do that.

Q. Did they explain why they felt that way?

A. Yeah, because what if they needed something between three and five [laughs], so . . .

Q. They see that as a job that had to be done right now?

A. Well, actually I might end up doing that job anyway, because they haven't found anyone who they think will be good at it who wants to do it.

Q. So, they're rethinking?

A. Well, kind of by default, but, it's . . . I almost have more responsibility than some of the full-time people.

Even contracting, which, in the past at least, has thrived most vigorously in the more routine aspects of technical work such as drafting, showed no signs of routinization amongst our sample. While a few suspected that they had, at least at times, been offered jobs that were routine or unimportant, most stressed that they normally were pleased with the variety and challenge of the jobs they were offered. Indeed, they stressed that one of the advantages of contract work was the ability to avoid repetitive assignments and to be able to choose what one did. Fairly typical is the experience of a female technical writer:

Q. So, you don't think that you're going to get crummier jobs or duller stuff to do, or smaller bits and pieces?

A. I don't know. I did take a project that nobody else wanted, for [an electronics company], so sometimes that could be the case that a lot of times they do float a project around with the writers, and if nobody wants it they contract it out, because I guess they figure you're getting paid more, and you will take anything.

Q. But, that hasn't been a consistent thing. Most of the jobs you've gotten you consider to be good jobs?

A. Yes, actually, I turn down quite a bit of work, because that's one of the things I like, being out on my own. I like being able to pick and choose what I do. I want to be happy with what I'm doing, and I can't be if I'm suffering on a project. I figure the money's not worth it to me, so I have turned down quite a bit. That doesn't seem to have hurt me thus far—at least not that I know of anyway.

A male engineer who had retired from a major automotive company and was now contracting on a part-time basis echoed this sentiment: "I can pick and choose more. I can turn people down. I'll do it if it's an interesting project. But, it has to be within my ability. I don't want to do something I've never done." In all, then, the sample of contractors, like the corporate part-timers, were engaged in highly complex technical work that seemed little different from that practiced by any similar sample of full-time, corporate technical staff.

A Challenge to Traditional Methods of Control

If not with routinization and deskilling, then how do managers manage these new types of workers? Many of the traditional techniques used to structure "responsible autonomy" (Friedman 1977)—work teams, time demands, well-rewarded career ladders, and so on—would seem, at first sight, to be of limited use when dealing with this new kind of technical professional.

Employers of technical professionals, for example, have long found *work teams* an effective method for the organization of technical work. They allow for cooperation among what are often highly specialized individuals; in matrix organizations, teams can be formed and reformed in different ways, depending upon the particular project or problem being tackled. Perhaps more importantly, teams provide an effective but not overly prescriptive means for controlling the work of technical professionals. Within a team, technical professionals can negotiate a division of labor that fits well with the various individuals' abilities and preferences. Though it may involve some direction by the team leader, it typically incorporates collegial discussion and allows professionals to do their actual work relatively free of direct oversight. The team, however, functions as a kind of supervisor (as students of quality circles have noted, in a rather different context) because of its interdependence. Individual team members depend on the others to get their work done, thus promoting both promptness and quality; meetings are occasions at which coordination problems can be raised, suggestions made, and so on. The result is an effective form of self-supervision by the team that allows for high levels of autonomy and eliminates much of the need for direct managerial oversight.

Part-timers, whether in-house or contractors, present obvious dilemmas for teams. When technical professionals are not continuously present in the workplace, the logistics of team coordination become more complex. Can individuals working three days a week keep up with those who are full-time, or will their reduced schedules delay the completion of their portion of projects, thereby delaying the team as a whole? Can meetings be scheduled if one or more members of a team are part-timers? Can teams continue to keep an informal eye on their members if individuals are not continuously present in the workplace, or, as in the case of home workers, not present at all? And if some technical work is being done by outside contractors, can teams be formed at all?

Similarly, organizations have long used *time demands* as a way of testing and controlling professional and managerial employees (Kanter 1977; Bailyn 1993). Professional career structures imply similar time demands (Serron and Ferris 1995; Epstein et al. 1999). The insistence on working extremely long hours, including odd hours such as weekends and holidays—what one recent study (Fried 1998) refers to as "the culture of overtime,"—forces employees to choose between loyalty to work or company and loyalty to something else. Individuals who "pass" these tests signal their commitment to work and organization and, thus, can be trusted to work in responsible positions without constant supervision.

The desire for part-time or reduced work is a direct challenge to these time demands. Employees who request part-time schedules or contractors who resist demands for a crash effort appear to be indicating that they are loyal to something else besides work. They are, in effect, refusing the organization's offer of high rewards in exchange for nearly unlimited demands on their time and asserting their desire that nonwork activities should not automatically be subordinated to work.

The provision of *high salaries and benefits* is another time-honored way of obtaining the loyalty of employees who are difficult to manage in other ways. Material rewards have the effect of rewarding employees for desired services and, as individuals' salaries rise above market rates, of tying them to their current employer. They also have traditionally been a sign of the employers' commitment to the employee, an indication that the individual is a valued asset that the employer wishes to retain.

The effect of such rewards has been weakened somewhat by changes in the contemporary economy. Downsizing, reengineering, and other forms of reorganization have led to layoffs even among highly paid staff, so that the meaning of high rewards is much more difficult to interpret and the exchange for loyalty less automatic. However, voluntary part-time work also tends to undermine the effect of this reward, even when its meaning is still clear. When a technical professional announces that she or he wishes to work part-time, they are explicitly acknowledging that material rewards are of secondary importance to them. At the very least, they know this will mean pro-rated rewards; in many cases, they know it will mean an even greater material sacrifice (since employers often "punish" their part-timers materially). Part-timers are considerably less responsive to the offer of high material rewards; while they obviously welcome them, their acceptance of them is always conditional on their ability to control their hours (and often place) of work.

Probably the most important traditional device for securing the loyalty of professional and managerial employees is the *internal labor market* or *career ladder*. Many studies have argued that upward mobility is the principal reward offered to such employees by organizations and that the condition for promotion is conformity to organizational agendas and a high degree of loyalty (Bailyn 1993; Kanter 1977; Jackall 1988). Because of the importance of mobility in the overall reward structure, corporations have labored long and hard to develop ways to offer promotions to technical professionals, especially engineers. The prospect of promotion into management is often dangled before staff engineers, and so-called dual career ladders have been developed to offer at least the impression of mobility to those for whom a management career is either not possible or desired (Goldner and Ritti 1967).

As in the case of material rewards, internal career ladders have been weakened as a motivational tool by the reality of flatter hierarchies and insecure employment. But these rewards also appear substantially less effective for part-timers, both in-house and contractual, whether or not they are growing scarcer. As indicated, in-house part-timers effectively assert their conditional acceptance of corporate rewards; similarly, they will accept promotion, but only if it is compatible with their other needs away from work. The attractiveness of promotions to them is likely to be weaker because of the heavy time demands built into many senior positions. Moreover, we have found a widespread (though not universal) perception that promotion into management is impractical for part-timers; so it appears that the likelihood of promotion being offered to them is relatively low (Meiksins and Whalley 1995). Contractors who insist on managing their time themselves are doubly insulated from the effects of career ladders, since they are rarely in a position to be promoted at all.

Organizational Responses

One might expect that the apparent control problems presented by part-time professional technical employees would lead employers to reject this new type of employment altogether. Yet this is not the case. Instead, responding to the pressure to provide such work arrangements, employers have innovated in limited ways that do not threaten traditional work arrangements. In part, this involves identifying effective control mechanisms for part-timers. Our research suggests that effective methods of control have, in fact, been developed: some are relatively new, but most are simply adaptations of more traditional methods. They include: (1) the use of portfolios and reputational networks as the basis for hiring such staff; (2) the role of both market pressures and contractual arrangements in controlling independent consultants; (3) the reframing of technical work as the assembling of particular expertise for particular projects, leading to a refocusing of technical workers onto their professional expertise rather than their corporate employer; (4) the use of electronic communication technologies to allow for the maintenance of team arrangements within a geographically dispersed workforce; and (5) the emergence of new forces promoting loyalty (including the very provision of flexible work arrangements themselves). These mechanisms were used in a variety of combinations. Indeed, we suspect that particular versions of them are becoming widespread for all technical professionals as the conditions of work of even full-timers become less corporate-focused and more flexible.

What is also notable, however, is that there appears to be a difference in approach to in-house part-timers and contractors. For a variety of reasons, among which, we argue, is the question of control, companies often seem more comfortable with contracting out (even if it means to part-timers) than with allowing their own employees to cut back on their work hours. Once we have discussed the various ways in which the control issue is handled for each of these categories of worker, the reasons for this difference will become more apparent.

Independent Contracting

Employers have long made use of contract technical professionals. Fluctuations in the need for particular kinds of expertise often make this a logical business strategy. Similarly, shortages of specific kinds of expertise may force employers, whether they like it or not, into using outside contractors. The downsizing of major employers has also increased contracting as they deal with the fact that their technical staff is relatively smaller than it once was. Most notably the practice has extended far beyond the traditional use of contractors to do routine work such as drafting. Indeed, particularly for computer specialists, it is often the most specialized and expert of work that is contracted. Moreover, a wider variety of technical professionals have discovered the possibility and virtues of working as independent contractors. Many of our contractor respondents said that they began as staff professionals, then discovered, often through moonlighting, that there was an external demand for their services. Desiring to work less than full-time, and/or at home or with more flexible schedules, they set out on their own, often winding up doing significant amounts of work for their former employers. Because of our focus on flexible working arrangements, our sample was particularly concentrated among contractors who were genuinely self-employed in the normal meaning of that term, rather than contractors employed by or through agencies, who, as the IRS is never tired of pointing out, are often self-employed in name only.

How then do employers manage these contractors while granting them the freedom to work relatively autonomously? This is, after all, the dilemma that transaction-cost theorists argue was initially responsible for the reliance on organizational rather than market methods for controlling technical work. It has long been assumed that technical performance, because it did not create a standardized product that could be readily bought and sold, could only be secured by traditional bureaucratic means. But what happens when many of these are undermined by new work arrangements?

One obvious control mechanism would be the development of *highly specific contractual arrangements* that would dictate how, when, and where contractors work. But these seem to be rare. Technical contractors typically do have some kind of written, contractual arrangement with their client/employer, although we encountered several cases of contractors who worked largely for a single company where this was not the case. Upon learning of a potential contract, they typically bid on the job and, if successful, enter into a written agreement specifying deadlines, expected outcomes, and the like. We were struck, however, by the degree to which contractors felt that they had a great deal of influence over the content of these contracts and by the high level of autonomy such contracts typically allowed them.

Technical consultants indicated that the bidding process was not rigid, which meant that they did not confront a situation where they had to respond passively to client demands. Rather, it was described as a kind of negotiation in which both parties had needs and through which a kind of mutually agreeable accommodation was reached. As one technical writer commented:

> I think a lot of freelancers—I don't know this for sure—try to act like they work for the company—like for [an electronics company], which I do, in a sense, but it's my own company, so I try to run it as a company rather than me freelancing for them. I don't want to run into—that's why I went off on my own, because I want them to consider me as a company, and not have to—or feel like they can—put deadlines and pressures on me.

Another female technical writer indicated that she experienced considerable variety in the type of contracts she signed; she added that clients are often not particularly knowledgeable about what they want, so that the contractor had to be proactive: "I start writing. I do installation: how to install, weight issues, access to the insides, visibility of LED displays (you can only see them from certain angles). I have to figure this out; the engineers don't tell you."

In some cases, contracts could be quite specific about how the work should be done, especially in those infrequent cases where a company had a standard format for their products (technical writers mentioned writing for the government as an example of this). Review procedures are also typically specified, and, in some cases, milestones are built into contracts. Some acknowledged that the reviews could be a battle in which the company typically "won," but it was equally common for respondents to say that reviews were "not a problem." Whether or not milestones were included varied considerably; indeed, several respondents, like this male engineer, indicated that they themselves insisted on milestones for their own reasons:

Q. Have they typically had review points or milestones or anything like that built into [the contracts]? You've had one that was long enough that that might have been a reasonable expectation.

A. More so ones that I've put in, because these other people didn't have the management sense that I had. Having been through a large company and seen some of the structure that they put on top of the projects, so the managers can get a handle on them, he [the manager] hasn't been through that, and doesn't have that kind of rigorous, and it shows in other things that he does.

Q. You're putting this in for your protection or for his?

A. My own sense of accomplishment. To feel like I am getting something done—so I can say, "Okay, I spent a week working on something. What do I have to show for it?" I'm going to give him a bill for this past month. I want to have something to show him that this is actually done, at the same time I give him the bill, so he has some sense that he's getting some value for his money.

Overall, the general impression is of a flexible negotiation process resulting in relatively open-ended contracts that allow considerable autonomy. One computer consultant concluded: "I think that I have more autonomy—certainly more autonomy than somebody in-house would have."

As we have argued, however, the absence of intrusive bureaucratic oversight and the presence of work autonomy are not imcompatible with controlling professional technical work. Our interviews with contractors revealed that a variety of other mechanisms combined to help "solve" the problem of controlling contractors, even those who worked part-time.

Perhaps paradoxically, *professional attitudes* themselves constituted an important source of control. All kinds of technical training have traditionally incorporated corporate values (Whalley 1986b). Magali Sarfatti Larson (1977, 199) has argued that "professionalism . . . functions as an internalized mechanism for the control of the subordinate expert." We found abundant evidence that contract technical professionals had strong professional attitudes that motivated them to work hard, complete work promptly, be responsive to clients, and so on. This is particularly likely in technical occupations, where practitioners tend to be committed to technical work per se and can frame their efforts on behalf of employers as "doing a good job" and "getting the technology right." Such attitudes are clearly evident in this statement made by a contract computer professional:

A. Like getting on the Web and things like that—some of these things, frankly, eventually result in increasing your skills, or increasing your . . . value to your clients. I know, quite frankly, the fact that I am on CompuServe, and there regularly, has made differences to . . . getting different drivers, for example, printer drivers for other people around there. Various things I have [done]—in a sense I provide a service to them, that they wouldn't have otherwise. I print their bar-code labels for them, partly because they don't want to do it themselves.

Q. So, there's a certain amount of that kind of work that is not formally paid for, but it makes you do the rest of your job better?

A. Yeah, actually, some of the stuff that I do kind of as a hobby, I think, people who are really into data-processing—the people who are at the top—they have data processing as a hobby too. In some ways, it amazes me when I hear of data processing managers that don't have a home computer. They do exist, but I'm surprised.

However, it is not professionalism alone that motivates technical contractors. Many of our respondents also talked about their *feelings of responsibility and loyalty* to the companies and/or individuals with which they contracted. The same computer contractor quoted above on professionalism later added that personal loyalties were at least as important:

Q. Well, here's kind of what I'm getting at. Is it the company itself, and its fate that you're at bottom really concerned about? Or is it that there are certain processes that you are working on that you feel ought to be done right, and you care about that—getting the computers right, or getting the networks right, or whatever it might be?

A. Well, it's been said that people in data processing have more loyalty to the field than they do to the company that they're with, and I guess, generally speaking, I like to do a professional, generally good, job.

Q. This is speculation, but is there any way you could weigh, in your own mind, which is the stronger loyalty?

A. I feel a pretty big responsibility to the people that I've been working for—not to, essentially, leave them in the lurch. I'm concerned right now, because [a metalworking company] has been taking so much of my time [and still] isn't getting what they need from me.

A technical writer added that there is a considerable degree of self-interest implicit in this. When asked why she exerted herself to do a good job for clients, she said: "I want them to stay in business [laughs]. There are a couple of reasons. I had clients who didn't want me to do as good a job as I did. I want to do a good job; I don't want someone to look at something I did and say, 'who did this?'" Technical consultants, thus, well illustrate the interpersonal dimensions of contractual relationships (Granovetter 1985). They appear to be strongly motivated by a combination of loyalties to technology itself, individuals, employers, and their own sense of identity with their product.

The other major force acting on contractors is the *market* itself. In part, the market coerces contractors, who know that their survival as contractors depends on their ability to find clients. This automatically tends to create a strong orientation to serving client needs; virtually every contractor with whom we spoke made a statement to the effect that "you do a good job or you don't work." Because these statements typically came in response to our inquiries about how clients control contractors, contractors clearly understand that the market is operating as an impersonal form of control.

Employers, however, obviously prefer to avoid trial and error in the market; they would rather select from the available universe of contractors those they can trust to do a good job the first time. Here again, the social structure of ostensibly impersonal market relationships becomes apparent, as respondents emphasize the importance of networks and reputation to success as a contractor. We have noted that many contractors built up relationships with future clients before they left organizational employment. And there was general agreement among contractors that the key to getting business was "being known" and "having a reputation"; as a result, contractors placed far more emphasis on networking and contacts than on advertising as a way of getting business. Once clients are reasonably familiar with an individual contractor, or when they are referred to them by someone they know, they have a relatively high level of trust in that contractor's ability and willingness to do what they want (what some recent organizational theorists [Lewicki and Bunker 1995] have referred to as "knowledge-based trust"). As a result, their inability to control directly what the contractor does becomes less of an issue. One technical writer made the connection between autonomy and reputation explicit: "They don't really keep tabs—I guess, because I've sort of become known for beating the deadlines."

Contracting, even in the genuine freelance style practiced by most of our respondents, is a growing phenomenon with, as yet, little examined consequences for organizational form or the long-term careers and lives of the professionals practicing it. It is growing despite the supposed difficulties of using market mechanisms to manage such discretionary activities. Instead the embeddedness of local labor markets in networks of reputation and trust serves as a functional alternative. For contractors, especially those most closely tied delivering a well-defined product—compiling a report, setting up a new system, writing a program, or solving a technical problem—negotiated contracts, but particularly professional training, portfolios, and reputational networks operating within the framework of a deeply socially embedded market, can provide mechanisms for ensuring employers get the kind of work they want.

Part-Time Corporate Work

The relative ease with which employers have accepted the growth of contracting has not, as yet, spilled over into their treatment of requests for part-time employment by their corporate technical staff. And such requests have become more frequent. In part, this is a reflection of the growing numbers of women in technical professions: many of our respondents were women who chose part-time work because they wanted to have children and be actively involved in their upbringing. The demand for part-time work also came from older workers who wished to reduce their work commitments, and from at least a few other men and women who saw part-time work as desirable for other, nonfamily reasons. In our respondents' experiences, employers' reactions to these requests are hesitant at best. Since this hesitancy plays a role in the controlling of part-time work, corporate attitudes toward part-time technical employment are worth discussing in some detail.[1]

We encountered few companies that had formal policies regarding part-time work for professionals and managers, so they treat requests on an individual basis, often inconsistently. Even in those companies with formal policies, individual managers vary dramatically in their attitudes toward part-time work, with the result that employees may have to shop around for an agreeable manager if they want such an arrangement (Fried 1998). Though some employers, especially high-tech companies, have found flexible employment practices to be cost-effective (Glass and Fujimoto 1995), it still appears that companies have only reluctantly confronted the possibility of salaried part-time work for professionals.

Moreover, the general thrust of their reaction to these requests has been to restrict part-time work quite severely. Managers' behavior suggests that they generally regard part-time work for high-level employees as problematic and accept it only under very specific circumstances. Many of our respondents indicated that they believed gender was a factor shaping managerial attitudes toward part-time work. The one "legitimate" reason for requesting part-time status was child care and then only if requested by women. Although some companies resist even this, many employers either had policies that allowed mothers to develop reduced work schedules or informally accepted this practice. Several respondents suggested that the willingness to accept part-time work for mothers reflected both the cultural acceptability of women "sacrificing" career to family and employers' desire to retain scarce female employees in whom they had invested considerable resources.

Individuals who do succeed in obtaining part-time employment usually find that employers see this arrangement as temporary. Typically, the companies for which our respondents worked allow such arrangements for a finite period, generally no more than a few years, on the assumption that employees will return to full-time schedules once their children have reached pre–school age. Part-timers frequently reported that they experienced subtle and not-so-subtle pressures to return to full-time work, even when they would prefer not to. A female engineer employed by a relatively progressive electronics manufacturer described her company's policy and her reaction to it:

> They just announced a policy over the phone. What word did they use? Assurance. An employee that requests part-time or flex-time for one of three reasons—elder care, child care, or . . . business reasons . . . is assured that they can have that for a period of three years. I have a problem with the three years. I guess [they] feel like if you're gonna give up your whole life for your kids, the time to do it is when they're an infant. Once they start getting school age, that's when you're needed more than ever. The basic moral learning [occurs] and that's when the real parenting skills kick in. So I have a problem with three years, I don't know. I'm being strongly encouraged right now to increase hours.

Another respondent was very reluctant to respond to our inquiry about when she intended to return to full-time work, indicating that "they [her company] would pay a lot of money to know that."

Typically, individuals who managed to obtain part-time salaried employment as technical professionals did so within companies where they had been working as full-time employees for some time. We encountered very few cases of a technical professional who started out as a part-timer, and our respondents perceived this scenario as unusual. A similar pattern prevails in other professional occupations (see, e.g., Epstein et al. 1999). As we shall see, this "rule" plays a role in the process of managing part-time technical professionals.

There are also penalties attached to part-time salaried work in many cases. Many respondents reported loss of benefits as a result of their part-time status. This was not an issue for most of them, as they were married to men who had family medical coverage and the like. However, it still represents a loss of security as well as a more tangible loss of items such as pension benefits. Many respondents also suffered economic penalties, either because they were switched from salaried to hourly status or because they did not get raises. We heard a number of reports that "raises stop" when one is part-time, though this was not the case in the more progressive electronics companies.

Several of our respondents reported being required to change job categories as part of their move to part-time schedules. This typically was related to the perception that there are certain kinds of jobs, particularly managerial jobs, that cannot be done on a part-time basis (but see Meiksins and Whalley [1995] for a discussion of the social construction of such "technical" constraints). We encountered several cases of technical professionals who had had managerial positions, trading jobs with a subordinate (who became their manager). We also heard of several technical professionals who had to shift laterally within their company in search of a unit that would accommodate their desire for part-time work.

Finally, in some cases an employer's reluctance to accommodate part-time employees translated into a suggestion that the employee become a contractual employee. Several employers described by our respondents routinely required that individuals who wanted to go from full-time to part-time status be reclassified as "peripheral" or "temporary" support (often with a corresponding loss of status and benefits). We also encountered a number of older technical professionals who continued to work for their employer on a part-time basis, but were allowed to do so only as contractors.

Our respondents, thus, found that their employers tended to define part-time technical employment as a limited, short-term option that they offered as a "benefit" to only certain scarce, highly valued employees. Employers' apparent suspicion of part-timers, however, did not translate into more aggressive forms of oversight of their work, nor to any sense that they were deskilled or assigned to the most routine jobs. Instead companies used a variety of mechanisms, to control these workers, some of which were similar to those used for contractors.

Part-time technical professionals report that, like independent contractors, *reputation* is an important factor affecting their ability to work in the way they do. As we have seen, employers are reluctant to extend part-time status to new employees, reserving it only for certain established individuals. As a female engineer stated: "That's another thing, and I've had managers tell me this, that I've been able to do what I've been doing because of the reputation I've built up over the fifteen years prior. There's no question, I could not come in from scratch and do this." In effect, this "rule" is about trust: from the employer's point of view, this individual had established that she was a good, loyal employee and could thus be trusted to work in unconventional ways. Past corporate performance thus served as an easily read "portfolio" for the corporate professional.

Similarly, like contractors, salaried part-timers are subject to the *disciplining effects of the market*. Part-time technical professionals generally valued their work highly; they were interested in technical work and had gone to considerable lengths to get technical jobs (this was especially true of the women, who were often pioneers in their fields) and to arrange part-time schedules so that they could continue to work. They thus feared losing their jobs and were aware that if they did, they were unlikely to be able to find other part-time positions. They also were concerned that, if they stopped working altogether, they might become obsolete and thus lose the ability to continue to function as technical professionals in the future.

As a result of this, many salaried part-timers expressed a deep sense of gratitude and loyalty to their employer. They perceive themselves as being "lucky" to have arranged a good part-time job and see their employers as benevolent for having accommodated them. One female engineer, who had traded her full-time managerial position for a part-time computer-engineering job, focused on how good her company had been during her pregnancy:

> I, unfortunately, was one of the women who were extremely sick during the pregnancy. I could throw up thirty times a day for nine months—I didn't believe in stopping after the first trimester. That turned into a real problem after two or three months, and everybody was saying, "Are you sure you shouldn't go to the hospital"—because I was so sick. Then I decided that we should tell them. We had wanted to wait. I would say that my immediate boss was extremely displeased at the fact that I was pregnant, because of the fact that this was a new business unit, I was heading it up, and they were going to have to find someone to replace me. Near the end of the pregnancy, I was put on bed rest, and the company was fantastic. I would come in as much as I could, and the rest I stayed home, and they paid my salary even when they knew I was not returning. They ended up determining that the reason I was so sick was that my gall bladder had failed. They scheduled me for surgery and I was not returning after the surgery, and they still went ahead and gave me full benefits throughout the surgery as well as sick leave after it, when technically they were well aware I was not coming back; that would not have been the norm. Those types of things created in me a real sense of loyalty to the company.

Another female engineer expressed a similar sense of gratitude, despite a degree of cynicism about how "enlightened" her employer actually was:

Q. Is there a sense that having the opportunity to go part-time has kept you at [a telecommunications company]? Would you have changed . . . or would you have planned to have stayed anyway?

A. Uh, I probably would have stayed anyway. While you're part-time, though, you're not going to even consider going anyplace else. Nobody else is gonna hire you part-time, so its a real benefit, and I'm real grateful.

Q. Is there a sense that other places don't offer part-time or that you just don't get hired at part-time?

A. Uh, the sense is, and I don't know how much of this is based on actual fact, the perception [is] that they won't hire you at part-time. The part-time is the benefit of being good employees, just to help them out temporarily in a situation, not as a career option.

Many salaried, part-time technical professionals also expressed a commitment to *professional values* quite similar to those that helped motivate independent contractors. They talked about liking difficult jobs and wanting challenges. Several respondents complained that their part-time jobs didn't keep them busy enough, because their employers weren't sure how much work to assign them. Many indicated that they felt that they had a responsibility to work hard because they were part-timers:

Q. Why isn't the work load cut down, why are you working full-time if they're paying [you for thirty-two hours]; is it the nature of the particular job or how the work is allocated or how you choose to do your job?
A. Uh, yeah, I guess it's probably more me than anything. Because you know, I want to pull my own weight, so it's probably me putting pressure on myself more than my employer.

Another female engineer noted her surprise and disapproval when she discovered how much time she wasted while working full-time:

When you're full-time, you have no concept of the value of time. People stand around shooting the breeze, they put in more hours, but they're down in the cafeteria talking with the boys 'til 8:30 and [talking] an hour-and-a half lunch. They work 'til 6:00, but half that time is. . . . I'm very, "Let's go, let's go, I have five minutes, let's get it done." I don't stand around and shoot the breeze, hardly ever. Maybe twice in the last year have I gone with anybody to lunch. You're just more aware of the value of time.

And home workers, whether salaried or not, frequently claimed that they were much more productive working at home because they were not distracted by "unproductive" schmoozing and "office politics."

The disciplining effect of *teams*, although somewhat attenuated, does continue to work on part-timers. When technical professionals choose to go part-time, problems may arise in incorporating them within teams. Several of our respondents reported that they had been assigned less work or work that was more self-contained to facilitate their schedule. However, many continued to function as parts of teams, and in some cases as team leaders. What this required was a degree of flexibility on the part of both companies and team members. Meetings had to be scheduled for when the part-timer was on-site. Other team members sometimes had to pinch-hit for part-timers who couldn't attend meetings or be present on certain days. Managers had to give individuals and teams sufficient advance notice of work requirements so that part-timers could schedule their time (i.e., no last-minute crises if at all possible). These kinds of adjustments did not always get made and, even when they did, could cause a degree of friction between part-timers and others. But they frequently were made, with the result that part-timers continued to be incorporated within teams that, in turn, continued to oversee their work. Indeed, the fact that adjustments had been made tended to increase part-timers' sense of obligation to the group, making them particularly responsive to group requirements in some ways.

It was also possible to facilitate the participation of part-timers in groups through the use of *communication technology*. Electronic mail, modems, beepers, and even conventional telephones all helped to link some part-timers to the workplace at times when they either were not working or were working at home or off-site. Sometimes this integration could be seamless. As one respondent who had been logging in from home on her (unpaid) days put it:

> They didn't know I was part-time because I was so responsible at times. And so they asked me to review their design on a day that I'm not in; they asked my supervisor, for some reason, not me. And she responded back to [them], in a copy to me, "She's not in those days, try to reschedule on another day." . . . And that was a real good sign for me. I said, "I never told you guys, I work part-time." They were like, "We never knew; we got answers from you all the time."

Here the technology allowed the employee to put in extra, and unpaid, work that helped her to maintain her professional commitment to her job. Similarly, another gave colleagues her personal home number:

> They can ask me questions about [any problem], or they can send me mail. . . . . At work everyone usually has their office number listed; I have my home phone number listed. It's the personal home number, so even Mondays, when I'm not working, I take phone calls like that and stuff. And there's e-mail; even on days I don't work sometimes I log in just to read my e-mail to see if there's anything important, but sometimes if you wait from Friday till the following Wednesday to work again, the e-mail can really build up, so I'll log in on other days just for that.

Not surprisingly, some companies actively encourage this; for example, one employer provided its employees with a variety of equipment to use at home. One technical writer who worked at home in a rural area was given a modem, tape drive, and sophisticated computer so that she could continue to interact with the engineers on whom she depended. Similarly, the female engineer discussed earlier, who had traded her full-time managerial job for a part-time engineering job, was able to resume her role as project manager despite working at home only three days a week by making use of company-subsidized electronic communications media such as e-mail.

The technology is not being used to monitor these professionals directly. Their hours at work are not being measured by the amount of time they log on, though some indicated that this was a theoretical possibility. Rather, the technology blurred the boundaries between home and work. From one perspective, this permitted employees to carry out their jobs more professionally despite being at home. From another, of course, this permitted employers to take advantage of employees during hours for which they were not being paid. When combined with a common argument that part-time employees are more productive than their full-time equivalents because they "waste" less time, it is clear that part-time work often represents a good value for employers, who gain more work for less pay.

Conclusion

Despite the evidence that part-time corporate professionals are quite loyal to employers and work well without the need for obtrusive, bureaucratic forms of control—indeed, that they may be more productive per unit cost than full-time employees (see Perlow 1997)—our respondents indicate that their employers were reluctant to provide opportunities for part-time in-house employment and do so only under very specific circumstances (for child care reasons, for a limited time, etc.). In the absence of interviews with employers themselves, we can only speculate as to the reasons for this reluctance. We believe, however, that an examination of its consequences reveals that the reluctance itself is one form of unobtrusive control.

One of the results of employers' reluctance to grant part-time status to employees who desire it is that part-time jobs are scarce and highly valued. As we have seen, employees feel deeply grateful for the fact that they have been "allowed" to reduce their hours, even if it is only for a finite period. They are also acutely aware that it is very difficult to find another part-time job and that part-time opportunities typically are extended only to valued employees whom the employer wishes to retain. This combined sense of vulnerability and privilege is the source of the sense of loyalty to company discussed above.

But what would happen if part-time salaried employment were not scarce? What if employers did not frame it as a short-term arrangement appropriate only for women with children and semiretired employees? On the basis of our conversations with individuals who are currently working part-time, we believe that a more liberal attitude toward part-time employment would greatly expand the numbers of voluntary part-time workers. We heard many stories regarding the difficulties individuals had in developing part-time jobs as well as about others who were unable to persuade their employers to offer them such jobs on acceptable terms. As Tilly (1992) has noted, there clearly are significant numbers of employees who want but cannot get part-time employment. And, at least in the case of technical professionals, the obstacle is often not purely economic, since, as we have seen, many of them are married to high-income individuals with family benefit packages. Greater opportunities for part-time employment would mean significantly larger numbers of part-time technical professionals.

Moreover, we believe that more part-time opportunities would also mean that part-time work might slowly become something more than a temporary phase for some technical professionals. We have been struck by the large number of our respondents who indicate that they like working part-time and would like to continue doing so if they could. These individuals do not aspire to high management positions and are content with what they find are manageable, technically challenging jobs that allow them also to enjoy their lives as parents. If part-time work were more readily available, such individuals would be likely to ask for extended periods of part-time employment and might be inclined to shop around for those part-time jobs that best suited their needs.

Were this to occur, employers would have to rethink significantly their approach to rewarding and controlling technical professionals. As it stands now, with salaried part-time work restricted, employers can make use of relatively familiar unobtrusive controls, such as high rewards and promotions (for in-house technical professionals), and markets and reputations (for contractors). In-house part-time work can be bracketed as a limited, temporary interruption to normal career patterns. But if salaried part-time work became more possible, the loyalty to company created by scarcity would be weakened, and employees' responsiveness to career and economic motivations might be significantly reduced. Employers would have to think more explicitly about issues mentioned by some of our respondents, such as making sure that part-timers are given sufficient responsibility and appropriate amounts of work to ensure the kind of loyalty they traditionally gained through the use of internal labor markets. They might also have to reduce the economic penalties on part-timers, which would compound the control issue by making part-timers more expensive.

Perhaps most importantly they would have to rethink the equation of full-time with commitment that has been built into the normative expectations of both corporate and professional work during the male monopoly of such positions. In the absence of measures of productivity, or of ways of directly observing work, corporations have come to rely on time at work as at least a short-run measure of commitment; a phenomenon observable in settings as different as the corporate law firm, medical internships, and the R&D departments of electronic giants. Corporations have been willing to hire contractors in part because such an arrangement does not challenge this equation for corporate staff. Corporate part-time work, however, requiring as it does at least some prima facie specification of what counts as full-time, threatens to undermine the process. Hence, perhaps, the willingness of corporations to allow staff to work part-time if they, in turn, are willing to accept the market constraints of independent contractor status.

As we have argued, the growth of corporate part-time employment does not automatically mean that employers lose control of part-time technical professionals. Our respondents' experiences suggest that other forms of unobtrusive control still operate. And employers could, perhaps, enhance such positions by exploring the more flexible approach to careers and work advocated by management theorists such as Lotte Bailyn (1993). They could experiment with ways of helping their employees to develop what Fred Block and Larry Hirschhorn (1979, 379) have called "a fluid, flexible life course built around work that provides continuous opportunities for learning." They could pursue the implications of recent research showing that allowing employees to enjoy positive experiences at home can have a positive spillover at work (Galinsky 1999). But our respondents indicate that few employers are moving rapidly in this direction. Despite the predictions of management futurists such as Charles Hecksher (1995), few companies appear to be moving away from the use of tests of loyalty and career ladders as the principal mechanisms for motivating staff employees. When forced to, they appear far more comfortable with using relatively familiar market control mechanisms than they do with confronting the possibility of different relationships with their in-house technical staff.

Notes

Acknowledgments: This research was funded by a grant from the Alfred P. Sloan Foundation. The authors gratefully acknowledge the foundation's support. Thanks are also due to Cynthia Negrey, who provided us with an insightful critique of an earlier draft of this chapter.

1. We need to be clear that, in this essay at least, we are reporting on corporate attitudes only as they are revealed to us through interviews with employees or contractors. Though we have talked to a number of employers, our research has been focused on the experiences and strategies of technical professionals themselves. For the purpose of this discussion we think our respondents are better able to describe companies' "revealed preferences" than would official policy statements.

References

Bailyn, Lotte. 1993. *Breaking the Mold: Women, Men, and Time in the New Corporate World.* New York: Free Press.

Bell, Trudy. 1993. "Jobs at Risk." *IEEE Spectrum,* 30: 18–35.

Block, Fred, and Larry Hirschhorn. 1979. "New Productive Forces and the Contradictions of Contemporary Capitalism." *Theory and Society,* 7(3): 363–395.

Epstein, Cynthia Fuchs, et al. 1999. *The Part-Time Paradox: Time Norms, Professional Life, Family, and Gender.* New York: Routledge.

Fried, Mindy. 1998. *Taking Time: Parental Leave Policy and Corporate Culture.* Philadelphia: Temple University Press.

Friedman, Andrew. 1977. *Industry and Labour.* London: Macmillan.

Galinsky, Ellen. 1999. *Ask the Children: What America's Children Really Think About Working Parents.* New York: William Morrow and Company.

Glass, Jennifer, and Tetsushi Fujimoto. 1995. "Employer Characteristics and the Provision of Family Responsive Policies." *Work and Occupations,* 22(4): 380–411.

Goldner, Fred, and R. Richard Ritti. 1967. "Professionalism as Career Immobility." *American Journal of Sociology,* 72: 489–503.

Granovetter, Mark. 1985. "Economic Action and Social Structure: The Problem of Embeddedness." *American Journal of Sociology,* 91: 481–510.

Heckscher, Charles. 1995. *White Collar Blues.* New York: Basic Books.

Jackall, Robert. 1988. *Moral Mazes.* New York: Oxford University Press.

Kanter, Rosabeth Moss. 1977. *Men and Women of the Corporation.* New York: Harper.

Larson, Magali Sarfatti. 1977. *Professionalism: A Sociological Analysis.* Berkeley: Univeristy of California Press.

Lewicki, Roy, and Barbara Benedict Bunker. 1995. "Developing and Maintaining Trust in Work Relationships." Pp. 114–39 in *Trust in Organizations: Frontiers of Theory and Research.* edited by Roderick Kramer and Tom Tyler. Thousand Oaks, CA: Sage Publications.

Meiksins, Peter, and Chris Smith. 1996. *Engineering Labour: Technical Workers in Comparative Perspective.* London: Verso Books.

Meiksins, Peter, and James Watson. 1989. "Professional Autonomy and Organizational Constraint: The Case of Engineers." *Sociological Quarterly,* 30(4): 561–586.

Meiksins, Peter, and Peter Whalley. 1995. "Technical Workers and Reduced Work: Limits and Possibilities." Paper presented at the meetings of American Sociological Association, Washington, DC.

Osterman, Paul. 1988. *Employment Futures.* Oxford: Oxford University Press.w

———. 1996. *Broken Ladders: Managerial Careers in the New Economy.* New York: Oxford University Press.

Perlow, Leslie. 1997. *Finding Time: How Corporations, Individuals, and Families Can Benefit from New Work Practices.* Ithaca: ILR Press.

Perrow, Charles. 1967. "A Framework for the Comparative Analysis of Organizations." *American Sociological Review,* 32: 194–208.

Salzman, Hal, and Stephen Rosenthal. 1993. *Software by Design.* New York: Oxford University Press.

Schoenberger, Erica. 1988. "The Ambiguous Future of Professional and Technical Workers in Manufacturing." *Acta Sociologica,* 31: 241–247.

Serron, Carol, and Kerry Ferris. 1995. "Negotiating Professionalism: The Gendered Social Capital of Flexible Time." *Work and Occupations,* 22: 22–47.

Tilly, Chris. 1992. "Dualism in Part-Time Employment." *Industrial Relations,* 31: 330–347.

Vincenti, Walter. 1990. *What Engineers Know and How They Know It: Analytical Studies from Aeronautical History.* Baltimore: Johns Hopkins University Press.

Whalley, Peter. 1986a. "Markets, Managers, and Technical Autonomy." *Theory and Society,* 15:1–2.

———. 1986b. *The Social Production of Technical Work.* London: Macmillan.

———. 1991. "Negotiating the Boundaries of Engineering: Professionals, Managers, and Manual Work." *Research in the Sociology of Organizations,* 8: 191–215.

CHAPTER 12

Net-Working for a Living: Irish Software Developers in the Global Workplace

Seán Ó Riain

It is 4:15 in the afternoon. On the wall of the software test group in the Irish offices of USTech, a prominent Silicon Valley computer company, there are four clocks. At the moment they show that it is 8:15 A.M. in Silicon Valley, California, 10:15 in Austin and Fort Worth, Texas, and 11:15 in Montreal, Canada. Silicon Valley has just "opened for business" and the software developers and managers in Ireland begin a hectic few hours of discussion with their American counterparts. The row of clocks evokes a smoothly working global economy, held back only by time zones, and a software operation which seamlessly manages a variety of transnational connections.

I hurry downstairs as I have a conference call to the United States at 4:30 P.M. Irish time (8:30 A.M. their time in Silicon Valley). Thirty minutes later I am sitting in an open plan cubicle along with five members of a software development team. Employed by USTech, they are developing a software product for a Silicon Valley start-up company called Womble Software. I have been writing a user guide for the product and am deep in discussion with Jane, the technical writing editor in Silicon Valley, and Ramesh, an immigrant from India and the "chief architect" of the program, living in St. Louis, the heart of middle America. As my manager comes into the team area I put the conference call on the speaker phone. Now the whole "Womble team" can hear the conversation.

As the conversation unfolds so does the mime drama around me as the team reacts to the flow of global communication into this cubicled "local" space. When Ramesh suggests adding new features (creating more work for the developers around me) there is an explosion of displeased sign language including a variety of abusive gestures directed at the speaker phone. Since Ramesh can hear everything on our end, this pantomime is conducted in complete silence. I have a hard time not bursting out laughing . . . . When Jane points out to Ramesh that it is difficult to write a user guide when the final screen designs for the software program have not been decided upon (a common complaint within the development team two weeks before the product is released) there is an explosion of mimed cheering and barely controlled laughter around me.

This is just another day in the global informational workplace, a workplace which is home to increasing numbers of employees around the world. The dominant image of these workplaces is that of places lifted out of time and space, places where communication and innovation are free from the drag of local cultures and practices and untainted by power relations. Robert Reich (1991) argues that new information and communication technologies make it possible and even necessary to reorganize firms into "global webs" and employees into global telecommuters. For Reich these webs operate smoothly, destroying constraints of space and social structure, moving in conjunction with the ever-circling hands of the clocks on the USTech wall. The global workplace is "lifted out" of its temporal and spatial contexts and becomes a "pure" space for communication based on shared rules of interaction and understanding.[1]

Others argue that this perspective is too benign. The speeding up of the global economy destroys local space—the fact that Ramesh and the Womble team can participate in the same conversation at the same time means that they essentially share the same social and economic space, despite the physical distance between them. Time annihilates space, melting away "solid" local places into the "air" of the global economy. (Berman 1982; Harvey 1989; Castells 1996).[2] This is not a neutral process, however, as the once autonomous local space of the worker is increasingly dominated by global corporations and the ever more rapid pace of economic life under capitalism. (Bluestone and Harrison 1982; Burawoy 1985; Shaiken 1990). Ramesh's presence on a phone call, an e-mail message or a plane trip away, undermines the autonomy provided these workers by their local space.

The Womble team is certainly connected to other global workplaces—including Silicon Valley and St. Louis on this particular afternoon. They also experience the pressure of the global economy through the demands of Ramesh for new features. However, local space is not destroyed by these global connections. The Womble cubicle takes on a culture of its own, manifested in the mimed hostility to Ramesh's suggestions but also in the information-sharing, problem-solving, and solidarity building within the team on an everyday basis. In fact, the demands of the global economy for increased flexibility and specialized learning actually make the local context and interactions of the global workplace even more critical. Efficient production and constant innovation require the construction of shared physical spaces where workers can interact and communicate on a face-to-face basis and where shared goals and meanings can be created and maintained.[3]

Global connections bring the pressures of the world economy into the heart of workplaces such as the Womble team cubicle. However, these pressures actually make local space and social context all the more important. The speed up of time and the extension of social space across physical distance in the global economy do not destroy space but in fact intensify the impact of space in constituting successful global workplaces.

However, this does not herald a return to an era of workplaces dominated by localized social relations. This is because the importance of local social relations to innovation creates a dilemma for the global corporations who rely on this innovation. The local character of their work teams is essential to their efficiency, but also poses a problem of regulating such localized relations from a distance. Ramesh may be aware that his proposals are not meeting with happy grins on the other end of the phone, but he is also unable to directly regulate the team's behavior because of his distance from the team and his only partial incorporation into the social space of the team. The typical managerial answer to this dilemma of control in the global workplace is to attempt to control the instrument of speed up and pressure within the global economy—time itself. The politics of the contemporary workplace is increasingly the politics of time.[4]

The most important instrument used to control time in the global workplace is the project deadline. Although Ramesh cannot control the everyday behavior of the Womble team, the parameters within which the team can operate are set by the demands of the deadline. The team members have a great deal of autonomy in how they work but the supervisor looking over their shoulder is time itself, with every decision measured against its impact on meeting the deadline. Ramesh's requests for new features are not considered on their technical merits but on the basis of their impact on the team's ability to meet the deadline. Even as the importance of space is intensified in the global workplace so too is time, in its manifestation as the dominant mode of control in these workplaces. Global workplaces are subject to a process of time-space intensification.

This chapter explores in detail the characteristic structures and dynamics of the global workplace under conditions of time-space intensification. The first part of the analysis shows the dilemmas posed for innovation in the global workplace due to the pressures placed on it by the intersection of the high mobility careers of software developers and highly mobile software firms. It documents how intense cooperation in localized workplaces makes it possible for such highly mobile workers and firms to forge an alliance in the pursuit of innovation and profit. A tension persists within this structure, however—a tension between place-bound cooperation based on group solidarity and individual careers based on high rates of mobility between firms and places. This tension is reconciled through the dynamics of the workplace, which is analyzed in the second part of the chapter. The period prior to the project deadline is one of team solidarity and cohesion, while the post-deadline phase is characterized by the fragmentation of the team as they use their social networks to position themselves for the next move in their career. The globalization of the information technology (IT) industry is seen to result not in a virtual economy but in a global industry organized around and through certain key places and regions. Within these global workplaces relations among workers constantly cycle through phases of cohesion and fragmentation as worker solidarity is mobilized for purposes of innovation but disarmed by the structure of careers in the labor market. The globalization of knowledge workplaces becomes an object of tension and conflict in the workplace, not simply an ever expanding process of increasingly pure communication and innovation nor an inexorable advance of the dominance of capital. Power relations in these workplaces are forged out of the interplay of mobility and place and of time and space, which is examined through the rest of this chapter.

This chapter argues therefore that as the workplace stretches out across national borders local spaces such as the Womble team cubicle become all the more crucial to the operation of the global economy. Overcoming the constraints of international time differences allows organization across time and space but poses new problems of control from a distance—problems which are solved by the intensification of time through work team deadlines. Global informational workplaces are characterized not by the disappearance of time and space as realities of work life but by their increasing importance and intensification.

Dilemmas of the Global Workplace

Neither do these workplaces emerge tabula rasa onto the global stage, as a response to the prompting of the global market. In fact, the Womble team is the outcome of state development strategies, changing corporate structures and strategies, and the emergence of new industries organized around knowledge creation. Indeed, the routine phone and e-mail arguments between Ramesh and the Womble team would bring a glow to the heart of many industrial development agency officials in Ireland. The formation of connections to the global economy through attracting foreign high-technology investment has been the cornerstone of Ireland's industrial policy since the late 1950s. The connection to the United States has been particularly crucial—over four hundred American companies have located in Ireland and some three-quarters of jobs in electronics and software in Ireland are in foreign-owned companies. Through the 1970s and 1980s transnational electronics and computer hardware firms located primarily low-level functions in Ireland and developed few links to the local economy (O'Malley, 1989). Many of the transnational corporations used Ireland as an "export-processing zone" within the European market, taking advantage of low tax and wage rates and Ireland's position within European Union tariff barriers. Irish plants were at best weakly integrated into the core activities of the corporate parents, as the typical Irish operation's activities were routine and relations with the parent hierarchical.

However, the past five to ten years have seen a shift in the nature of the activities and the character of some of the foreign investment in Ireland.[5] Encouraged by the state industrial development agencies, many hardware operations began to grow software development centers as the information technology industry moved towards a focus on software and software became the strategic technology for these corporations. Local managers, usually Irish-born, were able to carve out strategic positions for their operations within the parent companies although their position always remained precarious. In cases such as USTech, local managers often developed relationships with customers well before discussing these new lines of business with their colleagues at headquarters. In recent years, subcontracting and business partnership relationships between American and Irish firms have expanded and the two economies have become increasingly closely integrated. Indeed, the apparent shortage of computer skills in Silicon Valley was one of the reasons the Womble software contract went to the USTech Ireland office. Companies such as USTech Ireland were still limited by their place in the international corporate structure and often still concentrated on testing, support, and consulting software work rather than on the strategic software development tasks. However, many were able to develop small- to medium-sized software development teams, closely integrated with the parent's operations.

USTech is well established in Ireland, having located there over fifteen years ago and becoming one of the early success stories of Irish industrial policy. For many years it was one of Ireland's primary computer hardware production operations, with a reputation for high quality. The hardware manufacturing operations of USTech Ireland were dismantled with massive layoffs in the early 1990s, leaving local management scrambling for the operation's survival and turning to a complete reliance on the local pool of software skills. Their links to the global economy have diversified with a proliferation of customers, partners, and internal corporate sponsors replacing their previous model of reporting directly to a single office in the United States. The software development contract for Womble reflects this change as there was little opportunity within the previous corporate structure for such arrangements.

Womble Software itself is a perfect example of the "global web" corporate structure which Reich (1991) argues is becoming the norm. Formed as a spin-off from a large hierarchical corporation, the company is part owned by the four founders, part by USTech itself, part by a major customer, and the rest by a venture capital fund in Silicon Valley. It has no more than fifteen employees of its own. The development team is based in Ireland and is officially contracted to provide software development services to Womble. The screens for the program are conceptualized by Ramesh but all the development work necessary to turn them into computer graphics is done in a small graphic design house just outside San Francisco. The help-desk staff, which users reach if they call with a problem, is staffed by the trained employees of a help-desk contracting company. The technical writers who write the on-screen help for users are all hired on a contract basis. In place of more rigid, hierarchical organizational structures, we have a shifting web of connections forged into a relatively fleeting alliance.

Mobility and Connections in the Global Labor Market

However, Womble not only is the prototype of the "global web" organization but also conforms to a new model of computer industry careers. In this model, the dominant metaphor of IBM's promise of lifetime employment has been replaced by the image of the freewheeling Silicon Valley engineers who expect little from their employers and will jump ship for more money or more challenging work at the drop of a hat. Both of course are stereotypes, but there is more than a grain of truth in the emergence of cross-firm careers as the dominant pattern in software companies both in Silicon Valley and in Ireland (Saxenian 1994; Baron, Burton, and Hannan 1996). These trends are intensified by a shortage of experienced personnel in most countries' software industries (Office of Technology Policy 1997). Certain skills are in particularly high demand—including the Unix, C++, database, and Java skills of the employees in the Womble team. The variety of local and global connections of the team reinforces the tendency towards mobility by providing the channels of information about new opportunities and the social contacts for facilitating moves to those emerging areas. Negotiating the commitment of highly mobile employees becomes the critical dilemma facing software firms, a dilemma which is addressed in the following sections of this chapter.

In industries such as software the typical career pattern now involves a number of moves between organizations during a career, and there has been a clear shift from internal labor markets to job-hopping between firms. Where employees stay with the same firm, their tasks and level of responsibility change on a regular basis. Furthermore, professional migration into both the United States and Ireland has been increasing, with transnational intra-firm and inter-firm careers expanding. The high mobility career pattern with little attachment to the employer (or to the employee for the firm) has become a reality for these particular software developers. Even in the still "semi-peripheral" region of Ireland, the careers of such software developers have converged quite significantly with those of their counterparts in the leading high-technology regions such as Silicon Valley or global cities such as New York and London. A survey of 250 software firms in Ireland in 1997 revealed that a quarter of the firms had employee turnover of 25 percent or more in the previous year (Ó Riain 1999).[7]

These trends were evident in the experience of the Womble software team members. The team consisted of six people (including myself) during the time I was there. Séamus, the team leader, has been at USTech for seven years. In that time he has held four completely different positions—working as a computer test engineer, software systems test engineer, information systems support engineer, and software development team leader. The rest of the team has been assembled over the past six to eighteen months. Conor, six months out of college, still receives job postings from his college career counseling service every two weeks. If he follows the industry pattern he will most likely leave USTech in eighteen months time or so, when another software company will be glad to pay him well for his skills and experience.

Jim and Paul are employed on a contract basis. Dan had also been a contractor and took a pay cut of almost 50 percent when he accepted a permanent post in order to get a mortgage from the bank. Paul's history is one of a "software cowboy," using a series of lucrative short-term contracts to see the world without being tied down by business, social, or personal obligation. Jim and Dan have pursued a different path—they have at times been employees, contractors, entrepreneurs, or a number of these statuses at the same time. The line between employer, self-employed, and employee begins to blur in such careers.

Transnational experience is a major part of the developers' careers. Dan is originally from Hong Kong and came to Ireland to study, subsequently pursuing a career in software. Almost all the contractors who work with the team while I am there have emigrated at one point or spent a significant amount of time working on contracts abroad. Indeed, it is the contractors who are most openly dependent on mobility for their career advancement. They are usually brought in for their quite specialized skills and are often given tasks working on relatively self-contained parts of the system being designed. Their need to communicate with other team members may be minimized, although this remains a critical part of their effectiveness. Sometimes, contractors stay with a team for a relatively long time. Jim, a contractor, had been with the team for longer than the two permanent staff and had successfully resisted efforts to make him take a permanent position. Indeed, he was the *de facto* deputy team leader. Mobility across organizational, employer/employee, and national boundaries has therefore been central to these workers' careers and is understood by all to be the background to workplace interactions and relationships.

Mobility is also the team members' key bargaining chip with their employers. One lunchtime Conor, Michael, the group manager, and I ended up sitting together for lunch. We had somehow got onto the topic of the difficulty of getting people for the jobs that were available within USTech. Conor went into great detail on the job offers he had received on leaving college and on the ever-improving job market for graduates, until Michael quietly finished his lunch and left. Conor turned to me and asked: "What did you make of that? I wanted him to know there are plenty of other jobs out there. What I didn't say is that I've been getting job offers every two weeks through the college."

Mobility then is the dominant career strategy within the software industry as a whole and within the Womble software team. There are also, however, constraints on the mobility system for both the firm and the employee. The firm will sometimes try to get contractors with crucial product knowledge to become permanent employees so that their knowledge is kept within the organization. In the Womble team Dan had gone permanent because he had to get a mortgage, whereas Jim, already having a mortgage, was able to resist the efforts of the project managers to have him become a permanent employee. Neither are employees completely free to exercise their mobility. Companies are reluctant to pay employees if they threaten to leave, as they are likely to set a series of threats in train which may spiral out of control. However, companies will make exceptions on occasion as long as they can keep them relatively secret. In general, the threat of mobility serves as a background possibility which keeps the company's mind focused on getting training for key employees, increasing their pay, and so on in order to put off the possibility of leaving before it arises.

Employees must also be careful not to get a reputation for being unlikely to stay at a company. "If you look at a CV and see that someone has moved every nine months or so, you have to wonder if they'll stay here any longer than that. But if they stay two or three years, then you know they will contribute something" (Séamus). The degree of demand for a developer's particular skills is the critical factor which affects their bargaining power through mobility. "When I was in Belfast, you would be on contract if you couldn't get a permanent job. Here, you would be permanent if you couldn't go on contract. It's just a question of how many jobs there are" (Paul). This can even override the threat of lost reputation if the demand is high enough—"They mightn't think you'll stay but if they need you badly enough they'll hire you anyway!" (Paul). Industry norms have developed around the "proper" way in which this mobility is to occur—mobility between jobs is not unlimited but is a strategy which must be carefully managed.

Mobility therefore becomes a taken-for-granted element of the composition of software teams such as the Womble team. Relations with co-workers develop in the context of a constant awareness that the members of the team might be dispersed at short notice. This can happen either by corporate decision (the team beside us was disbanded overnight when USTech in Silicon Valley halted development of the product on which they were working) or through the decision of individuals to leave the team. Mobility then is a double-edged sword—the advantage to employees of being able to leave with few repercussions is balanced against the lack of constraints on companies changing employees' responsibilities and even getting rid of them (within the bounds of the law). Indeed, the Womble team was itself eventually disbanded when development work was moved back to the United States and ultimately when Womble itself went out of business. These advantages and dangers are all the more significant for contractors. Nonetheless, these highly mobile careers seem to pose a clear threat to the ability of software developers to work together in a cohesive way while working on a common project. The intensification of space in the global workplace provides some of the critical elements of the answer to this organizational dilemma.

Putting Work in Its Place

While software developers may move quite regularly from job to job, they have an intense relationship with each other once in a particular job. In informational and design work, the labor process is usually organized in the form of teams working closely together on specific projects. Some see these as virtual teams interacting purely through cybertechnologies—the process of generating cooperation among employees is assumed to be unproblematic (Reich 1991). Indeed, Ramesh himself subscribed to the theory of the virtual economy in a "Thank you" e-mail message he sent to the contract graphic design firm in California:

> Our project team was truly an international virtual-team, with up to 8 hours of time-zone difference among the different team members. We expected you to work at such a hectic pace, yet, we also demanded extreme flexibility from you in all respects. It is very rare that anybody of your caliber would be able to excel on both these fronts.

Such teams are usually located in close proximity to one another, however, as this allows the team to handle the complex interdependencies between team members through easy and constant communication, and allows them to build a coherent collective identity which becomes the basis of cooperation within the team.

The sheer volumes of information and the dependence of each member of the team on the design decisions of the others make the easy interaction of the team members critical. As Jim at USTech worked on the user interface screens, he would intermittently call over to Paul two desks away: "What did you call the course number variable, Paul, I can't find it"; "Are you working on the database at the moment, it's a bit slow"; "who's doing the security screens?" The questions and answers are discussed on the way to and back from breakfast and lunch, although by common consent rarely during the break itself.

By contrast, information flows to the United States can be patchy and tend to be limited to broad strategic decisions. A developer in Silicon Valley would have great difficulty in developing this product along with the team around me. Indeed, my own easy ability to ask the developers around me for information fifteen times a day contrasts with the difficulties I have sharing information with Jane in Silicon Valley, leaving me idle for mornings or afternoons as I wait to be able to call her in the United States to clear up some minor misunderstandings. Where such transnational "virtual" relationships work, they are constantly supplemented by travel to meet the team(s) in the other country—Ramesh was a regular visitor to the USTech Ireland office. This clearly also affected how much employees could learn from their colleagues. The experience of working with the more experienced and skilled developers taught others the skills and tricks which turn a computer science graduate into an effective and innovative programmer.[8]

The accountability of team members to one another is also much more easily sustained in face-to-face interactions than in "virtual" communications. This can happen even in the most apparently "flat" and nonhierarchical of organizations. I was caught in a bind during the conference call when Ramesh asked me, an untrained technical writer with a long and largely irrelevant training in sociology, "Seán, are you happy with the proposal to put the toolbar in the help box?" While I was being formally asked to participate in a design decision, the social structure of this global organization made me think first not of the implications of my decision for the system itself but of my loyalties to the fuming developers around me. Even the periodical visits of Ramesh to Ireland do not solve the problems of miscommunication and alienation felt by the Irish team. As Michael, the business manager of the group, said, "Having a remote manager has made getting a process of communication in place a lot more difficult." Problems which would require solutions in a face-to-face context can be swept under the carpet or become a figure of fun in a context where communication is by phone and the Internet.

The issues which can be resolved in a daily phone call to the United States are those relating to the strategic technical decisions, which were hotly debated with Ramesh every day by Séamus, the team leader, and even the other members of the team. E-mail is generally used within the team to pass on relatively routine information to one another—whether that be between the team members or between Séamus, the team leader, and Ramesh. On one occasion, although we sat less than ten feet apart, Conor and I exchanged a series of e-mails about problems I had found with the program and the fixes he had made—without ever turning around to speak to one another. Only when it became clear that one of the problems was more complex than it appeared did we discuss the issue face-to-face. E-mail also appeared to be a valuable tool for the team members to stay in touch with their friends throughout the industry. I was able to combine my membership in the "global ethnography group" with participation in the Womble team, largely unbeknownst to anyone else on the team. Other team members seemed to use e-mail similarly—every now and then someone would read out a joke they had been sent by a friend or tell us about the bonuses being offered at other companies for recruiting a new employee. Overall, while face-to-face interactions were critical to conveying complex information or to building and sustaining trust, computer-supported communication seemed "especially suited to maintaining intermediate-strength ties between people who cannot see each other frequently" (Wellman et al. 1996, 231).

USTech is also located within one of the locations best known for information technology within Ireland. Located in a city which is attractive to the young people which dominate the software industry, USTech also benefits from access to a large pool of local skilled labor and from the connections of the Womble team members to the broader "culture of innovation" within the region. The Womble team members, especially those who have had more mobile career patterns, have many connections to people through the local industry and will often recount stories of people they know in common, people who could be hired by the team, other developers they met around the city and discussed their work with, and so on. Their high-mobility careers are also sustained through social ties to others in the industry who can provide the team members with information on job opportunities and can provide formal or informal recommendations to employers regarding the team members' competence. It turns out that both the high-mobility careers and the face-to-face interactions which mitigate their corrosive effect on workplace cohesion are supported by the emergence of this regional "innovative milieu."[9]

Face-to-face interaction, localized social relations, and electronic networks each structures the global workplace in important but different ways. Clearly face-to-face interaction does not guarantee good communication or cooperative working relationships. However, it makes it a lot easier than trying to achieve these across eight time zones and numerous digital interactions. Ease of communication and mutual accountability at "work" ensure that spaces defined by face-to-face interaction remain a critical component of the global workplace, even as virtual spaces proliferate.

A Globalized Local Culture

These globalized places also take on a distinct culture which reinforces the cooperation and cohesion produced by the organization of work itself. In many ways even these human paradigms of the global economy are "global locals", bringing distinct local cultures to the global stage and remaking both global and local social relations in the process. This small, open-plan team area may be a globalized space, but it is one which has a clearly defined local identity and which interacts with the global economy with caution and at times with difficulty. Some have argued that such tensions between the local and the global are born out of a traditionalist resistance by the local to the cosmopolitanism of the global (see, e.g., Kanter 1995; Castells 1996). However, the Womble team do not resist the global in and of itself but contest how the global should operate, showing disdain for the mismanagement of the global by the remote managers.

This can be seen most clearly in their perceptions of American software developers and managers. As an Irish manager at USTech told me:

> The test group here was the best in the corporation and they were really saving USTech with their customers in the field. So we had all these American managers coming over telling them they were the greatest and how they were the best thing since sliced pan. That's OK the first time but after a while the people here started saying among themselves, "Quit the bullshit—if you think we're so great give us a raise or at least buy us a few pints."

This disjuncture was shown up dramatically after one particular bout of giving out about the United States managers of the team. Séamus, the team leader, summed up the relationship to the United States's parent ironically:

SÉAMUS. It's not as if there's "us and them" or anything. . . . It's not even that, it's just "them" really!
JIM (wearily). Yep, they're the enemy!

Nonetheless, the Irish managers and developers tend to work very successfully with their American counterparts, accepting some aspects of United States corporate culture while maintaining a clear rejection of many aspects of the Americanized environment in which they find themselves.

The developers themselves comment on their own homogenous team culture, despite the fact that Dan is from Hong Kong:

JIM. What would we do if a black guy joined the group, who would we pick on?
Conor. Or a woman?
JIM. Séamus, you can't ever hire a black woman!
SEÁN. There's always Americans to pick on. . . .
SÉAMUS. Yeah, but they're too easy, there's no challenge in that [laughter].

The mention of a "black guy" is largely rhetorical as I never heard any comment within the team directed against "black guys." The team culture was clearly masculine and there is no doubt that this culture could be self-perpetuating.[10] "American" is also somewhat ambiguous as Ramesh, the "American" with whom the Womble team members have the most interaction, is originally from India. On a different occasion, three members of a different team discuss their Indian boss in the U.S. with Conor and me:

PAT. We have one too—Ranjit.
CONOR. Ranjit that, sounds like something out of Aladdin.
PETER. [Says something imitating Ramesh's accent.] That's racist, that is [i.e., criticizing himself, very serious about it].

BOB. Yeah, that's an "ism," that is. That's racism.

PAT. They're [Indian software developers] probably over there saying, "Those bloody Micks."

AIDAN. Yeah, saying, "Drinking pints of Guinness over their computers."

"Difference" on a global scale is an everyday part of these software developers' milieu although it is negotiated within a strong homogenous local culture. This was also evident in the team's relationship to Dan (from Hong Kong). In fact, while the culture of the team was strongly male and Irish, members of the team was highly aware of this culture and most would criticize racism and sexism which they saw elsewhere. On one occasion two other team members and I were both shocked and amused on hearing Dan, who had been born in Hong Kong, slander a visiting technical trainer who was himself Pakistani. "The other" was accepted as an everyday part of life for Irish software developers and helped to define the team identity. When Dan revealed his own criticisms of another Asian ethnic group, this disrupted the assumption of a single "other" and was both surprising and funny to us as team members. It also revealed the unspoken assumption within the team that Dan's behavior and attitudes regarding race were subject to different rules than those of the Irish-born team members.

While the team members worked relatively easily with people of a variety of national, ethnic, and racial backgrounds, they consciously maintained a strong local team culture. Operating in the global workplace requires them to work with and around "difference," but by the same token the less hierarchical forms of economic domination also allow them to maintain their local culture within these global connections. There is also a strong pragmatic element to this ability of people from different backgrounds to work together in the global workplace. One of the Womble Software managers took us out for a meal when she was visiting from the United States. Half-way through the evening I commented to Pat, a contractor, "She seems OK, decent enough," to which Pat replied, "Well, when you come to discover the jungle you have to play with the natives."

Not only then are the Womble developers' "global locals," but they also think of themselves as such. Their highly mobile careers and relatively fleeting association with one another in the workplace demand an intense experience of a shared space and culture in order for them to create a cohesive work team. The team members use elements of a shared culture from outside the team to create this solidarity but are also able to incorporate aspects such as Dan's non-Irish racial and ethnic background into the team through the overriding emphasis on work and technical competence. While these local team cultures are quite likely to be exclusionary of women and other ethnic groups, as indicated in the quotes above, they are also flexible enough to accommodate the presence of such groups within the dominant team culture when necessary. Place, mobility, and the global workplace are not necessarily in tension with one another, as they might appear on first glance, but are in fact symbiotic, underpinning one another's importance and sustainability.

In short then, globalization does not mean the end of place. Instead it creates places which are increasingly "between" other places and have ever-deepening connections to other places. The high-mobility career pattern typical of the software industry poses a threat to the work team cooperation, commitment, and cohesion necessary for innovation. The intensification of space through the dense social networks of the team and the region provides a solution of sorts to this dilemma. However, local networks also serve to reproduce mobility as developers use their connections to engineer their next move. Mobility and place sustain one another but also remain in tension within the structure of the global workplace. In order to understand how this tension is resolved we need to go beyond the intensification of space in the structure of the global workplace to an analysis of the dynamics of that workplace, set in train by the control, regulation, and intensification of time.

The Dynamics of the Global Workplace

The mechanism for controlling the software development team is the project deadline. As it is impossible for the final design specifications to provide solutions to every issue faced by the team and the actual work done by the team is difficult for management to supervise directly, the deadline becomes the focus of management and team efforts. "Do what needs to be done to get this specification working by the deadline" is the broad task of the team. The deadline is the mechanism by which management brings the intensification of time into the heart of the team. It is also an attractive mechanism of control since direct authority over the work process is undermined by the expertise of the employees and the need for rapid communication and cooperation. In contrast time can be regulated through the use of the deadline with only a limited local managerial presence and with relatively little ongoing exercise of managerial authority. This deadline then becomes the stimulus which sets the dynamics of time-space intensification in motion in the global workplace—leading to a pre-deadline phase of team introversion and a post-deadline phase of extroversion.

The Womble team schedule had three main phases—a middle period of "normal work," a hectic period before releasing the product at the deadline, and a beginning period of rest and negotiation after the deadline and the release have passed. The character of the team and the issues it faces change as the team members go through these stages of the cycle together. I join the team, as I did in my fieldwork, in the hectic pre-release phase and leave them as the post-release phase winds down.

Introversion Before the Deadline: A Team Against the World

In the weeks before March 1st, the release date for our product, life in the Womble cubicle becomes busier and busier. The team works longer hours and becomes more and more isolated from the life of the company around them. Internally, the team becomes more cohesive, communication becomes more urgent, technical arguments take on a new edge, and any delay or new instruction from outside the team is met with a barrage of criticism. The graphics for the screens of the system (i.e., what the user sees when using the system) are delayed in coming in from the graphic design house outside San Francisco. The Womble developers grow more and more impatient, furiously criticizing management and the graphic designers for their incompetence. The time allotted for particular development tasks is counted in weeks and then in days. From time to time, a particular problem is put aside for the March 10th release which will contain the fixes for the initial bugs (errors) in the system, creating some dissatisfaction among the developers:

CONOR. We're all tired, we've been at it for two months really. It's a lot of pressure. Something every day. There's no time to take a day and research something. We need a week to go over some of the bigger issues, have some meetings, go over things, you know. There's some dodgy code in there too.

While not as long as the hours worked by some other software development firms in Ireland the work hours do start to creep up toward sixty a week. Séamus, the team leader, works constantly, often late into the evening and the night. Weeks earlier, Conor had told me:

I've a feeling this is the calm before the storm. My attitude when it's calm is get out of here at 4 or 5, cos when it gets busy . . . . You have to draw the line yourself as far as hours go, you have to say once in a while, "Sorry, I have something on tonight, I can't stay." You have to keep your standard hours around thirty-nine, forty. If you let your standard hours go up to forty-five, then they'll still come to you and ask you to do a few extra hours that evening, they won't think about that extra six hours you're doing as part of your standard. It's up to yourself to draw the line.

As the deadline nears, however, he ends up staying late and coming in two weekends in a row. While he is not impressed at having to work these long hours, they are largely accepted as the industry norm. In the Irish economy as a whole managerial and professional workers, especially in small firms, tend to work the longest hours and work a great deal of unrenumerated overtime. As Brian Fynes and his colleagues (1996) observe, "Ireland may be a long way from the Japanese or North American patterns of executive working time, which involves managers working particularly long hours . . . as a normal feature of managerial careers, but the trajectory of change is in this direction." They further argue that the same findings apply to professional workers, although the trend is somewhat weaker. Among the Womble team members, proposed legislation limiting working hours is discussed ironically:

SÉAMUS. I wonder does Ramesh know about the European Social Charter limiting the working week? Forty-three hours per week or something.
CONOR. Great!
JIM. It's forty-eight.
CONOR. F#*!, that long
JIM. Yeah, forty-eight for each company, forty-eight for Womble, and forty-eight for USTech!

Such hours and constant pressure take their toll—the week after the release I bumped into Paul on our way in to work:

PAUL. I was feeling crap lately cos I've been under a lot of pressure and everything. But now I feel great after having that day off.

The impact on the developers' personal lives is also clear from a conversation weeks later before Ramesh arrives in Ireland to take us to a promised celebration dinner.

JIM. Maybe we'll all meet up. I hope he doesn't meet my wife. She has it in for him.
SÉAMUS. Herself and Linda should get together so. They have a lot in common actually—they're both vegetarians too.
SEAN. Except when it comes to Ramesh! (Laughter)
JIM: I see you've met my wife!

However, what appears to be deep antagonism to Ramesh during the pre-release stage fades away in the post-release phase. While the developers' complaints about management making their life more difficult persist, their intensity wanes so that when Ramesh comes on a visit to Ireland after the release, he is quite warmly welcomed (he is also quite well liked by the team members on a personal basis). Apparently, however, the complaints do not fade as quickly for the developers' families, who experience only the long hours and intense demands on their personal life without sharing in the collective team "buzz" of getting the product out in time and working well together.

As well as attempting (with little success) to limit their hours, the developers try to protect themselves against the follies of management in other ways. The team responds to the pressures from Ramesh and the outside world by turning in on themselves, by becoming increasingly introverted. Having a manager on the other side of the world allows the team, including the team leader, to screen information from Ramesh in order to let the team balance the technical and time demands to their own satisfaction. Having encountered a particularly thorny problem, the team finally found a solution:

JIM. So we're going to do that then. Ramesh never needs to know about it. So we can have it set up the way we want it and he'll have it the way he wants too.
PAUL. So we're going to do it the sneaky bastard way
SÉAMUS. I like the sneaky bastard way!
PAUL. And Ramesh never needs to know
SÉAMUS. No, no. Well done, gentlemen!
JIM. Just don't say anything about this on Monday when Ramesh is here!

In many cases the reason for this screening of information was to avoid Ramesh's interference with a solution which the team considered to be the most technically effective. At other times, the goal was to avoid any extra tasks being given to the team before the deadline. On one occasion Ramesh sent an e-mail about a "work around" the team would have to do around a problem in the database they were using. Not realizing that Dan had been working on this issue for a while now, he set aside a day the week before the release for Dan to work on it.

JIM. Dan will have that done today.

SÉAN. So what about the day Ramesh is setting aside for it next week?

JIM. Oh God, I'm not going to tell him we already have a solution. He's already expecting it to slip a bit, so if we get it in on time he'll be really happy. I think we're a little bit ahead of schedule but he thinks we're a bit behind, so that suits us.

In general, team members were careful to protect themselves from undue interference from HQ in the United States, and left the negotiation of deadlines and larger technical issues to Séamus, the team leader. As Conor advised me when I had sent an e-mail to Ramesh about a problem in the help screens:

CONOR. Be careful what you send to Ramesh. Cc it to Séamus or better yet send it to Séamus first, let him decide. That's what I do. You have to look after your own behind first you know. I try to get involved as little as possible with Silicon Valley; I give it to Séamus. That way I have a buffer between me and the United States.

The team could also use the product technical specification (PTS) as a rhetorical device with which they could, if necessary, justify not doing certain tasks. The technical specification for the product was a detailed document outlining the technical basis and logic of the system and supposedly defining the key aspects of the actual development process. However, in contrast to the expectations of formal models of software engineering, the specification document was necessarily vague in places and could not capture all the technical dilemmas which arose during the development process.

Dan, sitting beside me, constantly justified his resistance to certain new tasks which arrived in before the deadline with the refrain, "If it's not in the specs, I'm not doing it." On one occasion Jim and Paul discussed a new requirement for the system which had come in from Ramesh in an e-mail that morning:

JIM. Is it in the specs?

PAUL. No.

JIM. Well, screw it then, we don't need to do it.

However, they later came up with a solution to the problem which they knew was not strictly compatible with the technical requirements of the PTS but which would solve the problem satisfactorily. In this case they were willing to drop their apparent dedication to following the specs in order to try to slip a different solution past Ramesh:

PAUL. I have a feeling we're going to get f#*!ed on this. I think the thing to do is to keep our mouths shut, do this what I'm doing now, present it to them without saying anything and then if they come back saying, "We're not supporting that," then OK. Cos if I just say it to him, he'll just say, "Noooo . . . ."

JIM. Yeah, he does that.

At times the dissatisfaction extended into banter about collective action among the employees. When new changes to the computer graphics for the screens arrived one week before the deadline, the team was furious:

CONOR. I'm going on strike

SÉAN. That'll make history, the first strike in the software industry. [Dan laughs ironically.]

CONOR. You know what last-minute changes means, it means you work your arse off.

DAN. If it's something we've agreed already, I'll work my ass off. But if its last-minute changes, I won't. It has to be reasonable, or else it's "See you later."

Later at breakfast Conor brought up the issue again:

CONOR. I'm going on strike. I say, "In with the union."

JIM. Well, if it's minor changes to what we still have to do, then we'll do it. But if it's changing stuff we've done already, then we're not doing it.

The others on the team agreed. Conor's view was that the developers themselves were not an elite as it was the companies who were making the real money. Of course, software developers are generally relatively well paid:

JIM. Maybe we should join SIPTU [the largest national union] and get union rates. But who wants that kind of pay cut?

Conor was, however, the only team member who put the complaints of the team in the language of collective action. Despite the close ties between the team members and the generous cooperation and help they gave to one another, the solidarity of the team is cast almost entirely in negative terms. They need to protect themselves from the interference of management and less competent designers and developers in order to get a technically good job done under reasonable conditions. This is achieved largely by controlling the flow of information out of the team as best they can. Collective efforts to negotiate what such reasonable conditions might be are not on the agenda, as industry norms around hours, unreasonable deadlines, and so on are rarely challenged. However, as the team comes together to resist the pressures of time intensification they create the team cohesion and work intensity which allow them to meet the challenges of innovation in the global economy. Ironically, it is the team's resistance to corporate interference which creates the conditions under which the team manages to meet corporate innovation goals.

Extroversion After the Deadline: A Team in the World

After the release the team goes into temporary collapse with the work pace slowing dramatically. As work starts to pick up again, I notice that the solidarity of the team in the pre-deadline, introverted phase has fractured somewhat. During the period after the release, individual team members begin to negotiate their roles in the next phase of product development. The team begins to fragment as the focus of the team shifts from getting the work done to building a career and as the team members become extroverted, looking outwards to their future opportunities within and beyond the team.

The next deadline is three to four months away and requires the implementation of the system in the Java programming language. Implementing it in Java should make it possible for the system to run on any computer and to use any database system where training content is stored. This move to Java is critical for the product, although difficult, because a new language, Java development skills are in short supply and many products do not have Java "drivers" which will enable them to work with a system designed in Java. From the team members' point of view this is a great opportunity—training in Java and experience in developing a complex product in the language will be a huge resource for them in the labor market.

However, the distribution of opportunities for training and for valuable experience is not determined by the technical requirements of the product. It is an object of negotiation within the team, negotiation which takes place through the social networks among team members and between team members and the team leader and managers. The issue is rarely mentioned publicly, let alone discussed collectively. Furthermore, the move to Java is a gradual one and each stage produces different sets of conflicts.

The move to Java represents an opportunity for the Irish team but also a threat. As the team moves to a new technical phase in the development, this opens a "window of locational opportunity" for Womble Software. Despite the Irish team's advantages of knowledge and experience of the system, there is still a danger that development work could move back to the United States. One team meeting discussing the move to Java produced the following exchange:

MICHAEL [business manager]: We had to get a Java person in Ireland. Ramesh had someone in the United States, but we couldn't let that happen, we couldn't let it go there.

PAUL. Yeah, you don't want to let the development stuff leak back to the US. If it starts, it'll all end up back there eventually.

The Irish team scrambles to gather together Java skills and to give Ramesh the impression that we have more skills than we do. Later it is my clear impression that Ramesh knows the level of skills in the Irish team but that he has developed a trust in the Irish team that they will be able to get up to speed on Java in time.

Of course, even keeping the Java work in Ireland does not solve the issue of how exactly the need for Java knowledge will be solved for the team. This issue arises first in relation to a totally different problem. The system can now run only on computers which have Unix or Windows NT operating system software. The system needs to be able to also run on computers with Apple's Macintosh operating system. One quick way to achieve this is to buy a software product from another company which can compile the computer code so that it will work on Macintosh systems. However, this will add £2,000 to the cost of each copy of the product for Mac. Instead it is decided to adjust some parts of the system using Java, which will achieve two goals: make the system work on Mac and begin the process of implementing the system in Java. The team must look for a contract developer to do this work before the release date.

MICHAEL. I think we'll have to get a contractor. Pat is up there with the porting team at the moment, he should be able to do it.

JIM. Yeah, Pat is very good.

MICHAEL. Under normal circumstances we'd put that £ 2,000 into training some-body on the team so that they could do it, but we don't have the time at the moment because of the release date coming up. So I think we should get Pat.

There are many ways, therefore, to incorporate new skills and sources of knowl-edge into the team. The strategy of buying a product made by another company which embodies that knowledge is rejected in this case due to its cost. Training cur-rent employees is always an option but is often overlooked in the hectic development schedule. No one can be let go to a week-long course with the deadline hanging over the team. The team also missed out on other training opportunities while I was there due to this pressure of time. Finally, bringing in someone with the necessary knowl-edge is chosen as the strategy, less than satisfactory in the longterm but necessary given the time constraints.

The issue of hiring contractors versus training employees is of course a sensitive one:

CONOR. Be careful we don't keep getting contractors to do Java stuff and none of us get to go to the training on it.

JIM. Sure, I know. I'm thinking if we get someone on Java he'll have lots of ideas about things to do in Java and that'll create lots of work for us to do in Java.

This is a particular danger, as while contractors may only come for a short while, they often stay longer as they develop a knowledge of a particular piece of the prod-uct or become valuable to the team in a particular area. Even I, as a novice technical writer, become valuable in that having developed a knowledge of the system, I would be able to write the help for future editions more quickly than some professional "tech writers" with no knowledge of the product.

This tension between contract and permanent employees becomes clear in the negotiation of team roles and opportunities for working with Java. It is in this inter-nal competition for Java work that the fragmentation of team solidarity and the shift from an introverted to an extroverted orientation within the team are clearest. When Paul, a contractor, declares that he is starting to teach himself Java and wants to do a Java implementation of his part of the system, this meets with some (private) concern from some other members of the team: "I thought he was just here to do that section of the system and not to do this Java stuff." Dan is particularly worried about the involvement of contractors in Java work to the exclusion of permanent employees:

DAN. The three contract people are doing Java and the two permanent people are doing everything else. It is not right. Conor and myself were told in our one-on-one reviews with Michael that the permanent people would get Java training, they would get priority over the contractors. Michael said that they didn't want to give it to the contractors first, cos they could just leave and take it somewhere else. But that's not how it's going to be—over the next few months they will be doing Java and we will be doing everything else. I was talking to Conor about it yesterday. He is aware of it.

SÉAN. Will you say anything about it?

DAN. What can I say? My attitude is if something is wrong and I can't change it, then I just leave and go somewhere else. It's as simple as that. It doesn't make sense from USTech's point of view. They are paying all this money for contractors and they are not paying for training for permanent staff. In the end they just pile up the costs for themselves. It's crazy from USTech's point of view. And from my point of view [laughs ironically].

Dan did eventually talk to Séamus, the team leader, about this and received assurances that he would be doing Java work. Paul's growing interest in other advanced technical areas also helped defuse the situation to some extent. However, the negotiations continued as I left. Indeed on Ramesh's second visit he treated the whole team to a dinner and a night out on the town. Each one of us, as we sat over dinner and wound our way through the city streets, discussed our future roles with Ramesh—I myself talked over the possibility of doing some further technical writing on a contract basis once my fieldwork was over; Paul discussed his hopes to do some field consulting on the product; Jim and Paul, their plans to work on a new technical area of the product; Conor, his desire to do work with Java in a particular application of our system. Indeed we also put in a good word with Ramesh for each other, where the different roles seemed complementary. In competition over certain areas, the team members helped each other out in others.

We can see, therefore, that the team solidarity of the pre-release phase becomes more fractured as opportunities for training and learning become a focus of conflict within the team. However, the conflict is submerged and operates through a complex set of social networks and shifting alliances among team members. These ties interact with the formal categories of permanent and contract employees to produce a politics of learning and skills within the team. These local dynamics are intimately connected to the nature of the opportunities in the global market for knowledge embodied (in this case) in the skills of American developers and the products (software tools) available to carry out certain tasks.

The pre-release phase revealed the nature of the local and global solidarities of the team, with local solidarities increasingly pitted against global interference as the local team fought for the space to achieve the "global" goal of releasing a good product in the way that they saw fit. The post-release phase reveals more schisms within the team and shows how the local team is forged out of a range of alliances between local and global employees and managers. The mobility of team members through various learning paths within the team and outside of it is negotiated in this phase, laying the foundation for the next pre-release phase in three to four months time.

Time-Space Intensification as the Politics of Globalization

The emergence of a global information economy has transformed the character of the workplace for many employees, including those within informational industries such as software. Many authors argue that the globalization of work destroys place and locality, creating a placeless virtual workplace. Against this view, this chapter has argued for a concept of globalization which emphasizes the organization of the global economy through particular places and regions and the critical importance of patterns of mobility of people, information, and resources within and between these regions. These changes in the territorial organization of capitalism interact with an organizational restructuring characterized by the decentralization of work and firms. While some authors argue that these organizational changes will bring relative equality and a rough-and-ready economic democracy, this chapter has shown that new forms of power operate within these new organizational forms. Ethnography reveals that we cannot simply "read off" concrete social practices and power relations from a particular organizational and territorial structure of work. Instead we find that a new ground is emerging upon which the struggles of the global informational economy will be waged—a new set of social identities, resources, interests, and issues are created which will be the basis of the politics of the global workplace in the years to come.

This new "contested terrain" of the global workplace is a system of time-space intensification where workers in the global workplace experience not the "end of time and space" but their raising to a new level of intensity. Space is intensified by the necessity of local cooperation and the increased use of project teams in the face of the challenges posed by the global economy. Time becomes an ever more pressing reality in the deadline-driven workplace. This time-space intensification shapes the structure of both work and careers in the global workplace. Careers are built using mobility between firms to bargain for improved wages and access to technical learning, and these mobile careers only increase the importance of close interactions and strong local cooperation while working on any particular project. Out of these underlying structures emerges a set of dynamics, organized around the project deadline, which give the global workplace its dynamism but also generate certain costs and dilemmas for the participants in the global workplace. Conflicts over these dilemmas of time-space intensification constitute the new politics of the globalization of knowledge work.

What then will be the central controversies on this new contested terrain? The two phases of time-space intensification create characteristics advantages and dilemmas for knowledge workers such as the software developers in this chapter, for firms such as USTech and Womble Software and for the (largely invisible) social actors beyond the industry with an interest in its social organization. While these dynamics and dilemmas have been recognized for some time in the global informational industries, globalization intensifies them.[11]

Certain characteristic organizational problems are likely to emerge—these are the internal organizational dilemmas of time-space intensification. In the pre-release phase the introversion of the team, the intensification of time and the pressures imposed by the deadline create the conditions which lead to employee burnout—manifested in the exhaustion of the team members up to and after the deadline, and also in the decision made by Ramesh (some five months after I left the team) to resign due to overwork. This creates problems for the organization as the team's introversion cuts it off from the rest of the organization and raises the danger of organizational involution and the distancing of teams from one another, even teams working on related technical or business issues. For the Womble team, this can be seen in the antagonistic attitude to the graphics team in California, a set of relationships which, if more cooperative, could have been very valuable in improving the product under development.

In the post-deadline phase the team solidarity fragments and the team members begin to look beyond the team for future opportunities. The extroverted phase is when employees can turn to the labor market to gain the rewards of their new-found expertise, and the organization can assemble a new group of employees with new sets of skills and resources into a project team for the next phase of the development effort. However, there is also a significant cost associated with the high levels of employee turnover within the industry. The accumulated knowledge of the Womble software product which has built up within the team is now dissipated throughout the industry. This constitutes a significant loss of firm-specific knowledge from Womble's point of view and also a loss of the effort put into developing effective working relationships within the team. There are, therefore, clear organizational costs attached to failure to address these internal dilemmas.[12]

Time-space intensification also causes certain external social dilemmas. The pressure and introverted character of the pre-deadline phase, and the resulting insulation of such workers and the organization of work from any kind of broader social accountability, make it all the more difficult to reconcile the team structure and culture with broader social concerns. This is manifested in at least two areas. The most directly obvious is the work-family nexus, where work demands come to dominate family life, leaving very little space for workers to negotiate alternative work and family time arrangements. Secondly, as technology increasingly penetrates our everyday social practices, the involvement of users in decisions regarding these technologies becomes more and more crucial. However, the isolation and insulation of the developers during their most creative and innovative phase militate strongly against any meaningful interaction with social actors from outside the team. To the extent that we might fear the arrival of the Weberian "iron cage" in the form of a society dominated by large, centralized organizations there is some promise in the decentralized organizational forms compatible with this high-mobility system. However, although organizations no longer have the same rigid bureaucratic structures insulating them from social accountability, the intensification of time ultimately results in a similar outcome.

The post-deadline phase of high mobility creates a very high degree of volatility and insecurity in the labor market so that employees lack strong employment guarantees. This is not currently a major issue in the Irish industry given the generally very high demand for software skills. Even in the current tight labor market, "employment security" gives way to "employability security."[13] However, when career gains are based on the threat of mobility, this seems to inevitably lead to increased labor market inequality, as the threat to leave is only effective when replacing the employee is difficult. As it is inherently based on scarcity, the limits of mobility as a universal career strategy are clear. This seems likely to be a contributing factor to the spiraling wage inequality in Ireland over the past ten years.[14]

These internal and external dilemmas of time-space intensification are all the more crucial given that the economic success of the Republic of Ireland over the past ten years has been built upon the success of industries such as software.[15] The politics of the conference call became the new politics of the global workplace—distant yet closely integrated into operations in the core, less hierarchical but nonetheless subject to new forms of power relations. As these global workplaces spread through economies such as Ireland's, the dilemmas of time-space intensification will become central economic and social issues for societies incorporated into new, deeper processes of globalization. The value of global ethnography is its ability to reveal these dilemmas as aspects of a "contested terrain" of globalization, rather than as inevitable outcomes of an apolitical process.

Notes

Acknowledgments: My thanks to my comrades at USTech for letting me pry into their lives for three months. Thanks to Becky King for making comments and going to Dublin. I received helpful comments at presentations of earlier versions of this at the Economic and Social Research Institute (ESRI), Dublin; the Center for Work, Technology, and Organizing, Stanford University; the labor process conference on "Work, Difference and Social Change," SUNY-Binghamton; and the Department of Sociology, University of California at Berkeley. Mike Hout and Anno Saxenian provided incisive comments and great encouragement. Material support was provided by the ESRI, Forfás and Forbairt in Ireland. This research was assisted by a grant from the Joint Committee on Western Europe of the American Council of Learned Societies and the Social Science Research Council, with funds provided by the Ford and Mellon foundations.

1. Anthony Giddens (1991) argues that globalization occurs in a process of *time-space distanciation* as space and time are "distanciated" from (lifted out of) their local contexts. There are two main mechanisms through which this happens: the use of *symbolic tokens* (universal media of exchange/interaction such as money) and of *expert systems* (shared bodies of technical knowledge that can be applied in a wide variety of contexts).

2. David Harvey (1989) argues that globalization is characterized by a process of *time-space compression,* where the speed up of time in the global economy also serves to compress the autonomy of local space and social context as different places are integrated into an increasingly universal capitalist economy.

3. We might refer to this perspective as *time-space embedding,* as embeddedness of workplaces in their local social contexts appears to provide a solution to the speed up of the global economy, giving the successful workplaces some insulation from these pressures and perhaps even reembedding time itself in local contexts (see Piore and Sabel 1984; Saxenian 1994; Storper 1997).

4. For detailed empirical analyses of these issues in a software workplace, see Perlow 1997, 1998.

5. For a more detailed analysis of this process see Ó Riain 1997a, b; 1999.

6. IBM's employment guarantee collapsed with a reduction of 140,000 in a workforce of

400,000 between 1986 and 1993. For an analysis of corporate culture in such workplaces see Kunda 1993.

7. For discussion of labor markets in agglomerated industries in core regions, see Sassen 1990; Saxenian 1994.

8. Much of this learning, especially in a team context, derives from what Jean Lave and Etienne Wenger (1992) call "situated learning."

9. For a discussion of this concept and a review of a variety of examples, see Castells and Hall 1994.

10. For a more detailed analysis of these processes, based on a case study of a software company in Ireland in the mid-1980s, see Tierney 1995.

11. For a classic account of these dynamics in a computer design workplace in the 1970s, see Kidder 1981.

12. For an organizational and management theory perspective, see Brown and Eisenhardt 1997.

13. For a discussion of this concept as developed in a study of a software company in Massachusetts, see Kanter 1995.

14. For a detailed analysis of trends from 1987 to 1994, see Barrett, Callan, and Nolan, 1999.

15. For a more detailed analysis of the growth of the Irish software industry, with particular reference to the potential and limits of state-society alliances in shaping the industry's development and impact, see Ó Riain 1999.

References

Baron, James, M. Diane Burton, and Michael Hannan. 1996. "The Road Taken: Origins and Early Evolution of Employment Systems in Emerging Companies." *Industrial and Corporate Change,* 5: 239–275.

Barrett, Alan, Tim Callan, and Brian Nolan. 1999. "Rising Wage Inequality, Returns to Education, and Labor Market Institutions: Evidence from Ireland." *British Journal of Industrial Relations,* 37: 77–100.

Berman, Marshall. 1982. *All That Is Solid Melts into Air: The Experience of Modernity.* London: Penguin.

Bluestone, Barry, and Bennett Harrison. 1982. *The Deindustrialization of America.* New York: Basic Books.

Brown, Shona, and Kathleen Eisenhardt. 1997. "The Art of Continuous Change." *Administrative Science Quarterly,* 42: 1–34.

Burawoy, Michael. 1985. *The Politics of Production. Factory Regimes Under Capitalism and Socialism.* London: Verso.

Castells, Manuel. 1996. *The Rise of the Network Society.* Vol. 1. Cambridge, MA: Blackwell.

Castells, Manuel, and Peter Hall. 1994. *Technopoles of the World.* New York: Routledge.

Fynes, Brian, Tim Morrissey, William K. Roche, Brendan J. Whelan, and James Williams. 1996. *Flexible Working Lives: The Changing Nature of Working Time Arrangements in Ireland.* Dublin: Oak Tree Press.

Giddens, Anthony. 1991. *The Consequences of Modernity.* Oxford: Blackwell.

Harvey, David. 1989. *The Condition of Postmodernity.* Oxford: Blackwell.

Kanter, Rosabeth Moss. 1995. *World Class.* New York: Simon and Schuster.

Kidder, Tracy. 1981. *The Soul of a New Machine*. New York: Avon Books.

Kunda, Gideon. 1993. *Engineering Culture*. Philadelphia: Temple University Press.

Lave, Jean, and Etienne Wenger. 1993. *Situated Learning: Legitimate Peripheral Participation*. Cambridge: Cambridge University Press.

Office of Technology Policy. 1997. *America's New Deficit: The Shortage of Information Technology Workers*. Washington, DC: U.S. Department of Commerce, Technology Administration. Available at http://www.ta.doc.gov/reports/itsw/itsw.pdf.

O'Malley, Eoin. 1989. *Industry and Economic Development*. Dublin: Gill and Macmillan.

Ó Riain, Seán. 1997a. "The Birth of a Celtic Tiger? *Communications of the ACM*, 40: 11–16.

———. 1997b. "An Offshore Silicon Valley?" *Competition and Change*, 2: 175–212.

———. 1999. "Remaking the Developmental State: The Irish Software Industry in the Global Economy." Ph.D. dissertation, Department of Sociology, University of California, Berkeley.

Perlow, Leslie. 1997. *Finding Time*. Cornell: ILR Press.

———. 1998. "Boundary Control: The Social Ordering of Work and Family Time in a High-Tech Corporation." *Administrative Science Quarterly*, 43: 328–357.

Piore, Michael, and Charles Sabel. 1984. *The Second Industrial Divide*. New York: Basic Books.

Reich, Robert. 1991. *The Work of Nations*. New York: Vintage Books.

Sassen, Saskia. 1990. *The Global City*. Princeton: Princeton University Press.

Saxenian, AnnaLee. 1994. *Regional Advantage*. Cambridge: Harvard University Press.

Shaiken, Harley. 1990. *Mexico in the Global Economy*. San Diego: Center for US–Mexican Studies.

Storper, Michael. 1997. *The Regional World: Territorial Development in a Global Economy*. London: Guilford Press.

Tierney, Margaret. 1995. "Negotiating a Software Career: Informal Work Practices and the Lads in a Software Installation." In *The Gender-Technology Relation: Contemporary Theory and Research*, edited by K. Grint and R. Gill. London: Taylor and Francis.

Wellman, Barry, Janet Salaff, Dimitrina Dimitrova, Laura Garton, Milena Gulia, and Caroline Haythornthwaite. 1996. "Computer Networks as Social Networks." *Annual Review of Sociology*, 22: 213–238.

About the Contributors

RICK BALDOZ is an assistant professor of sociology at the University of Hawaii–Manoa. His work has recently been published in *Critical Sociology* and *International Labor and Working Class History*. In his current research on Filipino migrant workers in the United States from the 1920s to the 1960s, he explores the interplay of racialization and class formation in shaping the socioeconomic mobility of Filipino-Americans.

EDNA BONACICH is a professor of sociology and ethnic studies at the University of California, Riverside. Her work focuses on issues surrounding race, class, and labor. She has written two books on the apparel industry, *Global Production: The Apparel Industry in the Pacific Rim* (a co-edited and co-authored volume published by Temple University Press) and (with Richard Appelbaum) *Behind the Label: Inequality in the Los Angeles Apparel Industry*.

MICHAEL BURAWOY teaches sociology at the University of California, Berkeley. For the last decade he has been studying Russia's efforts to establish a capitalist economy. He is one of the authors of *Global Ethnography,* an attempt to grapple with the forces, connections, and imaginations of the postmodern world.

JENNIFER JIHYE CHUN is a Ph.D. candidate at the Department of Sociology at the University of California, Berkeley. She is currently writing her dissertation on the racialized and gendered global migrant workforce, focusing on case studies of workers in the United States and South Korea.

JEFFREY HAYDU is the author of *Between Craft and Class: Skilled Workers and Factory Politics in the United States and Britain, 1890–1922* (1988) and *Making American Industry Safe for Democracy: Comparative Perspectives on the State and Employee Representation in the Era of World War I* (1997). His current research examines civic associations, class formation, and ideologies of work among late-nineteenth-century American employers. He is a professor of sociology at the University of California, San Diego.

CHARLES KOEBER is an assistant professor of sociology at Wichita State University. His work has recently been published in *Critical Sociology* and *International Labor and Working Class History*. His current research examines the impact of corporate "restructuring" and "downsizing" on the nature and organization of work and on the lives of workers.

PHILIP KRAFT teaches sociology at the State University of New York at Binghamton. He has studied a wide range of computer-intensive occupations and management control systems and is currently working with Richard Sharpe on a study of the software and telecommunications industries.

PEI-CHIA LAN was born and raised in Taiwan and received her Ph.D. in sociology at Northwestern University. She is currently a postdoctoral research fellow at the Center for Working Families at the University of California, Berkeley. She has published articles in *Feminist Studies* and *Taiwanese Sociological Review*. Her recent research explores labor control, symbolic struggles, and identity formation involved in the interactions between Filipina migrant domestic workers and their Taiwanese employers.

PETER MEIKSINS is an associate professor and the chair of sociology at Cleveland State University. He is the author (with Peter Whalley) of *Getting A Life: Customizing Work Time Among Technical Professionals* (forthcoming) and (with Chris Smith) of *Engineering Labour: Technical Workers in Comparative Perspective* (1996). He also is the editor (with Ellen Meiksins Wood and Michael Yates) of *Rising from the Ashes: Labor in the Age of Global Capitalism* (1999).

EVELYN NAKANO GLENN is professor of women's studies and ethnic studies and director of the Beatrice Bain Research Group on Gender at the University of California, Berkeley. She has written extensively on the political economy of households and the intersection of race and gender, labor immigration, and women of color in the United States. She is the author of *Issei, Nisei, War Bride* (Temple) and editor (with Grace Chang and Linda Forcey) of *Mothering: Ideology, Experience and Agency*. She is completing a comparative study of the race-gender construction of labor and citizenship in the South, Southwest, and Hawaii from 1870 to 1930.

SEÁN Ó RIAIN is an assistant professor of sociology at the University of California, Davis. He received his Ph.D. from UC-Berkeley in 1999; in his dissertation he argued that globalization is not destroying but in fact remaking the role of states in shaping socioeconomic development. He developed this argument in recent articles in *Politics and Society* and the *Annual Review of Sociology*. He is a co-author of *Global Ethnography: Forces, Connections and Imaginations in a Postmodern World* (2000).

JAMES RINEHART, professor emeritus at the University of Western Ontario, specializes in labor studies. He is the author of *The Tyranny of Work: Alienation and the Labour Process* and a co-author of *Just Another Car Factory? Lean Production and Its Discontents*.

RICHARD SHARPE has been researching, analyzing, reporting on, and lecturing about the world of information technology since 1970. His books include *The Computer World, Software Agents*, and *UK IT Skills in 2003*. His articles have been published in *The Financial Times, The Times* (London), *The Daily Telegraph, The Herald Tribune*, and numerous specialist publications. Recently he has written "Citizens' Preferences: Measuring the Acceptability of E-Channels" and a report on the role of public sector IT in UK Transport Plans. He occasionally lectures at the University of East London on IT developments.

ANGELO SOARES has a Ph.D. in sociology from Université Laval and is an associate professor at the Centre d'Étude des Interactions Biologiques entre la Santé et l'Environnement (CINBIOSE) of the Université du Québec à Montreal (UQAM). He is the editor of *Stratégies de Résistance et Travail des Femmes* (1997) and he is currently engaged in research on emotional labor and its effects on mental health. He is also conducting research on bullying in the workplace.

EDWARD WEBSTER is a professor of sociology and director of the Sociology of Work Unit at the University of the Witwatersrand in Johannesburg , South Africa. He is author of *Cast in a Racial Mould: Labour Process and Trade Unionism in the Foundries,* and he recently co-edited a collection of essays on trade unions and democratization in South Africa from 1985 to 1997. In 1995 he was a Fulbright scholar at the University of Wisconsin, Madison.

PETER WHALLEY is an associate professor and the chair of the Department of Sociology and Anthropology at Loyola University in Chicago. He is the author of *The Social Production of Technical Work* (1986) and a number of articles on engineers. He has also researched and published work on independent inventors. He has recently completed a book with Peter Meiksins entitled *Getting A Life* (forthcoming), about the customization of work time by technical professionals.